150 LEADING CASES

Obligations:
THE LAW OF TORT

SECOND EDITION

D G CRACKNELL
LLB, of the Middle Temple, Barrister

OLD BAILEY PRESS

OLD BAILEY PRESS
at Holborn College, Woolwich Road,
Charlton, London, SE7 8LN

First published 1998
Second edition 2002

ISBN 1 85836 459 0

British Library Cataloguing-in-Publication

A catalogue record for this book is available from the British
Library.

Printed and bound in Great Britain

Contents

Acknowledgements   *v*

Preface   *vii*

Table of Cases   *ix*

1   Introduction   *1*

2   Parties to an Action in Tort   *2*

3   Joint and Several Tortfeasors   *7*

4   Vicarious Liability   *10*

5   Liability for Independent Contractors   *19*

6   Negligence: The Duty of Care   *22*

7   Negligence: Breach of the Duty   *81*

8   Negligence: Causation   *92*

9   Negligence: Remoteness of Damage   *98*

10 Contributory Negligence   *104*

11 Volenti Non Fit Injuria   *107*

12 Breach of Statutory Duty   *111*

13 Employers' Liability   *118*

14 Product Liability   *121*

15 Occupiers' Liability   *122*

16 Private Nuisance   *131*

17 Public Nuisance   *138*

18 The Rule in *Rylands* v *Fletcher*   *141*

19 Fire   *147*

20 Animals   *149*

21 Defamation   *152*

22 Trespass to the Person   *161*

23 Trespass to Land   *164*

24 Deceit   *166*

25 Malicious Falsehood   *169*

26 Passing Off   *173*

27 The Economic Torts   *176*

28 Remedies   *179*

29 Miscellaneous Defences and Limitation   *205*

30 Torts to Chattels   *209*

31 Malicious Prosecution   *211*

Acknowledgements

The publishers and author would like to thank the Incorporated Council of Law Reporting for England and Wales for kind permission to reproduce extracts from the Weekly Law Reports, and Butterworths for their kind permission to reproduce extracts from the All England Law Reports.

Preface

Old Bailey Press casebooks are intended as companion volumes to the textbooks but they also comprise invaluable reference tools in themselves. Their aim is to supplement and enhance a student's understanding and interpretation of a particular area of law and provide essential background reading. Companion Revision WorkBooks and Statutes are also published.

The *Obligations: The Law of Tort* casebook is designed for use by any undergraduates who have Tort within their syllabus. It will be equally useful for all CPE/LLDip students who must study Tort Law as one of the 'core' subjects.

In order to comply with the series limitation of 150 cases, as a general rule authorities more recent in date and higher in terms of status have been chosen. An attempt has been made to include cases, and extracts from judgments, which most helpfully and memorably establish, illustrate or explain the underlying principles.

Of course, many more than 150 cases are covered in the sense that reference is made to them in judgments and commentary.

Recent cases include decisions of the House of Lords in *Arthur J S Hall & Co* v *Simons* [2000] 3 All ER 673 (advocates' immunity), *Lister* v *Hesley Hall Ltd* [2001] 2 All ER 769 (vicarious liability) and *Kuddus* v *Chief Constable of Leicestershire Constabulary* [2001] 3 All ER 193 (misfeasance in public office).

The law is stated on the basis of cases fully reported on or before 1 March 2002. No account has been taken of cases where leave has been given for a further appeal.

Table of Cases

Cases in bold type are the leading cases. Page numbers in bold indicate the main references to them.

A (Children) (Conjoined Twins: Surgical Separation), Re [2000] 4 All ER 961   *82*

AB *v* South West Water Services Ltd [1993] 1 All ER 609   *190, 191*

Abramzik *v* Brenner (1967) 65 DLR (2d) 651   *58*

Acton *v* Graham Pearce & Co [1997] 3 All ER 909   *93*

Adams *v* Ursell [1913] 1 Ch 269   *131*

Adamson *v* Jarvis (1827) 4 Bing 66   *185*

Addie (R) & Sons (Collieries) Ltd *v* Dumbreck [1929] AC 358   *124*

Addis *v* Crocker [1960] 2 All ER 629   *211*

Airedale NHS Trust *v* Bland [1993] 2 WLR 316   *81*

Alcock *v* Chief Constable of South Yorkshire [1992] 1 AC 310; [1991] 3 WLR 1057; [1991] 4 All ER 907   *23, 25, 29, 35, 38, 39, 59, 67*

Aldred's Case (1610) 9 Co Rep 57b   *132*

Alexandrou *v* Oxford [1993] 4 All ER 328   *34, 37, 47*

Al-Kandari *v* J R Brown & Co [1988] QB 665; [1988] 2 WLR 671; [1988] 1 All ER 833   *22*

Al-Nakib Investments (Jersey) Ltd *v* Longcroft [1990] 3 All ER 321   *32, 71*

Al Saudi Banque *v* Clarke Pixley (A Firm) [1990] 2 WLR 344; [1989] 3 All ER 361   *32, 71*

Allen *v* Bloomsbury Health Authority [1993] 1 All ER 651   *179*

Allen *v* Flood [1898] AC 1   *1*

Allen *v* Gulf Oil Refining Ltd [1981] AC 1001; [1980] QB 156; [1981] 1 All ER 353   *72, 138*

Alliance & Leicester Building Society *v* Edgestop Ltd [1993] 1 WLR 1462   *104*

Allied Maples Group Ltd *v* Simmons & Simmons [1995] 1 WLR 1602   *92*

Ambergate, Nottingham and Boston and Eastern Junction Rly Co *v* Midland Rly Co (1853) 2 E & B 793   *183*

Ancell *v* McDermott [1993] 4 All ER 355   *25, 47*

Anderson *v* Gorrie [1895] 1 QB 668   *4*

Anns *v* Merton London Borough Council [1978] AC 728; [1977] 2 WLR 1024; [1977] 2 All ER 492   *30, 33, 42, 49, 53, 62, 63, 64, 73*

Armory *v* Delamirie (1722) 5 Stra 505   *210*

Arthur *v* Anker [1996] 3 All ER 783   *181*

Arthur J S Hall & Co *v* Simons; Barratt *v* Ansell; Harris *v* Scholfield Roberts & Hill [2000] 3 All ER 673   *vii, 27*

Ashton *v* Turner [1981] QB 137   *110*

Atkinson *v* Newcastle Waterworks Co (1877) 2 Ex D 441   *111*

Attorney-General *v* Guardian Newspapers Ltd (No 2) [1990] 1 AC 109; [1988] 2 WLR 805; [1988] 3 All ER 545   *153, 154, 157*

Attorney General *v* PYA Quarries Ltd [1957] 2 QB 169   *139*

Attorney-General (ex rel Gray's Inn Society) *v* Doughty (1752) 2 Ves Sen 453   *132*

Baker *v* Willoughby [1970] AC 467; [1970] 2 WLR 50   *93, 95*

Baldwin *v* Rushbridger (2001) The Times 23 July   *156*

Balfour *v* Barty-King [1957] 1 QB 496; [1957] 2 WLR 84; [1957] 1 All ER 156   *19, 147, 148*

Ball *v* London County Council [1949] 1 All ER 1056   *123*

Barnett *v* Chelsea & Kensington Hospital Management Committee [1969] 1 QB 428; [1968] 2 WLR 422   *93, 95*

Barrett *v* Enfield London Borough Council [1999] 3 All ER 193   *51, 78*

Barrett *v* Ministry of Defence [1995] 1 WLR 1217; [1995] 3 All ER 87   *37*

Bayley *v* Manchester, Sheffield and Lincolnshire Railway Co (1873) LR 8 CP 148   *10, 18*

Beaulieu *v* Finglam (1401) YB 2 Hen 4   *147*

Bell *v* Department of Health and Social Security (1989) The Times 13 June   *89*

Benjamin *v* Storr (1874) LR 9 CP 400   *115*

Beresford *v* White (1914) 30 TLR 591   *160*

Berkoff *v* Burchill [1996] 4 All ER 1008   *152*

Bernstein of Leigh (Lord) *v* Skyviews & General Ltd [1978] QB 479; [1977] 3 WLR 136   *164*

Billings (A C) and Sons Ltd *v* Riden [1958] AC 240; [1957] 3 WLR 596; [1957] 3 All ER 1   *122, 133*

Bland *v* Moseley (1587) 9 Co Rep 58a   *132*

Blue Circle Industries plc *v* Ministry of Defence [1998] 3 All ER 385   *64, 93*

Blyth *v* Birmingham Waterworks Co (1856) 11 Ex 781   *82*

Bognor Regis UDC *v* Campion [1972] 2 WLR 983   *154*

Bolam *v* Friern Hospital Management Committee [1957] 1 WLR 582; [1957] 2 All ER 118   *40, 81, 83, 84, 88, 89*

Bolitho *v* City and Hackney Health Authority [1997] 4 All ER 771   *82*

Bolton *v* Stone [1951] AC 850; [1951] 1 All ER 1078 (HL); [1950] 1 KB 201; [1949] 1 All ER 237 (QBD)   *61, 85, 100*

Bondarenko *v* Sommers (1968) 69 NR (NSW) 269   *109*

Bonnard *v* Perryman [1891] 2 Ch 269   *154, 155*

Bonnington Castings Ltd *v* Wardlaw [1956] AC 613; [1956] 1 All ER 615   *68, 84*

Boulcott Golf Club Inc *v* Engelbrecht [1945] NZLR 556   *147*

Bourgoin SA *v* Ministry of Agriculture, Fisheries and Food [1985] 3 All ER 585   *53*

Bourhill (or Hay) *v* Young [1943] AC 92; [1942] 2 All ER 396   *23, 28, 57, 67*

Bowater *v* Rowley Regis Corporation [1944] KB 476   *107*

Bradburn *v* Lindsay [1983] 2 All ER 408   *136*

Bradford *v* Robinson Rentals Ltd [1967] 1 WLR 337   *99*

Bradford Corporation *v* Pickles [1895] AC 587   *1*

Bridges *v* Hawkesworth (1851) 21 LJQB 75   *210*

Bridlington Relay Ltd *v* Yorkshire Electricity Board [1965] Ch 436; [1965] 1 All ER 264   *132*

British Racing Drivers Club Ltd *v* Hextall Erskine & Co [1996] 3 All ER 667   *94*

British Railways Board *v* Herrington [1972] AC 877; [1972] 2 WLR 537; [1972] 1 All ER 749   *123, 126, 129*

British Transport Commission *v* Gourley [1956] AC 185; [1956] 2 WLR 41   *184*

Broadley *v* Guy Clapham & Co [1994] 4 All ER 439   *207*

Brooke *v* Bool [1928] 2 KB 578   *7, 19, 20*

Burmah Oil Co (Burmah Trading) *v* Lord Advocate [1965] AC 75; [1964] 2 All ER 348   *60*

Burnside *v* Emerson [1968] 3 All ER 471   *113*

Burrows *v* Rhodes [1899] 1 QB 816   *185*

Byrne *v* Hall Pain & Foster [1999] 2 All ER 400   *205*

Calveley *v* Chief Constable of Merseyside Police [1989] AC 1228; [1989] 2 WLR 624; [1989] 1 All ER 1025   *29, 78*

Cambridge Water Co Ltd *v* Eastern Counties Leather plc [1994] 2 WLR 53   *141, 146*

Canadian Pacific Railway Co *v* Lockhart [1942] AC 591   *17*

Candler *v* Crane, Christmas & Co [1951] 2 KB 164   *32, 70*

Cann *v* Willson (1888) Ch D 39   *31*

Caparo Industries plc *v* Dickman [1990] 2 AC 605; [1990] 2 WLR 358; [1990] 1 All ER 568   *30, 34, 38, 56, 77, 94*

Capital and Counties plc *v* Hampshire County Council; Digital Equipment Co Ltd *v* Hampshire County Council; John Munroe (Acrylics) Ltd *v* London Fire and Civil Defence Authority; Church of Jesus Christ of Latter Day Saints (Great Britain) *v* West Yorkshire Fire and Civil Defence Authority [1997] 2 All ER 865   *32, 33, 74, 129*

Carr-Glynn *v* Frearsons [1998] 4 All ER 225   *79*

Cassell & Co Ltd *v* Broome [1972] AC 1027; [1972] 1 All ER 801   *158, 190, 191*

Century Insurance Co Ltd *v* Northern Ireland Road Transport Board [1942] AC 509   *10*

Chadwick *v* British Transport Commission [1967] 1 WLR 912   *58, 59*

Chastey *v* Ackland [1895] 2 Ch 389   *132*

Clark *v* Associated Newspapers Ltd [1998] 1 All ER 959   *173*

Clark *v* MacLennan [1983] 1 All ER 416   *90*

Clayards *v* Dethick & Davis (1848) 12 QB 439   *122, 123*

Clough *v* Bussan (West Yorkshire Police Authority, third party) [1990] 1 All ER 431   *26, 47, 80*

Clunis *v* Camden and Islington Health Authority [1998] 3 All ER 180   *74, 184*

Cocks *v* Thanet District Council [1983] 2 AC 286; [1982] 3 All ER 1135   *54*

Collingwood *v* Home and Colonial Stores Ltd
[1936] 3 All ER 200   *147*

Coltman *v* Bibby Tankers Ltd [1988] AC 276;
[1987] 3 WLR 1181   *118*

Condon *v* Basi [1985] 1 WLR 866; [1985] 2 All
ER 453   *86*

Conway *v* George Wimpey & Co Ltd [1951] 2 KB
266   *12*

Corporacion Nacional del Cobre de Chile *v*
Sogemin Metals Ltd [1997] 2 All ER 917
105

Costello *v* Chief Constable of Derbyshire
Constabulary [2001] 3 All ER 150   *210*

Costello *v* Chief Constable of Northumbria [1999]
1 All ER 550   *77*

Credit Lyonnais Bank Nederland NV *v* Export
Credits Guarantee Department [1999] 1 All
ER 929   *15*

Crofter Hand Woven Harris Tweed Co Ltd *v*
Veitch [1942] AC 435   *116, 177*

Crook *v* Derbyshire Stone Ltd [1956] 2 All ER
447   *11*

Cross *v* Kirklees Metropolitan Borough Council
[1998] 1 All ER 654   *114*

Cummings *v* Grainger [1977] QB 397; [1976] 3
WLR 842   *149*

Cunningham *v* Harrison [1973] QB 942; [1973] 3
All ER 463   *187, 196*

Curtis *v* Betts [1990] 1 WLR 459; [1990] 1 All
ER 769   *149*

Cutler *v* United Dairies (London) Ltd [1933] 2 KB
297   *90–91*

Cutler *v* Wandsworth Stadium Ltd [1949] AC
398   *41, 111*

D & F Estates Ltd *v* Church Commissioners for
England [1989] AC 177; [1988] 3 WLR 368
63, 65, 66

Daish *v* Wanton [1972] 1 All ER 25   *184*

Dalton *v* Henry Angus & Co, Comrs of HM
Works and Public Buildings v Henry Angus
and Co (1881) 8 App Cas 740   *132*

Dann *v* Hamilton [1939] 1 KB 509   *90, 91, 108*

Darker *v* Chief Constable of West Midlands Police
[2000] 4 All ER 193   *2*

Davey *v* Harrow Corporation [1958] 1 QB 60;
[1957] 2 WLR 941   *131, 136*

Davie *v* New Merton Board Mills Ltd [1959] AC
604; [1959] 2 WLR 331   *118*

Davis *v* Ministry of Defence (1985) The Times 7
August   *206*

Davis *v* Radcliffe [1990] 1 WLR 821   *41, 80,
112*

Deeny *v* Gooda Walker Ltd (No 2) [1996] 1 All
ER 993   *184*

**Department of the Environment *v* Thomas
Bates & Son Ltd** [1991] 1 AC 499; [1990] 3
WLR 457   *42, 64, 65*

Delaware Mansions Ltd *v* Westminster City
Council [2001] 4 All ER 737   *131*

**Derbyshire County Council *v* Times
Newspapers Ltd** [1993] 2 WLR 449   *153*

Dews *v* National Coal Board [1988] AC 1; [1987]
2 All ER 545   *196*

Dobbie *v* Medway Health Authority [1994] 1
WLR 1234; [1994] 4 All ER 450   *205*

Doe d Bishop of Rochester *v* Bridges (1831) 1
B & Ad 847   *115*

Donnelly *v* Joyce [1974] QB 454   *187, 187–188*

Donoghue (or McAlister) *v* Stevenson [1932]
AC 562   *24, 29, 43, 48, 54, 99, 121*

Doughty *v* Turner Manufacturing Co Ltd [1964] 2
WLR 240   *99, 102*

Downs *v* Chappell [1996] 3 All ER 344   *166,
199*

Doyle *v* Olby (Ironmongers) Ltd [1969] 2 QB
158; [1969] 2 All ER 119   *167, 168*

Dulieu *v* White & Sons [1901] 2 KB 669   *67*

Dutton *v* Bognor Regis United Building Co Ltd
[1972] 2 WLR 299   *62, 63*

Dyer *v* Munday [1895] 1 QB 742   *14, 18*

East Suffolk Rivers Catchment Board *v* Kent
[1941] AC 74; [1940] 1 KB 319; [1940] 4 All
ER 527   *36, 37, 38*

Edward Wong Finance Co Ltd *v* Johnson, Stokes
& Master [1984] AC 296   *85*

Edwards *v* Railway Executive [1952] AC 737
124

Elguzouli-Daf *v* Metropolitan Police
Commissioner [1995] 2 WLR 173; [1995] 1
All ER 883   *78, 117*

**Emanuel (H & N) Ltd *v* Greater London
Council** [1971] 2 All ER 835   *19, 147*

Emeh *v* Kensington and Chelsea and Westminster
Area Health Authority [1985] QB 1012;
[1984] 3 All ER 1044   *179, 180, 181*

Esterhuizen *v* Allied Dunbar Assurance plc (1998)
The Times 10 June   *80*

Evans *v* London Hospital Medical College [1981]
1 WLR 184; [1981] 1 All ER 715   *2*

F *v* West Berkshire Health Authority [1990] 2 AC
1; [1989] 2 WLR 1025; [1989] 2 All ER 545
81

Ferguson *v* Welsh [1987] 1 WLR 1533; [1987] 3
All ER 777   *125*

Filliter *v* Phippard (1847) 11 QBD 347   *147*
Fish *v* Kelly (1864) 17 CBNS 194   *45*
Fishmongers' Co *v* East India Co (1752) 1 Dick
     164   *132*
Fitzgerald *v* Lane [1989] AC 328; [1987] QB
     781   **105**
Flack *v* Hudson (2000) The Times 22 November
     151
Forbes *v* Wandsworth Health Authority [1996] 4
     All ER 881   *208*
Foster *v* Warblington UDC [1906] 1 KB 648
     133, 134
Frenchay Healthcare NHS Trust *v* S [1994] 2 All
     ER 403   *81*

Galoo Ltd *v* Bright Grahame Murray [1994] 1
     WLR 1360; [1994] 1 All ER 16   *32*, **94**
Gardiner *v* Mountfield (1989) 5 BMLR 1   *179*
Gardner *v* Marsh & Parsons [1997] 3 All ER 871
     194
Gaskill *v* Preston [1981] 3 All ER 427   *197*
Geddis *v* Proprietors of Bann Reservoir (1878) 3
     App Cas 430   *39, 49*
General Cleaning Contractors *v* Christmas
     [1953] AC 180; [1953] 2 WLR 6   **118, 119**
**General Engineering Services Ltd *v* Kingston
     and Saint Andrew Corp** [1989] 1 WLR 69
     11
Giles *v* Walker (1890) 24 QBD 656   *136*
**Gillingham Borough Council *v* Medway
     (Chatham) Dock Co Ltd** [1993] QB 343
     138
Glasgow Corporation *v* Taylor [1922] 1 AC 448
     99
Glinski *v* McIver [1962] AC 726; [1962] 2 WLR
     862   *214*
Goldman *v* Hargrave [1967] 1 AC 645; [1966] 3
     WLR 513; [1966] 2 All ER 989   *136, 147*
Goldsmith *v* Bhoyrul [1997] 4 All ER 268   *154*
Goodes *v* East Sussex County Council [2000] 3
     All ER 603   **112**
Goodwill *v* British Pregnancy Advisory Service
     [1996] 2 All ER 161   *80*
Gorely *v* Codd [1966] 3 All ER 891   *3*
Grant *v* Australian Knitting Mills Ltd [1936]
     AC 85   **121**
Gray *v* Barr (Prudential Assurance Co Ltd, third
     party) [1971] 2 All ER 949   *185, 186*
Green *v* Chelsea Waterworks Co (1894) 70 LT
     547   *146*
Green *v* Fibreglass Ltd [1958] 2 All ER 521   *20*
Gregory *v* Portsmouth City Council [2000] 1 All
     ER 560   *30, 213*

Grobbelaar *v* News Group Newspapers Ltd [2001]
     2 All ER 437   *159*

Hague *v* Deputy Governor of Parkhurst Prison,
     Weldon *v* Home Office [1991] 3 All ER 733
     16, 117
Halford *v* Brookes [1991] 3 All ER 559   *206*
Halsey *v* Esso Petroleum Co Ltd [1961] 1 WLR
     683   *139*
Hambrook *v* Stokes Bros [1925] 1 KB 141; [1924]
     All ER 110   *57, 58, 67*
Hardwick *v* Hudson [1999] 3 All ER 426
     188
Harris *v* Birkenhead Corporation [1976] 1
     WLR 279; [1976] 1 All ER 341   *124*, **125**
Harris *v* Wyre Forest District Council *see* Smith *v*
     Eric S Bush
Harrison *v* Duke of Rutland [1893] 1 QB 142
     164
Harrison *v* Michelin Tyre Co Ltd [1985] 1 All ER
     918   *11*
Hatton *v* Sutherland [2002] 2 All ER 1   *120*
Hay (or Bourhill) *v* Young *see* Bourhill (or Hay) *v*
     Young
Haydon *v* Kent County Council [1978] 2 All ER
     97   *113, 114*
Haynes *v* Harwood [1935] 1 KB 146   *48, 91*
Heaven *v* Pender (1883) 11 QBD 503   *123*
**Hedley Byrne & Co Ltd *v* Heller & Partners
     Ltd** [1964] AC 465; [1963] 3 WLR 101;
     [1963] 2 All ER 575   *4, 5, 31, 35, 36,* **43,**
     45, 48, 63, 65, 70, 79
Heil *v* Rankin [2000] 3 All ER 138   *188*
Henderson *v* Henry E Jenkins & Sons [1970]
     AC 282; [1969] 3 WLR 732   **86**
Henderson *v* Merrett Syndicates Ltd [1994] 3 WLR
     761; [1994] 3 All ER 506   *4, 35, 36*
Hevican *v* Ruane [1991] 3 All ER 65   *25*
Hickman *v* Maisey [1900] 1 QB 752   *164*
Hill *v* Chief Constable of West Yorkshire
     [1989] AC 53; [1988] 2 All ER 238   *26, 31,
     34, 35, 38, 39,* **46,** *49, 50, 52, 75, 78, 162*
Hodgson *v* Trapp [1989] AC 807; [1988] 3 WLR
     1281   *192*
Holbeck Hall Hotel Ltd *v* Scarborough Borough
     Council [2000] 2 All ER 705   *32, 136*
Holley *v* Smyth [1998] 1 All ER 853   *154*
Holliday *v* National Telephone Co [1899] 2 QB
     392   *9,* **19,** *21*
Holman *v* Johnson (1775) 1 Cowp 341   *184*
Home Brewery plc *v* William Davis & Co
     (Loughborough) Ltd [1987] QB 339; [1987] 2
     WLR 117   *136*

Home Office *v* Dorset Yacht Co Ltd [1970] AC
   1004; [1970] 2 WLR 1140; [1970] 2 All ER
   294   *35, 39, 43, 46,* **47***, 73, 80*
**Honeywill & Stein Ltd *v* Larkin Bros
   (London's Commercial Photographers) Ltd**
   [1934] 1 KB 191   *9,* **20**
Hooper *v* Fynmores (2001) The Times 19 July
   79
Hotson *v* East Berkshire Area Health Authority
   [1987] 3 WLR 232   **94**
Hucks *v* Cole (1968) [1993] 4 Med LR 393   *85*
Hughes *v* Lord Advocate [1963] AC 837; [1963]
   2 WLR 779; [1963] 1 All ER 705   *61,* **98,**
   100
Hughes *v* National Union of Mineworkers
   [1991] 4 All ER 278   *47,* **49,** *60*
Humphries *v* Cousins (1877) 2 CPD 237   *142*
Hunt *v* Severs [1994] 2 All ER 385   **186,** *196*
Hunter *v* British Coal Corp [1998] 2 All ER 97
   25
**Hunter *v* Canary Wharf Ltd; Hunter *v* London
   Docklands Development Corp** [1997] 2 All
   ER 426   *123,* **131,** *134, 139*
Hunter *v* Chief Constable of West Midlands
   [1982] AC 529; [1981] 3 All ER 727   *27*
Hussain *v* Lancaster City Council [1999] 4 All ER
   125   *74, 134*
Hussain *v* New Taplow Paper Mills Ltd [1988]
   AC 514; [1988] 2 WLR 266; [1988] 1 All ER
   541   *187,* **188,** *192, 196, 197*

Ilkiw *v* Samuels [1963] 2 All ER 879   *14*
IM Properties plc *v* Cape & Dalgleish [1998] 3 All
   ER 203   *194*
Imperial Chemical Industries Ltd *v* Shatwell
   [1965] AC 656   *108*
Invercargill City Council *v* Hamlin [1996] 1 All
   ER 756   *64*
Issa *v* Hackney London Borough Council
   [1997] 1 All ER 999   **114,** *116*

Jackson *v* Harrison (1978) 138 CLR 438   *110*
Jaensch *v* Coffey (1984) 54 ALR 417   *24*
Jefferson *v* Derbyshire Farmers Ltd [1921] 2 KB
   281   *11*
Jobling *v* Associated Dairies Ltd [1982] AC 794;
   [1981] 3 WLR 155   *93,* **95**
John *v* MGN [1996] 2 All ER 35   *158, 204*
Jolley *v* Sutton London Borough Council [2000]
   3 All ER 409   **99,** *103*
Jones *v* Department of Employment [1989] QB
   1; [1988] 2 WLR 493; [1988] 1 All ER 725
   50

Joyce *v* Sengupta [1993] 1 WLR 337   **169**
Junior Books Ltd *v* Veitchi Co Ltd [1983] 1 AC
   520; [1982] 3 WLR 477   *64, 65*

Kane *v* New Forest District Council [2001] 3 All
   ER 914   **51,** *115*
Kay *v* Ayrshire and Arran Health Board [1987]
   2 All ER 417   **96,** *97*
Kennaway *v* Thompson [1981] QB 88; [1980] 3
   WLR 361   **134**
Kent *v* Griffiths [2000] 2 All ER 474   *41*
Khodaparast *v* Shad [2000] 1 All ER 545   *172*
Khorasandjian *v* Bush [1993] 3 All ER 669   *134*
Kiam *v* MGN Ltd [2002] 2 All ER 219   *159*
King *v* Phillips [1953] 1 QB 429; [1953] 1 All ER
   617   *66, 67*
Kirkham *v* Chief Constable of Greater Manchester
   Police [1990] 2 QB 283; [1990] 2 WLR 987;
   [1990] 3 All ER 246   *37*
Knightley *v* Johns [1982] 1 WLR 349; [1982] 1
   All ER 851   *35, 39, 50, 77,* **101**
Koursk, The [1924] P 140   *7, 8*
Kowal *v* Ellis (1977) 76 DLR (3d) 546   *210*
**Kuddus *v* Chief Constable of Leicestershire
   Constabulary** [2001] 3 All ER 193   *vii,*
   189

Lam *v* Brennan and Borough of Torbay [1997]
   PIQR P488   *51*
Lamb *v* Camden London Borough Council
   [1981] QB 625; [1981] 2 WLR 1038   **52**
Latimer *v* AEC Ltd [1953] 2 All ER 449   *113*
Law Society *v* KPMG Peat Marwick [2000] 4 All
   ER 540   *32*
Le Lievre *v* Gould [1893] 1 QB 49   *31*
Leach *v* Chief Constable of Gloucestershire
   Constabulary [1999] 1 All ER 215   *47*
**Leakey *v* National Trust for Places of Historic
   Interest or Natural Beauty** [1980] QB 485;
   [1980] 2 WLR 265   *131,* **135,** *143, 146*
Lee *v* Leeds City Council (2002) The Times 29
   January   *127–128*
Letang *v* Cooper [1965] 1 QB 232; [1964] 2 All
   ER 929   *129*
Limpus *v* London General Ombibus Co (1862)
   1 H & C 526   **12**
Lincoln *v* Daniels [1962] 1 QB 237; [1961] 3 All
   ER 740   *159, 160, 211*
Lincoln *v* Hayman [1982] 1 WLR 488; [1982] 2
   All ER 819   *197*
Lippiatt *v* South Gloucestershire Council [1999] 4
   All ER 149   *134*
Lister *v* Hesley Hall Ltd [2001] 2 All ER 769
   vii, **13**

Lloyd *v* DPP [1992] 1 All ER 982   *183*
Lloyd *v* Grace, Smith & Co [1912] AC 716
  11, 15
Longden *v* British Coal Corp [1988] 1 All ER 289
  196, 197
Lonrho Ltd *v* Shell Petroleum Co Ltd [1981] 3
  WLR 33   *115, 176, 177*
Lonrho Ltd *v* Shell Petroleum Co Ltd (No 2)
  [1982] AC 173; [1981] 2 All ER 456   *114*
Lonrho plc *v* Fayed [1992] 1 AC 448; [1991] 3
  WLR 188 (HL); [1990] 2 QB 479 (CA)
  116, 176
Lonrho plc *v* Tebbit [1992] 4 All ER 280   *53*
Loutchansky *v* Times Newspapers Ltd [2001] 4
  All ER 115   *155*
Loutchansky *v* Times Newspapers Ltd (No 2)
  [2002] 1 All ER 652   *155*
Lumley *v* Gye (1853) 2 E & B 216   *177, 178*
Luxmoore-May *v* Messenger May Baverstock
  [1990] 1 WLR 1009; [1990] 1 All ER 1067
  86

McAlister (or Donoghue) *v* Stevenson *see*
  Donoghue (or McAlister) *v* Stevenson
McAuley *v* Bristol City Council [1992] 1 QB
  134; [1992] 1 All ER 749   *126*
McCamley *v* Cammell Laird Shipbuilders Ltd
  [1990] 1 WLR 963; [1990] 1 All ER 854
  189, 191
McFarlane *v* E E Caledonia Ltd [1994] 2 All ER 1
  25, 67
McFarlane *v* Tayside Health Board [1999] 4 All
  ER 961   *32, 54*
McGhee *v* National Coal Board [1973] 1 WLR
  1; [1972] 3 All ER 1008   *68, 96*
McHale *v* Watson [1966] ALR 513; (1966) 115
  CLR 199   *60, 87*
McKay *v* Essex Area Health Authority [1982] QB
  1166; [1982] 2 All ER 771   *180*
McLoughlin *v* O'Brian [1983] 1 AC 410; [1982]
  2 WLR 982; [1982] 2 All ER 298   *23, 24,
  25, 29, 57, 67*
Mahon *v* Rahn (No 2) [2000] 4 All ER 41
  156, 211
Malone *v* Laskey [1907] 2 KB 141   *123, 133*
Malz *v* Rosen [1966] 1 WLR 1008   *213*
Marc Rich & Co AG *v* Bishop Rock Marine Co
  Ltd, The Nicholas H [1996] 1 AC 211; [1995]
  3 All ER 307; [1994] 1 WLR 1071   *33*
Marcic *v* Thames Water Utilities Ltd [2002] 2 All
  ER 55   *136*
Mariola Marine Corporation *v* Lloyd's Register of
  Shipping, The Morning Watch [1990] 1
  Lloyd's Rep 547   *32*

Marshall *v* Osmond [1983] QB 1034; [1983] 2 All
  ER 225   *38*
Martin *v* Watson [1995] 3 All ER 559   *212*
Maynard *v* West Midlands Regional Health
  Authority [1984] 1 WLR 634; [1985] 1 All
  ER 635   *83, 84, 87*
Meah *v* McCreamer [1985] 1 All ER 367   *185,
  186*
Meah *v* McCreamer (No 2) [1986] 1 All ER 943
  185, 186
Meering *v* Grahame-White Aviation Co Ltd
  (1919) 122 LT 44   *161*
Merrington *v* Ironbridge Metal Works Ltd [1952]
  2 All ER 1101   *107*
Merryweather *v* Nixon (1799) 8 Term Rep 186
  185
Mersey Docks and Harbour Board Trustees *v*
  Gibbs (1866) LR 1 HL 93   *39, 72*
Metall und Rohstoff AG *v* Donaldson Lufkin &
  Jenrette Inc [1990] 1 QB 391; [1989] 3 WLR
  563   *176, 177*
Michaels *v* Taylor Woodrow Development Ltd
  [2000] 4 All ER 645   *116*
Mid Kent Holdings plc *v* General Utilities plc
  [1996] 3 All ER 132   *116*
Miller *v* Jackson [1977] QB 966; [1977] 3 WLR
  20   *135*
Mills *v* Winchester Diocesan Board of Finance
  [1989] Ch 428; [1989] 2 All ER 317   *51*
Morgan Crucible Co plc *v* Hill Samuel Bank Ltd
  [1991] 1 All ER 148; [1990] 3 All ER 330
  32, 94
Morris *v* C W Martin & Sons Ltd [1966] 1 QB
  716; [1965] 3 WLR 276   *13, 14, 15*
Morris *v* Murray [1991] 2 WLR 195   *107*
Morriss *v* Marsden [1952] 1 All ER 925   *2*
Mount Isa Mines *v* Pusey (1970) 125 CLR 383
  77
Mulcahy *v* Ministry of Defence [1996] 2 WLR
  474; [1996] 2 All ER 758   *50, 59, 119*
Mullin *v* Richards [1998] 1 All ER 920   *60*
Murphy *v* Brentwood District Council [1991] 1
  AC 398; [1990] 3 WLR 414; [1990] 2 All ER
  908   *42, 43, 53, 62, 65, 66, 73*
Murray *v* Ministry of Defence [1988] 2 All ER
  521   *161*
Musgrove *v* Pandelis [1919] 2 KB 43   *19, 147*

Nabi *v* British Leyland (UK) Ltd [1980] 1 All ER
  667   *196*
Nash *v* Eli Lily & Co [1993] 4 All ER 383   *207*
National Coal Board *v* J E Evans & Co (Cardiff)
  Ltd [1951] 2 KB 861   *3*

Nelson Holdings Ltd *v* British Gas plc (1997) The Times 7 March   *38, 41*

Nettleship *v* Weston [1971] 2 QB 691; [1971] 3 WLR 370   *91, 108*

Newcastle-under-Lyme Corp *v* Wolstanton Ltd [1946] 2 All ER 447   *133*

Newton *v* Edgerley [1959] 1 WLR 1031   *3*

NHS Trust A *v* M [2001] 1 All ER 801   *82*

Nitrigin Eireann Teoranta *v* Inco Alloys Ltd [1992] 1 WLR 498; [1992] 1 All ER 854   *43, 64*

Noble *v* Harrison [1926] 2 KB 332   *146*

Nocton *v* Lord Ashburton [1914] AC 932   *45*

Nykredit Mortgage Bank plc *v* Edward Erdman Group Ltd (No 2) [1998] 1 All ER 305   *192*

O'Connor *v* Waldron [1935] AC 76   *211*

Ogopogo, The [1971] 2 Lloyd's Rep 410   *37*

Ogwo *v* Taylor [1988] AC 431; [1987] 3 WLR 1145; [1987] 3 All ER 961   *36, 99, 128*

OLL Ltd *v* Secretary of State for Transport [1997] 3 All ER 897   *41*

Olutu *v* Home Office [1997] 1 All ER 385   *116*

Osman *v* Ferguson [1993] 4 All ER 344   *37, 47*

Osman *v* United Kingdom (1998) 5 BHRC 293   *51*

Overseas Tankship (UK) Ltd *v* Morts Dock & Engineering Co Ltd, The Wagon Mound (No 1) [1961] AC 388; [1961] 1 All ER 404   *48, 82, 99, 100, 101, 102*

Overseas Tankship (UK) Ltd *v* The Miller Steamship Co Pty Ltd, The Wagon Mound (No 2) [1967] 1 AC 617; [1966] 3 WLR 498   *86, 100, 101, 102, 143*

Owens *v* Brimmell [1977] QB 859   *108*

Page *v* Smith [1995] 2 WLR 644; [1995] 2 All ER 736   *29, 66, 68*

Page *v* Smith (No 2) [1996] 1 WLR 855; [1996] 3 All ER 272   *68, 96, 97*

Pannett *v* P McGuinness & Co Ltd [1972] 3 WLR 386   *124*

Pape *v* Cumbria County Council [1992] 3 All ER 211; [1992] ICR 132   *119*

Parker *v* British Airways Board [1982] 1 QB 1004   *209, 210*

Parkinson *v* St James and Seacroft University Hospital NHS Trust [2001] 3 All ER 97   *56*

Parry *v* Cleaver [1970] AC 1; [1969] 2 WLR 821; [1969] 1 All ER 555   *184, 187, 189, 194, 196, 197*

Patel *v* Hooper & Jackson [1999] 1 All ER 992   *199*

Paterson Zochonis & Co Ltd *v* Merfarken Packaging Ltd [1986] 3 All ER 522   *49*

Peabody Donation Fund (Governors of) *v* Sir Lindsay Parkinson & Co Ltd [1985] AC 210; [1984] 3 All ER 529   *31*

Pearce *v* Round Oak Steel Works Ltd [1969] 3 All ER 680   *86*

Pemberton *v* Southwark London Borough Council [2000] 3 All ER 924   *134*

Performance Cars Ltd *v* Abraham [1962] 1 QB 33; [1961] 3 WLR 749   *97*

Perl (P) (Exporters) Ltd *v* Camden London Borough Council [1984] QB 342   *72*

Phelps *v* Hillingdon London Borough Council [2000] 4 All ER 504   *16, 112*

Philcox *v* Civil Aviation Authority (1995) The Times 8 June   *34*

Photo Production Ltd *v* Securicor Transport Ltd [1980] 1 All ER 556   *13, 14*

Pitts *v* Hunt [1991] 1 QB 24; [1990] 3 WLR 542; [1990] 3 All ER 344   *108, 130*

Platform Home Loans Ltd *v* Oyston Shipways Ltd [1999] 1 All ER 833   *199*

Poland *v* John Parr & Sons [1927] 1 KB 240   *18*

Polemis and Furness, Withy & Co, Re [1921] 3 KB 560   *48, 102*

Pontardawe Rural District Council *v* Moore-Gwyn [1929] 1 Ch 656   *136*

Port Swettenham Authority *v* TW Wu & Co (M) Sdn Bhd [1978] 3 All ER 337   *13*

Possfund Custodian Trustee Ltd *v* Diamond [1996] 2 All ER 774   *32*

Practice Note [1996] 4 All ER 766   *82*

Praed *v* Graham (1889) 24 QBD 53   *156*

Punjab National Bank *v* de Boinville [1992] 1 WLR 1138   *32*

Quinn *v* Leathem [1901] AC 495   *104, 116, 176*

R *v* Associated Octel Co Ltd [1996] 4 All ER 846   *10*

R *v* Colohan (2001) The Times 14 June   *162*

R *v* Governor of Brockhill Prison, ex parte Evans (No 2) [2000] 4 All ER 15   *117*

R *v* Ireland [1997] 4 All ER 225 (HL); [1997] 1 All ER 112 (CA)   *162*

R *v* Meade and Belt (1823) 1 Lew CC 184   *162*

R *v* Wilson [1955] 1 WLR 493; [1955] 1 All ER 744   *162*

Racz *v* Home Office [1994] 2 WLR 23   *15*

Rainham Chemical Works Ltd *v* Belvedere Fish Guano Co [1921] 2 AC 465   *142, 143*

Rantzen v Mirror Group Newspapers (1986) Ltd [1993] 3 WLR 953; [1993] 4 All ER 975 *156, 200*

Ravenscroft v Rederiaktiebolaget Transatlantic [1992] 2 All ER 470; [1991] 3 All ER 73   *25*

RCA Corp v Pollard [1982] 3 WLR 1007   *116*

Read v J Lyons & Co Ltd [1947] AC 156   *144*

Reckitt & Colman Products Ltd v Bordern Inc [1990] 1 WLR 491   *174*

Redgrave v Hurd (1881) 20 Ch D 1   *104*

Rees v Darlington Memorial Hospital NHS Trust (2002) The Times 20 February   *56*

Rees v Skerrett (2001) The Times 18 June   *137*

Reeves v Commissioner of Police of the Metropolis [1999] 3 All ER 897   *41*

Revill v Newbery [1996] 2 WLR 239; [1996] 1 All ER 291   *110, 124, 126,* **129**

Reynell v Champernoon (1631) Cro Car 228 *182*

Reynolds v Times Newspapers Ltd [1999] 4 All ER 609   *155*

Rickards v Lothian [1913] AC 263   *144, 148*

Rigby v Chief Constable of Northamptonshire [1985] 1 WLR 1242; [1985] 2 All ER 985 *35, 39, 50*

Rondel v Worsley [1969] 1 AC 191; [1967] 3 WLR 1666; [1967] 3 All ER 993 (HL); [1966] 3 WLR 950 (CA)   *27, 28, 47*

Rookes v Barnard [1964] AC 1129; [1964] 1 All ER 367   *155, 176, 189, 190, 191*

Rose v Plenty [1976] 1 WLR 141; [1976] 1 All ER 97   *12, 14*

Ross v Caunters [1980] Ch 297; [1979] 3 All ER 580   *79*

Rowe v Herman [1997] 1 WLR 1390   *21*

Rowling v Takaro Properties [1988] AC 473; [1988] 1 All ER 163   *31, 53, 54*

Roy v Kensington and Chelsea and Westminster Family Practitioner Committee [1992] 1 All ER 705   *54*

Royal Aquarium and Summer and Winter Garden Society Ltd v Parkinson [1892] 1 QB 431 *159, 211*

Royscot Trust Ltd v Rogerson [1991] 3 All ER 294   *167*

Rylands v Fletcher (1868) LR 3 HL 330; affirming (1866) LR 1 Ex 265   *21, 136, 141, 142, 143, 144,* **145,** *148*

Saif Ali v Sydney Mitchell & Co [1980] AC 198; [1978] 3 WLR 849; [1978] 3 All ER 1033 *27, 40*

St Helens Colliery Co Ltd v Hewitson [1924] AC 59   *17*

Salmon v Seafarer Restaurants Ltd [1983] 1 WLR 264; [1983] 3 All ER 729   *128, 129*

Salsbury v Woodland [1970] 1 QB 324   *9, 19, 20*

Sasea Finance Ltd v KPMG [2000] 1 All ER 676 *94*

Scott v London and St Katherine Docks Co (1865) 3 H & C 596   *87*

Scott v Shepherd (1733) 2 Wm Bl 892   *103*

Sedleigh-Denfield v O'Callaghan [1940] AC 880 *136*

Shakoor v Situ [2000] 4 All ER 181   *85*

Shelfer v City of London Electric Lighting Co Ltd [1895] 1 Ch 287   *135*

Sidaway v Bethlem Royal Hospital Governors [1985] AC 871   **88**

Simms v Leigh Rugby Football Club Ltd [1969] 2 All ER 923   *86*

Sirros v Moore [1975] QB 118; [1974] 3 WLR 459   **3**

Slater v Clay Cross Co Ltd [1956] 2 QB 264 *108*

Smith v Baker & Sons [1891] AC 325   *182*

Smith v Eric S Bush, Harris v Wyre Forest District Council [1989] 2 WLR 790   **70**

Smith v Jenkins (1970) 119 CLR 397   *109*

Smith v Littlewoods Organisation Ltd [1987] AC 241; [1987] 2 WLR 480   **71**

Smith v Stages [1989] AC 928; [1989] 2 WLR 529   **16**

Smith New Court Securities Ltd v Scrimgeour Vickers (Asset Management) Ltd [1996] 4 All ER 769   **166**

Smoker v London Fire and Civil Defence Authority; Wood v British Coal Corp [1996] 2 WLR 1052; [1991] 2 All ER 449 **196,** *197*

Sochacki v Sas [1947] 1 All ER 344   *147*

South Australia Asset Management Corp v York Montague Ltd; United Bank of Kuwait plc v Prudential Property Services Ltd; Nykredit Mortgage Bank plc v Edward Erdman Group Ltd [1996] 3 WLR 87; [1996] 3 All ER 365   *166,* **197**

South Hetton Coal Co Ltd v North-Eastern News Association Ltd [1894] 1 QB 133   *153*

Southwark London Borough Council v Mills [1999] 4 All ER 449   *134*

Spring v Guardian Assurance plc [1994] 3 WLR 355; [1994] 3 All ER 129   *45, 77*

Stafford v Conti Commodity Services Ltd [1981] 1 All ER 691   *88, 90*

Stear v Scott [1992] RTR 226   *183*

Stephens *v* Anglian Water Authority [1987] 3 All
  ER 379   *1*
Stovin *v* Wise [1996] 3 WLR 389; [1996] 3 All
  ER 801   *33, 39, 51, 64,* **72,** *186*
Sturge *v* Hackett [1962] 3 All ER 166   *19, 147*
Sutcliffe *v* Pressdram [1990] 1 All ER 269   *156*
Sutherland Shire Council *v* Heyman (1985) 60
  ALR 1   *31, 33, 53, 64*
Swingcastle Ltd *v* Alastair Gibson (A Firm)
  [1991] 2 All ER 353   *198*
**Swinney *v* Chief Constable of Northumbria
  Police** [1996] 3 All ER 449   *49,* **74**

Targett *v* Torfaen Borough Council [1992] 3 All
  ER 27   *64*
Taylor *v* Serious Fraud Office [1998] 4 All ER
  801 (HL); [1997] 4 All ER 887 (CA)   *2,
  213*
Tetley *v* Chitty [1986] 1 All ER 663   *135*
Thake *v* Maurice [1986] QB 669; [1986] 1 All ER
  497   *179, 180*
**Thomas *v* National Union of Mineworkers
  (South Wales Area)** [1985] 2 WLR 1081
  139
Thomas *v* News Goups Newspapers Ltd (2001)
  The Times 25 July   *162*
**Thompson *v* Commissioner of Police of the
  Metropolis; HSU *v* Commissioner of Police
  of the Metropolis** [1997] 2 All ER 762
  158, **199**
Thompson-Schwab *v* Costaki [1956] 1 All ER 652
  133
Thornton *v* Kirklees Metropolitan Borough
  Council [1979] QB 626; [1979] 3 WLR 1
  112
Three Rivers District Council *v* Bank of England
  (No 3) [2000] 3 All ER 1   *16, 78*
Tojo Maru, The [1971] 1 All ER 1110   *38*
Torquay Hotel Co Ltd *v* Cousins [1969] 2 Ch 106;
  [1969] 1 All ER 522   *178*
Trapp *v* Mackie [1979] 1 All ER 489   *211*
Trotman *v* North Yorkshire County Council
  [1999] LGR 584   *15*
Tuberville *v* Savage (1699) 1 Mod Rep 3   **162**
Tuberville *v* Stampe (1697) 1 Ld Raym 264
  147

**Van Oppen *v* Clerk to the Bedford Charity
  Trustees** [1990] 1 WLR 235   **75**
Vandyke *v* Fender [1970] 2 WLR 929   *17*
Vaughan *v* Menlove (1837) 3 Bing NC 468   *147*
Vernon *v* Bosley (No 1) [1997] 1 All ER 577
  25

Vine *v* Waltham Forest London Borough Council
  [2000] 4 All ER 169   *184*

W *v* Essex County Council [2000] 2 All ER 237
  25, 78
Wagon Mound (No 1), The *see* Overseas
  Tankship (UK) *v* Morts Dock & Engineering
  Co
Wagon Mound (No 2), The *see* Overseas
  Tankship (UK) Ltd *v* The Miller Steamship
  Co Pty Ltd
Walker *v* Geo H Medlicott & Son [1999] 1 All ER
  685   *80*
Walkin *v* South Manchester Health Authority
  [1995] 4 All ER 132   *181*
Wallace *v* Newton [1982] 1 WLR 375   **150**
Wandsworth London Borough Council *v* Railtrack
  plc (2001) The Times 2 August   *139*
Waple *v* Surrey County Council [1998] 1 All
  ER 624   *2,* **159**
Ward *v* Cannock Chase District Council [1985] 3
  All ER 537   *52*
Ward *v* T E Hopkins & Son Ltd [1959] 1 WLR
  966; [1959] 3 All ER 225   *91*
Ward *v* Tesco Stores Ltd [1976] 1 WLR 810
  88
Warren *v* Henlys Ltd [1948] 2 All ER 935   *10,
  14,* **17**
**Waters *v* Commissioner of Police of the
  Metropolis** [2000] 4 All ER 934   *30, 47,* **76**
Watson *v* M'Ewan, Watson *v* Jones [1905] AC
  480   *159, 160*
Waverley Borough Council *v* Fletcher [1995] 3
  WLR 772; [1995] 4 All ER 756   *210*
Wells *v* Wells [1997] 1 All ER 673   *188*
Welsh *v* Chief Constable of the Merseyside Police
  [1993] 1 All ER 692   *37*
West *v* Bristol Tramways Co [1908] 2 KB 14
  142
Wheat *v* E Lacon & Co Ltd [1966] AC 552;
  [1966] 2 WLR 581   *148*
White *v* Blackmore [1972] 2 QB 651; [1972] 3
  WLR 296   *91*
White *v* Chief Constable of Yorkshire Police
  [1999] 1 All ER 1   *25, 59, 68, 77*
White *v* Jones [1995] 2 WLR 187; [1995] 1 All
  ER 691   *32,* **79**
Whitehouse *v* Jordan [1981] 1 WLR 246   **89**
Wilkinson *v* Ancliff (BLT) Ltd [1986] 3 All ER
  427   *206*
Wilks *v* The Cheltenham Home Guard Motor
  Cycle Light Car Club [1971] 1 WLR 668   *91*
Williams *v* Jones (1865) 3 H & C 602   *11*

Williams *v* Ladner (1798) 8 Term Rep 72
  183
Williams *v* Natural Life Health Foods [1998] 2
  All ER 577 (HL); [1997] 1 BCLC 131 (CA)
  4, 9, 45
Wilsher *v* Essex Area Health Authority [1988] AC
  1074; [1987] 2 WLR 425; [1988] 1 All ER
  871   *68, 84*
Wilson *v* Pringle [1987] QB 237; [1986] 2 All ER
  440   *162*
Wisely *v* John Fulton (Plumbers) Ltd [2000] 2 All
  ER 545   *189*
Wood *v* British Coal Corp *see* Smoker *v* London
  Fire and Civil Defence Authority
Woods *v* Martins Bank Ltd [1958] 3 All ER 166
  45

Wooldridge *v* Sumner [1963] 2 QB 43; [1963] 3
  WLR 616   *90*

X (Minors) *v* Bedfordshire County Council; M *v*
  Newham London Borough Council; E *v*
  Dorset County Council; Christmas *v*
  Hampshire County Council; Keating *v*
  Bromley London Borough Council [1995] 3
  WLR 152; [1995] 3 All ER 353   *2, 38, 39,*
  40, 73, 78, 117

Yianni *v* Edwin Evans & Sons [1982] QB 438
  71
**Yuen Kun Yeu *v* Attorney-General of Hong
  Kong** [1988] AC 175; [1987] 3 WLR 776;
  [1987] 2 All ER 705   *26, 31, 41, 80, 112*

1 Introduction

Bradford Corporation v Pickles
[1895] AC 587 House of Lords
(Lords Halsbury LC, Watson,
Ashbourne and Macnaghten)

* *Lawful act, improper motive*

Facts
The defendant prevented water percolating under his land from flowing to the plaintiffs' adjoining land from which it drew its supply.

Held
His lawful act was not rendered unlawful even if he had done it with the sole object of compelling the plaintiffs to acquire rights in the water at his own price.

Lord Halsbury LC:

'This is not a case where the state of mind of the person doing the act can affect the right to do it. If it was a lawful act, however ill the motive be, he had a right to do it. If it was an unlawful act, however good his motive might be, he would have no right to do it.'

Comment
In *Allen* v *Flood* [1898] AC 1 Lord Watson said that Lord Halsbury LC's statement was confined to the class of case then before the House, but he apprehended that what was said was not applicable only to rights of property, but was equally applicable to the exercise by an individual of his other rights. *Pickles* was applied in *Stephens* v *Anglian Water Authority* [1987] 3 All ER 379 (landowner entitled to exercise right to abstract subterranean water flowing in undefined channels under his land regardless of consequences, physical or pecuniary, to neighbours and regardless of motive or intention or whether he anticipated damage).

2 Parties to an Action in Tort

Evans v *London Hospital Medical College* [1981] 1 WLR 184 High Court (Drake J)

- *Witness – immunity from civil action*

Facts
At the request of the police the defendants carried out a post-mortem on the plaintiff's infant son: they reported that they had found morphine in the organs examined by them and the plaintiff was subsequently charged with her son's murder. A pathologist engaged by the plaintiff found no traces of morphine in other organs examined by him. At the plaintiff's trial the prosecution offered no evidence against her and she was acquitted: she claimed damages for negligence or malicious prosecution.

Held
Her action would fail, as to malicious prosecution because the law had not been set in motion by the defendants and, as to both grounds, because the defendants were covered by the absolute immunity from any civil action conferred on a witness in criminal proceedings in respect of his evidence.

Drake J:

'I think it essential that the immunity given to a witness should also extend to cover statements he makes prior to the issue of a writ or commencement of a prosecution, provided that the statement is made for the purpose of a possible action or prosecution and at a time when a possible action or prosecution is being considered. In a large number of criminal cases the police have collected statements from witnesses before anyone is charged with an offence; indeed sometimes before it is known whether or not *any* criminal offence has been committed.'

Comment
Approved in *X (Minors)* v *Bedfordshire County Council* [1995] 3 All ER 353 (immunity of psychiatrist's report on child allegedly sexually abused). Distinguished in *Darker* v *Chief Constable of the West Midlands Police* [2000] 4 All ER 193 (immunity of witnesses from civil action does not extend to deliberate fabrication of police evidence).

See also *Taylor* v *Serious Fraud Office* [1998] 4 All ER 801 and *Waple* v *Surrey County Council* [1998] 1 All ER 624.

Morriss v *Marsden* [1952] 1 All ER 925 High Court (Stable J)

- *Liability of person of unsound mind*

Facts
The defendant violently attacked the plaintiff, a hotel manager. On a charge of criminal assault, the defendant was found unfit to plead and was directed to be detained to await His Majesty's pleasure. The plaintiff claimed damages for assault and battery and it was found that, although the defendant knew the nature and quality of his act, his mental illness was such that he did not know that what he was doing was wrong.

Held
The plaintiff was entitled to damages.

Stable J:

'I have come to the conclusion that knowledge of wrongdoing is an immaterial averment, and that, where there is the capacity to know the nature and quality of the act, that is sufficient although the mind directing the hand that did the wrong was diseased.'

Comment
Applied: *National Coal Board* v *J E Evans & Co (Cardiff) Ltd* [1951] 2 KB 861.

Newton v *Edgerley* [1959] 1 WLR 1031 High Court (Lord Parker CJ)

• *Parent's liability*

Facts
The defendant allowed his son, aged 12, to buy himself a .410 gun and showed him how to use it, but he told him that he must not take the gun off the farm where they lived and that he was not to use the gun when other children were present. The defendant did not instruct the boy how to handle the gun in the presence of others. The boy disobeyed his father and another boy, the plaintiff, was shot in the head when the gun went off.

Held
The defendant was liable in negligence. He could not possibly have ensured that his orders would be obeyed and he had failed to teach his son how to handle the gun when others were present.

Lord Parker CJ:

'I hold that there was a failure on the part of the defendant to use reasonable care to prevent his son using a gun at all, or alternatively, if the son was to be allowed to use a gun, not to instruct him as to its use if the boy succumbed to temptation and went out with others.'

Comment
Distinguished in *Gorely* v *Codd* [1966] 3 All ER 891 (defendant had given 16½-year-old son proper and adequate instruction in use of air rifle, so not liable).

Sirros v *Moore* [1974] 3 WLR 459 Court of Appeal (Lord Denning MR, Buckley and Ormrod LJJ)

• *Judicial immunity*

Facts
The plaintiff, a citizen of Turkey, was brought before a magistrate for breach of the Aliens Order 1953. He was fined £50 and the magistrate recommended that he be deported, adding that he should not be detained pending the Home Secretary's final decision as to deportation. The plaintiff's appeal to the Crown Court against the deportation recommendation was dismissed, but the circuit judge ordered police officers to detain the plaintiff and he was taken away in custody. The plaintiff sued the defendants, the circuit judge and the police officers, for damages for assault and false imprisonment.

Held
Although the plaintiff's detention had been unlawful (the appeal against the magistrate's order having merely been dismissed), the plaintiff had no cause of action against the circuit judge as he had acted judicially and under the honest (though mistaken) belief that his act was within his jurisdiction. No action lay against the police officers as they had acted at the judge's direction, not knowing it was wrong.

Lord Denning MR:

'Today we are concerned with judges of a new kind. The judges of the Crown Court. It is, by definition, a superior court of record: see s4(1) of the [Courts Act 1971]. The judges of it should, in principle, have the same immunity as all other judges, high or low. The Crown Court is manned by judges of every rank. Judges of the High Court, circuit judges, recorders, justices of the peace, all sit there. No distinction can or should be drawn between them. Each one shares responsibility for the decisions given by the court. If the High Court judge is not liable to an action, it should be the same with the circuit judge, the recorder or the justice of the peace. No distinction can be taken on the seriousness of the case. Any one of them may sit on one day on a case of trifling importance, on the next on a case of the utmost gravity. No distinction can be taken as to the nature of the case. It may be a matter triable only on indictment, or it may be a man up for sentence, or an appeal from magistrates. If they are not liable in trials on indictment, they should not be liable on other matters. But, whatever it is, the immunity of the judges – and each of them – should rest on the same principle. Not liable for acts done by them in a judicial capacity. Only liable for acting in bad faith, knowing they have no jurisdiction to do it.'

Comment

Considered: *Anderson* v *Gorrie* [1895] 1 QB 668. As to the immunity of justices of the peace and justices' clerks, see ss51 and 52 of the Justices of the Peace Act 1997. See also s69 of the Courts and Legal Services Act 1990 (exemption from liability of Lord Chancellor and designated judges).

Williams v *Natural Life Health Foods Ltd* [1998] 2 All ER 577 House of Lords (Lords Goff of Chieveley, Steyn, Hoffmann, Clyde and Hutton)

• *Company director – liability for company's negligent advice*

Facts

Mr Mistlin, the second defendant, formed the defendant company, of which he was managing director and the principal shareholder, in order to franchise the concept of retail health food shops. The plaintiffs entered into a franchise agreement, but their business failed. They were awarded damages for negligent advice. The defendant company having been dissolved, the question was whether Mr Mistlin was personally liable.

Held

On the facts, this was not the case.

Lord Steyn:

'*The theory of the extended Hedley Byrne principle …*
It is clear, and accepted by counsel on both sides, that the governing principles are stated in the leading speech of Lord Goff of Chieveley in *Henderson* v *Merrett Syndicates Ltd* [1994] 3 All ER 506. First in *Henderson*'s case it was settled that the assumption of responsibility principle enuciated in *Hedley Byrne & Co Ltd* v *Heller & Partners Ltd* [1963] 2 All ER 575 is not confined to statements but may apply to any assumption of responsibility for the provision of services. The extended *Hedley Byrne* principle is the rationalisation or technique adopted by English law to provide a remedy for the recovery of damages in respect of economic loss caused by the negligent performance of services. Secondly, it was established that once a case is identified as falling within the extended *Hedley Byrne* principle, there is no need to embark on any further inquiry whether it is "fair, just and reasonable" to impose liability for economic loss (see [1994] 3 All ER 506 at 521). Thirdly, and applying *Hedley Byrne*, it was made clear that –

"reliance upon [the assumption of responsibility] by the other party will be necessary to establish a cause of action (because otherwise the negligence will have no causative effect …" (See [1994] 3 All ER 506 at 520)

Fourthly, it was held that the existence of a contractual duty of care between the parties does not preclude the concurrence of a tort duty in the same respect.

It will be recalled that [when this case was in the Court of Appeal] Waite LJ took the view that in the context of directors of companies the general principle must not "set at naught" the protection of limited liability. …

What matters is not that the liability of the shareholders of a company is limited but that a company is a separate entity, distinct from its directors, servants or other agents.

The trader who incorporates a company to which he transfers his business creates a legal person on whose behalf he may afterwards act as director. For present purposes, his position is the same as if he had sold his business to another individual and agreed to act on his behalf. Thus the issue in this case is not peculiar to companies. Whether the principal is a company or a natural person, someone acting on his behalf may incur personal liability in tort as well as imposing vicarious or attributed liability upon his principal. But in order to establish personal liability under the principle of *Hedley Byrne*, which requires the existence of a special relationship between plaintiff and tortfeasor, it is not sufficient that there should have been a special relationship with the principal. There must have been an assumption of responsibility such as to create a special relationship with the director or employee himself. ... it is important to make clear that a director of a contracting company may only be held liable where it is established by evidence that he assumed personal liability and that there was the necessary reliance. ...

Applying the principle to the facts

Mr Mistlin owned and controlled the company. The company held itself out as having the expertise to provide reliable advice to franchisees. The brochure made clear that this expertise derived from Mr Mistlin's experience ... In my view these circumstances were insufficient to make Mr Mistlin personally liable to the plaintiffs. Stripped to essentials ... the arguments of counsel for the plaintiffs can be considered under two headings. First, it is said that the terms of the brochure, and in particular its description of the role of Mr Mistlin, are sufficient to amount to an assumption of responsibility by Mr Mistlin. In his dissenting judgment [in the Court of Appeal] ([1997] 1 BCLC 131 at 156) Sir Patrick Russell rightly pointed out that in a small one-man company "the managing director will almost inevitably be the one possessed of qualities essential to the functioning of the company". By itself this factor does not

convey that the managing director is willing to be personally answerable to the customers of the company. Secondly, great emphasis was placed on the fact that it was made clear to the franchisees that Mr Mistlin's expertise derived from his experience in running [his] Salisbury shop for his own account. ... The point will simply not bear the weight put on it. Postulate a food expert who over ten years gains experience in advising customers on his own account. Then he incorporates his business as a company and he so advises his customers. Surely, it cannot be right to say that in the new situation his earlier experience on his own account is indicative of an assumption of personal responsibility towards his customers. In the present case there were no personal dealings between Mr Mistlin and the plaintiffs. There were no exchanges or conduct crossing the line which could have conveyed to the plaintiffs that Mr Mistlin was willing to assume personal responsibility to them. Contrary to the submissions of counsel for the plaintiffs, I am also satisfied that there was not even evidence that the plaintiffs believed that Mr Mistlin was undertaking personal responsibility to them. Certainly, there was nothing in the circumstances to show that the plaintiffs could reasonably have looked to Mr Mistlin for indemnification of any loss. For these reasons I would reject the principal argument of counsel for the plaintiffs.

The joint tortfeasor point

Counsel for the plaintiffs tried to support the judgment of the Court of Appeal ([1997] 1 BCLC 131) on the alternative ground that Mr Mistlin had played a prominent part in the production of the negligent projections and had directed that the projections be supplied to the plaintiffs. Accordingly, he submitted, Mr Mistlin was a joint tortfeasor with the company, the latter being liable to the plaintiffs on the extended *Hedley Byrne* principle.

... the argument is unsustainable. A moment's reflection will show that, if the argument were to be accepted in the present case, it would expose directors, officers and employees of companies carrying on business as providers of services to a plethora of new tort claims. The fallacy in the argument is clear. In the present case liability of the company is dependent on a special relationship with the plaintiffs giving rise to an assumption of responsibility. Mr Mistlin was a stranger to that particular relationship.

He cannot therefore be liable as a joint tortfeasor with the company. If he is to be held liable to the plaintiffs, it could only be on the basis of a special relationship between himself and the plaintiffs. There is none. I would therefore reject this alternative argument.'

3 Joint and Several Tortfeasors

Brooke v Bool [1928] 2 KB 578 High Court (Salter and Talbot JJ)

- *Joint tortfeasors*

Facts
The plaintiff tenant of a lock-up shop had asked her landlord, who lived in adjoining premises, to visit the shop occasionally at night to see that everything was secure. When the defendant landlord's lodger (Morris) complained of a smell of gas from the shop, both went to investigate. Both used naked lights, but the lodger's caused an explosion and the plaintiff sought damages from the defendant in respect of damage to her goods.

Held
The plaintiff's action should succeed.

Salter J:

'In my opinion there are three grounds on which it was competent in law for the learned [county court] judge to find that the defendant was responsible for what was obviously a grossly reckless act on the part of Morris – namely, holding a naked light near to a place where he suspected an escape of gas. First, I think that there was evidence of agency. The defendant desired to examine this pipe, and examined it himself so far as he could in a most reckless and dangerous way with a naked light. He then desired to examine the upper part of it. Now the defendant was an old man of nearly eighty years of age, and he had in his company a much younger man. I think that there was ample evidence that the defendant impliedly invited and instructed Morris to get up on to the counter and complete the examination, when it was not convenient for him to continue it himself, and that Morris

did what he did on the instructions of the defendant. The maxim Qui facit per alium facit per se applies, and on that first ground I think that there was evidence on which the judge could have found the defendant responsible.

Secondly, he could have been held responsible on the score of the control which he exercised over the proceedings. It is necessary to bear in mind the difference between the position of the defendant and that of Morris. The defendant was on the premises lawfully, at the request of the plaintiff, whereas Morris was a trespasser, unless the defendant had a right to invite him there to help. There was ample evidence on which the judge could find that the invitation by the plaintiff to the defendant to keep a watch over the premises extended to the right to bring in someone to help him on an occasion of that kind. In my opinion, Morris was there by the permission and invitation of the defendant, since otherwise he would have been a trespasser, and the defendant was in control of the enterprise. ...

Thirdly, I think that there was here a joint enterprise on the part of the defendant and Morris, and that the act which was the immediate cause of the explosion was their joint act done in pursuance of a concerted enterprise. A case in which the question of joint tortfeasors was much discussed was *The Koursk* [1924] P 140. There there had been a collision between vessels called the *Clan Chisholm* and the *Koursk* in consequence of separate and independent acts of negligence on the part of those controlling each vessel, and in direct consequence of that collision and without any intervening act of negligence the *Clan Chisholm* ran into and sank the plaintiffs' vessel. The plaintiffs, having recovered judgment against the owners of the *Clan Chisholm* (who limited their liability) then brought an action against the owners of the *Koursk*. It was set up on behalf of the owners of the *Koursk* that the owners of the *Clan Chisholm* and the owners of the *Koursk* were joint tortfeasors, and that the judgment recovered against the former barred any subsequent judgment against the latter. In that case the Court of Appeal considered the law in regard to joint torts and joint tortfeasors, and there are two passages in the judgment of Scrutton LJ to which I desire to refer. The first occurs where the Lord Justice is discussing the true meaning of joint tortfeasors, and is as follows ([1924] P at p155):

> "The substantial question in the present case is: What is meant by 'joint tortfeasors?' and one way of answering it is: 'Is the cause of action against them the same?' Certain classes of persons seem clearly to be 'joint tortfeasors': the agent who commits a tort within the scope of his employment for his principal, and the principal; the servant who commits a tort in course of his employment, and his master; two persons who agree on common action, in the course of which, and to further which, one of them commits a tort. These seem clearly joint tortfeasors; there is one tort committed by one of them on behalf of, or in concert with, another."

This case falls within the third class to which the learned Lord Justice refers. Here the defendant and Morris went into the room, obviously proceeding by tacit agreement to examine this pipe and both employing the same negligent means. I think that what Morris did negligently was done by him in concert with the defendant and in pursuance of their common enterprise. In the other passage to which I wish to refer, Scrutton LJ, says ([1924] P at p156):

> "I am of opinion that the definition in *Clerk and Lindsell on Torts* (7th edn) 59, is much nearer the correct view: 'Persons are said to be joint tortfeasors when their respective shares in the commission of the tort are done in furtherance of a common design ... but mere similarity of design on the part of independent actors, causing

independent damage, is not enough: there must be concerted action to a common end.' "

That appears to me precisely to describe this case, and on that third ground also I think that the county court judge was fully entitled in law to find for the plaintiffs.'

Talbot J:

'I am of the same opinion, and I do not differ from the judgment just delivered or from any part of it. There is, I think, another principle on which the liability of the defendant can be satisfactorily based. The evidence in this case shows that the defendant was, by arrangement with the plaintiff, in charge of the shop occupied by her during business hours, in the sense that he had the right, and possibly on occasions the duty, to enter it and see that it was safe and to do anything which needed to be done at once there in order to make it safe. Morris, on the other hand, had no right to enter the shop; and accordingly when he noticed a smell of gas which he thought came from the shop he went to the defendant for leave to go in and investigate. Thereupon the defendant got up, went with Morris into the shop, and there proceeded to ascertain for the protection, both of the plaintiff's premises and of his own, whether gas was escaping by means of lighted matches. It is obvious that to examine a place in which an escape of gas is suspected is highly dangerous, unless proper care is taken, and that one of the necessary precautions against disaster is to avoid the use of a naked light.

In my opinion, the defendant having undertaken this examination was under a duty to take reasonable care to avoid damage resulting from it to the shop and its contents; and, if so, he could not escape liability for the consequences of failure to discharge this duty by getting (as he did) someone to make the examination, or part of it, for him, whether that person was an agent or a servant or a contractor or a mere voluntary helper. ... The principle is that if a man does work on or near another's property which involves danger to that property unless proper care is taken, he is liable to the owner of the property for damage resulting to it from the failure to take proper care, and is equally liable if, instead of doing the work himself, he procures another, whether agent, servant, or otherwise, to do it for him. A like principle applies to work done in or near a highway involving damage to those who use it; see, for example, *Holliday* v *National Telephone Co* [1899] 2 QB 392.

It appears to me, therefore, that the defendant is liable to the plaintiff for damage caused to her property by the negligence of Morris, who, by the defendant's authority, continued the examination of the premises which the defendant had undertaken and begun. ... It was the defendant's duty to take care that the dangerous operation which he had undertaken was done safely; and he is as much liable for the carelessness of Morris in doing part of the work as he would have been if he had done it himself in the same way.'

Comment

Approved and applied in *Honeywill & Stein Ltd* v *Larkin Bros (London's Commercial Photographers) Ltd* [1934] 1 KB 191. See also *Salsbury* v *Woodland* [1970] 1 QB 324.

Williams v *Natural Life Health Foods Ltd* [1998] 2 All ER 577

See Chapter 2.

4   Vicarious Liability

Bayley v Manchester, Sheffield and Lincolnshire Railway Co (1873) LR 8 CP 148 Court of Exchequer Chamber (Kelly CB, Martin, Cleasby and Pigott BB, Blackburn, Mellor and Lush JJ)

- *Scope of porter's authority*

Facts

The plaintiff was violently pulled from one of the defendants' carriages by one of the defendants' porters, just after the train had started: the porter had erroneously believed that the plaintiff was travelling in the wrong train. The plaintiff fell and suffered injuries. While it was part of porters' duties to prevent passengers going by wrong trains so far as they were able to do so, the defendants' byelaws expressly provided that they (passengers) were not to be removed.

Held

The defendants were liable as the porter had acted within the scope of his authority.

Kelly CB:

'When we look for the principle which governs all the cases, the result is that, where a servant, acting within the scope of his authority, does even that which he is told not to do, his master, who gave him the general authority, is responsible. The defendants had given a general authority to their servants to prevent passengers from travelling in wrong carriages as far as possible; and it was the duty of each servant to act on this general authority and to prevent travellers from so travelling accordingly. It could not be said that a servant was not acting within the scope of his authority

when, in order to prevent this, he pulled a passenger out of a carriage by force; for there might be circumstances – where a carriage is too full for instance – in which a porter might really think it is his duty to use force. The cases in which the servant has been held not to have acted within the scope of his authority are cases where the act complained of was an isolated act, done in disobedience of an express or implied injunction, and are on that ground distinguishable from the present case. There is, indeed, here a statement in byelaw 6 that it is not the duty of the porters to remove passengers from wrong trains or carriages; but where a porter finds inconsistent directions, such as this and the other to do his best to prevent persons from travelling in wrong carriages, he may well follow one and disregard the other. This porter was interfering in a state of things in which, acting on the discretion which the defendants had given him, it was his duty to interfere. Consequently, the defendants are responsible for what he did.'

Comment

See also *Warren* v *Henlys Ltd* [1948] 2 All ER 935. An employer's vicarious liability is not to be confused with the duty imposed by s3 of the Health and Safety at Work etc Act 1974 upon the employer himself: see *R* v *Associated Octel Co Ltd* [1996] 4 All ER 846.

Century Insurance Co Ltd v Northern Ireland Road Transport Board [1942] AC 509 House of Lords (Viscount Simon LC, Lords Wright, Romer, Porter)

- *Vicarious liability – course of employment*

Facts

The defendants' employee, a petrol tanker driver, was waiting by his tanker whilst the tanks of a petrol station were being filled. He lit a cigarette and threw the match on the ground, causing an explosion and fire. The plaintiffs, the defendants' insurers, argued that the negligent act of the driver was not done in the course of his employment so as to make the defendants vicariously liable.

Held

This argument would be rejected.

Lord Wright:

'The act of a workman in lighting his pipe or cigarette is an act done for his own comfort and convenience and at least, generally speaking, not for his employer's benefit. That last condition, however, is no longer essential to fix liability on the employer (*Lloyd* v *Grace, Smith & Co* [1912] AC 716). Nor is such an act prima facie negligent. It is in itself both innocent and harmless. The negligence is to be found by considering the time when and the circumstances in which the match is struck and thrown down. The duty of the workman to his employer is so to conduct himself in doing his work as not negligently to cause damage either to the employer himself or his property or to third persons or their property, and thus to impose the same liability on the employer as if he had been doing the work himself and committed the negligent act. This may seem too obvious as a matter of common sense to require either argument or authority. I think that what plausibility the contrary argument might seem to possess results from treating the act of lighting the cigarette in abstraction from the circumstances as a separate act. This was the line taken by the majority judgment in *Williams* v *Jones* (1865) 3 H & C 602, from which Mellor and Blackburn JJ, as I think, rightly dissented. I also agree with the decision of the Court of Appeal in *Jefferson* v *Derbyshire Farmers Ltd* [1921] 2 KB 281, which is in substance indistinguishable on the facts from the present case.'

Comment

Distinguished in *Crook* v *Derbyshire Stone Ltd* [1956] 2 All ER 447 (lorry driver's negligence during a refreshment stop not in course of his employment). Followed in *Harrison* v *Michelin Tyre Co Ltd* [1985] 1 All ER 918 (employers liable for employee's horseplay in pushing a truck).

General Engineering Services Ltd v *Kingston and Saint Andrew Corp*
[1989] 1 WLR 69 Privy Council
(Lords Bridge of Harwich, Templeman, Ackner, Oliver of Aylmerton and Sir John Stephenson)

- *Intentional wrongful acts*

Facts

The plaintiffs' property was completely destroyed by fire and the damage was increased by the fact that the firemen who answered the plaintiffs' emergency call were involved in a 'go-slow' in support of a pay claim and took 17 minutes rather than three-and-a-half minutes to reach the plaintiffs' property. The plaintiffs alleged that the defendants, who were the employers of the firemen, were vicariously liable for the acts of the firemen.

Held

This was not the case.

Lord Ackner:

'It is, of course, common ground that a master is not responsible for a wrongful act done by his servant unless it is done in the course of his employment. Further, it is well established that the act is deemed to be so done if it is either (1) a wrongful act authorised by the master, or (2) a wrongful and unauthorised mode of doing some act authorised by the master ...

Their Lordships have no hesitation in agreeing ... that the members of the fire brigade were not acting in the course of their employment when they, by their conduct ...

permitted the destruction of the building and its contents. Their unauthorised and wrongful act was so to prolong the time taken by the journey to the scene of the fire, as to ensure that they did not arrive in time to extinguish it, before the building and its contents were destroyed. Their mode and manner of driving, the slow progression of stopping and starting, was not so connected with the authorised act, that is driving to the scene of the fire as expeditiously as reasonably possible, as to be a mode of performing that act ...

Here the unauthorised and wrongful act by the firemen was a wrongful repudiation of an essential obligation of their contract of employment, namely the decision and its implementation not to arrive at the scene of the fire in time to save the building and its contents. This decision was not in furtherance of their employers' business. It was in furtherance of their industrial dispute, designed to bring pressure on their employers to satisfy their demands, by not extinguishing fires until it was too late to save the property.

Such conduct was the very negation of carrying out some act authorised by the employer, albeit in a wrongful and unauthorised mode. Indeed in preventing the provision of an essential service, members of the fire brigade were ... guilty of a criminal offence.'

Limpus v *London General Omnibus Co* (1892) 1 H & C 526 Court of Exchequer Chamber (Wightman, Williams, Crompton, Willes, Byles and Blackburn JJ)

• *Vicarious liability – course of employment*

Facts
The defendant's drivers were expressly forbidden to obstruct or race with other buses. One of them did so and caused damage to the plaintiff's bus and horses. At first instance,

Martin B had directed the jury that where the relation master and servant existed, the master was responsible for the reckless and improper conduct of the servant in the course of the service, and that if they believed that the defendants' driver, being irritated with the plaintiff's driver, whether justly or unjustly, by reason of what had occurred, and in that state of mind acted recklessly, wantonly and improperly, but in the course of his service and employment and in doing that which he believed to be for the interests of the defendants, then the defendants were responsible. The learned baron also said that the instructions given to the defendants' driver were immaterial if he did not pursue them, and that, if the true character of the act of the defendants' servant was that it was an act of his own, done to effect a purpose of his own, the defendants' were not responsible.

Held (Wightman J dissenting)
The direction to the juriy had been correct and the defendants were vicariously liable.

Williams J:

'If a master employs a servant to drive and manage a carriage, the master is, in my opinion, answerable for any misconduct of the servant in driving or managing which can fairly be considered to have resulted from the performance of the functions entrusted to him, and especially if he was acting for his master's benefit, and not for any purpose of furthering his own interest, or for any motive of his own caprice or inclination. I think the summing-up of Martin B, was substantially in accordance with that doctrine ...'

Comment
Distinguished in *Conway* v *George Wimpey & Co Ltd* [1951] 2 KB 266 (plaintiff trespasser in defendants' vehicle). Applied in *Rose* v *Plenty* [1976] 1 All ER 97 (employers liable to boy riding on milkman's float, contrary to express prohibitions).

Lister v *Hesley Hall Ltd* [2001] 2 All ER 769 House of Lords (Lords Steyn, Clyde, Hutton, Hobhouse of Woodborough and Millett)

- *Vicarious liability – sexual abuse by school warden*

Facts

When aged between 12 and 15, the appellants were residents in the boarding house of the respondents' school. While there, they were sexually abused by the warden of the boarding house, an employee of the respondents. In the appellants' actions for personal injury, the question arose as to whether the respondents were vicariously liable for the torts of their employee.

Held

The respondents were so liable.

Lord Millett:

'My Lords, the question in this appeal is whether in principle the owner of a residential school for boys can, without fault on its part, be held vicariously liable for indecent assaults carried out by the warden of the school on the boys in his care. … it raises in a particularly stark form the question in what circumstances an employer may be vicariously liable for the deliberate and criminal wrongdoing of his employee, wrongdoing in which the employee indulged for his own purposes and which the employer must be taken to have expressly or at least impliedly prohibited.

Vicarious liability is a species of strict liability. It is not premised on any culpable act or omission on the part of the employer; an employer who is not personally at fault is made legally answerable for the fault of his employee.

Cases of intentional wrongdoing have always proved troublesome. At one time it was thought that the employer could not be held vicariously liable for his employee's deliberate wrongdoing. This view was not maintained …

In *Morris* v *CW Martin & Sons Ltd* [1965] 2 All ER 725 a firm of cleaners was held vicariously liable to a customer whose fur was stolen by one of its employees. The firm was a sub-bailee for rewards, but the decision was not based on the firm's own failure to take care of the fur and deliver it upon termination of the bailment. It was held vicariously liable for the conversion of the fur by its employee. Diplock LJ said, that he based his decision –

"on the ground that the fur was stolen *by the very servant* whom the defendants as bailees for reward had employed to take care of it and to clean it" … (my emphasis.)

Salmon LJ too … was anxious to make it plain that the conclusion which he had reached depended on the fact that the thief was "the servant through whom the defendants chose to discharge their duty to take reasonable care of the plaintiff's fur". … The employee's position gave him the opportunity to steal the fur, but as Diplock LJ was at pains to make clear … this was not enough to make his employer liable. What brought the theft within the scope of his employment and made the firm liable was that in the course of its business the firm had entrusted him with the care of the fur, and he stole it while it was in his custody as an employee of the firm.

As my noble and learned friend Lord Steyn has observed, *Morris'* case has consistently been held to be an authority on vicarious liability generally and not confined to cases of bailment. The case was expressly approved by the Privy Council in *Port Swettenham Authority* v *TW Wu & Co (M) Sdn Bhd* [1978] 3 All ER 337 at 341, not altogether surprisingly as the opinion of the board was delivered by Lord Salmon. There was another case of bailment. But in *Photo Production Ltd* v *Securicor Transport Ltd* [1980] 1 All ER 556, where a patrolman employed by a security firm deliberately set fire to the premises he was employed to protect, neither Lord Wilberforce nor Lord Salmon saw any difficulty in holding the employer vicariously liable on the principle stated in *Morris'* case. …

Just as an employer may be vicariously liable for deliberate and criminal conduct on the part of his employee, so he may be vicariously liable for acts of the employee which he has expressly forbidden him to do. In *Ilkiw* v *Samuels* [1963] 2 All ER 879 a lorry driver was under strict instructions from his employers not to allow anyone else to drive the lorry. He allowed a third party, who was incompetent, to drive it without making any inquiry into his competency to do so. The employers were held vicariously liable for the resulting accident. ...

The case was followed in *Rose* v *Plenty* [1976] 1 All ER 97 where despite strict instructions not to do so a milk roundsman employed a boy to help him deliver milk and let him accompany him on his float. The employer was held liable for injuries sustained by the boy when he fell off the float as a result of the roundsman's negligent driving. ...

So it is no answer to say that the employee was guilty of intentional wrongdoing, or that his act was not merely tortious but criminal, or that he was acting exclusively for his own benefit, or that he was acting contrary to express instructions, or that his conduct was the very negation of his employer's duty. The cases show that where an employer undertakes the care of a client's property and entrusts the task to an employee who steals the property, the employer is vicariously liable. ...

Employers have long been held vicariously liable in appropriate circumstances for assaults committed by their employees. Clearly an employer is liable where he has placed the employee in a situation where he may be expected on occasions to have to resort to personal violence: see *Dyer* v *Munday* [1895] 1 QB 742, where an employer was held vicariously liable for a criminal assault committed by his employee while attempting to repossess his employer's property. Equally clearly the employer is not liable for an assault by his employee on a customer merely because it was the result of a quarrel arising out of his employment: see *Warren* v *Henleys Ltd* [1948] 2 All ER 935, where a petrol pump attendant assaulted a customer as a result of a dispute over payment. The case was decided partly on the ground that the customer had paid for the petrol and was driving away when he was assaulted, and partly on the ground that he was assaulted because he had threatened to report the attendant to his employer. The reasoning has been criticised, and the better view may be that the employer was not liable because it was no part of the duties of the pump attendant to keep order. Attention must be concentrated on the closeness of the connection between the act of the employee and the duties he is engaged to perform broadly defined. ...

In the present case the warden's duties provided him with the opportunity to commit indecent assaults on the boys for his own sexual gratification, but that in itself is not enough to make the school liable. The same would be true of the groundsman or the school porter. But there was far more to it than that. The school was responsible for the care and welfare of the boys. It entrusted that responsibility to the warden. He was employed to discharge the school's responsibility to the boys. For this purpose the school entrusted them to his care. He did not merely take advantage of the opportunity which employment at a residential school gave him. He abused the special position in which the school had placed him to enable it to discharge its own responsibilities, with the result that the assaults were committed by the very employee to whom the school had entrusted the care of the boys. ...

I would hold the school vicariously liable for the warden's intentional assaults, not (as was suggested in argument) for his failure to perform his duty to take care of the boys. That is an artificial approach based on a misreading of *Morris'* case. The cleaners were vicariously liable for their employee's conversion of the fur, not for his negligence in failing to look after it. Similarly in the *Photo Production* case the security firm was vicariously liable for the patrolman's arson, not for his negligence. The law is mature enough to hold an employer vicariously liable for deliberate, criminal wrongdoing on the part of an employee without indulging in sophistry of this kind. I would also not base liability on the warden's failure to report his own wrongdoing to his employer, an approach which I regard as both artificial and unrealistic. Even if such a duty did exist, on which I prefer to express no opinion, I am inclined to think that it would be a duty owed exclusively to the employer and not a duty for breach of which the employer could be vicariously liable. The same reasoning would not, of course, necessarily apply to the duty to report the wrongdoing of fellow employees, but it is not necessary to decide this.'

Comment
Overruled: *Trotman v North Yorkshire County Council* [1999] LGR 584.

Lloyd v Grace, Smith & Co [1912] AC 716 House of Lords (Lord Loreburn LC, Earl of Halsbury, Lord Macnaghten, Lord Atkinson, Lord Shaw and Lord Robson)

• *Vicarious liability – employee's fraud*

Facts
Authorised to undertake conveyancing matters on the firm's behalf, a managing clerk defrauded a client in the course of a conveyancing transaction. The client sued the solicitors, the clerk's employers.

Held
Although the solicitors were innocent of the fraud and it was committed for the clerk's, not their, benefit, they were liable as it had been committed in the course of the clerk's employment and not outside the scope of his authority.

Lord Shaw:

'In the present case ... it has been clearly found that the fraud was committed in the course of, and within the scope of, the duties with which the respondents had intrusted ... their managing clerk. In my opinion, they

must in these circumstances stand answerable in law for their agent's misconduct.'

Comment
Applied in, inter alia, *Morris v C W Martin & Sons Ltd* [1965] 3 WLR 276 (defendant cleaners liable for theft by employee of customer's fur coat).

In *Credit Lyonnais Bank Nederland NV v Export Credits Guarantee Department* [1999] 1 All ER 929 the House of Lords said that where an employee is a joint tortfeasor, his employer is vicariously liable only if the combined conduct of both tortfeasors is sufficient to constitute a tort in the course of the employee's employment. Their Lordships also concluded that there is no basis for holding that an act carried out with the intent of assisting a tort can itself amount to a free-standing tort.

Racz v Home Office [1994] 2 WLR 23 House of Lords (Lords Templeman, Goff of Chieveley, Jauncey of Tullichettle, Browne-Wilkinson and Mustill)

• *Misfeasance in public office – whether Home Office vicariously liable*

Facts
The plaintiff, a remand prisoner, alleged that he had been ill-treated by prison officers: he brought an action against the Home Office for damages for assault and battery, misfeasance in public office and false imprisonment. The defendants sought to strike out the plaintiff's claim relating to misfeasance in public office: this application was granted by Ebsworth J and upheld by the Court of Appeal. The plaintiff appealed against this decision.

Held
The appeal would be allowed.

Lord Jauncey of Tullichettle:

'The Court of Appeal ordered ... the ...

statement of claim to be struck out because in law the defendant could not be vicariously liable for misfeasance in public office by the prison officers. The Court of Appeal reached that conclusion because of the decision of this House in *Hague* v *Deputy Governor of Parkhurst Prison, Weldon* v *Home Office* [1991] 3 All ER 733 and, in particular, of certain observations therein of Lord Bridge of Harwich. In order to see whether that conclusion was justified it is necessary to look at the case in come detail.

In *Hague*'s case a convicted prisoner, Weldon, claimed damages against the Home Office for assault and battery and false imprisonment by certain prison officers. He averred, inter alia, that he was removed from his cell without good cause to one in the punishment block and was then removed to a strip cell where his clothes were taken from him. The Home Office application to strike out so much of the averments as related to false imprisonment was dismissed, both by the assistant recorder and by the Court of Appeal. This House allowed the appeal of the Home Office, holding that there could be no false imprisonment of a prisoner who was lawfully confined under s12(1) of the Prison Act 1952 and that a restraint upon movement, which was not in accordance with the Prison Rules 1964 did not confer on a prisoner a cause of action for breach of statutory duty under the rules … the tort of misfeasance in public office did not arise in *Hague*'s case … I therefore conclude that *Hague*'s case does not support the proposition that the Home Office could not be vicariously liable for acts of prison officers which amounted to misfeasance in public office. …

My Lords, in my view, striking out … of the claim could only be justified if the inevitable result of proof of the averments therein was that the unauthorised acts of the prison officers were so unconnected with their authorised duties as to be quite independent of and outside those duties. … [Counsel for the plaintiff], in argument and in his written case, pointed out that it is likely to be a question of fact and degree whether the prison officers were engaged in a misguided and authorised method of performing their authorised duties or were engaged in what was tantamount to an unlawful frolic of their own. My Lords, I consider that there is substance in [this] submission. I am in no doubt that it is impossible to determine the precise character of the actions of the prison officers upon which will depend the liability or otherwise of the defendants for their acting from a perusal of the pleadings alone and that this can only be done after the facts have been established. It follows that, there being no compulsitor to strike out … by reason of *Hague*'s case, the case must go to trial on the whole pleadings as they stand.'

Comment
As to the ingredients of the tort of misfeasance in public office, see *Three Rivers District Council* v *Bank of England (No 3)* [2000] 3 All ER 1. The House of Lords found there are two alternative ways in which the tort can be established, namely (a) where a public officer performs an act with the object of injuring the plaintiff (which may be called targeted malice), and (b) where he performs an act which he knows that he has no power to perform and which he knows will injure the plaintiff. Compare, eg, *Phelps* v *Hillingdon London Borough Council* [2000] 4 All ER 504 (educational psychologist employed by defendants failed to identify claimant as dyslexic: psychologist had owed claimant a duty of care to diagnose her condition and take appropriate action and for breach of this duty defendants vicariously liable).

Smith v *Stages* [1989] 2 WLR 529 House of Lords (Lords Keith of Kinkel, Brandon of Oakbrook, Griffiths, Goff of Chieveley and Lowry)

- *Different place of work*

Facts
Two peripatetic laggers were working on a

power station in the Midlands when they were sent to carry out urgent work in Wales. No stipulation was made as to the mode of travel, but they were paid for the travelling time and the equivalent of the rail fare. They travelled in the car of one of the laggers, the first defendant, and the other lagger was injured on the return journey when, as a result of the first defendant's negligence, his car crashed through a brick wall. The first defendant was uninsured: were the employers, the second defendants, also liable?

Held

They were as the laggers had been travelling in their (the employers') time.

Lord Lowry:

'The paramount rule is that an employee travelling on the highway will be acting in the course of his employment if, and only if, he is at the material time going about his employer's business. One must not confuse the duty to turn up for one's work with the concept of already being "on duty" while travelling to it.

It is impossible to provide for every eventuality and foolish, without the benefit of argument, to make the attempt, but some prima facie propositions may be stated with reasonable confidence. (1) An employee travelling from his ordinary residence to his regular place of work, whatever the means of transport and even if it is provided by the employer, is not on duty and is not acting in the course of his employment, but, if he is obliged by his contract of service to use the employer's transport, he will normally, in the absence of an express condition to the contrary, be regarded as acting in the course of his employment while doing so. (2) Travelling in the employer's time between workplaces (one of which may be the regular workplace) or in the course of a peripatetic occupation, whether accompanied by goods or tools or simply in order to reach a succession of workplaces (as an inspector of gas meters might do), will be in the course of the employment. (3) Receipt of wages (though not receipt of a travelling allowance) will indicate that the employee is travelling in the employer's time and for his benefit and is acting in the course of his employment, and in such a case the fact that the employee may have discretion as to the mode and time of travelling will not take the journey out of the course of his employment. (4) An employee travelling in the employer's time from his ordinary residence to a workplace other than this regular workplace or in the course of a peripatetic occupation or to the scene of an emergency (such as a fire, an accident or a mechanical breakdown of plant) will be acting in the course of his employment. (5) A deviation from or interruption of a journey undertaken in the course of employment (unless the deviation or interruption is merely incidental to the journey) will for the time being (which may include an overnight interruption) take the employee out of the course of his employment. (6) Return journeys are to be treated on the same footing as outward journeys.

All the foregoing propositions are subject to any express arrangements between the employer and the employee or those representing his interests. They are not, I would add, intended to define the position of salaried employees, with regard to whom the touchstone of payment made in the employer's time is not generally significant.'

Comment

Applied: *St Helens Colliery Co Ltd* v *Hewitson* [1924] AC 59 and *Canadian Pacific Railway Co* v *Lockhart* [1942] AC 591.

Approved: *Vandyke* v *Fender* [1970] 2 WLR 929.

Warren v *Henlys Ltd* [1948] 2 All ER 935 High Court (Hilbery J)

• *Vicarious liability – assault on customer*

Facts

Mistakenly believing that the plaintiff had tried to drive away without paying for his petrol, the pump attendant (Beaumont) had used violent language when calling on him to stop. The plaintiff told the attendant that he would report him to his employers (the defendants) and the attendant 'gave him one on the chin to get on with'.

Held

The defendants were not liable for Beaumont's assault.

Hilbery J:

'Without going through a lot of authorities, it seems to me that I cannot do better than adopt the general statement of the law expressly cited and approved by the Court of Appeal through the mouth of Bankes LJ, in his judgment in *Poland* v *John Parr & Sons* [1927] 1 KB 240. ... It is in these terms:

"A master is not responsible for a wrongful act done by his servant unless it is done in the course of his employment. It is deemed to be so done if it is either (a) a wrongful act authorised by the master, or (b) a wrongful and unauthorised *mode* of doing some act authorised by the master."

I think that accurately states the law, so I ask myself: Is there any evidence on which a jury could find that this assault, committed in the circumstances which I have just given, was so connected with the acts which the servant was expressly or impliedly authorised to do as to be a mode of doing those acts? It seems to be the answer must be "No". Of course, as in *Dyer* v *Munday* [1895] 1 QB 742, if a manager, who, in the course of the very duties in the business goes to recover furniture, so conducts himself in recovering the furniture that he commits an assault, that is a tortious mode of doing the class of act which he is autho-rised to do. Without multiplying the ways in which this matter has been expressed and judges have sought to mark the limitations or bounds within which a master is to be held liable, I may use one more quotation. It is from Scrutton LJ, in *Poland* v *John Parr & Sons*:

"To make an employer liable for the act of a person alleged to be his servant the act must be one of a class of acts which the person was authorised or employed to do. If the act is one of that class the employer is liable, though the act is done negligently or, in some cases, even if it is done with excessive violence. But the excess may be so great as to take the act out of the class of acts which the person is authorised or employed to do."

Clearly, there is no evidence here that this act belonged to the class of acts that Beaumont was authorised to do. In extension of what Scrutton LJ has said, I have also [asked] whether, although it was not of the class of acts which Beaumont was authorised to do, it was so connected with that class of acts as to be a mode of doing some act within that class. It seems to me that it was an act entirely of personal vengeance. He was personally inflicting punishment, and intentionally inflicting punishment, on the plaintiff because the plaintiff proposed to take a step which might affect Beaumont in his own personal affairs. It had no connection whatever with the discharge of any duty for the defendants. The act of assault by Beaumont was done by him in relation to a personal matter affecting his personal interests, and there is no evidence that it was otherwise.'

Comment

See also *Bayley* v *Manchester, Sheffield and Lincolnshire Railway Co* (1873) LR 8 CP 148.

5 Liability for Independent Contractors

Balfour v *Barty-King* [1957] 2 WLR 84 Court of Appeal (Lord Goddard CJ, Morris LJ, Vaisey J)

• *Escape of fire – negligence of independent contractor*

Facts

Part of a large country house had been converted into separate dwelling-houses. The plaintiff owned one of these and the defendants occupied the adjoining premises which had also been converted. There was a severe frost and the pipes in the defendant's loft became frozen. At the request of the defendants, some builders undertook to thaw the pipes and their workmen, neither of whom was a plumber, set about their task with a blow-lamp which, in the circumstances, was a highly dangerous operation. Some felt lagging caught fire and the flames spread to the plaintiff's premises and caused a great amount of damage.

Held

The defendants were liable because the fire was caused by the negligence of the independent contractors who were invited by them to do the work and for this reason the fire did not begin 'accidentally' within the meaning of s86 of the Fires Prevention (Metropolis) Act 1774, and it was not the act of a stranger.

Comment

Applied: *Musgrove* v *Pandelis* [1919] 2 KB 43.

Applied in *Emanuel (H & N) Ltd* v *Greater London Council* [1971] 2 All ER 835 (occupier only not liable when negligence act or omission of stranger) and *Sturge* v *Hackett* [1962] 3 All ER 166 (assured liable simply as occupier).

Holliday v *National Telephone Co* [1899] 2 QB 392 Court of Appeal (Earl of Halsbury LC, A L Smith and Vaughan Williams LJJ)

• *Negligence – independent contractor*

Facts

When laying telephone wires in trenches under a highway, the defendants engaged a plumber – an independent contractor – to carry out some aspects of the work. Due to the negligence of the plumber's employee, there was an explosion and molten solder flew out and injured the plaintiff who was passing along the footway.

Held

The defendants were liable.

A L Smith LJ:

'Where a person is executing work upon a public highway, he cannot escape liability by employing an independent contractor, because there is a duty cast upon him to see that the work upon the highway is so carried out as not to injure persons who are using the highway.'

Comment

See also *Brooke* v *Bool* [1928] 2 KB 578 and *Salsbury* v *Woodland* [1970] 1 QB 324.

Honeywill & Stein Ltd v *Larkin Bros (London's Commercial Photographers) Ltd* [1934] 1 KB 191 Court of Appeal (Lord Hewart CJ, Lord Wright and Slesser LJ)

• *Independent contractor – negligence*

Facts
After they had installed sound reproduction apparatus in a cinema, the plaintiffs employed the defendants to take photographs of the cinema's interior. The defendants negligently set light to the cinema's curtains and the plaintiffs sought to recover from the defendants the compensation which they (the plaintiffs) had voluntarily paid to the cinema's owners.

Held
The plaintiffs should succeed as they were themselves liable to the cinema owners for the defendants' negligence.

Slesser LJ:

'To take a photograph in the cinema with a flashlight was, on the evidence stated above, a dangerous operation in its intrinsic nature, involving the creation of fire and explosion on another person's premises, that is, in the cinema, the property of the cinema company. The plaintiffs, in procuring this work to be performed by their contractors, the defendants, assumed an obligation to the cinema company which was, as we think, absolute, but which was at least an obligation to use reasonable precautions to see that no damage resulted to the cinema company from those dangerous operations. That obligation they could not delegate by employing the defendants as independent contractors, but they were liable in this regard for the defendants' acts. For the damage actually caused the plaintiffs were, accordingly, liable in law to the cinema company, and are entitled to claim and recover from the defendants damages for their breach of contract or negligence in performing their contract to take photographs.'

Comment
Approved and applied: *Brooke* v *Bool* [1928] 2 KB 578. See also *Green* v *Fibreglass Ltd* [1958] 2 All ER 521.

Salsbury v *Woodland* [1970] 1 QB 324 Court of Appeal (Harman, Sachs and Widgery LJJ)

• *Independent contractor – negligence*

Facts
Defendant one (D1), the occupier of a house, employed defendant two (D2), an apparently competent tree-feller, to cut down a large tree in the front garden. D2 did so negligently so that the tree brought down some telephone wires which fell onto the road. The plaintiff went to remove the wires from the road and seeing a car driven by defendant three approaching and believing that the car would collide with the wires and possibly cause him (the plaintiff) injury, he threw himself to the ground and suffered injury as a result of the fall. The question arose, inter alia, as to whether D1 was vicariously liable for the negligence of D2.

Held
This was not the case.

Widgery LJ:

'In truth, according to the authorities there are a number of well-determined classes of case in which this direct and primary duty on an employer [of an independent contractor] to see that care is taken exists. Two such classes are directly relevant for consideration in this case. The first class concerns what have sometimes been described as "extra hazardous acts" – acts commissioned by an employer which are so hazardous in their character that the law has thought it proper to impose this direct obligation on the employer to see that care is taken. An example of such a case is *Honeywill and Stein Ltd* v *Larkin Bros (London's Commercial Photographers) Ltd* [1934] 1 KB 191. Other cases which one finds in the books are cases where the activity commissioned by the employer is the keeping of dangerous things, within the rule in *Rylands* v *Fletcher* (1868) LR 3 HL 330, and where liability is not dependent on negligence at all.

I do not propose to add to the wealth of authority on this topic by attempting further to define the meaning of "extra hazardous acts"; but I am confident that the act commissioned in the present case, if done with ordinary elementary caution by skilled men, presented no hazard to anyone at all.

The second class of case which is relevant for consideration of the present dispute concerns dangers created in a highway. There are a number of cases on this branch of the law, a good example of which is *Holliday* v *National Telephone Co* [1899] 2 QB 392. These, on analysis, will all be found to be cases where work was being done in a highway and was work of a character which would have been a nuisance unless authorised by statute. It will be found in all these cases that the statutory powers under which the employer commissioned the work were statutory powers which left on the employer a duty to see that due care was taken in the carrying out of the work, for the protection of those who passed on the highway. In accordance with principle, an employer subject to such a direct and personal duty cannot excuse himself if things go wrong merely because the direct cause of the injury was the act of the independent contractor.

This again is not a case in that class. It is not a case in that class because in the instant case no question of doing work on the highway, which might amount to a nuisance if due care was not taken, arises. In my judgment, the present case is clearly outside the well-defined limit of the second class to which I have referred. Counsel for the plaintiff accordingly invited us to say that there is a third class into which the instant case precisely falls and he suggested that the third class comprised those cases where an employer commissions work to be done *near* a highway in circumstances in which, if due care is not taken, injury to passers-by on the highway may be caused. If that be a third class of case to which the principle of liability of the employer applies, no doubt the present facts would come within the description. The question is, is there such a third class? ... in my judgment, there is no third class of cases of the kind put forward by counsel for the plaintiff ...'

Comment

Applied in *Rowe* v *Herman* [1997] 1 WLR 1390 (employer not liable where independent contractor engaged for work on his land causes obstruction of the public highway which was not a necessary part of the contract work).

See also s2(4)(b) of the Occupiers' Liability Act 1957 (damage caused to visitors).

6 Negligence: The Duty of Care

Al-Kandari v J R Brown & Co
[1988] 2 WLR 671 Court of Appeal
(Lord Donaldson of Lymington MR,
Dillon and Bingham LJJ)

• *Negligence – solicitor's duty of care*

Facts
The plaintiff was married to a Kuwaiti national and their two children were included on his passport. In 1981 the couple separated and the husband abducted the children to Kuwait. He was persuaded to return with them: the wife was given custody, care and control of the children and the husband undertook to deposit his passport with his solicitors, the defendants. Wishing to return to Kuwait, the husband wanted to have the children's names removed from it. To this end, the defendants forwarded the passport to London agents with instructions to take it to the Kuwait embassy. While it was there, the husband persuaded the embassy to release it to him. He then arranged for the plaintiff to be kidnapped and he used the passport to take the children to Kuwait. The plaintiff claimed damages for, inter alia, negligence.

Held
She was entitled to succeed. The defendants owed the plaintiff a duty to take reasonable care to keep the passport in their possession and they had been in breach of that duty. The damage suffered by the plaintiff had been a natural and probable consequence of the breach of duty.

Bingham LJ:

'In the ordinary course of adversarial litigation a solicitor does not owe a duty of care to his client's adversary. The theory underly-

ing such litigation is that justice is best done if each party, separately and independently advised, attempts within the limits of the law and propriety and good practice to achieve the best result for himself that he reasonably can without regard to the interests of the other party. The duty of the solicitor, within the same limits, is to assist his client in that endeavour, although the wise solicitor may often advise that the best result will involve an element of compromise or give and take or horse trading. Ordinarily, however, in contested civil litigation a solicitor's proper concern is to do what is best for his client without regard to the interests of his opponent.

It may nevertheless happen, even in the course of contested civil litigation, that a solicitor for a limited purpose steps aside from his role as solicitor and agent of one party and assumes a different role, either independent of both parties or as agents of both …

In … holding the passport the defendants were not acting as solicitors and agents of Mr Al-Kandari, their client, but as independent custodians subject to the directions of the court and the joint directions of the parties. I have no doubt that in this situation the defendants owed the plaintiff a duty of care, since the purpose of holding the passport at all was to protect her lawful rights.
…

The judge found against the plaintiff on the ground that it was not reasonably foreseeable that Mr Al-Kandari would be given any opportunity to abduct the children. The correct approach is to consider the breach of duty which has been proved and to ask whether an ordinarily competent solicitor in the defendants' position would have foreseen damage of the kind which actually occurred as a not unlikely result of that breach ... In my judgment such a solicitor would have foreseen the damage which the plaintiff has in fact suffered as a possible and by no means fanciful consequence of the breach of duty established. I would not, therefore, agree with the judge that this damage was too remote to be recoverable in law.'

Alcock v *Chief Constable of the South Yorkshire Police* [1991] 3 WLR 1057 House of Lords (Lords Keith of Kinkel, Ackner, Oliver of Aylmerton, Jauncey of Tullichettle and Lowry)

• *Negligence – persons entitled to damages for nervous shock*

Facts
The defendant admitted liability in negligence in respect of the 95 deaths and over 400 physical injuries in the Hillsborough Stadium disaster. Scenes from the ground were broadcast live on television from time to time and later on television news. News of the disaster was also broadcast over the radio. None of the television broadcasts depicted the suffering or dying of recognisable individuals. Sixteen persons, some of whom were at the match but not in the area where the disaster occurred, and all of whom were relatives, or in one case the fiance, of persons who were in that area, brought actions against the defendant claiming damages for nervous shock resulting in psychiatric illness alleged to have been caused by seeing or hearing news of the disaster. The Court of Appeal having decided against all of the plaintiffs, ten of them made a final appeal.

Held
Their appeals would be dismissed, either because the plaintiffs had not been at the match or their relationship to a victim had not been sufficiently close.

Lord Keith of Kinkel:

'The question of liability in negligence for what is commonly, if inaccurately, described as "nervous shock" has only twice been considered by this House, in *Hay (or Bourhill)* v *Young* [1943] AC 92 and in *McLoughlin* v *O'Brian* [1983] 1 AC 410. In the latter case ... Lord Wilberforce ... expressed the opinion that foreseeability did not of itself and automatically give rise to a duty of care owed to a person or class of persons and that considerations of policy entered into the conclusion that such a duty existed. He then considered the arguments on policy which had led the Court of Appeal to reject the plaintiff's claim, and concluded that they were not of great force. ...

Lord Bridge of Harwich, with whom Lord Scarman agreed ... appears to have rested his finding of liability simply on the test of reasonable foreseeability of psychiatric illness affecting the plaintiff as a result of the consequences of the road accident ... Lord Edmund-Davies and Lord Russell of Killowen both considered the policy arguments which had led the Court of Appeal to dismiss the plaintiff's claim to be unsound ... Neither speech contained anything inconsistent with that of Lord Wilberforce.

It was argued for the appellants in the present case that reasonable foreseeability of the risk of injury to them in the particular form of psychiatric illness was all that was required to bring home liability to the respondent. In the ordinary case of direct physical injury suffered in an accident at work or elsewhere, reasonable foreseeability of the risk is indeed the only test that need be applied to determine liability. But injury by psychiatric illness is more subtle, as Lord Macmillan observed in *Bourhill* v *Young*. In the present type of case it is a secondary sort of injury brought about by the infliction of physical injury, or the risk of physical injury, upon another person. That can affect those closely connected with that person in various ways. One way is by subjecting a close relative to the stress and strain of caring for the injured person over a prolonged period, but psychiatric illness due to such stress and strain has not so far been treated as founding a claim in damages. So I am of the opinion that in addition to reasonable foreseeability liability for injury in the particular form of psychiatric illness must depend in addition upon a requisite relationship of proximity between the claimant and the party said to owe the duty. Lord Atkin in *M'Alister (or Donoghue)* v *Stevenson* [1932] AC 562 at 580, described those to whom a duty of care is owed as being –

> "persons who are so closely and directly affected by my act that I ought reasonably to have them in contemplation as being so affected when I am directing my mind to the acts or omissions which are called in question."

The concept of a person being closely and directly affected has been conveniently labelled "proximity", and this concept has been applied in certain categories of cases, particularly those concerned with pure economic loss, to limit and control the consequences as regards liability which would follow if reasonable foreseeability were the sole criterion.

As regards the class of persons to whom a duty may be owed to take reasonable care to avoid inflicting psychiatric illness through nervous shock sustained by reason of physical injury or peril to another, I think it sufficient that reasonable foreseeability should be the guide. I would not seek to limit the class by reference to particular relationships such as husband and wife or parent and child. The kinds of relationship which may involve close ties of love and affection are numerous, and it is the existence of such ties which leads to mental disturbance when the loved one suffers a catastrophe. They may be present in family relationships or those of close friendship, and may be stronger in the case of engaged couples than in that of persons who have been married to each other for many years. It is common knowledge that such ties exist, and reasonably foreseeable that those bound by them may in certain circumstances be at real risk of psychiatric illness if the loved one is injured or put in peril. The closeness of the tie would, however, require to be proved by a plaintiff, though no doubt being capable of

being presumed in appropriate cases. The case of a bystander unconnected with the victims of an accident is difficult. Psychiatric injury to him would not ordinarily, in my view, be within the range of reasonable foreseeability but could not perhaps be entirely excluded from it if the circumstances of a catastrophe occurring very close to him were particularly horrific.

In the case of those within the sphere of reasonable foreseeability the proximity factors mentioned by Lord Wilberforce in *McLoughlin* v *O'Brian* must, however, be taken into account in judging whether a duty of care exists. The first of these is proximity of the plaintiff to the accident in time and space. For this purpose the accident is to be taken to include its immediate aftermath, which in *McLoughlin*'s case was held to cover the scene at the hospital which was experienced by the plaintiff some two hours after the accident. In *Jaensch* v *Coffey* (1984) 54 ALR 417 the plaintiff saw her injured husband at the hospital to which he had been taken in severe pain before and between his undergoing a series of emergency operations, and the next day stayed with him in the intensive care unit and thought he was going to die. She was held entitled to recover damages for the psychiatric illness she suffered as a result. Deane J said:

> "... the aftermath of the accident extended to the hospital to which the injured person was taken and persisted for so long as he remained in the state produced by the accident up to and including immediate post-accident treatment ... Her psychiatric injuries were the result of the impact upon her of the facts of the accident itself and its aftermath while she was present at the aftermath of the accident at the hospital."

As regards the means by which the shock is suffered, Lord Wilberforce said in *McLoughlin*'s case that it must come through sight or hearing of the event or of its immediate aftermath. He also said that it was surely right that the law should not compensate shock brought about by communication by a third party. On that basis it is open to serious doubt whether *Hevican v Ruane* [1991] 3 All ER 65 and *Ravenscroft v Rederiaktiebolaget Transatlantic* [1991] 3 All ER 73 were correctly decided, since in both of these cases the effective cause of the psychiatric illness would appear to have been the fact of a son's death and the news of it.

Of the present appellants two, Brian Harrison and Robert Alcock, were present at the Hillsborough ground, both of them in the West Stand, from which they witnessed the scenes in pens 3 and 4. Brian Harrison lost two brothers, while Robert Alcock lost a brother-in-law and identified the body at the mortuary at midnight. In neither of these cases was there any evidence of particularly close ties of love or affection with the brothers or brother-in-law. In my opinion the mere fact of the particular relationship was insufficient to place the plaintiff within the class of persons to whom a duty of care could be owed by the defendant as being foreseeably at risk of psychiatric illness by reason of injury or peril to the individuals concerned. The same is true of other plaintiffs who were not present at the ground and who lost brothers, or in one case a grandson. I would, however, place in the category of members to which risk of psychiatric illness was reasonable foreseeable Mr and Mrs Copoc, whose son was killed, and Alexandra Penk, who lost her fiance. In each of these cases the closest ties of love and affection fall to be presumed from the fact of the particular relationship, and there is no suggestion of anything which might tend to rebut that presumption. These three all watched scenes from Hillsborough on television, but none of these depicted suffering of recognisable individuals, such being excluded by the broadcasting code of ethics, a position known to the defendant. In my opinion the viewing of these scenes cannot be equiparated with the viewer being within "sight or hearing of the event or of its immediate aftermath", to use the words of Lord Wilberforce in *McLoughlin v O'Brian*, nor can the scenes reasonably be regarded as giving rise to shock, in the sense of a sudden

assault on the nervous system. They were capable of giving rise to anxiety for the safety of relatives known or believed to be present in the area affected by the crush, and undoubtedly did so, but that is very different from seeing the fate of the relative or his condition shortly after the event. The viewing of the television scenes did not create the necessary degree of proximity.'

Comment

See also *Ravenscroft v Rederiaktiebolaget Transatlantic* [1992] 2 All ER 470n (shock did not arise through sight or hearing of the accident or of its immediate aftermath so no liability), *McFarlane v E E Caledonia Ltd* [1994] 2 All ER 1 (nearness in time and place and a close relationship of love and affection required before a bystander or witness of horrific events could recover damages), *Vernon v Bosley (No 1)* [1997] 1 All ER 577 (ability of secondary victims to recover damages for post-traumatic stress disorder and pathological grief disorder) and *Hunter v British Coal Corp* [1998] 2 All ER 97 (plaintiff not present at the scene of an accident could not recover damages because he felt responsible for it when news of it was broken to him later).

Alcock was applied by the House of Lords in *White v Chief Constable of the South Yorkshire Police* [1999] 1 All ER 1 (police officers suffering post-traumatic stress disorder as a result of carrying the dead and helping the injured at the Hillsborough football disaster not entitled to damages) and both cases were considered by the House of Lords in *W v Essex County Council* [2000] 2 All ER 237 (claim for damages for psychiatric illness said to have arisen from placement of sex abuser foster child in family home should not have been struck out).

Ancell v *McDermott* [1993] 4 All ER 355 Court of Appeal (Norse and Beldam LJJ, Sir John Megaw)

• *Duty of care owed by police to road users*

Facts

The first defendant drove over an obstruction in the road, rupturing his fuel tank. He continued to drive without stopping to see whether his car had suffered any damage, leaving a trail of diesel fuel on the road. Some officers of Hertfordshire police noticed the diesel fuel and notified Bedfordshire police of the spillage. Some 20 minutes after the spillage commenced an officer of Bedfordshire police noticed the spillage and reported it to Bedfordshire highways department. Ten minutes later a car skidded on the diesel fuel and was involved in a collision. The passengers and husband of the driver who was killed as a result sued (inter alia) the Hertfordshire and Bedfordshire chief constables. The chief constables applied to strike out the claims against them, but this was refused by the judge on the grounds that whether a duty of care existed depended on the precise circumstances, including the nature of the hazard, the extent of the danger created and the likelihood of injury, and that those matters could only be determined at trial. The chief constables appealed.

Held

The appeal would be allowed.

Beldam LJ:

'I approach the question of the existence of a duty of care in the present case with these considerations in mind. Firstly, as Lord Keith pointed out in *Yuen Kun Yeu* v *A-G of Hong Kong* [1987] 2 All ER 705 at 711, there was clearly a special relationship between the prison officers and the owners of the yachts so close and direct that a duty to take reasonable care to prevent damage to the yachts arose. But ... it is exceptional to find in the law a duty to control another's actions to prevent harm to strangers and where they are found they arise from special relationships. When it is contended that such special relationship arises out of duties carried out in the performance of a public office, the court must have regard to the purpose and scope of the public duties,

whether they are intended to benefit a particular section of the public, eg investors or depositors, and whether such persons could reasonably place reliance on the fulfilment of the duties.

Secondly, such a duty of care would impose upon a police force potential liability of almost unlimited scope. Not only would the class of persons to whom the duty was owed be extensive, but the activities of police officers which might give rise to the existence of such a duty would be widespread. The constable on the beat who failed to notice a danger on the pavement or noticed it but dismissed it as insufficiently serious to warrant his attention, the officer who searched for but failed to find property when he might have done or the officer who misinterpreted a breathalyser reading might all be said to come under liability to anyone who could show that they suffered injury or loss as a result of failure. Further, I am not persuaded that there is any sufficient distinction from the reasoning which led the House of Lords to reject the existence of a duty in *Hill* v *Chief Constable of West Yorkshire* [1988] 2 All ER 238 ... to justify the imposition of a duty to act in the circumstances of the present case.

I find this conclusion supported by the decision of Kennedy J in *Clough* v *Bussan* [1990] 1 All ER 431, a case in which an attempt was made to impose liability on the police authority for failing to respond to information that traffic signals were out of order at a junction where a road accident subsequently occurred. Kennedy J struck out the defendant's claim in the third party proceedings as disclosing no cause of action.

[Counsel for the chief constables] also based his application [to strike out the claims] on the public policy considerations which formed the second ground of the rejection of the plaintiff's claim in *Hill* v *Chief Constable of West Yorkshire*: viz that to hold that the defendant owed such a duty would serve no useful purpose in advancing the general public interest, it would give rise to extensive investigation into the manner in which the police carried out their duties, would lead to many actions being brought against the police, which would cause much time, trouble and expense to be devoted to preparation of the defence and the attendance of witnesses at the trial. In my view these considerations apply with equal force in the present case. I have already indicated the extreme width and scope of the duty to take care contended for by the plaintiffs. The diversion of police resources and manpower if such a duty were held to exist would, in my judgment, extensively hamper the performance of ordinary police duties and create a formidable diversion of police manpower. I would accordingly hold that the police officers did not owe the plaintiffs a duty of care in the circumstances of this case ...'

Arthur J S Hall & Co v Simons; Barratt v Ansell; Harris v Scholfield Roberts & Hill [2000] 3 All ER 673 House of Lords (Lords Steyn, Browne-Wilkinson, Hoffmann, Hope of Craighead, Hutton, Hobhouse of Woodborough and Millett)

• *Advocates – immunity in their conduct of proceedings*

Facts
These three appeals gave rise, in the words of Lord Steyn, to the same two fundamental questions, namely: (1) Ought the current immunity of an advocate in respect of and relating to conduct of legal proceedings as enunciated by the House in *Rondel* v *Worsley* [1967] 3 All ER 993, and explained in *Saif Ali* v *Sydney Mitchell & Co (a firm) (P, third party)* [1978] 3 All ER 1033, to be maintained in England? (2) What is or ought to be the proper scope in England of the general principle barring a collateral attack in a civil action on the decision of a criminal court as enunciated in *Hunter* v *Chief Constable of West Midlands* [1981] 3 All ER 727?

Held
1. Although they were far from saying that

Rondel v *Worsley* had been wrongly decided at the time, in today's world the decision did not correctly reflect public policy. Advocates' immunity in civil and (Lords Hope, Hutton and Hobhouse dissenting) criminal proceedings would therefore be abolished.

2. If a convicted person succeeded in having his conviction set aside, an action against his original advocate in negligence would no longer be barred by the policy identified in *Hunter*, but the Civil Procedure Rules make provision for unsustainable actions to be struck out.

Lord Steyn:

'There would be benefits to be gained from the ending of immunity. First, and most importantly, it will bring to an end an anomalous exception to the basic premise that there should be a remedy for a wrong. There is no reason to fear a flood of negligence suits against barristers. The mere doing of his duty to the court by the advocate to the detriment of his client could never be called negligent. Indeed, if the advocate's conduct was bona fide dictated by his perception of his duty to the court there would be no possibility of the court holding him to be negligent. Moreover, when such claims are made courts will take into account the difficult decisions faced daily by barristers working in demanding situations to tight timetables. ... The courts can be trusted to differentiate between errors of judgment and true negligence. In any event, a plaintiff who claims that poor advocacy resulted in an unfavourable outcome will face the very great obstacle of showing that a better standard of advocacy would have resulted in a more favourable outcome. Unmeritorious claims against barristers will be struck out. ... Secondly, it must be borne in mind that one of the functions of tort law is to set external standards of behaviour for the benefit of the public. And it would be right to say that while standards at the Bar are generally high, in some respects there is room for improvement. An exposure of isolated acts of incompetence at the Bar will strengthen rather than weaken the legal system. Thirdly, and most importantly, public confidence in the legal system is not enhanced by the existence of the immunity. The appearance is created that the law singles out its own for protection no matter how flagrant the breach of the barrister. The world has changed since 1967. The practise of law has become more commercialised: barristers may now advertise. They may now enter into contracts for legal services with their professional clients. They are now obliged to carry insurance. ... It tends to erode confidence in the legal system if advocates, alone among professional men, are immune from liability for negligence. ... In combination these factors reinforce the already strong case for ending the immunity.

My Lords, one is intensely aware that *Rondel* v *Worsley* was a carefully reasoned and unanimous decision of the House. On the other hand, it is now clear that when the balance is struck between competing factors it is no longer in the public interest that the immunity in favour of barristers should remain. I am far from saying that *Rondel* v *Worsley* was wrongly decided. But on the information now available and developments since *Rondel* v *Worsley* I am satisfied that in today's world that decision no longer correctly reflects public policy. The basis of the immunity of barristers has gone. And exactly the same reasoning applies to solicitor advocates. There are differences between the two branches of the profession but not of a character to differentiate materially between them in respect of the issue before the House. I would treat them in the same way.'

Bourhill (or Hay) v *Young* [1943] AC 92 House of Lords (Lords Thankerton, Russell of Killowen, Macmillan, Wright and Porter)

• *Negligence – shock*

Facts

The appellant claimed damages against the estate of the respondent, now deceased, who due to his negligent riding of a motor-cycle was involved in a collision with a motor car. The appellant was getting off a tram when she heard the sound of the collision some fifty feet away. Shortly after she saw blood on the road. She sustained nervous shock and had a miscarriage. At no time was there any danger of physical injury to the appellant herself, who brought an action in negligence.

Held

The cyclist owed no duty of care to the appellant as he could not have reasonably foreseen the likelihood that the appellant, placed as she was, could be affected by his negligent act.

Lord Thankerton:

'Clearly (the duty of the motor-cyclist) is to drive the cycle with such reasonable care as will avoid the risk of injury to such persons as he can reasonably foresee might be injured by failure to exercise such reasonable care. It is now settled that such injury includes injury by shock although no direct physical impact or lesion occurs. If then the test of proximity or remoteness is to be applied, I am of the opinion that such a test involves that injury must be within that which the cyclist ought reasonably to have contemplated as the area of potential danger which would arise as the result of his negligence and the question in the present case is whether the appellant was within that area. I am clearly of the opinion that she was not ...'

Lord Wright:

'The general concept of reasonable foresight as the criterion of negligence or breach of duty ... may be criticised as too vague; but negligence is a fluid principle, which has to be applied to the most diverse conditions and problems of human life. It is a concrete, not an abstract idea. It has to be fitted to the facts of the particular case ... It is also always relative to the individual affected. This raises a serious additional difficulty in the cases where it has to be determined not merely whether the act itself is negligent against someone, but whether it is negligent vis-a-vis the plaintiff. This is a crucial point in cases of nervous shock. Thus, in the present case, John Young was certainly negligent in an issue between himself and the owner of the car which he ran into, but it is another question whether he was negligent vis-a-vis the appellant ...

I cannot accept that Young could reasonably have foreseen, or more correctly the reasonable hypothetical observer could reasonably have foreseen, the likelihood that anyone placed as the appellant was, could be affected in the manner in which she was.'

Lord Porter:

'The duty (of care) is not owed to the world at large ... In order to establish a duty towards herself, the pursuer must show that the cyclist should reasonably have foreseen emotional injury to her as a result of his negligent driving and I do not think she has done so ... The driver of a car or vehicle, even though careless, is entitled to assume that the ordinary frequenter of the streets has sufficient fortitude to endure such incidents as may from time to time occur in them, including the noise of a collision and the sight of injury to others and is not to be considered negligent towards one who does not possess the customary phlegm...'

Comment

See also *Page* v *Smith* [1995] 2 All ER 736, *McLoughlin* v *O'Brian* [1982] 2 WLR 982 and *Alcock* v *Chief Constable of the South Yorkshire Police* [1991] 3 WLR 1057.

Calveley v *Chief Constable of Merseyside Police* [1989] 2 WLR 624 House of Lords (Lords Bridge of Harwich, Ackner, Oliver of Aylmerton, Goff of Chieveley and Lowry)

• *Police disciplinary proceedings – duty of care to officers under investigation*

Facts
Following complaints, the plaintiff police officers had been suspended on full pay and allowances pending the outcome of investigations. In disciplinary proceedings the complaints had either been dismissed, quashed on appeal or discontinued, but the plaintiffs now sought general damages for anxiety, vexation and loss of reputation and special damages for loss of overtime pay, alleging, inter alia, that the investigating officer had been in breach of duty at common law in failing to proceed expeditiously.

Held
Their claims could not succeed.

Lord Bridge of Harwich:

'Leading counsel for the plaintiffs submitted that a police officer investigating any crime suspected to have been committed, whether by a civilian or by a member of a police force, owes to the suspect a duty of care at common law. It follows, he submits, that the like duty is owed by an officer investigating a suspected offence against discipline by a fellow officer. It seems to me that this startling proposition founders on the rocks of elementary principle. The first question that arises is: what injury to the suspect ought reasonably to be foreseen by the investigator as likely to be suffered by the suspect if the investigation is not conducted with due care which is sufficient to establish the relationship of legal neighbourhood or proximity in the sense explained by Lord Atkin in *Donoghue (or M'Alister)* v *Stevenson* [1932] AC 562 at 580-582 as the essential foundation of the tort of negligence? The submission that anxiety, vexation and injury to reputation may constitute such an injury needs only to be stated to be seen to be unsustainable. Likewise, it is not reasonably foreseeable that the negligent conduct of a criminal investigation would cause injury to the health of the suspect, whether in the form of depressive illness or otherwise. If the allegedly negligent investigation is followed by the suspect's conviction, it is obvious that an indirect challenge to that conviction by an action for damages for negligent conduct of the investigation cannot be permitted. One must therefore ask the question whether foreseeable injury to the suspect may be caused on the hypothesis either that he has never been charged or, if charged, that he has been acquitted at trial or on appeal, or that his conviction has been quashed on an application for judicial review. It is, I accept, foreseeable that in these situations the suspect may be put to expense, or may conceivably suffer some other economic loss, which might have been avoided had a more careful investigation established his innocence at some earlier stage. However, any suggestion that there should be liability in negligence in such circumstances runs up against the formidable obstacles in the way of liability in negligence for purely economic loss. Where no action for malicious prosecution would lie, it would be strange indeed if an acquitted defendant could recover damages for negligent investigation. Finally, all other considerations apart, it would plainly be contrary to public policy, in my opinion, to prejudice the fearless and efficient discharge by police officers of their vitally important public duty of investigating crime by requiring them to act under the shadow of a potential action for damages for negligence by the suspect.

If no duty of care is owed by a police officer investigating a suspected crime to a civilian suspect, it is difficult to see any conceivable reason why a police officer who is subject to investigation ... should be in any better position. Junior counsel for the plaintiffs, following, put the case in negligence on a very much narrower basis. He submitted that in the case of a police officer subject to investigation a specific duty of care is owed to him to avoid any unnecessary delay in the investigation precisely because the officer is, or is liable to be, suspended from duty until the investigation is concluded. The short answer to this submission is that suspension from duty is not in itself and does not involve any foreseeable injury of a kind capable of sustaining a cause of action in negligence ... In the light of the provision made by the relevant regulations suspension is not a foreseeable cause of even economic loss.'

Comment
Distinguished in *Waters* v *Commissioner of Police of the Metropolis* [2000] 4 All ER 934. See also *Gregory* v *Portsmouth City Council* [2000] 1 All ER 560 (malicious prosecution does not extend to domestic disciplinary proceedings).

Caparo Industries plc v *Dickman*
[1990] 2 WLR 358 House of Lords (Lords Bridge of Harwich, Roskill, Ackner, Oliver of Aylmerton and Jauncey of Tullichettle)

* *Auditor – duty of care*

Facts
The plaintiff shareholder in Fidelity plc received the accounts audited by the defendants and at first purchased more shares and then made a successful takeover bid. The plaintiffs alleged that the accounts had been inaccurate and misleading: instead of showing a pre-tax profit for the year of some £1.2m, they should have revealed a loss of over £400,000. Had the defendants owed the plaintiffs a duty of care?

Held
They had not, either as shareholders or potential investors.

Lord Bridge of Harwich:

'The most comprehensive attempt to articulate a single general principle [as to the existence and scope of a duty of care] is reached in the well-known passage from the speech of Lord Wilberforce in *Anns* v *Merton London Borough* [1977] 2 All ER 492 at 498 ... But since *Anns*'s case a series of decisions of the Privy Council and of your Lordships' House, notably in judgments and speeches delivered by Lord Keith, have emphasised the inability of any single general principle to provide a practical test which can be applied to every situation to determine whether a duty of care is owed and, if so, what is its scope: see *Peabody Donation Fund* v *Sir Lindsay Parkinson & Co Ltd* [1984] 3 All ER 529 at 533–534, *Yuen Kun Yeu* v *A-G of Hong Kong* [1987] 2 All ER 705 at 709–712, *Rowling* v *Takaro Properties Ltd* [1988] 1 All ER 163 at 172 and *Hill* v *Chief Constable of West Yorkshire* [1988] 2 All ER 238 at 241. What emerges is that, in addition to the foreseeability of damage, necessary ingredients in any situation giving rise to a duty of care are that there should exist between the party owing the duty and the party to whom it is owed a relationship characterised by the law as one of "proximity" or "neighbourhood" and that the situation should be one in which the court considers it fair, just and reasonable that the law should impose a duty of a given scope on the one party for the benefit of the other. But it is implicit in the passages referred to that the concepts of proximity and fairness embodied in these additional ingredients are not susceptible of any such precise definition as would be necessary to give them utility as practical tests, but amount in effect to little more than convenient labels to attach to the features of different specific situations which, on a detailed examination of all the circumstances, the law recognises pragmatically as giving rise to a duty of care of a given scope. Whilst recognising, of course, the importance of the underlying general principles common to the whole field of negligence, I think the law has now moved in the direction of attaching greater significance to the more traditional categorisation of distinct and recognisable situations as guides to the existence, the scope and the limits of the varied duties of care which the law imposes. We must now, I think, recognise the wisdom of the words of Brennan J in the High Court of Australia in *Sutherland Shire Council* v *Heyman* (1985) 60 ALR 1 at 43–44, where he said:

"It is preferable in my view, that the law should develop novel categories of negli-

gence incrementally and by analogy with established categories, rather than by a massive extension of a prima facie duty of care restrained only by indefinable considerations which ought to negative, or to reduce or limit the scope of the duty or the class of person to whom it is owed."

One of the most important distinctions always to be observed lies in the law's essentially different approach to the different kinds of damage which one party may have suffered in consequence of the acts or omissions of another. It is on thing to owe a duty of care to avoid causing injury to the person or property of others. It is quite another to avoid causing others to suffer purely economic loss. ...

The damage which may be caused by the negligently spoken or written word will normally be confined to economic loss sustained by those who rely on the accuracy of the information or advice they receive as a basis for action. The question what, if any, duty is owed by the maker of a statement to exercise due care to ensure its accuracy arises typically in relation to statements made by a person in the exercise of his calling or profession. In advising the client who employs him the professional man owes a duty to exercise that standard of skill and care appropriate to his professional status and will be liable both in contract and in tort for all losses which his client may suffer by reason of any breach of that duty. But the possibility of any duty of care being owed to third parties with whom the professional man was in no contractual relationship was for long denied because of the wrong turning taken by the law in *Le Lievre* v *Gould* [1893] 1 QB 49 in overruling *Cann* v *Willson* (1888) Ch D 39. ... it was not until the decision of this House in *Hedley Byrne & Co Ltd* v *Heller Partners Ltd* [1963] 2 All ER 575 that the law was once more set on the right path. ...

Assuming for the purpose of the argument that the relationship between the auditor of a company and individual shareholders is of sufficient proximity to give rise to a duty of care, I do not understand how the scope of that duty can possibly extend beyond the protection of any individual shareholder from losses in the value of the shares which he holds. As a purchaser of additional shares in reliance on the auditor's report, he stands in no different position from any other investing member of the public to whom the auditor owes no duty.'

Lord Jauncey of Tullichettle:

' ... the purpose of annual accounts, so far as members are concerned, is to enable them to question the past management of the company, to exercise their voting rights, if so advised, and to influence future policy and management. Advice to individual shareholders in relation to present or future investment in the company is not part of the statutory purpose of the preparation and distribution of the accounts ...

If the statutory accounts are prepared and distributed for certain limited purposes, can there nevertheless be imposed on auditors an additional common law duty to individual shareholders who choose to use them for another purpose without the prior knowledge of the auditors? The answer must be No. Use for that other purpose would no longer be ... use for the "very transaction" which Denning LJ in *Candler v Crane, Christmas & Co* [1951] 2 KB 164 at 183 regarded as determinative of the scope of any duty of care. Only where the auditor was aware that the individual shareholder was likely to rely on the accounts for a particular purpose such as his present or future investment in or lending to the company would a duty of care arise. Such a situation does not obtain in the present case.

... it was argued that the relationship of the unwelcome bidder in a potential takeover situation was nearly as proximate to the auditor as was the relationship of a shareholder to whom the report was directed. Since I have concluded that the auditor owed no duty to an individual shareholder, it follows that this argument must also fail. The fact that a company may at a time when the auditor is preparing his report be vulnerable to a takeover bid cannot per se create a relationship of proximity between the auditor and the ultimate successful bidder. Not only is the auditor under no statutory duty to such a bidder but he will have reason at the material time to know neither of his identity nor of the terms of his bid. In this context the recent case of *Al Saudi Banque v Clark Pixley* [1990] 2 WLR 344 is in point. There Millett J held that the auditors of a company owed no duty of care to a bank which lent money to the company, regardless of whether the bank was an existing creditor or a potential one, because no sufficient proximity of relationship existed in either case between the auditor and the bank. I have no doubt that this case was correctly decided ...'

Comment

Applied in *Al-Nakib Investments (Jersey) Ltd v Longcroft* [1990] 3 All ER 321 (prospectus does not give rise to duty of care to purchaser of shares through stock market: cf *Possfund Custodian Trustee Ltd v Diamond* [1996] 2 All ER 774), *Galoo Ltd v Bright Grahame Murray* [1994] 1 All ER 16 (auditor could owe duty of care to identified bidder whom he knows and intends will rely on his work: see also *Morgan Cruicible Co plc v Hill Samuel Bank Ltd* [1991] 1 All ER 148) and *White v Jones* [1995] 1 All ER 691 (solicitor preparing will owes duty of care to intended beneficiary).

See also *Capital and Counties plc v Hampshire County Council* [1997] 2 All ER 865, *Mariola Marine Corporation v Lloyd's Register of Shipping, The Morning Watch* [1990] 1 Lloyd's Rep 547, *Punjab National Bank v de Boinville* [1992] 1 WLR 1138 and *McFarlane v Tayside Health Board* [1999] 4 All ER 961, *Law Society v KPMG Peat Marwick* [2000] 4 All ER 540 (accountants owed duty of care to Law Society) and *Holbeck Hall Hotel Ltd v Scarborough Borough Council* [2000] 2 All ER 705 (not fair, just and reasonable to impose liability for land slip).

Capital and Counties plc v Hampshire County Council; Digital Equipment Co Ltd v Hampshire County Council; John Munroe (Acrylics) Ltd v London Fire and Civil Defence Authority; Church of Jesus Christ of Latter Day Saints (Great Britain) v West Yorkshire Fire and Civil Defence Authority
[1997] 2 All ER 865 Court of Appeal (Stuart-Smith, Potter and Judge LJJ)

- *Negligence – fire brigade – liability*

Facts
The *Hampshire* case(s) arose out of a fire at a modern commercial building of which Capital and Counties plc were the developers and head lessees and Digital Equipment Co Ltd were occupiers as underlessees. The building was equipped with a heat-activated sprinkler system. Twenty-seven minutes after the fire brigade's arrival the sprinkler system was shut down on their instructions. Almost immediately, the fire went out of control and the building became a total loss. The trial judge found that, in having the sprinklers turned off, the fire brigade had been negligent and that a total loss would have been averted had the fire brigade left the sprinklers on and fought the fire. He was unable to say what would have happened if the fire brigade had not turned up at all. The plaintiffs were awarded damages: see [1996] 4 All ER 336.

In the *London Fire Brigade* case, a film company caused a deliberate explosion on wasteland near the plaintiff's premises. Burning debris was scattered over a wide area and some was seen to fall onto the plaintiff's industrial site. The fire brigade left without inspecting the plaintiff's premises and fire broke out there later in the day, causing severe damage. The judge found that the fire brigade had not owed the plaintiff a duty of care: see [1996] 4 All ER 318.

The *West Yorkshire* case concerned a fire which broke out in a classroom adjoining the plaintiff's chapel. If fire hydrants had worked or been located by the fire brigade, said the plaintiff, the fire would have been contained within the classroom: as it was, the chapel was destroyed as well. The judge dismissed the action, holding, inter alia, that it would not be just, fair and reasonable to impose a duty of care on the fire brigade: see (1996) The Times 9 May.

Since similar questions of law were involved, appeals against these decisions were consolidated.

Held
All of the appeals would be dismissed.

Stuart-Smith LJ (delivering the judgment of the court):

> '*Is there a common law duty on the fire brigade to answer calls to fires or to take reasonable care to so do?*
> The question whether, in the absence of a statutory duty, a statutory power to act can be converted into a common law duty to exercise the power has been extensively considered by the House of Lords in *Stovin v Wise* [1996] 3 All ER 801 ...
> [Counsel] for the plaintiff in the *London Fire Brigade* case, submitted that he was entitled to rely on the doctrine of general reliance as giving rise to a duty to exercise statutory powers which have been granted and/or a duty of care to respond to the public's call for help. ... The principle of general reliance has been applied on a number of occasions in Australia. ... But the doctrine has received little if any support in English law. There appears to be no case, except *Anns v Merton London Borough* [1977] 2 All ER 492 itself, which could be said to be said to be an example of its application. And two of the examples suggested by Mason J [in *Sutherland Shire County v Heyman* (1985) 60 ALR 1] have been held not to give rise to a duty of care. In *Marc Rich & Co AG v Bishop Rock Marine Co Ltd, The Nicholas H* [1995] 3 All ER 307 a classification society in which a vessel was entered was held not to be under a duty of care to cargo owners in respect of a negli-

gent inspection of the vessel. And a similar conclusion was reached by the Court of Appeal in *Philcox* v *Civil Aviation Authority* (1995) The Times 8 June, the Civil Aviation Authority being held under no duty of care to the owner of an aircraft alleged to have been negligently inspected and improperly given a certificate of airworthiness. ...

In *Alexandrou* v *Oxford* [1993] 4 All ER 328 the plaintiff's clothing shop was burgled on a Sunday evening. The shop was equipped with a 999-type burglar alarm which rang in the police station on being activated and gave a recorded message as to the site of the burglary. The alarm sounded at 7.23pm and police officers went to investigate. The judge did not believe that they had inspected the rear of the premises as well as the front. The alarm bell ceased to ring at 9.26pm. The judge found that the burglary had been committed shortly before this, access being obtained through a window at the rear of the premises and egress with the stolen goods through a fire door also at the back. The judge also rejected the police evidence that at about 9.26pm they inspected the rear of the premises and nothing was amiss. He held that, if an inspection had been made at the rear as well as the front, as it should have been, the burglars would have been stopped. It is a case therefore on the facts where the police responded to the 999 call, but through negligent failure to inspect, they failed to prevent the loss to the plaintiff, their intervention being ineffectual. Glidewell LJ, with whose judgment Parker and Slade LJJ agreed, dealt with the argument that there was sufficient proximity between the plaintiff and the police to give rise to a duty of care. ... It is true that in that passage Glidewell LJ is concentrating on the question whether there was any duty to respond to the call; but he cannot have overlooked the fact that the police had intervened, albeit ineffectually. This will be a relevant matter when we come to consider the duty if any on the fire brigade once they have reached the fire ground. For present purposes *Alexandrou*'s case is clear authority for the proposition that there is no sufficient proximity simply on the

basis that an emergency call is sent to the police, even if there is a direct line from the premises to the police station. The decision is binding on us, unless it can be distinguished, and in our view on this aspect it cannot.

Glidewell LJ also held, following *Hill* v *Chief Constable of West Yorkshire* [1988] 2 All ER 238, that it was not just, fair and reasonable to impose a duty of care on the police in these circumstances. ... In our judgment the fire brigade are not under a common law duty to answer the call for help and are not under a duty to take care to do so. If therefore they fail to turn up or fail to turn up in time because they have carelessly misunderstood the message, got lost on the way or run into a tree, they are not liable.

Does the fire brigade owe a duty of care to the owner of property on fire, or anyone else to whom the fire may spread, once they have arrived at the fire ground and started to fight the fire?

There are to be found some general statements to the effect that they do owe such a duty. ... Before decisions the subject of the present appeals, however, there have been no reported cases on the point in this country. ... It is therefore necessary to approach this question from first principles.

Counsel for the plaintiffs in the *Hampshire* case submit that there are two approaches in principle which lead to the conclusion of liability in their case.

First it is said that, although the correct method for deciding whether there is a duty of care at common law is to adopt the approach advocated by Lord Bridge in *Caparo Industries plc* v *Dickman* [1990] 1 All ER 568 at 573–574, namely: (i) foreseeability of damage arising from the negligent performance of the relevant operation, (ii) the existence of a sufficient relationship of proximity between the parties, and (iii) whether or not as a matter of legal policy it is "fair, just and reasonable" that a duty of care should exist, the direct infliction of foreseeable physical damage is an established category of case where a duty exists. It is argued that Station Officer Mitchell's act of switching off the sprinklers was a positive act of misfeasance which foreseeably caused the fire to get out of control and spread and cause the loss [of parts of the premises] which would not otherwise have been affected. It was on this basis that Judge Havery found in the plaintiff's favour. By reason of the differing circumstances in each appeal this line of argument is only of direct assistance to the plaintiffs in the *Hampshire* case.

The alternative ground upon which it is said that proximity will arise is where someone possessed of a special skill undertakes, quite irrespective of contract, to apply that skill for the assistance of another person who relies upon such skill, and there is direct and substantial reliance by the plaintiffs on the defendant's skill (see *Henderson v Merrett Syndicates Ltd, Hallam-Eames v Merrett Syndicates Ltd, Hughes v Merrett Syndicates Ltd, Arbuthnott v Feltrim Underwriting Agencies Ltd, Deeny v Gooda Walker Ltd (in liq)* [1994] 3 All ER 506 at 518–520 per Lord Goff of Chieveley, adopting what was said by Lord Morris of Borth-y-Gest and Lord Devlin in *Hedley Byrne & Co Ltd v Heller & Partners Ltd* [1963] 2 All ER 575 at 594, 608).

We turn to consider the first of these submissions. The peculiarity of fire brigades, together with other rescue services, such as ambulance or coastal rescue and protective services such as the police, is that they do not as a rule create the danger which causes injury to the plaintiff or loss to his property. For the most part they act in the context of a danger already created and damage already caused, whether by the forces of nature, or the acts of some third party or even of the plaintiff himself, and whether those acts are criminal, negligent or non-culpable.

But where the rescue/protective service itself by negligence creates the danger which caused the plaintiff's injury there is no doubt in our judgment the plaintiff can recover. There are many examples of this. In *Rigby v Chief Constable of Northamptonshire* [1985] 2 All ER 985 the plaintiff's gun shop was at risk from a lunatic. The police

came to deal with the situation; they fired a CS canister of gas into the shop, though it caused a high risk of fire, without ensuring that the fire engine which had previously been available was there to put out any fire that resulted. In *Knightly v Johns* [1982] 1 All ER 851 in the course of traffic control following an accident two police constables were instructed to take a course which involve them riding against the traffic flow from round a blind bend causing a collision in which the plaintiff was injured. In *Home Office v Dorset Yacht Co Ltd* [1970] 2 All ER 294 the defendant's prison officers had brought the borstal boys who had a known propensity to escape into the locality where the yachts were moored and so had created a potential situation of danger for the owners of those yachts, in which they failed to exercise proper supervision over the boys (see *Hill v Chief Constable of West Yorkshire* [1988] 2 All ER 238 at 242 per Lord Keith of Kinkel). Similarly in *Alcock v Chief Constable of South Yorkshire* [1991] 4 All ER 907 where the question in issue was the liability of the police to those suffering shock as a result of the Hillsborough disaster. There was never any dispute that the police were liable to the primary victims because they had created the danger by incompetent crowd control.

These are all cases, however, where a new or different danger has been created from that which the police were seeking to guard against, except perhaps in *Alcock*. A comparable situation would be if, on arrival at the scene of a fire, the fire engine was negligently driven into the owner's car parked in the street. But it seems to us there is no difference in principle if, by some positive negligent act, the rescuer/protective service substantially increases the risk; he is thereby creating a fresh danger, albeit of the same kind or of the same nature, namely fire. The judge held that at the time the sprinkler systems were turned off, the fire was being contained, but that once they were turned off it rapidly went out of control, spreading to [parts of the premises] which had been deprived of their own sprinkler protection.

In answer to both way in which [counsel]

put the case for Digital, [counsel for the fire brigade] relies on the decision in *East Suffolk Rivers Catchment Board* v *Kent* [1940] 4 All ER 527. The facts are well known. Owing to a very high tide, a breach was made in the sea wall as a consequence of which the respondent's land was flooded. The appellants, in the exercise of their statutory powers, undertook the repair of the wall, but carried out the work so inefficiently that the flooding continued for 178 days thereby causing serious damage to the respondent's pasture land. By the exercise of reasonable skill in carrying out the work of repair the breach in the wall could have been repaired in 14 days.

The trial judge ([1939] 2 All ER 207) and the majority of the Court of Appeal ([1939] 4 All ER 174) held the appellants liable. In the House of Lords it was held that where a statutory authority embarks upon the execution of the power to do work, the only duty owed to any member of the public is not thereby to add to the damages which that person would have suffered had the authority done nothing. ...

We think that the true analogy between the *Hampshire* case and the *East Suffolk* case would be this: suppose that after the main sea wall had been breached the plaintiff had constructed a temporary wall which contained the floodwater to a relatively small area, and that the defendants then came upon the land to repair the main wall and negligently destroyed the plaintiff's temporary wall so that the area of the flooding increased before the repairs were completed. In such circumstances the defendants would at least prima facie be liable for the extra damage unless they could show (and the burden would be upon them) that the damage would have occurred in any event, even if they had never come upon the scene. If they were unable to discharge that burden, then they would be liable. Similarly in the present case, the judge's inability to make such a finding in their favour must in our view render the defendants liable. ...

We now turn to consider the second submission made on behalf of all the plaintiffs that the requisite proximity exists. It involves

the concept of assumption of responsibility by the fire brigade and particular reliance by the owner. As a general rule a sufficient relationship of proximity will exist when someone possessed of special skill undertakes to apply that skill for the assistance of another person who relies upon such skill and there is direct and substantial reliance by the plaintiff on the defendant's skill (see *Hedley Byrne & Co Ltd* v *Heller & Partners* and *Henderson* v *Merrett Syndicates Ltd*). There are many instances of this. The plaintiffs submit that that which is most closely analogous is that of doctor and patient or health authority and patient. There is no doubt that once the relationship of doctor and patient or hospital authority and admitted patient exists, the doctor or the hospital owe a duty to take reasonable care to effect a cure, not merely to prevent further harm. The undertaking is to use the special skills which the doctor and hospital authorities have to treat the patient. ...

Plaintiffs' counsel argue that the provisions of subss(3) and (2) of s30 [of the Fire Services Act 1947] which confer on the senior fire brigade officer present sole charge and control of fire fighting operations and make it a criminal offence wilfully to obstruct or interfere with any member of a fire brigade engaged in fire fighting, establish a proximate relationship, once responsibility for fighting the fire is taken over by the brigade. ...

But it seems to us that the statute imposes control of operations on the senior officer for the benefit of the public generally where there may be conflicting interests. By taking such control that officer is not to be seen as undertaking a voluntary assumption of responsibility to the owner of the premises on fire, whether or not the latter is in fact reliant upon it. ...

It has been held that a property owner owes a duty of care to firemen not by his negligence to start a fire or create special hazards to fire fighting operations (see *Ogwo* v *Taylor* [1987] 3 All ER 961). That being so, it was submitted that there ought to be a reciprocal duty on the part of the fire brigade to the property owner, the argument being that if there is proximity in one direction it ought to be in both. But the reason why a duty is owed to rescuers is because the law recognises, that if A by his negligence puts the person or property of B at risk, it is reasonably foreseeable that some courageous and public spirited person C will come to the assistance of B. C is the secondary victim of A's negligence and the duty is owed to C as well as B. A has created the danger which causes injury to both B and C. But simply by attending the fire and conducting fire fighting operations the fire brigade do not, save in exceptional circumstances such as the *Hampshire* case, create or increase the danger.

It is not clear why a rescuer who is not under an obligation to attempt a rescue should assume a duty to be careful in effecting the rescue merely by undertaking the attempt. It would be strange if such a person were liable to the dependants of a drowning man who but for his carelessness he would have saved, but without the attempt would have drowned anyway. In Canada it has been held that he is not (see *The Ogopogo* [1971] 2 Lloyd's Rep 410). This is consistent with the *East Suffolk* case. It is also, as we have pointed out, the effect of *Alexandrou* v *Oxford* because the ineffective intervention by the police in incompetently inspecting the plaintiff's premises did not create a relationship of proximity.

There are a number of cases where the courts have held that the relationship of proximity arises so as to give rise to a duty of care for the plaintiff's physical safety which are based on assumption of responsibility and reliance. In *Kirkham* v *Chief Constable of the Greater Manchester Police* [1990] 3 All ER 246 the plaintiff's husband was taken into custody by the police. The police were told by the plaintiff that her husband was a suicide risk. When the husband was remanded in custody to the prison authorities that information was not passed on to the prison authority. The husband committed suicide and the police were held liable to the plaintiff. ... It is not altogether clear whether the reliance in that

case was that of the plaintiff or her husband. But the reasoning was clear.

In *Welsh* v *Chief Constable of the Merseyside Police* [1993] 1 All ER 692 Tudor Evans J held that there was arguably a breach of duty by the Crown Prosecution Service which had undertaken to pass on certain information to the court relating to the plaintiff's case, but failed to do so.

In *Osman* v *Ferguson* [1993] 4 All ER 344 a great deal of information had been given to the police by the victim's family identifying P as a potentially dangerous criminal, but the police failed to apprehend him. McCowan and Simon Brown LJJ considered that there was arguably a sufficiently close degree of proximity between the police and the victim's family to give rise to a special relationship. Beldam LJ expressed no opinion on this. The action was struck out on the basis that it would be contrary to public policy to impose a duty of care on the police.

In *Barrett* v *Ministry of Defence* [1995] 3 All ER 87 the deceased, a 30-year-old naval airman, engaged in a bout of heavy drinking; having become unconscious, [he] was placed on a bunk lying in the recovery position, but his condition was not checked and he was later found dead having asphyxiated on his vomit. The defendant officer was not liable for preventing the deceased abusing alcohol or for anything prior to his collapse. Beldam LJ said ([1995] 3 All ER 87 at 96):

"Thereafter, when the appellant assumed responsibility for him, it accepts that the measures taken fell short of the standard reasonably to be expected. It did not summon medical assistance and its supervision of him was inadequate."

It is apparent that the point was conceded. But it is not surprising, having regard to the fact that the deceased was under command of the officer concerned.

These are all examples of where the court has considered on the special facts of the case that there is sufficiently close relationship of proximity to give rise to a duty of care. But we do not think they are anywhere near the circumstances that arise in these appeals. In our judgment, a fire brigade does not enter into a sufficient proximate relationship with the owner or occupier of premises to come under a duty of care merely by attending at the fire ground and fighting the fire; this is so, even though the senior officer actually assumes control of the fire-fighting operation.

Is it just, fair and reasonable to impose a duty of care? – public policy immunity
In the *Hampshire* case Judge Havery held that it was just and reasonable to hold the defendant liable for negligent actions of Station Officer Mitchell. Rougier J in the *London Fire Brigade* case held both that there was no sufficient proximity to give rise to a duty of care, and also that it would not be just, fair and reasonable to impose such a duty. Rimer J in *Nelson Holdings Ltd* v *British Gas plc* (1997) The Times 7 March followed the same course. In the *West Yorkshire* case Judge Crawford held there was sufficient proximity, but it was not just, fair and reasonable to impose the duty of care.

In the light of our conclusion that there is not sufficient proximity in the *London Fire Brigade* case and *West Yorkshire* case it is perhaps not necessary to consider in either case whether the third test in the *Caparo* case is satisfied or not, since treated separately, the third test only arises, following the conclusion of the court that the test of proximity is prima facie satisfied. However, the second and third test in *Caparo* are closely inter-related. …

We consider first, therefore, whether there is any reason of policy why the Hampshire fire authority should not be liable. The starting point is that "the public policy consideration which has first claim on the loyalty of the law is that wrongs should be remedied, and that very potent counter-considerations are required to override that policy" (per Lord Browne-Wilkinson in *X and Others (Minors)* v *Bedfordshire CC* [1995] 3 All ER 353 at 380). Counsel for the fire brigades have placed much reliance on the police cases, on the basis that there is a similarity between fire brigades answering

rescue calls and the police answering calls for help and protection from the public. But it is clear from the leading case of *Hill* v *Chief Constable of West Yorkshire* [1988] 2 All ER 238 that the police do not enjoy blanket immunity. … Other examples would be *Alcock* v *Chief Constable of South Yorkshire* [1991] 4 All ER 907 (the Hillsborough case) and *Marshall* v *Osmond* [1983] 2 All ER 225. These are cases, as we have already pointed out, where the police created danger and are closely analogous to the *Hampshire* case.

There is no general immunity for professionals or others carrying out difficult tasks in stressful circumstances. Doctors, barristers (save for immunity in court), salvors (*The Tojo Maru* [1971] 1 All ER 1110), police (save in certain circumstances) and prison officers do not have immunity.

In the *East Suffolk* case, it is clear that the board would have been liable if through their negligence they had added to the damage the plaintiff would otherwise have suffered. The dividing line between liability and non-liability is thus defined and there is no need to pray in aid any concept of public policy. We agree with [counsel for Digital] that the courts should not grant immunity from suit to fire brigades simply because the judge may have what he describes as a visceral dislike for allowing possibly worthless claims to be made against public authorities, whose activities involve the laudable operation of rescuing the person or property of others in conditions often of great danger. Such claims may indeed be motivated by what is sometimes perceived to be the current attitude to litigation – "if you have suffered loss and can see a solvent target – sue it". None the less, if a defendant is to be immune for suit such immunity must be based upon principle.

It seems to use that in those cases where the courts have granted immunity or refused to impose a duty of care it is usually possible to discern a recognition that such a duty would be inconsistent with some wider object of the law or interest of the particular parties. Thus if the existence of a duty of care would impede the careful performance of the relevant function, of if the investigation of the allegedly negligent conduct would itself be undesirable and open to abuse by those bearing grudges, the law will not impose a duty. ...

On the other hand liability has been imposed when, in the course of carrying out their duties, the police have themselves created the danger (see *Rigby* v *Chief Constable of Northamptonshire, Knightley* v *Johns, Alcock* v *Chief Constable of South Yorkshire* and *Marshall* v *Osmond*).

In our judgment, there is no doubt on which side of the line a case such as the *Hampshire* case falls. It is one where the defendants, by their action in turning off the sprinklers, created or increased the danger. There is no ground for giving immunity in such a case.

Rougier J in the *London Fire Brigade* case, after citing from the speeches of Lord Keith and Lord Templeman in *Hill*'s case, set out a number of reasons why in his judgment it was not appropriate to impose a common law duty to take care on fire brigades. ... Judge Crawford in the *West Yorkshire* case added a number of others ...

In our judgment there is considerable force in the criticisms made. If we had found a sufficient relationship of proximity in the *London Fire Brigade* and *West Yorkshire* cases, we do not think that we would have found the arguments for excluding a duty of care on the grounds that it would not be just, fair and reasonable convincing. ... We do not think that the principles which underlie those decisions where immunity has been granted can be sufficiently identified in the case of fire brigades.

Statutory immunity
The argument for the defendant authorities is that s30 confers immunity or creates a statutory defence against liability for negligence or breach of statutory duty by the fire brigade and firemen involved in extinguishing a fire. If that is correct, the plaintiffs' claims would fail. Liability for activities which caused damage at the scene is said to be limited to cases of deliberate bad faith, which is not in question in any of the present cases.

There is a clear distinction to be observed at this stage of the argument between the general question whether the plaintiffs are entitled to maintain an action at common law and the question currently under consideration, which is whether, assuming that the 1947 Act would otherwise be appropriate to sustain an action for negligence at common law or breach of statutory duty, s30 precludes any such liability.

Liability of a public authority in tort may be restricted or avoided by appropriate statutory language. Section 30 itself provides a clear example of language which authorises what would otherwise be a tortious interference with property. ...

However, it is an elementary principle repeated in different language in numerous authorities that a public body is normally expected to use its statutory powers with reasonable care (see *Mersey Docks and Harbour Board Trustees* v *Gibbs* (1866) LR 1 HL 93, *Geddis* v *Proprietors of Bann Reservoir* (1878) 3 App Cas 430 and the more recent examples of *Home Office* v *Dorset Yacht Co Ltd* [1970] 2 All ER 294, *X and Others (Minors)* v *Bedfordshire CC* [1995] 3 All ER 353 and *Stovin* v *Wise* [1996] 3 All ER 801) ...

Accordingly, liability for negligence or breach of a statutory duty by a public body in the course of fulfilling its statutory obligations may only be excluded by express language or by necessary implication.

It is common ground between the parties that fire authorities are not expressly required to respond to emergency calls and attend the scene of each fire and to extinguish it. There is, however, a reasonable public expectation that normally the emergency call will be answered and the fire extinguished. In addition to their fire-fighting duties, fire officers attend and assist at emergencies where their fire-fighting skills as such are not required (s3(1)(e)).

Each member of a fire brigade on duty who attends the scene of any fire in order to extinguish it is granted specific powers directly concerned with fire fighting (s30(1)) and sole charge and control of all operations for the extinction of the fire is given to the senior fire brigade officer present at the scene (s30(3)). ...

Section 30 therefore removes potential impediments to efficient fire fighting. ...

Although the powers are very wide, there is nothing in s30 which permits them to be exercised negligently. If it had been intended to exclude liability for negligence express provision could readily have been made. None was, and the omission in a section which otherwise expressly exonerates firemen from potential liability in tort for trespass is striking. ...

In our view those words in s30 which empower a fire officer to do all such things as he may deem necessary for extinguishing the fire etc are no more than the adoption of a comprehensive formula to enable the officer to do all those things which might otherwise amount to trespass to property person or goods, or other infringements of private rights in the course of fire fighting.

The language of s30 is not apt to establish an implied immunity from proceedings in negligence, whether brought by those whose property has been damaged, or indeed other fireman working at the scene, or individuals present who have suffered personal injury as a result of negligence in the course of fire fighting.

Section 13

The particular relevance of s13 arises in relation to the *West Yorkshire* appeal. There are certain distinctions between that appeal and the other two before the court in the following respects. First, there is a claim for breach of statutory duty simpliciter under s13, which provides:

> "A fire authority shall takes all reasonable measures for ensuring the provision of an adequate supply of water, and for securing that it will be available for use, in case of fire."

Secondly unlike the crucial allegation in the *Hampshire* case, the allegations made against this defendant consists of omissions rather than positive acts. Thirdly, save for an allegation of failing to locate the hydrants close to the chapel on arrival at the fire,

none of the allegations relates to conduct in the course of fighting the fire, but rather to the failure of the defendants to take reasonable steps to ensure that the necessary plant and equipment was in place to enable the fire to be fought. ...

The proper approach must be to take a fresh look at the terms of s13 in its statutory context, guided by the recent restatement by Lord Browne-Wilkinson in *X and Others (Minors)* v *Bedfordshire CC* [1995] 3 All ER 353 at 364–365, under the heading "Breach of statutory duty simpliciter": ...

Considered in that light, we do not consider that s13 is intended to confer a right of private action upon a member of the public injured by a breach. The duty propounded in s13 is in no way "limited and specific" in the sense contemplated by Lord Browne-Wilkinson; it is more in the nature of a general administrative function of procurement placed on the fire authority in relation to supply of water for fire fighting generally. There is no reference to any specific measure contemplated, nor any reference, whether expressly or by implication, to any class of person short of the public as a whole being ear-marked for protection under the section. ... We therefore consider that in the *West Yorkshire* case no action lies for breach of statutory duty under s13. ...

Negligence in law

[Counsel for the fire brigade's] final grounds of appeal in the *Hampshire* case relate to the judge's finding that Station Officer Mitchell's conduct in turning off the sprinklers did not amount to negligence in law. The judge applied as his benchmark the test laid down in *Bolam* v *Friern Hospital Management Committee* [1957] 2 All ER 118. This is a very high threshold in establishing negligence, namely, it must be established that the error was one that no reasonably well-informed and competent fireman could have made (see *Saif Ali* v *Sydney Mitchell & Co* [1978] 3 All ER 1033 at 1043 per Lord Diplock). ... But the judge considered with great care the reasons advanced by Station Officer Mitchell for departing from the normal rule, namely to prevent damage to Digital's computers and because the sprinklers were hampering the fire-fighters, he gave unassailable reasons for not accepting them. The third reason, namely the sprinklers were not assisting in fighting the fire, is obviously no reason at all and was completely untenable. In our view the judge's conclusion that Station Officer Mitchell's conduct amounted to negligence cannot be disturbed.'

Comment

These cases were applied in *OLL Ltd* v *Secretary of State for Transport* [1997] 3 All ER 897 (liability of coastguard in relation to emergency calls same as that of fire brigade) but distinguished in *Kent* v *Griffiths* [2000] 2 All ER 474 (ambulance service owed duty of care in responding to 999 call: liability established since arrival of ambulance delayed without good reason).

In *Nelson Holdings Ltd* v *British Gas plc* (1997) The Times 7 March, on arrival at a fire a gas leak was identified. The brigade asked British Gas to cut off the supply but some two hours later, before they arrived, there was a gas explosion and a further fire which caused substantial additional damage. Rimer J struck out a claim that the brigade had been negligent in failing to turn off the gas supply.

See also *Reeves* v *Commissioner of Police of the Metroplis* [1999] 3 All ER 897 (man in police custody committed suicide: police negligent but damages reduced by one half on account of man's contributory negligence).

Davis v *Radcliffe* [1990] 1 WLR 821 Privy Council (Lords Keith of Kinkel, Brandon of Oakbrook, Templeman, Goff of Chieveley and Lowry)

• *Licensing of banks – duty of care*

Facts

By statute, and subject to the directions of the Isle of Man Finance Board, the Treasurer had power to issue, revoke and suspend banking licences: he issued such a licence to Savings and Investment Bank Ltd (SIB) with which the plaintiffs deposited money. SIB was wound up and it appeared that the plaintiffs would receive no more than a small dividend from the liquidator. The plaintiffs sued the Treasurer and the Board alleging negligence and/or breach of statutory duty: their claim was struck out: they appealed.

Held

Their appeal would be dismissed as the defendants had not owed them a duty of care.

Lord Goff of Chieveley:

'Their Lordships feel great sympathy for those who, like the [plaintiffs], have deposited substantial sums of money with a bank in the confident expectation that a bank is a safe place for their money, only to find that the bank has become insolvent and that the most they can expect to receive is a small dividend payable in its winding up. But, when it is sought to make some third person responsible in negligence for the loss suffered through the bank's default, the question whether that third person owes a duty of care to the depositor has to be decided in accordance with the established principles of the law of negligence. In the present case the [judge], having reviewed the authorities with care, concluded that neither the members of the Finance Board nor the Treasurer owed any such duty to the [plaintiffs], and so struck out their statement of case as disclosing no reasonable cause of action. Their Lordships are in no doubt that [he] was right to reach that conclusion, substantially for the reasons given by him. Indeed they are in agreement with him that the present case is, for all practical purposes, indistinguishable from the decision of their Lordships' Board in *Yuen Kun Yeu* v *A-G of Hong Kong* [1987] 3 WLR 776 ... The [judge] also dismissed, in a terse paragraph, an alternative plea based on breach of statutory duty, on the principle set out in *Cutler* v *Wandsworth Stadium Ltd* [1949] AC 398. Their Lordships entirely agree with [his] conclusion on this point, which was plainly right.'

Department of the Environment v *Thomas Bates & Son Ltd* [1990] 3 WLR 457 House of Lords (Lords Keith of Kinkel, Brandon of Oakbrook, Ackner, Oliver of Aylmerton and Jauncey of Tullichettle)

• *Negligence – economic loss – no personal danger*

Facts

The plaintiffs were underlessees of the upper storeys of an office block built by the defendants in 1970 and 1971. In 1981 and 1982 it was discovered that low-strength concrete had been used in the pillars which, although they could support the existing load, could not support the design load safely. The plaintiffs strengthened the pillars and sought to recover the cost from the defendants; the trial judge found, inter alia, that there had been no imminent danger to the health or safety of the plaintiffs' employees or the public.

Held

The plaintiffs could not succeed as the cost of the remedial work was purely economic loss.

Lord Keith of Kinkel:

'The foundation of the plaintiffs' case is *Anns* v *Merton London Borough* [1977] 2 WLR 1024 ... It has been held by this House in *Murphy* v *Brentwood DC* [1990] 3 WLR 414 that *Anns* was wrongly decided and should be departed from, by reason of the erroneous views there expressed as to the scope of any duty of care owed to purchasers of houses by local authorities when exercising the powers conferred on them for the purpose of securing compliance with building regulations. The process of reasoning by which the House reached its conclusion necessarily included close examination of the position of the builder who was primarily responsible, through lack of care in the construction process, for the presence of defects in the building. It was the unanimous view that, while the builder would be liable under the principle of *Donoghue* v *Stevenson* [1932] AC 562 in the event of the defect, before it had been discovered, causing physical injury to persons or damage to property other than the building itself, there was no sound basis in principle for holding him liable for the pure economic loss suffered by a purchaser who discovered the defect, however such discovery might come about, and who was required to expend money in order to make the building safe and suitable for its intended purpose.

In the present case it is clear that the loss suffered by the plaintiffs is pure economic loss. At the time the plaintiffs carried out the remedial work on the concrete pilars the building was not unsafe by reason of the defective construction of these pillars. It did, however, suffer from a defect of quality which made the plaintiffs' lease less valuable than it would otherwise have been, in respect the the building could not be loaded up to its design capacity unless any occupier who wished so to load it had incurred the expenditure necessary for the strengthening of the pillars. It was wholly uncertain whether during the currency of their lease the plaintiffs themselves would ever be likely to require to load the building up to its design capacity, but a purchaser from them might well have wanted to do so. Such a purchaser, faced with the need to strengthen the pillars, would obviously have paid less for the lease than if they had been sound. This underlines the purely economic character of the plaintiffs' loss. To hold in favour of the plaintiffs would involve a very significant extension of the doctrine of *Anns* so as to cover the situation where there existed no damage to the building and no imminent danger to personal safety or health. If *Anns* was correctly decided, such an extension could reasonably be regarded as entirely logical. The undesirability of such an extension, for the reasons stated in in *Murphy*, formed an important part of the grounds which led to the conclusion that *Anns* was not correctly decided. That conclusion must lead inevitably to the result that the plaintiffs' claim fails.'

Comment
See also *Murphy v Brentwood District Council* [1990] 3 WLR 414 and *Nitrigin Eireann Teoranta v Inco Alloys Ltd* [1992] 1 WLR 498.

Donoghue (or McAlister) v Stevenson [1932] AC 562 House of Lords (Lords Buckmaster, Atkin, Tomlin, Thankerton and Macmillan)

• *Negligence – duty of care*

Facts
The appellant went, together with her friend, to a cafe, where the friend purchased a bottle of ginger beer which was sealed and in opaque glass. Both drank from the ginger beer before realising that it contained a dead snail. The appellant suffered gastro-enteritis and shock as a result and sued the manufacturer of the ginger beer for damages on the ground that he had been negligent in the production of the product. The only question before the House of Lords was whether the respondent (manufacturer) owed a duty of care to the appellant.

Held (Lords Buckmaster and Tomlin dissenting)
The respondent owed the appellant a duty of care, although he did not know the product to be dangerous and no contractual relationship existed between the parties. On proof of the facts the appellant would be entitled to damages.

Lord Atkin:

'You must take reasonable care to avoid acts or omissions which you can reasonably foresee would be likely to injure your neighbour. Who then, in law, is my neighbour? The answer seems to be – persons who are so closely and directly affected by my act that I ought reasonably to have them in contemplation as being so affected when I am directing my mind to the acts or omissions which are called in question.'

Lord Macmillan:

'In the daily contacts of social and business life, human beings are thrown into, or place themselves in, an infinite variety of relations with their fellows; and the law can refer only to the standards of the reasonable man in order to determine whether any particular relation gives rise to a duty to take care, as between those who stand in that relation to each other. The grounds of action may be as various and manifold as human errancy; and the conception of legal responsibility may develop in adaptation to altering social conditions and standards. The criterion of judgment must adjust and adapt itself to the changing circumstances of life. The categories of negligence are never closed.'

Comment
In *Home Office v Dorset Yacht Co Ltd* [1970] 2 All ER 294 Lord Reid described *Donoghue v Stevenson* as a milestone in the development of the law of negligence and said that Lord Atkin's words should be regarded as a statement of principle. Frequent reference has been and is still made to both the decision itself and Lord Atkin's statement.

Harris v Wyre Forest District Council see *Smith v Eric S Bush*

Hay (or Bourhill) v Young see *Bourhill (or Hay) v Young*

Hedley Byrne & Co Ltd v Heller & Partners Ltd [1963] 3 WLR 101 House of Lords (Lords Reid, Morris of Borth-y-Gest, Hodson, Devlin and Pearce)

• *Negligence – duty of care in relation to information or advice*

Facts
The appellants, becoming doubtful about the financial position of Easipower Ltd, asked their bank to communicate with Easipower's

bankers, the respondents. This they did by telephone asking the respondents 'in confidence, and without liability on [the respondents'] part', whether Easipower would be good for a contract of £8,000 to £9,000. The respondents replied that they believed Easipower 'to be respectably constituted and considered good for its normal business engagements'. Six months later the appellants' bank wrote to the respondents to ask whether they considered Easipower trustworthy, in the way of business, to the extent of a £100,000 per annum contract and the respondents replied: 'Respectably constituted company, considered good for its ordinary business engagements'. The appellants relied upon the respondents' statements and as a result lost over £17,000 when Easipower Ltd went into liquidation. The appellants sought to recover this loss from the respondents as damages on the ground that the respondents' replies were given negligently and in breach of the respondents' duty to exercise care in giving them.

Held

Assuming that negligence could be established, persons in the respondents' position might have been liable but the disclaimer here was adequate to exclude their assumption of a legal duty of care.

Lord Reid:

'A reasonable man, knowing that he was being trusted or that his skill and judgment were being relied on, would, I think, have three courses open to him. He could keep silent or decline to give the information or advice sought: or he could give an answer with a clear qualification that he accepted no responsibility for it or that it was given without that reflection or inquiry which a careful answer would require: or he could simply answer without any such qualification. If he chooses to adopt the last course he must, I think, be held to have accepted some responsibility for his answer being given carefully, or to have accepted a relationship with the inquirer which requires him to

exercise such care as the circumstances require.'

Lord Morris of Borth-y-Gest:

'I consider that ... it should now be regarded as settled that if someone possessed of a special skill undertakes, quite irrespective of contact, to apply that skill for the assistance of another person who relies on such skill, a duty of care will arise. The fact that the service is to be given by means of, or by the instrumentality of, words can make no difference. Furthermore if, in a sphere in which a person is so placed that others could reasonably rely on his judgment or his skill or on his ability to make careful inquiry, a person takes it on himself to give information or advice to, or allows his information or advice to be passed on to, another person who, as he knows or should know, will place reliance on it, then a duty of care will arise. ...

There was in the present case no contemplation of receiving anything like a formal and detailed report such as might be given by some concern charged with the duty (probably for reward) of making all proper and relevant inquiries concerning the nature, scope and extent of a company's activities and of obtaining and marshalling all available evidence as to its credit, efficiency, standing and business reputation. There is much to be said, therefore, for the view that if a banker gives a reference in the form of a brief expression of opinion in regard to credit-worthiness he does not accept, and there is not expected from him, any higher duty than that of giving an honest answer. I need not, however, seek to deal further with this aspect of the matter, which perhaps cannot be covered by any statement of general application, because in my judgment the bank in the present case, by the words which they employed, effectively disclaimed any assumption of a duty of care.'

Lord Devlin:

'It is the relationship between the parties in this case that it can be brought within a category giving rise to a special duty? As always in English law the first step in such an inquiry is to see how far the authorities have gone, for the new categories in the law do not spring into existence overnight.

It would be surprising if the sort of problem that is created by the facts of this case had never until recently arisen in English law. As a problem it is a by-product of the doctrine of consideration. If the respondents had made a nominal charge for the reference, the problem would not exist. If it were possible in English law to construct a contract without consideration, the problem would move at once out of the first and general phase into the particular; and the question would be, not whether on the facts of the case there was a special relationship, but whether on the facts of the case there was a contract.

The respondents in this case cannot deny that they were performing a service. Their sheet anchor is that they were performing it gratuitously and therefore no liability for its performance can arise. My lords, in my opinion this is not the law. A promise given without consideration to perform a service cannot be enforced as a contract by the promisee; but if the service is in fact performed and done negligently, the promisee can recover in an action in tort. This is the foundation of the liability of a gratuitous bailee. ...

I think ... that there is ample authority to justify your lordships in saying now that the categories of special relationships, which may give rise to a duty to take care in word as well as in deed, are not limited to contractual relationships or to relationships of fiduciary duty, but include also relationships which in the words of Lord Shaw in *Nocton v Ashburton* [1914] AC 932 are "equivalent to contract" that is, there is an assumption of responsibility in circumstances in which, but for the absence of consideration, there would be a contract. ...

I am satisfied for the reasons which I have given that a person for whose use a banker's reference is furnished is not, simply because no consideration has passed, prevented from contending that the banker is responsible to him for what he has said.'

Lord Pearce:

"There is ... in my opinion a duty of care created by special relationships which, though not fiduciary, give rise to an assumption that care as well as honesty is demanded.

'Was there such a special relationship in the present case as to impose on the respondents a duty of care to the appellants as the undisclosed principals for whom National Provincial Bank Ltd was making the inquiry? The answer to that question depends on the circumstances of the transaction. If, for instance, they disclosed a casual social approach to the inquiry no such special relationship or duty of care would be assumed (see *Fish v Kelly* (1864) 17 CBNS 194). To import such a duty the representation must normally, I think, concern a business or professional transaction whose nature makes clear the gravity of the inquiry and the importance and influence attached to the answer. It is conceded that Salmon J rightly found a duty of care in *Woods v Martins Bank Ltd* [1958] 3 All ER 166, but the facts in that case were wholly different from those in the present case. A most important circumstance is the form of the inquiry and of the answer. Both were here plainly stated to be without liability.'

Comment

The principle established by this decision has been widely applied and reference to it is frequently made: see, eg, *Williams v Natural Life Health Foods Ltd* [1998] 2 All ER 577 and *Spring v Guardian Assurance plc* [1994] 3 All ER 129 (employer liable to former or present employee in respect of reference negligently given to prospective employer). In the latter case, Lord Goff of Chieveley said: 'In my opinion, the source of duty of care lies in the principle derived from *Hedley Byrne*, viz an assumption of responsibility by [the employers] to the plaintiff in respect of the reference, and reliance by the plaintiff upon the exercise by them of due care and skill in respect of its preparation.' His Lordship left open the question as to whether the employers owed a duty of care to the recipient of the reference.

Hill v *Chief Constable of West Yorkshire* [1989] AC 53 House of Lords (Lords Keith of Kinkel, Brandon of Oakbrook, Templeman, Oliver of Aylmerton and Goff of Chieveley)

• *Negligence – police – duty of care*

Facts
A claim brought on behalf of the estate of Jacqueline Hill for damages under the Law Reform (Miscellaneous Provisions) Act 1934, against the Chief Constable of an area where the 'Yorkshire Ripper' had murdered many women, Jacqueline Hill being his last victim. The Chief Constable sought to strike out the claim on the ground that the statement of claim did not disclose a cause of action and the trial judge decided in his favour.

Held
The proceedings had been properly struck out.

Lord Keith of Kinkel:

'It has been said almost too frequently to require repetition that foreseeability of likely harm is not in itself a sufficient test of liability in negligence. Some further ingredient is invariably needed to establish the requisite proximity of relationship between the plaintiff and defendant, and all the circumstances of the case must be carefully considered and analysed in order to ascertain whether such an ingredient is present. The nature of the ingredient will be found to vary in a number of different categories of decided cases ...

It is plain that vital characteristics which were present in *Home Office* v *Dorset Yacht Co Ltd* [1970] 2 WLR 1140 and which led to the imposition of liability are here lacking. Sutcliffe was never in the custody of the police force. Miss Hill was one of a vast number of the female general public who might be at risk from his activities but was at no special distinctive risk in relation to them, unlike the owners of yachts moored off Brownsea Island in relation to the foreseeable conduct of the borstal boys. It appears from the ... speech of Lord Diplock in the *Dorset Yacht* case that in his view no liability would rest on a prison authority, which carelessly allowed the escape of an habitual criminal, for damage which he subsequently caused, not in the course of attempting to make good his getaway, to persons at special risk, but in further pursuance of his general criminal career to the person or property of members of the general public. The same rule must apply as regards failure to recapture the criminal before he had time to resume his career. In the case of an escaped criminal his identity and description are known. In the instant case the identity of the wanted criminal was at the material time unknown and it is not averred that any full or clear description of him was ever available. The alleged negligence of the police consists in a failure to discover his identity. But, if there is no general duty of care owed to individual members of the public by the responsible authorities to prevent the escape of a known criminal or to recapture him, there cannot reasonably be imposed on any police force a duty of care similarly owed to identify and apprehend an unknown one. Miss Hill cannot for this purpose be regarded as a person at special risk simply because she was young and female. Where the class of potential victims of a particular habitual criminal is a large one the precise size of it cannot in principle affect the issue. All householders are potential victims of a habitual burglar, and all females those of a habitual rapist. The conclusion must be that although there existed reasonable foreseeability of likely harm to such as Miss Hill if Sutcliffe were not identified and apprehended, there is absent from the case any such ingredient or characteristic as led to the liability of the Home Office in the *Dorset Yacht* case. Nor is there present any additional characteristic such as might make up the deficiency. The circumstances of the case are therefore not capable of establishing a duty of care owed towards Miss Hill by the West Yorkshire police.

That is sufficient for the disposal of the appeal. But in my opinion there is another reason why an action for damages in negligence should not lie against the police in circumstances such as those of the present case, and that is public policy ... I consider that ... the police were immune from an action of this kind on grounds similar to those which in *Rondel* v *Worsley* [1969] 1 AC 191 were held to render a barrister immune from actions for negligence in his conduct of proceedings in court.'

Comment

Applied: *Rondel* v *Worsley* [1969] 1 AC 191.

Applied in *Clough* v *Bussan* [1990] 1 All ER 431, *Hughes* v *National Union of Mineworkers* [1991] 4 All ER 278, *Ancell* v *McDermott* [1993] 4 All ER 355 (in which *Clough* v *Bussan* was approved), *Osman* v *Ferguson* [1993] 4 All ER 344 and *Alexandrou* v *Oxford* [1993] 4 All ER 328.

Distinguished: *Home Office* v *Dorset Yacht Co Ltd* [1970] 2 WLR 1140.

Distinguished in *Waters* v *Commissioner of Police of the Metropolis* [2000] 4 All ER 934.

See also *Leach* v *Chief Constable of Gloucestershire Constabulary* [1999] 1 All ER 215 (police had not assumed responsibility to an independent voluntary worker whom they had asked to be an 'appropriate adult' at the interview of Frederick West, a multiple murder suspect, although it was arguable that they had a duty to offer her counselling during or within a short time after this harrowing experience) and *Costello* v *Chief Constable of the Northumbria Police* [1999] 1 All ER 550 (without undermining the general principle in *Hill*, defendant vicariously liable when police inspector stood by and did nothing as plaintiff woman constable attacked by woman prisoner in police cell).

Home Office v *Dorset Yacht Co Ltd*

[1970] 2 WLR 1140 House of Lords (Viscount Dilhorne, Lords Reid, Morris of Borth-y-Gest, Pearson and Diplock)

• *Negligence – escape of trainees*

Facts

The appellants were responsible for the operation and running of a Borstal institution. Several inmates were on a training exercise under the supervision of three Borstal officers when they escaped one night, boarded a yacht which collided with and damaged the respondents' yacht which was moored nearby. Did the appellants owe any duty of care to the respondents?

Held (Viscount Dilhorne dissenting)
They did.

Lord Reid:

'The case for the Home Office is that under no circumstances can borstal officers owe any duty to any member of the public to take care to prevent trainees under their control or supervision from injuring him or his property. If that is the law then enquiry into the facts of this case would be a waste of time and money because whatever the facts may be the respondents must lose. That case is based on three main arguments. First, it is said that there is virtually no authority for imposing a duty of this kind. Secondly, it is said that no person can be liable for a wrong done by another who is of full age and capacity and who is not the servant or acting on behalf of that person. And thirdly, it is said that public policy (or the policy of the relevant legislation) requires that these officers should be immune from any such liability.

The first would at one time have been a strong argument. ... In later years there has been a steady trend towards regarding the law of negligence as depending on principle so that, when a new point emerges, one should ask not whether it is covered by authority but whether recognised principles apply to it. *Donoghue v Stevenson* [1932] AC 562 may be regarded as a milestone, and the well-known passage in Lord Atkin's speech [at 580] should I think be regarded as a statement of principle. ... where negligence is involved the tendency has been to apply principles analogous to those stated by Lord Atkin (cf *Hedley Byrne & Co Ltd v Heller & Partners Ltd* [1964] AC 465). And when a person has done nothing to put himself in any relationship with another person in distress or with his property mere accidental propinquity does not require him to go to that person's assistance. There may be a moral duty to do so, but it is not practicable to make it a legal duty. ...

Even so it is said that the respondents must fail because there is a general principle that no person can be responsible for the acts of another who is not his servant or acting on his behalf. But here the ground of liability is not responsibility for the acts of the escaping trainees; it is liability for damage caused by the carelessness of these officers in the knowledge that their carelessness would probably result in the trainees causing damage of this kind. So the question is really one of remoteness of damage. And I must consider to what extent the law regards the acts of another person as breaking the chain of causation between the defendants' carelessness and the damage to the plaintiff.

There is an obvious difference between a case where all the links between the carelessness and the damage are inanimate so that, looking back after the event, it can be seen that the damage was in fact the inevitable result of the careless act or omission, and a case where one of the links is some human action. In the former case the damage was in fact caused by the careless conduct, however unforeseeable it may have been at the time that anything like this would happen. At one time the law was that unforeseeability was no defence (*Re Polemis and Furness, Withy & Co Ltd* [1921] 3 KB 560). But the law now is that there is no liability unless the damage was of a kind which was foreseeable (*Overseas Tankship (UK) Ltd v Morts Dock & Engineering Co Ltd, The Wagon Mound* [1961] AC 388).

On the other hand, if human action (other than an instinctive reaction) is one of the links in the chain, it cannot be said that, looking back, the damage was the inevitable result of the careless conduct. No one in practice accepts the possible philosophic view that everything that happens was predetermined. Yet it has never been the law that the intervention of human action always prevents the ultimate damage from being regarded as having been caused by the original carelessness. The convenient phrase novus actus interveniens denotes those cases where such action is regarded as breaking the chain and preventing the damage from being held to be caused by the careless conduct. But every day there are many cases where, although one of the connecting links is deliberate human action, the law has no difficulty in holding that the defendant's conduct caused the plaintiff loss. ...

But if the intervening action was likely to happen I do not think it can matter whether that action was innocent or tortious or criminal. Unfortunately tortious or criminal action by a third party is often the "very kind of thing" [per Greer LJ in *Haynes v Harwood* [1935] 1 KB 146] which is likely to happen as a result of the wrongful or careless act of the defendant. And in the present case, on the facts which we must assume at this stage, I think that the taking of a boat by the escaping trainees and their unskilful navigation leading to damage to another vessel were the very kind of thing that these borstal officers ought to have seen to be likely.

There was an attempt to draw a distinction between loss caused to the plaintiff by failure to control an adult of full capacity and loss caused by failure to control a child or mental defective. As regards causation, no doubt it is easier to infer novus actus interveniens in the case of an adult but that seems to me to be the only distinction. In the present case on the assumed facts there would in my view be no novus actus when the trainees damages the respondents' property and I would therefore hold that damage to have been caused by the borstal officers' negligence.

If the carelessness of the borstal officers was the cause of the respondents' loss what justification is there for holding that they had no duty to take care? The first arguments was that their right and power to control the trainees was purely statutory and that any duty to exercise that right and power was only a statutory duty owed to the Crown. I would agree but there is very good authority for the proposition that, if a person performs a statutory duty carelessly so that he causes damage to a member of the public which would not have happened if he had performed his duty properly, he may be liable. In *Geddis* v *Proprietors of Bann Reservoir* (1878) 3 App Cas 430 Lord Blackburn said:

> "For I take it, without citing cases, that it is now thoroughly well established that no action will lie for doing that which the legislature has authorised, if it be done without negligence, although it does occasion damage to anyone; but an action does lie for doing that which the legislature has authorised, if it be done negligently." ...

In my view there can be no liability if the discretion is exercised with due care. There could only be liability if the person entrusted with discretion either unreasonably failed to carry out his duty to consider the matter or reached a conclusion so unreasonable as again to show failure to do his duty. It was suggested that these trainees might have been deliberately released at the time when they escaped and then there could have been no liability. I do not agree. Presumably when trainees are released either temporarily or permanently some care is taken to see that there is no need for them to resort to crime to get food or transport. I could not imagine any more unreasonable exercise of discretion than to release trainees on an island in the middle of the night without making any provision for their future welfare. ...

It was suggested that a decision against the Home Office would have very far reaching effects; it was indeed suggested in the

Court of Appeal that it would make the Home Office liable for the loss occasioned by a burglary committed by a trainee on parole or a prisoner permitted to go out to attend a funeral. But there are two reasons why in the vast majority of cases that would not be so. In the first place it would have to be shown that the decision to allow any such release was so unreasonable that it could not be regarded as a real exercise of discretion by the responsible officer who authorised the release. And secondly it would have to be shown that the commission of the offence was the natural and probable, as distinct from merely a foreseeable, result of the release – that there was no novus actus interveniens. ...

Finally, I must deal with public policy. It is argued that it would be contrary to public policy to hold the Home Office or its officers liable to a member of the public for this carelessness – or indeed any failure of duty on their part. The basic question is who shall bear the loss caused by that carelessness – the innocent respondents or the Home Office who are vicariously liable for the conduct of their careless officers? ... I can see no good ground in public policy for giving this immunity to a government department.'

Comment
Inter alia: applied in *Anns* v *Merton London Borough Council* [1977] 2 All ER 492, *Paterson Zochonis & Co Ltd* v *Merfarken Packaging Ltd* [1986] 3 All ER 522 (no duty owed by printer to take reasonable care to prevent infringement of copyright) and *Swinney* v *Chief Constable of Northumbria Police* [1996] 3 All ER 449; distinguished in *Hill* v *Chief Constable of West Yorkshire* [1988] 2 All ER 238 and *Alexandrou* v *Oxford* [1993] 4 All ER 328.

Hughes v *National Union of Mineworkers* [1991] 4 All ER 278
High Court (May J)

- *Negligence – duty of care*

Facts

On duty at a colliery during a strike, the plaintiff police officer sustained injuries when the police were attacked by some 4,000 mineworkers. The plaintiff alleged that the officer in charge had been negligent in the deployment of the police, but the chief constable sought to have his action struck out on the ground that he had not owed the plaintiff a duty of care.

Held

The plaintiff's claim was bound to fail and it would be struck out.

May J:

'The plaintiff was one of a number of police officers deployed to control serious public disorder by a vast number of picketing miners. He was injured by some of those disorderly miners. Having considered *Hill* v *Chief Constable of West Yorkshire* [1988] 2 All ER 238 on the one hand and *Knightley* v *Johns* [1982] 1 All ER 851 and *Rigby* v *Chief Constable of Northamptonshire* [1985] 2 All ER 985 on the other, in my judgment, as a matter of public policy, if senior police officers charged with the task of deploying what may or may not be an adequate force of officers to control serious public disorder are to be potentially liable to individual officers under their command if those individuals are injured by attacks from rioters, that would be significantly detrimental to the control of public order.

It will no doubt often happen that in such circumstances critical decisions have to be made with little or no time for considered thought and where many individual officers may be in some danger of physical injury of one kind or another. It is not, I consider, in the public interest that those decisions should generally be the potential target of a negligence claim if rioters do injure an individual officer, since the fear of such a claim would be likely to affect the decisions to the prejudice of the very task which the decisions are intended to advance. Accordingly, in my judgment, public policy requires that senior police officers should not generally

be liable to their subordinates who may be injured by rioters or the like for on the spot operational decisions taken in the course of attempts to control serious public disorder. That, in my judgment, should be the general rule in cases of policing serious public disorders. There may be exceptions where the plaintiff's injuries arise, as in *Knightley* v *Johns*, from specifically identified antecedent negligence or specific breach of identified regulations, orders or instructions by a particular senior officer. There is no such specific allegation in the statement of claim in this case and none has been suggested in argument. It follows that the plaintiff's claim against the [chief constable] taken at its pleaded highest is bound to fail and that the claim should be struck out.'

Comment

See also *Mulcahy* v *Ministry of Defence* [1996] 2 All ER 758.

Jones v *Department of Employment*
[1988] 2 WLR 493 Court of Appeal (Slade, Glidewell LJJ and Caulfield J)

• *Adjudication officer's alleged negligence*

Facts

The plaintiff's claim for unemployment benefit was disallowed by the adjudication officer but allowed by the appeal tribunal. The plaintiff sought damages alleging negligence on the part of the adjudication officer.

Held

His action could not succeed as, inter alia, the adjudication officer had not owed the plaintiff a duty of care.

Glidewell LJ:

'The question ... is whether, taking all [the] circumstances into account, it is just and reasonable that the adjudication officer should be under a duty of care at common law to the claimant to benefit. Having regard to the non-judicial nature of the adjudication officer's responsibilities, and in particular to the fact that the statutory framework provides a right of appeal which, if a point of law arises, can eventually bring the matter to this court, it is my view that the adjudication officer is not under any common law duty of care. In other words ... his decision is not susceptible of challenge at common law unless it be shown that he is guilty of misfeasance.

Indeed, in my view, it is a general principle that, if a government department or officer, charged with the making of decisions whether certain payments should be made, is subject to a statutory right of appeal against his decisions, he owed no duty of care in private law. Misfeasance apart, he is only susceptible in public law to judicial review or to the right of appeal provided by the statute under which he makes his decision.'

Comment
Followed in *Mills* v *Winchester Diocesan Board of Finance* [1989] 2 All ER 317 (Charity Commissioners do not owe duty of care in respect of their advice).

Kane v *New Forest District Council*
[2001] 3 All ER 914 Court of Appeal (Simon Brown, May and Dyson LJJ)

• *Planning authority – liability for danger on highway*

Facts
An agreement between a developer (Wilcon) and the respondent planning authority required the former to construct a footpath before commencing the development. The footpath ended on the inside bend of a road and, although provision had been made for the eventual improvement of the sightlines, at the material time this work had not been carried out. Mr Kane, the appellant, emerged from the footpath and he was struck by a car. His proceedings for negligence against the respondents were dismissed as having no real

prospect of success and he appealed against that decision.

Held
The appeal would be allowed: the appellant's prospects of success were not merely realistic, he had a positively powerful case.

May LJ:

'It is, to my mind, evident from the facts ... that the respondent district council required, by the [agreement] the construction of what was to become a public footpath whose exit onto Main Road would, if nothing were done to improve matters, be dangerous. They thereby assumed a responsibility to those, including the claimant, who might wish to use the footpath to see that it was not open until the danger was removed. That is, in my view, an entirely orthodox application of common law principles of negligence. There is nothing in *Stovin* v *Wise (Norfolk CC, third party)* [1996] 3 All ER 801 which suggests a different conclusion. In *Stovin* v *Wise*, the county council had not created the hazard. In the present case the respondents had created the hazard. Nor on the facts of this case are the respondents immune from a claim in negligence because they were exercising a statutory function under planning legislation. It may be, depending on the facts, that the ordinary exercise of a statutory power to grant or refuse planning permission would not create a duty of care at common law carrying with it a liability to pay compensation to those affected by this – see *Lam* v *Brennan and Borough of Torbay* [1997] PIQR P488. But I reject [counsel for the respondents'] submission that a planning authority has blanket immunity from claims for negligence whatever the facts. That is simply not consonant with recent developments of the law both in this jurisdiction and in Strasbourg – see for example *Barrett* v *Enfield London BC* [1999] 3 All ER 193 and *Osman* v *UK* (1998) 5 BHRC 293.

There is no question but that the respondents were aware of the danger. Although preliminary steps were taken to enable the danger to be removed, the relevant works were not carried out when the footpath was opened. The respondents had the effective power to require Wilcon not to open the footpath until it was safe to do so. It is, in my view, at best an unpersuasive quibble to suggest … that the respondents were powerless to do this. I am sure that in the real world a suitable letter to Wilcon telling them to bar use of the footpath until its exit onto the road was safe would have achieved that result. Wilcon had no interest whatever other than to satisfy the respondents' request in relation to this footpath, which, after all, the respondents had required in the first place by means of the … agreement. This seems to me to be a solid basis in law for the claimant's case that his accident was caused by the respondents' breach of the duty of care which, in my judgment, they assumed.'

Comment

In *Osman* v *UK*, above, the European Court of Human Rights said that the rule in *Hill* v *Chief Constable of West Yorkshire* [1988] 2 All ER 238, in so far as it acted as an absolute defence to an action in negligence and thereby prevented a court considering the competing public interests in a case before it, constituted a disproportionate inference with a person's right to have a determination on the merits of an action against the police in a deserving case in breach of art 6(1) of the European Convention for the Protection of Human Rights and Fundamental Freedoms.

Lamb v *Camden London Borough Council* [1981] 2 WLR 1038 Court of Appeal (Lord Denning MR, Oliver and Watkins LJJ)

• *Damage – foreseeability*

Facts

In 1972, the plaintiff let her house while she spent some time abroad. In 1973 an employee of the defendants negligently fractured a water main outside her house which flooded the

foundations and caused the house to subside. The tenants consequently moved out and squatters moved in during 1974, though they were subsequently evicted. In 1975, there was a second 'invasion' by squatters who ripped out fixtures in the house and the central heating. The plaintiff brought an action against the defendant council for negligence, including a claim for the damage which had been caused to the house by the squatters.

Held

The plaintiff could not recover damages for the actions of the squatters, since they were not reasonably foreseeable.

Oliver LJ:

'Few things are less certainly predictable than human behaviour, and if one is asked whether in any given situation a human being may behave idiotically, irrationally or even criminally the answer must always be that that is a possibility, for every society has its proportion of idiots and criminals. It cannot be said that you cannot foresee the possibility that people will do stupid or criminal acts, because people are constantly doing stupid or criminal acts. But the question is not what is foreseeable merely as a possibility but what would the reasonable man actually foresee if he thought about it … If the instant case is approached as a case of negligence and one asks the question, did the defendants owe a duty not to break a water pipe so as to cause the plaintiff's house to be invaded by squatters a year later, the tenuousness of the linkage between act and result becomes apparent. I confess that I find it inconceivable that the reasonable man, wielding his pick in the road in 1973, could be said reasonably to foresee that his puncturing of a water main would fill the plaintiff's house with uninvited guests in 1974.'

Comment

Distinguished in *Ward* v *Cannock Chase District Council* [1985] 3 All ER 537 where it was found that there was a chain of causation from breach of duty to damage.

Lonrho plc v *Tebbit* [1992] 4 All ER 280 Court of Appeal (Dillon and Stocker LJJ and Sir Michael Kerr)

• *Duty of care – minister's delay in releasing plaintiffs from their undertaking to him*

Facts

The plaintiffs gave an undertaking to the defendants that they would not acquire more than 30 per cent of the share capital of House of Fraser pending a reference to the Monopolies and Mergers Commission (MMC). In November 1984 the plaintiffs sold the vast majority of their 29.9 per cent shareholding to a company controlled by the Al-Fayed brothers. On 14 February 1985 the MMC reported that the proposed merger between the plaintiffs and House of Fraser would not be contrary to the public interest. On 4 March the company controlled by the Al-Fayed brothers made a public offer for the remainder of the shares in House of Fraser which enabled them to acquire more than 50 per cent of the shares. When the defendants released the plaintiffs from their undertaking on 14 March it was too late for them to make a successful bid for House of Fraser. The plaintiffs sought to recover damages from the defendants on the ground that the Secretary of State had been negligent in the exercise of his statutory power because of his delay in releasing the plaintiffs from their undertaking. The defendants sought to strike out the plaintiffs' claim but Sir Nicolas Browne-Wilkinson V-C refused their application. The defendants appealed to the Court of Appeal.

Held

The appeal would be dismissed.

Dillon LJ:

'... there is, as I have said, no allegation of bad faith against the defendants, but it is alleged that they acted ultra vires, that is to say beyond their powers, in deferring the release of the undertaking until 14 March 1985 when the MMC report had become available on or about 14 February. If that is so, the likely conclusion is that the defendants acted as they did in good faith, believing that they were entitled to time for consideration and to look at the matter in the round and consider at the same time whether the undertaking given by Lonrho should be released, and whether the bid by Holdings for House of Fraser should be referred to the MMC. Reference was made to an apparently unlimited dictum of Nourse LJ in *Bourgoin SA* v *Ministry of Agriculture, Fisheries and Food* [1985] 3 All ER 585 at 633:

> "In this country the law has never allowed that a private individual should recover damages against the Crown for an injury caused to him by an ultra vires order made in good faith."

But the fields of law with which we are concerned in this case are difficult and developing. [Counsel for the defendants] gave us an admirable summary of the principal authorities. In the law of negligence he referred us to the two-stage test suggested by Lord Wilberforce in *Anns* v *Merton London Borough* [1977] 2 All ER 492 at 500, and showed how that had been rejected in later authorities and particularly in *Murphy* v *Brentwood DC* [1990] 2 All ER 908. The preferred approach is now what is called "the incremental approach" as stated by Brennan J in *Sutherland Shire Council* v *Heyman* (1985) 60 ALR 1 at 43-44 ...

[Counsel] referred us also to authorities which show that a civil action for damages cannot be brought as a result of a "policy decision" of a public authority and to judgments where a distinction is suggested between "policy decisions" which cannot be justiciable and "operational decisions" which may be justiciable. But in *Rowling* v *Takaro Properties Ltd* [1988] 1 All ER 163 ... some of the difficulties of that approach are explored in the opinion of Lord Keith and the conclusion of their Lordships seems to be that the question whether a duty of care should be imposed is a question of an intensely pragmatic character, well-suited for gradual development but requiring most careful analysis (see [1988] 1 All ER 163 at 172). That is in line with the incremental approach to the development of the tort of negligence.

The imposition of the undertaking on Lonrho in 1981 was of course a matter of public law in the public interest when the MMC had considered that the acquisition by Lonrho of the share capital of House of Fraser might be expected to operate against the public interest. The public interest in having the undertaking released when the acquisition by Lonrho of the share capital of House of Fraser was no longer expected to operate against the public interest is considerably more remote and sophisticated. But the private interest of Lonrho in having the undertaking released as soon as it was no longer needed in the public interest is obvious. It does not therefore appal me that it should be suggested that, if the Secretary of State imposes the restrictions of the undertaking on Lonrho in the public interest, the Secretary of State should thereby assume a private law duty to Lonrho to release the undertaking when it is no longer needed and that the restriction on Lonrho's freedom to conduct its business no longer has a rationale. There is an arguable case for Lonrho, therefore, against which may have to be set the sort of considerations militating against the imposition of liability which Lord Keith rehearses in *Rowling* v *Takaro Properties Ltd*. These raise questions which the court in *Rowling* v *Takaro* did not have to resolve. Moreover, the nature of any private law duty would have to be carefully defined. Is it, for instance, an absolute duty to release the undertaking when no longer required in the public interest, or is it only a duty of care, within the field of the tort of negligence – with the result in the latter case that there would be no liability on the defendants if delay in releasing the undertaking was due to an error of law which was not negligent?

In these circumstances, I agree with Browne-Wilkinson V-C that Lonrho's claim should not be struck out as disclosing no reasonable cause of action. Lonrho faces considerable difficulties, and others may arise on the facts as the evidence emerges at a trial, but I cannot say that Lonrho has no arguable case, or ... that the claim is obviously foredoomed to fail.

I turn to the final question whether, if Lonrho's claim is not struck out on the ground that it discloses no reasonable cause of action, it ought none the less to be struck out as an abuse of the process of the court on the ground that Lonrho ought to be required to get a ruling by way of judicial review before it starts any proceedings by way of writ and civil action against the defendants.

[Counsel for the defendants] founds this submission on *Cocks* v *Thanet DC* [1982] 3 All ER 1135. He says in effect that it is a matter of public law for the plaintiff to establish the necessary public law basis on which it can ground a private right, as in *Cocks*'s case. Therefore the plaintiff must obtain a declaration in proceedings for judicial review on which to found a claim to a private right or for breach of a private law duty.

I see the matter differently. The plaintiff is asserting a private law right, albeit arising out of a background of public law. That can be asserted in an action by writ as in *Roy* v *Kensington and Chelsea and Westminster Family Practitioner Committee* [1992] 1 All ER 705. If the plaintiff fails to establish the private law right claimed, the action will fail. But it is not necessary to apply for judicial review before bringing the action.'

McAlister (or Donoghue) v *Stevenson* see *Donoghue (or McAlister)* v *Stevenson*

McFarlane v *Tayside Health Board* [1999] 4 All ER 961 House of Lords (Lords Slynn of Hadley, Steyn, Hope of Craighead, Clyde and Millett)

• *Vasectomy – unwanted pregnancy – entitlement to damages*

Facts

Following the husband's vasectomy and advice that the operation had achieved its purpose, the wife conceived and gave birth to a healthy daughter. In an action for damages for negligence, the couple sought damages for the costs of rearing the child and for the pain and distress suffered by the wife in carrying and giving birth to her.

Held

The first claim would fail but the second (including financial loss associated with the pregnancy) would be successful.

Lord Slynn of Hadley:

'The facts are that Mr McFarlane underwent a vasectomy operation on 16 October 1989; by letter of 23 March 1990 he was told that his sperm counts were negative. In September 1991 (following the resumption of intercourse without contraceptive measures), Mrs McFarlane became pregnant and their fifth child, Catherine, was born on 6 May 1992. They claim that Mrs McFarlane suffered pain and distress from the pregnancy and birth and that they both have incurred and will incur costs in rearing Catherine, all due to the negligence of the defenders. They put Mrs McFarlane's claim at £10,000 and their claim as parents at £100,000 for the cost of maintaining the child. It is right to say at once that despite their claim the respondents have loved and cared for Catherine as an integral member of the family. ...

My Lords, I do not find real difficulty in deciding the claim for damages in respect of the pregnancy and birth itself. The parents did not want another child for justifiable economic and family reasons; they already had four children. They were entitled lawfully to take steps to make sure that that did not happen, one possible such step being a vasectomy of the husband. It was plainly foreseeable that if the operation did not succeed, or recanalisation of the vas took place, but the husband was told that contraceptive measures were not necessary, the wife might become pregnant. It does not seem to me to be necessary to consider the events of an unwanted conception and birth in terms of "harm" or "injury" in its ordinary sense of the words. They were unwanted and known by the health board to be unwanted events. The object of the vasectomy was to prevent them happening. It seems to me that in consequence the wife, if there was negligence, is entitled by way of general damages to be compensated for the pain and discomfort and inconvenience of the unwanted pregnancy and birth, and she is also entitled to special damages associated with both – extra medical expenses, clothes for herself and equipment on the birth of the baby. She does not claim, but in my view in principle she would have been entitled to prove, compensation for loss of earnings due to the pregnancy and birth. It is not contended that the birth was due to her decision not to have an abortion which broke the chain of causation or made the damage too remote or was a novus actus interveniens. If it were suggested, I would reject the contention and I see no reason in principle why the wife should not succeed on this part of the claim.

Whether the parents should be entitled as a matter of principle to recover for the costs of maintaining the child is a much more difficult question. Logically, the position may seem to be the same. If she had not conceived because of the board's negligence there would not have been a baby and then a child and then a young person to house, to feed and to educate. I would reject (had it been suggested, which it was not) that a failure to arrange adoption (like an abortion) was a new act which broke the chain of causation or which made the damage necessarily too remote. There was no legal or moral duty to arrange an abortion or an adoption of an unplanned child.

The question remains whether as a matter of legal principle the damages should include, for a child by then loved, loving and fully integrated into the family the costs of shoes at 14 and a dress at 17 and everything then can reasonably be described as necessary for the upbringing of the child until the end of school, university, independence, maturity? ...

As to this I do not accept the argument that no damages should be awarded as otherwise children will learn that their birth was not wanted and this will have undesirable psychological consequences. An unplanned conception is hardly a rare event and it does not follow that if the conception is unwanted the baby when it is born, or the baby as it integrates into the family, will not be wanted. Nor do I attach weight to the argument that if damages claims of this kind are allowed, doctors to protect themselves will encourage late abortions. Such an event is possible but the ethical standards of the medical profession (coupled with insurance) should be a sufficient protection in such cases, which ought to be rare if proper care is taken.

The real question raised here is more fundamental. It is to be remembered on this part of the case that your Lordships are concerned only with liability for economic loss. It is not enough to say that the loss is foreseeable as I have accepted it is foreseeable. Indeed if foreseeability is the only test there is no reason why a claim should necessarily stop at the date when a statutory duty to maintain a child comes to an end. There is a wider issue to consider. I agree ... that the question is not simply one of the quantification of damages, it is one of liability, of the extent of the duty of care which is owed to the husband and wife.

It is to be remembered that in relation to liability the House has recognised that, in respect of economic loss, in order to create liability there may have to be a closer link between the act and the damage that foreseeability provides in order to create liability. Thus in *Caparo Industries plc* v *Dickman* [1990] 1 All ER 568, Lord Bridge said that there should be a relationship of "neighbourhood" or "proximity" between the person said to owe the duty and the person to whom it is said to be owed. That relationship depends on whether it is "fair, just and reasonable" for the law to impose the duty. ... the alternative test is to ask whether the doctor or the board has assumed responsibility for the economic interest of the claimant "with concomitant reliance by the claimant".

The doctor undertakes a duty of care in regard to the prevention of pregnancy: it does not follow that the duty includes also avoiding the costs of rearing the child if born and accepted into the family. Whereas I have no doubt that there should be compensation for the physical effects of the pregnancy and birth, including of course solatium for consequential suffering by the mother immediately following the birth, I consider that is is not fair, just or reasonable to impose on the doctor or his employer liability for the consequential responsibilities, imposed on or accepted by the parents to bring up a child. The doctor does not assume responsibility for those economic losses. If a client wants to be able to recover such costs he or she must do so by an appropriate contract.

This conclusion is not the result, as it is in some of the American cases of the application of "public policy" to a rule which would otherwise produce a different conclusion; it comes from the inherent limitation of the liability relied on. A line is to be drawn before such losses are recoverable.'

Comment

See also *Parkinson* v *St James and Seacroft University Hospital NHS Trust* [2001] 3 All ER 97 (where child's significant disabilities flowed foreseeably from unwanted conception resulting from negligently-performed sterilisation, damages recoverable for the costs of providing for child's special needs and care attributable to those disabilities, but not for ordinary costs of upbringing) and *Rees* v *Darlington Memorial Hospital NHS Trust* (2002) The Times 20 February (disabled mother entitled to recover damages uniquely referable to her disability when negligently performed sterilisation led to her giving birth to healthy child), both decisions of the Court of Appeal.

McLoughlin v *O'Brian* [1982] 2 WLR 982 House of Lords (Lords Wilberforce, Edmund-Davies, Russell of Killowen, Scarman and Bridge of Harwich)

• *Negligence – foreseeable harm*

Facts

The plaintiff's husband and three young children were involved in a serious road accident caused by the negligence of the defendant. The plaintiff's husband and two of her children were very badly injured. The other child was killed. At the time that the accident occurred, the plaintiff was at home two miles away. She was informed of the accident by a neighbour and was taken to the hospital where she saw the extent of the injuries of her family and was told of her daughter's death. In consequence of seeing and hearing the results of the accident, the plaintiff suffered severe and persistent nervous shock. The plaintiff claimed damages against the defendant for nervous shock, distress and injury to health caused by the negligence of the defendant.

Held

The test of liability for damages for nervous shock was simply reasonable foreseeability of the plaintiff being injured by the defendant's negligent act or omission. Applying this test, the plaintiff was entitled to recover damages because even though the plaintiff was not at or near the scene of the accident, either at the time or shortly afterwards, the nervous shock suffered by the plaintiff was a reasonably foreseeable consequence of the defendant's negligence.

Lord Wilberforce:

' ... Although we continue to use the hallowed expression "nervous shock", English law, and common understanding, have moved some distance since recognition was given to this symptom as a basis for liability. Whatever is unknown about the mind-body relationship (and the area of ignorance

seems to expand with that of knowledge), it is now accepted by medical science that recognisable and severe physical damage to the human body and system may be caused by the impact, through the senses, of external events on the mind. There may thus be produced what is as identifiable an illness as any that may be caused by direct physical impact. It is safe to say that this, in general terms, is understood by the ordinary man or woman who is hypothesised by the courts in situations where claims for negligence are made. Although in the only case which has reached this House (*Hay (or Bourhill)* v *Young* [1943] AC 92), a claim for damages in respect of "nervous shock" was rejected on its facts, the House gave clear recognition to the legitimacy, in principle, of claims of that character. As the result of that and other cases, assuming that they are accepted as correct, the following position has been reached:

1. While damages cannot, at common law, be awarded for grief and sorrow, a claim for damages for "nervous shock" caused by negligence can be made without the necessity of showing direct impact or fear of immediate personal injuries for oneself ...

2. A plaintiff may recover damages for "nervous shock" brought on by injury caused not to him or herself but to a near relative, or by the fear of such injury ...

3. Subject to the next paragraph, there is no English case in which a plaintiff has been able to recover nervous shock damages where the injury to the near relative occurred out of sight and earshot of the plaintiff. In *Hambrook* v *Stokes Bros* an express distinction was made between shock caused by what the mother saw with her own eyes and what she might have been told by bystanders, liability being excluded in the latter case.

4. An exception from, or I would prefer to call it an extension of, the latter case has been made where the plaintiff does not see or hear the incident but comes on its immediate aftermath ...

5. A remedy on account of nervous shock has been given to a man who came on a

serious accident involving people immediately thereafter and acted as a rescuer of those involved (*Chadwick* v *British Transport Commission* [1967] 1 WLR 912). 'Shock' was caused neither by fear for himself nor by fear or horror on account of a near relative. The principle of 'rescuer' cases was not challenged by the respondents and ought, in my opinion, to be accepted. But we have to consider whether, and how far, it can be applied to such cases as the present.

If one continues to follow the process of logical progression it is hard to see why the present plaintiff also should not succeed. She was not present at the accident, but she came very soon after on its aftermath. If, from a distance of some 100 yards she had found her family by the roadside, she would have come within principle 4 above. Can it make any difference that she comes on them in an ambulance, or, as here, in a nearby hospital, when as the evidence shows, they were in the same condition, covered with oil and mud, and distraught with pain? If Mr Chadwick can recover when, acting in accordance with normal and irresistable human instinct, and indeed moral compulsion, he goes to the scene of an accident, may not a mother recover if, acting under the same motives, she goes to where her family can be found? ... To argue from one factual situation to another and to decide by analogy is a natural tendency of the human and legal mind. But the lawyer still has to inquire whether, in so doing, he has crossed some critical line behind which he ought to stop ... Foreseeability which involves a hypothetical person, looking with hindsight at an event which has occurred, is a formula adopted by English law, not merely for defining, but also for limiting the persons to whom duty may be owed, and the consequences for which an actor may be held responsible. It is not merely an issue of fact to be left to be found as such. When it is said to result in a duty of care being owed to a person or a class, the statement that there is a "duty of care" denotes a conclusion into the forming of which considerations of policy have entered. That foreseeability

does not of itself and automatically lead to a duty of care is, I think, clear ... cases of "nervous shock" and the possibility of claiming damages for it are not necessarily confined to those arising out of accidents in public roads. To state, therefore, a rule that recoverable damages must be confined to persons on or near the highway is to state not a principle in itself but only an example of a more general rule that recoverable damages must be confined to those within sight and sound of an event caused by negligence or, at least, to those in close, or very close, proximity to such a situation.

The policy arguments against a wider extension can be stated under four heads. First, it may be said that such extension may lead to a proliferation of claims, and possibily fraudulent claims, to the establishment of an industry of lawyers and psychiatrists who will formulate a claim for nervous shock damages, including what in America is called the customary miscarriage, for all, or many road accidents and industrial accidents. Second, it may be claimed that an extension of liability would be unfair to defendants, as imposing damages out of proportion to the negligent conduct complained of. In so far as such defendants are insured, a large additional burden will be placed on insurers, and ultimately on the class of persons insured: road users or employers. Third, to extend liability beyond the most direct and plain cases would greatly increase evidentiary difficulties and tend to lengthen litigation. Fourth, it may be said (and the Court of Appeal agreed with this) that an extension of the scope of liability ought only to be made by the legislature, after careful research. This is the course which has been taken in New South Wales and the Australian Capital Territory ... In *Hambrook* v *Stokes Bros* [1924] All ER 110, indeed it was said that liability would not arise in such a case, and this is surely right. It was so decided in *Abramzik* v *Brenner* (1967) 65 DLR (2d) 651. The shock must come through sight or hearing of the event or of its immediate aftermath. Whether some equivalent of sight or hearing, eg through simultaneous television, would suffice may have to be considered.

My Lords, I believe that these indications, imperfectly sketched, and certainly to be applied with common sense to individual situations in their entirety, represent either the existing law, or the existing law with only such circumstantial extension as the common law process may legitimately make. They do not introduce a new principle. Nor do I see any reason why the law should retreat behind the lines already drawn. I find on this appeal that the appellant's case falls within the boundaries of the law so drawn. I would allow her appeal.'

Comment

Distinguished in *Alcock* v *Chief Constable of the South Yorkshire Police* [1991] 3 WLR 1057.

In *White* v *Chief Constable of the South Yorkshire Police* [1999] 1 All ER 1 Lord Steyn said that Waller J's decision in *Chadwick* v *British Transport Commission* [1967] 1 WLR 912 had been correct since there had clearly been a risk that a railway carriage might collapse on the plaintiff rescuer.

Mulcahy v *Ministry of Defence*
[1996] 2 All ER 758 Court of Appeal (Neill, McCowan LJJ and Sir Iain Glidewell)

• *Negligence – soldier owes duty of care to fellow soldier?*

Facts

While sharing in the firing of a howitzer during the Gulf War, the plaintiff suffered injury as a result, allegedly, of the gun commander's negligence.

Held

His action against the defendants, the gun commander's employers, would be struck out as disclosing no cause of action.

Sir Iain Glidewell:

'[Counsel] for the defendants defined the

issue before the court in these words: "Does one soldier owe to another a duty of care when engaging the enemy in the course of hostilities?" I agree that ... this is a correct formulation of the issue.

It may seem surprising that this question has not previously been decided by a court in this country, but the reason is not far to seek. An action in negligence by one member of the armed forces of the Crown against another would have been barred by the doctrine of common employment until that doctrine was abolished by the Law Reform (Personal Injuries) Act 1948. When that happened, the Crown Proceedings Act 1947 was already in force. ... The terms of s10 clearly required the question posed by [counsel] to be answered "No". Thus it was not until s10 of the 1947 Act was itself suspended by s1 of the Crown Proceedings (Armed Forces) Act 1987 that the answer to the question depended, for the first time, on the general common law principles of the law of negligence.

[Counsel for the defendants] accepts that, if the plaintiff proves the facts alleged in his statement of claim (as, for the purposes of this appeal, we must assume he can do) the first two criteria for establishing that [the gun commander] owed the plaintiff a duty of care, namely proximity between the parties and foreseeability of damages, are satisfied. Thus, such a duty of care would be owed unless considerations of public policy require that, in the course of hostilities, it should not.

... it is in my judgment clear that public policy does require that, when two or more members of the armed forces of the Crown are engaged in the course of hostilities, one is under no duty of care in tort to another. Indeed, it could be highly detrimental to the conduct of military operations if each soldier had to be conscious that, even in the heart of battle, he owed such a duty to his comrade. ... If during the course of hostilities no duty of care is owed by a member of the armed forces to civilians or their property, it must be even more apparent that no such duty is owed to another member of the armed forces. This conclusion is wholly consistent with, and supported by, the decision of the House of Lords in *Burmah Oil Co (Burmah Trading)* v *Lord Advocate* [1964] 2 All ER 348 and depends upon similar reasoning to that adopted by May J in relation to police officers in *Hughes* v *National Union of Mineworkers* [1991] 4 All ER 278. In my judgment, therefore, at common law, one soldier does not owe to another a duty of care when engaging the enemy in the course of hostilities.

[Counsel] for the plaintiff sought to amend his pleading to allege that the defendants were not merely vicariously liable for any breach of duty (if duty there was) by [the gun commander], but also directly liable for failure to maintain a safe system of work. ... such an amendment makes no difference. The reasons which result in the first question being answered "No" result in the same answer to the second issue. Having reached this decision as a matter of principle, I agree ... that the plaintiff's claim is pleaded with sufficient clarity to make it clear that no further process of fact finding could result in success in his action.'

Mullin v *Richards* [1998] 1 All ER 920 Court of Appeal (Butler-Sloss, Hutchinson LJJ and Sir John Vinelott)

* *Negligence – child – test of foreseeability*

Facts

Two 15-year-old schoolgirls, Teresa and Heidi, while sitting at their desk had a 'sword fight' with their plastic rulers. One of the rulers snapped and a fragment of plastic entered Teresa's right eye, causing loss of its useful sight. Teresa sued Heidi and the local education authority. The claim against the latter was dismissed (on the facts, the class teacher had not been guilty of negligence) but the judge concluded that both girls had been negligent, that Teresa's injury was the foreseeable result and that her claim against Heidi would succeed subject to a 50 per cent reduction for contributory negligence. Heidi appealed, contending, inter alia, that the judge had erred when considering foreseeability by failing to take account of the fact that she was not an adult.

Held

The appeal would be allowed.

Hutchinson LJ:

'The judge ... had to determine whether negligence had been proved against either defendant; if so, whether the plaintiff's injury was foreseeable; and whether there was contributory negligence on the part of the plaintiff. ...

So far as negligence is concerned, the relevant principles are well settled ... I would summarise the principles that govern liability in negligence in a case such as the present as follows. In order to succeed the plaintiff must show that the defendant did an act which it was reasonably foreseeable would cause injury to the plaintiff, that the relationship between the plaintiff and the defendant was such as to give rise to a duty of care, and that the act was one which caused injury to the plaintiff. In the present case, as it seems to me, no difficulty arose as to the second and third requirements because Teresa and Heidi were plainly in a sufficiently proximate relationship to give rise to a duty of care and the causation of the injury is not in issue. The argument centres on foreseeability. The test of foreseeability is an objective one; but the fact that the first defendant was at the time a 15-year-old schoolgirl is not irrelevant. The question for the judge is not whether the actions of the defendant were such as an ordinarily prudent and reasonable adult in the defendant's situation would have realised gave rise to a risk of injury, it is whether an ordinarily prudent and reasonable 15-year-old schoolgirl in the defendant's situation would have realised as much. In that connection both counsel referred us to, and relied upon, the Australian decision of *McHale* v *Watson* (1966) 115 CLR 199, especially at 213–214 in the judgment of Kitto J. ...

Then, even if the requirements that I have so far summarised are satisfied with the consequence that negligence has been proved, the defendant will not be liable if the injury actually sustained is not foreseeable, that is to say is of a different kind from that which the defendant ought to have foreseen as the likely outcome of his want of care (see in that regard *Hughes* v *Lord Advocate* [1963] 1 All ER 705).

Applying those principles to the facts of the present case the central question to which this appeal gives rise is whether on the facts found by the judge and in the light of the evidence before him he was entitled to conclude that an ordinary reasonable 15-year-old schoolgirl in the first defendant's position would have appreciated that by participating to the extent that she did in a play fight, involving the use of plastic rulers as though they were swords, gave rise to a risk of injury to the plaintiff of the same general kind as she sustained. In that connection I emphasise that a mere possibility is not enough as passages in the well-known case of *Bolton* v *Stone* [1951] 1 All ER 1078 ... make clear. ...

However the question of actual foreseeability (that is to say the application of that correct approach in law to the facts) raises, in my judgment, great difficulties. First, there certainly was no evidence as to the propensity or otherwise of such rulers to break or any history of their having done so. There was evidence which the judge does not say he rejects and which he may, since it was an admission against interest, be taken to have accepted, that ruler fencing was commonplace. ...

This was in truth nothing more than a schoolgirls' game such as on the evidence was commonplace in this school and there was, I would hold, no justification for attributing to the participants the foresight of any significant risk of the likelihood of injury. They had seen it done elsewhere with some frequency. They had not heard it prohibited or received any warning about it.

They had not been told of any injuries occasioned by it. They were not in any sense behaving culpably. So far as foresight goes, had they paused to think they might, I suppose, have said: "It is conceivable that some unlucky injury might happen", but if asked if there was any likelihood of it or any real possibility of it, they would, I am sure, have said that they did not foresee any such possibility. Taking the view therefore that the learned judge – who, as I have said, readily and almost without question accepted that on his findings of fact there was negligence on the part of both these young ladies – was wrong in his view and there was no evidence on which he could come to it, I would allow the appeal and direct that judgment be entered for [Heidi].'

Butler-Sloss LJ:

'I would like to conclude with another passage of Kitto J (at 216) particularly relevant to today –

"... in the absence of relevant statutory provision, children, like everyone else, must accept as they go in society the risks from which ordinary care on the part of others will not suffice to save them. One such risk is that boys of twelve may behave as boys of twelve ..."

– and I would say that girls of 15 playing together may play as somewhat irresponsible girls of 15.'

Comment

Hutchinson LJ observed that neither defendant had argued volenti non fit injuria, though the particulars of contributory negligence referred to Teresa as being a willing participant in the game. The trial judge had adverted to the absence of any such contention in terms which suggested that he thought it would not have been a possible defence, something on which Hutchinson LJ expressed no opinion. He simply noted that the question had not arisen because it was never raised.

Murphy v *Brentwood District Council* [1990] 3 WLR 414 House of Lords (Lords Mackay of Clashfern LC, Keith of Kinkel, Bridge of Harwich, Brandon of Oakbrook, Ackner, Oliver of Aylmerton and Jauncey of Tullichettle)

• *Negligence – local authority's statutory powers – economic loss*

Facts

The plaintiff purchased a house in 1970 from builders who had constructed it in 1969. The house was built upon a single concrete raft foundation because the site had been filled and levelled. The foundation raft was designed by a firm of civil engineers but its design was inadequate and differential settlement of the ground beneath the raft caused it to distort and caused cracks to appear in the building. When the plaintiff discovered the extent of the damage to the house he decided that it was impractical to have the necessary remedial work performed himself and so he sold it, at a price considerably below the market price of a house which was sound, to a builder who knew the cause of the damage. The plaintiff then brought an action against the local authority alleging that they had been negligent in passing plans which were inadequate. The defendants had in fact referred the plans to a firm of consulting engineers, independent contractors, and, in reliance upon their report, had passed the plans. The trial judge found as a fact that the plaintiff had been exposed to an imminent risk to health and safety. He concluded that the defendants were liable for the consulting engineers' negligence and, by way of damages, awarded the plaintiff the loss on the sale of the house plus expenses. The Court of Appeal ([1990] 2 WLR 944), being bound by the decision of the House of Lords in *Anns* v *Merton London Borough Council* [1978] AC 728, dismissed the defendants' appeal. The defendants appealed against this decision to the House of Lords.

Held

The appeal would be allowed.

Lord Mackay of Clashfern LC:

'We are asked to depart from the judgment of this House in *Anns* v *Merton London Borough* ...

As I read the speech of Lord Wilberforce [in *Anns*] the cause of action which he holds could arise in the circumstances of that case can only do so when damage occurs to the house in question as a result of the weakness of the foundations and therefore no cause of action arises before that damage has occurred even if as a result of information obtained about the foundations it may become apparent to an owner that such damage is likely.

The person to whom the duty is owed is an owner or occupier of the house who is such when the damage occurs. And therefore an owner or occupier who becomes aware of the possibility of damage arising from a defective foundation would not be within the class of persons on whom the right of action is conferred.

As had been demonstrated in the speeches of my noble and learned friends, the result of applying these qualifications to different factual circumstances is to require distinctions to be made which have no justification on any reasonable principle and can only be described as capricious. It cannot be right for this House to leave the law in that state.

Two options call for consideration. The first is to remove altogether the qualifications on the cause of action which *Anns* v *Merton London Borough* held to exist. This would be in itself a departure from *Anns* since these qualifications are inherent in the decision. The other option is to go back to the law as it was before *Anns* was decided and this would involve also overruling *Dutton* v *Bognor Regis United Building Co Ltd* [1972] 2 WLR 299.

Faced with the choice I am of the opinion that it is relevant to take into account that Parliament has made provisions in the Defective Premises Act 1972 imposing on builders and others undertaking work in the provision of dwellings obligations relating to the quality of their work and the fitness for habitation of the dwelling. For this House in its judicial capacity to create a large new area of responsibility on local authorities in respect of defective buildings would in my opinion not be a proper exercise of judicial power. I am confirmed in this view by the consideration that it is not suggested, and does not appear to have been suggested in *Anns*, that the Public Health Act 1936, in particular Pt II, manifests any intention to create statutory rights in favour of owners or occupiers of premises against the local authority charged with responsibility under that Act. The basis of the decision in *Anns* is that the common law will impose a duty in the interests of the safety and health of owners and occupiers of buildings since that was the purpose for which the 1936 Act was enacted. While of course I accept that duties at common law may arise in respect of the exercise of statutory powers or the discharge of statutory duties I find difficulty in reconciling a common law duty to take reasonable care that plans should conform with byelaws or regulations with the statute which has imposed on the local authority the duty not to pass plans unless they comply with the byelaws or regulations and to pass them if they do.

In these circumstances I have reached the clear conclusion that the proper exercise of the judicial function requires this House now to depart from *Anns* in so far as to affirmed a private law duty of care to avoid damage to property which causes present or imminent danger to the health and safety of owners, or occupiers, resting on local authorities in relation to their function of supervising compliance with building byelaws or regulations, that *Dutton* v *Bognor Regis United Building Co Ltd* should be overruled and that all decisions subsequent to *Anns* which purported to follow it should be overruled. I accordingly, reach the same conclusion as do my noble and learned friends.

I should make it clear that I express no opinion on the question whether, if personal injury were suffered by an occupier of defective premises as a result of a latent defect in those premises, liability in respect of that personal injury would attach to a local authority which had been charged with the public law duty of supervising compliance with the relevant building byelaws or regulations in respect of a failure properly to carry out such duty.'

Lord Bridge of Harwich:

'... these considerations lead inevitably to the conclusion that a building owner can only recover the cost of repairing a defective building on the ground of the authority's negligence in performing its statutory function of approving plans or inspecting buildings in the course of construction if the scope of the authority's duty of care is wide enough to embrace purely economic loss. The House has already held in *D & F Estates Ltd* v *Church Commissioners for England* [1988] 3 WLR 368 that a builder, in the absence of any contractual duty or of a special relationship of proximity introducing the *Hedley Byrne & Co Ltd* v *Heller & Partners Ltd* [1963] 3 WLR 101 principle of reliance, owes no duty of care in tort in respect of the quality of his work. As I pointed out in *D & F Estates*, to hold that the builder owed such a duty of care to any person acquiring an interest in the product of the builder's work would be to impose on him the obligations of an indefinitely transmissible warranty of quality.

By s1 of the Defective Premises Act 1972 Parliament has in fact imposed on builders and others undertaking work in the provision of dwellings the obligations of a transmissible warranty of the quality of their work and of the fitness for habitation of the completed dwelling. But, besides being limited to dwellings, liability under that Act is subject to a limitation period of six years from the completion of the work and to the exclusion provided for by s2. It would be remarkable to find that similar obligations in the nature of a transmissible warranty of quality, applicable to buildings of every kind and subject to no such limitations or exclusions as are imposed by the 1972 Act, could be derived from the builder's common law duty of care or from the duty imposed by building byelaws or regulations. In *Anns* Lord Wilberforce expressed the opinion that a builder could be held liable for a breach of statutory duty in respect of buildings which do not comply with the byelaws. But he cannot, I think, have meant that the statutory obligation to build in conformity with the byelaws by itself gives rise to obligations in the nature of transmissible warranties of quality. If he did meant that, I must respectfully disagree. I find it impossible to suppose that anything less than clear express language such as is used in s1 of the 1972 Act would suffice to impose such a statutory obligation.

As I have already said, since the function of a local authority in approving plans or inspecting buildings in the course of construction is directed to ensuring that the builder complies with building byelaws or regulations, I cannot see how, in principle, the scope of the liability of the authority for a negligent failure to ensure compliance can exceed that of the liability of the builder for his negligent failure to comply.

There may, of course, be situations where, even in the absence of contract, there is a special relationship of proximity between builder and building owner which is sufficiently akin to contract to introduce the element of reliance so that the scope of the duty of care owed by the builder to the owner is wide enough to embrace purely economic loss. The decision in *Junior Books Ltd* v *Veitchi Co Ltd* [1983] 1 AC 520 can, I believe, only be understood on this basis.

In *Sutherland Shire Council* v *Heyman* (1985) 60 ALR 1 the critical role of the reliance principle as an element in the cause of action which the plaintiff sought to establish is the subject of close examination, particularly in the judgment of Mason J. The central theme of his judgment, and a subordinate theme in the judgments of Brennan and Dean JJ, who together with Mason J formed the majority rejecting the *Anns* doctrine, is that a duty of care of a scope sufficient to make the authority liable for damage of the kind suffered can only be based on the principle of reliance and that

there is nothing in the ordinary relationship of a local authority, as statutory supervisor of building operations, and the purchaser of a defective building capable of giving rise to such a duty. I agree with these judgments. It cannot, I think, be suggested, nor do I understand *Anns* or the cases which have followed *Anns* in Canada and New Zealand to be in fact suggesting, that the approval of plans or the inspection of a building in the course of construction by the local authority in performance of their statutory function and a subsequent purchase of the building by the plaintiff are circumstances in themselves sufficient to introduce the principle of reliance which is the foundation of a duty of care of the kind identified in *Hedley Byrne*.'

Comment

Applied in *Department of the Environment* v *Thomas Bates & Son Ltd* [1990] 3 WLR 457 (builder not liable in tort since loss purely economic and defective building not unsafe). Distinguished in *Targett* v *Torfaen Borough Council* [1992] 3 All ER 27 (weekly tenant's position entirely different) and *Blue Circle Industries plc* v *Ministry of Defence* [1998] 3 All ER 385. Not followed in *Invercargill City Council* v *Hamlin* [1996] 1 All ER 756 (New Zealand law applied). See also *Stovin* v *Wise* [1996] 3 All ER 801.

Nitrigin Eireann Teoranta v *Inco Alloys Ltd* [1992] 1 WLR 498 High Court (May J)

- *Negligence – economic loss and physical damage*

Facts

The first defendants had manufactured and supplied steel alloy tubing for the plaintiffs' chemical plant. An allegedly defective pipe was supplied in summer 1981. In 1983 the plaintiffs discovered that it was damaged by cracking. They were unable to find the cause but repaired the pipe. On 27 June 1984 the pipe burst and there was an explosion which caused damage to the structure of the plant around the pipe. A writ alleging negligent manufacture was issued on 21 June 1990 and the plaintiffs alleged it was issued within six years of the accrual of their cause of action in negligence. Did the plaintiffs have a cause of action in negligence and, if they did, was it statute-barred?

Held

They did have a cause of action which was not statute-barred.

May J:

'... the plaintiffs argued that the cracking to the pipe in 1983 was a defect in the quality of the pipe itself which did not cause personal injury or damage to other property. Accordingly, they had no cause of action in 1983. By contrast, the June 1984 explosion did cause damage to other property and a cause of action then arose which is not statute-barred. The first defendants firstly argue that, not withstanding the recent developments in the law of negligence ... a cause of action did accrue with the 1983 cracking. Secondly and alternatively they argue that the defect became apparent with the 1983 cracking so that ... the loss resulting in 1984 was purely economic and irrecoverable. ...

It would be intellectually dishonest in this case to attempt to distinguish *Junior Books Ltd* v *Veitchi Co Ltd* [1982] 3 WLR 477 and I do not do so. I simply decline to apply it on the basis that it is unique and that it depends on the *Hedley Byrne & Co Ltd* v *Heller & Partners Ltd* [1963] 3 WLR 101 doctrine of reliance. ... the relationship in the case before me is not a *Hedley Byrne* relationship.

I accordingly reject [counsel for the first defendants'] first submission and hold that on the assumed facts the cracking to the pipe in 1983 was damage to the pipe itself constituting a defect of quality resulting in economic loss irrecoverable in negligence. For this reason, a cause of action in negligence did not accrue to the plaintiffs in 1983.

[Counsel's] second argument derives from the law as stated in ... Lord Bridge's opinion in *D & F Estates Ltd* v *Church Commissioners for England* [1989] AC 177 at 206 ... He also referred to passages in *Murphy* v *Brentwood DC* [1991] 1 AC 398 at 464–465 in the opinions of Lord Keith and Lord Bridge respectively to like effect and to Lord Keith's summary of the effect of *Murphy*'s case in *Department of the Environment* v *Thomas Bates & Son* [1991] 1 AC 499 at 519. Once the defect is discovered, the plaintiff has the means of removing it by replacement or repair and the cost of doing so is irrecoverable economic loss. A latent defect which causes personal injury or damage to property other than the thing itself gives rise to a cause of action but once the defect is no longer latent the law as enunciated by Lord Bridge does not provide a cause of action in negligence. [Counsel] for the plaintiffs argues that there is a distinction between defect and damage and that, whereas the plaintiffs may have known that there was damage in 1983, on the assumed facts they were unaware of the cause of the cracking despite reasonable investigation and accordingly were not aware of the defect. [Counsel] argues that the explosion in 1984 did cause physical damage to property other than the pipe itself, and that this is precisely where a cause of action in negligence does arise and that the cracking in 1983 from a then undiagnosed cause did not, as he put it, quash the cause of action. There is support for this approach in Lord Keith's opinion in *Murphy* v *Brentwood DC* [1991] 1 AC 398 at 464, where he said:

"But that principle is not apt to bring home liability towards an occupier who knows the full extent of the defect yet continues to occupy the building."

It is argued that on assumed facts the plaintiffs did not know the full extent of the defect at any time before the explosion.

In my judgment, [counsel for the plaintiffs'] argument here fails. The passages relied on suppose that the defect is discovered before any damage is done and that it is repaired or replaced *before any damage is done*. The cost of so doing is then irrecoverable economic loss. But in this case physical damage to other property did occur. The plaintiffs did not diagnose the cause of the cracking and did not sufficiently repair the pipe to avoid the physical damage caused by the explosion. The damage caused by the explosion includes damage of the kind which gives rise to a cause of action in negligence. It may be supposed that, had the plaintiffs diagnosed the cause of the cracking in 1983, they would have dealt with it in a way which would have avoided the explosion. But they did not do so and on the assumed facts this was despite reasonable investigation. In my judgment, the fact of the cracking in 1983 does not turn what was in fact and in truth physical damage to other property into economic loss. It follows that a cause of action accrued to the plaintiffs on 27 June 1984 which is not statue-barred.

The question which is begged by this analysis and which needs to be addressed is what the position would be if the plaintiffs ought reasonably to have diagnosed the cause of the cracking in 1983. Would that affect the accrual of a cause of action in negligence? In my judgment it would not. The fact of sufficient physical damage to sustain the plaintiffs' cause of action would remain, but the first defendants could argue on appropriate facts that the plaintiffs' recovery should be reduced or extinguished by the plaintiffs' contributory negligence.'

Comment
The recent developments in the law of negligence to which May J referred were found in, and based upon, the decisions of the House of Lords in *D & F Estates* and *Murphy*.

Page v *Smith* [1995] 2 All ER 736
House of Lords (Lords Keith of Kinkel, Ackner, Jauncey of Tullichettle, Browne-Wilkinson and Lloyd of Berwick)

• *Nervous shock – no physical injury to primary victim – foreseeability – damages*

Facts
The plaintiff's car was involved in a collision with the defendant's car in which the plaintiff suffered no physical injury. For 20 years prior to the accident the plaintiff had suffered from ME (myalgic encephalomyelitis) which had manifested itself from time to time with different degrees of severity but was then in remission. The plaintiff claimed damages for his injuries, alleging that as a result of the accident his ME condition had become chronic and permanent. At first instance the High Court found for the plaintiff, and the Court of Appeal allowed the defendant's appeal on the grounds, inter alia, that the plaintiff's injury was not foreseeable. The plaintiff appealed to the House of Lords.

Held (Lords Keith of Kinkel and Jauncey of Tullichettle dissenting)
The appeal would be allowed.

Lord Lloyd of Berwick:

'I now come to *King* v *Phillips* [1953] 1 All ER 617, the case of the "unimaginative taxi cab driver", as it was called by Professor A L Goodhart (see (1953) 69 LQR 347). In the course of backing his taxi without looking, the defendant injured a small boy, and damaged his tricycle. His mother was at a window, about 80 yards away, when she heard a scream. She saw the taxi backing slowly onto the tricycle, but she could not see her son. She suffered severe shock. She brought an action on behalf of her son as the primary victim, and also on her own behalf. McNair J found in favour of the son. He was awarded £5 for his personal injuries and £10 for his tricycle. But the mother's action failed, and her appeal was dismissed.

It seems clear enough that the result nowadays would have been different. In particular, the ground on which Denning LJ decided the case, namely, that because the taxi was backing slowly, the damage was too remote, is indefensible. ... then comes Denning LJ's celebrated dictum ([1953] 1 All ER 617 at 623):

"Howsoever that may be, whether the

exemption for shock be based on want of duty or on remoteness, that can be no doubt that since *Bourhill* v *Young* [1942] 2 All ER 396 that the test for liability for shock is foreseeability of injury by shock."

The danger of any good phrase is that is gets repeated so often and applied so uncritically that in the end it tends to distort the law. Denning LJ's dictum is wrong in two respects. It is both too wide and too narrow. It is too wide where the plaintiff is the secondary victim, as she was in *King* v *Phillips*. For subsequent cases have shown that foreseeability of injury by shock is not the sole test (see *Alcock* v *Chief Constable of the South Yorkshire Police* [1991] 4 All ER 907 at 913 per Lord Keith of Kinkel and *McFarlane* v *E E Caledonia Ltd* [1994] 2 All ER 1). The test is also too narrow, where, as here, the plaintiff is the primary victim. There is nothing in *Bourhill* v *Young* to displace the ordinary rule that where the plaintiff is within the range of foreseeable physical injury the defendant must take his victim as he finds him. The whole point of *Bourhill* v *Young* was that the plaintiff was *not* within the range of foreseeable physical injury. She was not "involved" in the collision. There was, therefore, no way in which she could recover damages unless she could show that the defendant ought to have foreseen injury by shock. It is only in that limited sense that it was ever true to say that liability for shock depends on foreseeability of injury by shock. The dictum has no application where the plaintiff is the primary victim of the defendant's negligence. ...

I return to ... the present case ... The judge held ... that the collision was one of moderate severity. He had no doubt that the plaintiff suffered nervous shock in the broad sense of that word. He concluded that since the plaintiff was actually involved in the accident, it became a foreseeable consequence.

I have some difficulty in understanding how the Court of Appeal was justified in disturbing the judge's primary findings, or the inference which he drew from those findings. ...

In conclusion, the following propositions can be supported.

(1) In cases involving nervous shock, it is essential to distinguish between the primary victim and secondary victims.

(2) In claims by secondary victims the law insists on certain control mechanisms, in order as a matter of policy to limit the number of potential claimants. Thus, the defendant will not be liable unless psychiatric injury is foreseeable in a person of normal fortitude. These control mechanisms have no place where the plaintiff is the primary victim.

(3) In claims by secondary victims, it may be legitimate to use hindsight in order to be able to apply the test of reasonable foreseeability at all. Hindsight, however, has no part to play where the plaintiff is the primary victim.

(4) Subject to the above qualifications, the approach in all cases should be the same, namely, whether the defendant can reasonably foresee that his conduct will expose the plaintiff to the risk of personal injury, whether physical or psychiatric. If the answer is yes, then the duty of care is established, even though physical injury does not, in fact, occur. There is no justification for regarding physical and psychiatric injury as different "kinds of damage".

(5) A defendant who is under a duty of care to the plaintiff, whether as primary or secondary victim, is not liable for damages for nervous shock unless the shock results in some recognised psychiatric illness. It is no answer that the plaintiff was predisposed to psychiatric illness. Nor is it relevant that the illness takes a rare form or is of unusual severity. The defendant must take his victim as he finds him.

These propositions do not, I think, involve any radical departure from the law as it was left by Kennedy J in *Dulieu* v *White & Sons* [1901] 2 KB 669 and by the Court of Appeal in *Hambrook* v *Stokes Bros* [1925] 1 KB 141 and *King* v *Phillips*, although the decision in the latter case can no longer be supported on its facts. In *McLoughlin* v *O'Brian* [1982] 2 All ER 298 your Lordships had the opportunity to take the law forward by holding that the plaintiff could recover damages for nervous shock, even though she was two miles away at the time of the accident. No such opportunity offers in the present case. But it is at least as important that the law would not take a step backwards. This would, I fear, be the result if the decision of the Court of Appeal were allowed to stand.

In the result, I would restore the judgment of Otton J, but subject to one last caveat. One of the grounds of appeal from Otton J's judgment was that his finding on causation was against the weight of the evidence. Ralph Gibson LJ upheld this ground of appeal, but it was left open by Farquharson and Hoffmann LJJ. Unless, therefore, the claim can now be settled, the case will have to go back to the Court of Appeal for a finding on this issue.'

Comment
The case did indeed return to the Court of Appeal on the issue of causation: see *Page v Smith (No 2)* [1996] 3 All ER 272.

Applied in *White v Chief Constable of the South Yorkshire Police* [1999] 1 All ER 1.

Page v *Smith (No 2)* [1996] 3 All ER 272 Court of Appeal (Sir Thomas Bingham MR, Morritt and Auld LJJ)

• *Nervous shock – no physical injury to primary victim – causation – damages*

Facts
See *Page v Smith* [1995] 2 All ER 736 above. The House of Lords having remitted the issue of causation to the Court of Appeal, the defendant contended, by way of appeal against the decision at first instance in favour of the plaintiff, that the judge misdirected himself in law on the test to be applied and that on the facts he was not properly entitled to reach a decision in favour of the plaintiff.

Held
The appeal would be dismissed.

Sir Thomas Bingham MR:

'(1) *The test*
At the outset of his judgment the judge formulated the questions which he had to answer. The relevant question for present purposes was: "Did the road traffic accident cause or materially contribute to the condition that has prevailed since the accident?" The judge indicated his legal approach to answer this question:

"Putting all this evidence together and those submissions of law, it seems to me that the test is: did the accident, on the balance of probabilities, cause or materially contribute or materially increase the risk of the development or prolongation of the symptoms of CFS [chronic fatigue syndrome, in earlier proceedings referred to as ME] which he currently suffers? This is to be derived from the decisions of *Bonnington Castings Ltd* v *Wardlaw* [1956] 1 All ER 615, *McGhee* v *National Coal Board* [1972] 3 All ER 1008 and *Wilsher* v *Essex Health Authority* [1988] 1 All ER 871. I am satisfied on the balance of probabilities that the defendant's negligence materially contributed to the recrudescence of the CFS and converted that illness from a mild and sporadic state to one of chronic intensity and permanency. The vital element is that it should be a material contribution, ie it should not be merely a minimal or trivial or insignificant contribution. I have come to the conclusion that although they undoubtedly play their part in the make up of the plaintiff before and after the accident, none can be promoted to the sole cause or the 'joint sole cause' of the relapse, so as to exclude any significant contribution of the effects of the accident."

Various criticisms were made of this passage. First, it was said that the judge was wrong to refer to a material increase of the risk, which was clearly an echo of the difficult decision of the House of Lords in *Wilsher* v *Essex Health Authority* [1988] 1 All ER 871. I do not ... conclude that this criticism assists the defendant since, although the judge posed the question in terms which made reference to risk, he made it plain when answering that question that he was simply concluding whether the negligence had materially contributed to the plaintiff's symptoms, and not whether it had exposed him to an increased risk.

Secondly, it was argued that the judge had erred in asking whether on the balance of probabilities the defendant's negligence had materially contributed to the recrudescence of the plaintiff's symptoms. He should, it was said, have asked himself whether on the balance of probabilities the plaintiff would have suffered the injury for which he was claiming compensation but for the defendant's negligence. I do not for my part accept these criticisms. In a case in which other causes could have played a part in the causation of the plaintiff's exacerbated symptoms, it was in my view entirely appropriate for the judge to direct himself in the way that he did, reminding himself that a cause was only to be regarded as material if it was more than minimal or trivial or insignificant. I cannot in any event see that in a case such as this the outcome would be different whichever the test is formulated. The judge had already accepted the view expressed by one of the medical experts that the plaintiff's recovery would probably have continued but for the accident. The judge adopted a straightforward, pragmatic approach which was in my judgment entirely appropriate in the circumstances.

It was argued thirdly that the judge was wrong to address the question whether the accident was the sole cause or whether there was any other sole cause. Had the judge expressly or impliedly cast an onus on the defendant to eliminate other possible causes of the plaintiff's injury, that would certainly have been wrong. But the judge did not do that. Having formed a tentative view that the accident had probably caused the exacerbation of the plaintiff's symptoms, he turned to consider other possible causes with a view on seeing if any of them should be identified as the sole cause of the accident. He accordingly reviewed various suggestions that had been made in the course of argument and evidence: it had been suggested that the plaintiff had read medical literature relating to CFS and had, as a result, become unconsciously susceptible to a relapse; it had been suggested that he had found his occupation as a teacher stressful, and that accordingly he had been relieved to find that he would not have to return to work; it had been suggested that the stress of involvement in litigation was the cause of his exacerbated symptoms; it had been suggested that he was perfectly content to live without occupation as he was doing; and it had been suggested that a combination of some of these factors might account for his symptoms to the exclusion of any effect caused by the accident itself. The judge rejected some of these suggestions outright and rejected others as a sole cause of the plaintiff's symptoms. I discern no error in the judge's approach. Even if he had concluded, rightly, that some of these factors made some contribution to exacerbating the plaintiff's symptoms, that would not have been a ground for concluding that the defendant's negligence was not itself a material contributory cause. He was, of course, vividly alive to the fact that the plaintiff had been a victim of CFS from time to time throughout his adult life.

I reject this ground of appeal. ...

(2) *The facts*

There are two questions to be considered: first, whether CFS can be caused or exacerbated by a motor accident causing no physical injury; and secondly, if so, whether the plaintiff's condition was exacerbated by the accident in this case. These are different questions, since the answer to the first might be positive and the answer to the second negative. ...

On the strength of all [the] evidence, the judge was satisfied that the plaintiff did suffer from CFS for a substantial period of his life before the collision. He was satisfied ... that the defendant's negligence materially contributed to the recrudescence of the plaintiff's CFS and converted that illness from a mild and sporadic state to one of chronic intensity and permanence.

We have been referred in some detail to

the medical reports which were before the judge, and the evidence which witnesses gave before him. I am left with a very clear impression that the conclusion which the judge reached was one which was fully open to him. I am of opinion that the judge's conclusion on this issue is unassailable.'

Smith v Eric S Bush, Harris v Wyre Forest District Council [1989] 2 WLR 790 House of Lords (Lords Keith of Kinkel, Brandon of Oakbrook, Templeman, Griffiths and Jauncey of Tullichettle)

* *Valuation – duty of care*

Facts

In *Smith*, wishing to buy a terraced house at the lower end of the housing market, the plaintiff applied to the Abbey National Building Society for a mortgage. She paid an inspection fee and signed an application form which stated that she would receive a copy of the survey report and mortgage valuation; the form also contained a disclaimer of responsibility for the contents of the report and valuation. The society instructed the defendant surveyors to carry out the inspection: the plaintiff duly received a copy of their report and valuation which also included a disclaimer. On the strength of the report, which stated that no essential repairs were required, the plaintiff purchased the house, but the defendants had carried out their work negligently, overlooking a serious defect. Eighteen months later, as a result of that defect, some flues collapsed and caused substantial damage. The facts of *Harris* were essentially the same except that the inspection was carried out by their own surveyor.

Held

The defendants were liable: they had owed the plaintiff in tort a duty to exercise reasonable skill and care, they had been in breach of that duty and the disclaimer clauses were ineffective.

Lord Templeman said that in each case the valuer knew that the purchaser was providing the money for the valuation, that the purchaser would only contract to purchase the house if the valuation was satisfactory and that the purchaser might suffer injury or damage or both if the valuer did not exercise reasonable skill and care. In those circumstances his Lordship would expect the law to impose on the valuer a duty owed to the purchaser to exercise reasonable skill and care in carrying out the valuation. The considerations referred to by Denning LJ in *Candler* v *Crane, Christmas & Co* [1951] 2 KB 164, 176-181, whose dissenting judgment was subsequently approved by the House of Lords in *Hedley Byrne & Co Ltd* v *Heller & Partners Ltd* [1964] AC 465, applied to the valuers in the present appeals. The statutory duty of the council to value the house did not prevent the council coming under a contractual or tortious duty to the plaintiffs who in *Harris* were informed of the valuation and relied on it.

The contractual duty of a valuer to value a house for the Abbey National did not prevent the valuer coming under a tortious duty to Mrs Smith who was furnished with a report of the valuation and relied on it. In general, his Lordship was of the opinion that in the absence of a disclaimer of liability the valuer who valued a house for the purpose of a mortgage, knowing that the mortgagee would, and the mortgagor would probably rely on the valuation, knowing that the purchaser mortgagor had in effect paid for the valuation, was under a duty to exercise reasonable skill and care, and that duty was owed to both parties to the mortgage for which the valuation was made. Indeed, in both appeals the existence of such a dual duty was tacitly accepted and acknowledged because notices excluding liability for breach of the duty owed to the purchaser were drafted by the mortgagee and imposed on the purchaser. In those circumstances it was necessary to consider the second question which arose in the appeals, namely, whether the disclaimers of liability were notices which fell within the Unfair

Contract Terms Act 1977. In his Lordship's opinion, both ss11(3) and 13(1) supported the view that the 1977 Act required that all exclusion notices which would at common law provide a defence to an action for negligence must satisfy the requirement of reasonableness. Here, they did not and the evidence and findings of Mr Justice Park in *Yianni v Edwin Evans & Sons* [1982] QB 438, supported the view that it was unfair and unreasonable for a valuer to rely on an exclusion clause directed against a purchaser in the circumstances of the present appeals.

Lord Griffiths, concurring, said that it had to be remembered that each of the appeals concerned a dwelling house of modest value in which it was widely recognised by valuers that purchasers were in fact relying on their care and skill. It would obviously be of general application in broadly similar circumstances. But his Lordship expressly reserved his position in respect of valuations of quite different types of property for mortgage purposes, such as industrial property, large blocks of flats or very expensive houses. In such cases it might well be that the general expectation of the behaviour of the purchaser was quite different. With very large sums of money at stake prudence would demand that the purchaser obtain his own structural survey to guide him in his purchase and, in such circumstances, with such large sums of money at stake, it might be reasonable for the valuers acting on behalf of the mortgagees to exclude or limit their liability to the purchaser.

Comment
Applied in *Al Saudi Banque v Clark Pixley* [1989] 3 All ER 361 (insufficient relationship between auditors of company accounts and lenders to company to give rise to a duty of care) and *Al-Nakib Investments (Jersey) Ltd v Longcroft* [1990] 3 All ER 321.

Smith v Littlewoods Organisation Ltd [1987] 2 WLR 480 House of Lords (Lords Keith of Kinkel, Brandon of Oakbrook, Griffiths, Mackay of Clashfern and Goff of Chieveley)

• *Negligence – act of third party*

Facts
The defendants purchased a cinema in Dunfermline with a view to demolishing it and building a supermarket on the site. From June 1976 the site was empty and unattended. Vandals broke into the old cinema and attempted to set fire to the building. On 5 July 1976 a fire was started in the building and spread to neighbouring properties, including the plaintiffs' property. The plaintiffs sued the defendants in negligence, alleging that they had failed to take reasonable steps to prevent damage.

Held
The defendants were not liable. An occupier was under a general duty to exercise reasonable care in order to ensure that the condition of his premises was not a source of danger to neighbouring properties. Although it was expressly found that the damage by fire was foreseeable, the defendants had done all that a reasonable owner of the property could do in boarding up the cinema. There was no duty to patrol the premises all the time to keep vandals away.

Lord Griffiths:

'The fire in this case was caused by the criminal activity of third parties on Littlewoods' premises. I do not say that there will never be circumstances in which the law will require an occupier of premises to take special precautions against such a contingency but they would surely have to be extreme indeed. It is common ground that only a 24-hour guard on these premises would have been likely to prevent this fire, and even that cannot be certain, such is the determination and ingenuity of young vandals.

There was nothing of an inherently dangerous nature stored in the premises, nor can I regard an empty cinema stripped of its equipment as likely to be any more alluring to vandals than any other recently vacated premises in the centre of a town. No message was received by Littlewoods from the local police, fire brigade or any neighbour that vandals were creating any danger on the premises. In short, so far as Littlewoods knew, there was nothing significantly different about these empty premises from the tens of thousands of such premises up and down the country. People do not mount 24-hour guards on empty properties and the law would impose an intolerable burden if it required them to do so save in the most exceptional circumstances. I find no such exceptional circumstances in this case ...

I doubt myself if any search will reveal a touchstone that can be applied as a universal test to decide when an occupier is to be held liable for a danger created on his property by the act of a trespasser for whom he is not responsible. I agree that mere foreseeability of damage is certainly not a sufficient basis to found liability. But with this warning I doubt that more can be done than to leave it to the good sense of the judges to apply realistic standards in conformity with generally accepted patterns of behaviour to determine whether in the particular circumstances of a given case there has been a breach of duty sounding in negligence.'

Comment

When considering – and supporting – the Court of Appeal decision in *P Perl (Exporters) Ltd* v *Camden London Borough Council* [1984] QB 342, Lord Mackay of Clashfern here explained that the entry of thieves through the defendant's premises was a foreseeable possibility, not a foreseeable probable consequence of any breach of the defendant's duty.

Stovin v *Wise* [1996] 3 All ER 801 House of Lords (Lords Goff of Chieveley, Jauncey of Tullichettle, Slynn of Hadley, Nicholls of Birkenhead and Hoffmann)

* *Highway authority – duty of care*

Facts

The plaintiff sustained serious injury when his motor cycle collided with the defendant's car as it emerged from a side road. A bank of earth on British Rail land restricted the defendant's view to about 100 feet. The highway authority had offered to remove part of the bank at its own expense, but by the time of the accident (11 months after the offer had been made) British Rail had not responded and no action had been taken. The Court of Appeal decided that the highway authority had not been in breach of its statutory duty under s41 of the Highways Act 1980 as the bank did not form part of the highway. However, it had been in breach of its common law duty of care and it was liable for 30 per cent of the plaintiff's damages (the other 70 per cent being payable by the defendant). The highway authority appealed against this finding as to its common law duty of care.

Held (Lords Slynn of Hadley and Nicholls of Birkenhead dissenting)

The appeal would be allowed.

Lord Hoffmann:

'Since *Mersey Docks and Harbour Board Trustees* v *Gibbs* (1866) LR 1 HL 93 it has been clear law that, in the absence of express statutory authority, a public body is in principle liable for torts in the same way as a private person. But its statutory powers or duties may restrict its liability. For example, it may be authorised to do something which necessarily involves committing what would otherwise be a tort. In such a case it will not be liable (see *Allen* v *Gulf Oil Refining Ltd* [1981] 1 All ER 353). Or it may have discretionary powers which enable it to do things to achieve a statutory purpose notwithstanding that they involve a foreseeable risk of damage to others. In such a case, a bona fide exercise of the discretion will not attract liability (see *X and Others (Minors)* v *Bedfordshire CC* [1995] 3 All ER 353 and *Home Office* v *Dorset Yacht Co Ltd* [1970] 2 All ER 294).

In the case of positive acts, therefore, the liability of a public authority in tort is in principle the same as that of a private person but may be *restricted* by its statutory powers and duties. The argument in the present case, however, is that whereas a private person would have owed no duty of care in respect of an omission to remove the hazard at the junction, the duty of the highway authority is *enlarged* by virtue of its statutory powers. The existence of the statutory powers is said to create a "proximity" between the highway authority and the highway user which would not otherwise exist. ...

Until the decision of this House in *Anns* v *Merton London Borough* [1977] 2 All ER 492 there was no authority for treating a statutory power as giving rise to a common law duty of care. ...

Anns ... is the mainstay of Mrs Wise's argument ... So far as it held that the council owed a duty of care in respect of purely economic loss, the case has been overruled by *Murphy* v *Brentwood DC* [1990] 2 All ER 908. The House left open the question of whether the council might have owed a duty in respect of physical injury, although I think it is fair to say that the tone of their Lordships' remarks on this question was somewhat sceptical. Nevertheless, it is now necessary to ask whether the reasoning can support the existence of a duty of care owed by a public authority in respect of foreseeable physical injury which is founded upon the existence of statutory powers to safeguard people against that injury. ...

In summary ... I think that the minimum pre-conditions for basing a duty of care upon the existence of a statutory power, if it can be done at all, are, first, that it would in the circumstances have been irrational not to have exercised the power, so that there

was in effect a public law duty to act, and secondly, that there are exceptional grounds for holding that the policy of the statute requires compensation to be paid to persons who suffer loss because the power was not exercised. ...

I ... consider whether the council owed a duty of care which required it to take steps to improve the junction. Since the only basis for such a duty is the authority's statutory powers, both specifically under s79 of the 1980 Act and generally to carry out works of improvement with the consent of British Rail, I will start by asking whether, in the light of what the council knew or ought to have known about the injunction, it would have had a duty in public law to undertake the work. This requires that it would have been irrational not to exercise its discretion to do so. ... The judge ... made no finding as to whether it would have been irrational for the council not to have done the work. The unchallenged evidence of [the] head of the accident studies office, would have made it very difficult to do so. In evidence-in-chief, he was asked about [a previous] accident:

> "Q. So far as you are concerned, what difference, if any, would the significance of this accident have made in relation to priority given to carrying out work at this site, against the background of what had happened with British Rail? A. In practical terms, it would have made no difference at all to the priority within the accident remedial budget, because our attention and resources would have been directed to those many sites in the county which already had much higher accident records."

There was no suggestion in cross-examination that this was an unreasonable, let alone irrational, attitude to take.

It seems to me, therefore, that the question of whether anything should be done about the injunction was at all times firmly within the areas of the council's discretion. As they were therefore not under a public law duty to do the work, the first condition for the imposition of a duty of care was not satisfied. ...

But even if it were, I do not think that the second condition would be satisfied. Assuming that the highway authority ought, as a matter of public law, to have done the work, I do not think that there are any grounds upon which it can be said that the public law duty should give rise to an obligation to compensate persons who have suffered loss because it was not performed. There is no question here of reliance on the council having improved the junction. Everyone could see that it was still the same. Mr Stovin was not arbitrarily denied a benefit which was routinely provided to others. In respect of the junction, he was treated in exactly the same way as any other road user. The foundation for the doctrine of general reliance is missing in this case, because we are not concerned with provision of a uniform identifiable benefit or service. Every hazardous junction, intersection or stretch of road is different and requires a separate decision as to whether anything should be done to improve it. It is not without significance that the Canadian cases in which a duty of care has been held to exist have all involved routine inspection and maintenance rather than improvements. ...

Given the fact that the British road network largely antedates the highway authorities themselves, the court is not in a position to say what an appropriate standard of improvement would be. This must be a matter for the discretion of the authority. On the other hand, denial of liability does not leave the road user unprotected. Drivers of vehicles must take the highway network as they find it. Everyone knows that there are hazardous bends, intersections and junctions. It is primarily the duty of drivers of vehicles to take due care. And if, as in the case of Mrs Wise, they do not, there is compulsory insurance to provide compensation to the victims. There is no reason of policy or justice which requires the highway authority to be an additional defendant.'

Comment
Applied in *Capital and Counties plc* v

Hampshire County Council [1997] 2 All ER 865 and *Hussain* v *Lancaster City Council* [1999] 4 All ER 125. See also *Clunis* v *Camden and Islington Health Authority* [1998] 3 All ER 180 (since under the Mental Health Act 1983 the primary method of enforcement of the obligations under s117 (after-care) was by complaint to the Secretary of State, the wording of the section was not apposite to create a private law cause of action for failure to carry out the duties under the statute. Further, bearing in mind the ambit of the obligations under s117 and the statutory framework, it would not be fair, just and reasonable to impose a common law duty of care on an authority).

Swinney v *Chief Constable of Northumbria Police* [1996] 3 All ER 449 Court of Appeal (Hirst, Peter Gibson and Ward LJJ)

* *Police – duty of care to informant*

Facts
The plaintiff gave the police information in strict confidence as to the identity of a person implicated in the unlawful killing of a police officer. The police recorded this information in a document in which the plaintiff was named as informant and they knew that the person implicated in the crime was violent. The document was stolen from an unattended police vehicle and subsequently reached the person implicated. The plaintiff and her husband were threatened with violence and arson and they suffered psychiatric damage: they sued the police alleging negligence. The police contended that the proceedings should be struck out as disclosing no reasonable cause of action.

Held
This application had rightly been dismissed.

Ward LJ:

'The plaintiffs must establish only that it is arguable that they have a good cause of action. It seems to me that it is indeed properly arguable that: (1) the risk of theft of the documents from the police car is foreseeable, it being conceded that the harm to the plaintiffs in consequence of the theft is also foreseeable; (2) there is a special relationship between the plaintiffs and the defendant, which is sufficiently proximate. Proximity is shown by the police assuming responsibility, and the plaintiffs relying upon the assumption of responsibility, for preserving the confidentiality of the information which, if it fell into the wrong hands, was likely to expose the first plaintiff and members of her family to a special risk of damage from the criminal acts of others, greater than the general risk which ordinary members of the public must endure with phlegmatic fortitude; and (3) it is fair, just and reasonable that the law should impose a duty, there being no overwhelming dictate of public policy to exclude the prosecution of this claim. On the one hand there is, as more fully set out in *Hill* v *Chief Constable of West Yorkshire* [1988] 2 All ER 238 at 243–244, an important public interest that the police should carry out their difficult duties to the best of their endeavours without being fettered by, or even influenced by, the spectre of litigation looming over every judgment they make, every discretion they exercise, every act they undertake or omit to perform, in their ceaseless battle to investigate and suppress crime. The greater public good rightly outweighs any individual hardship. On the other hand, it is incontrovertible that the fight against crime is daily dependent upon information fed to the police by members of the public, often at real risk of villainous retribution from the criminals and their associates. The public interest will not accept that good citizens should be expected to entrust information to the police, without also expecting that they are entrusting their safety to the police. The public interest would be affronted were it to be the law that members of the public should be expected, in the execution of public service, to undertake the risk of harm to themselves without the police, in return, being expected to take no more than reason-

able care to ensure that the confidential information imparted to them is protected. The welfare of the community at large demands the encouragement of the free flow of information without inhibition. Accordingly, it is arguable that there is a duty of care, and that no consideration of public policy precludes the prosecution of the plaintiffs' claim, which will be judged on its merits later.'

Comment
Peter Gibson LJ said that it was not entirely clear to him that the informant's husband, the second plaintiff, had an equally arguable case.

Van Oppen v *Clerk to the Bedford Charity Trustees* [1990] 1 WLR 235 Court of Appeal (O'Connor, Croom-Johnson and Balcombe LJJ)

• *School – duty of care*

Facts
The plaintiff, when aged sixteen and a half, suffered injury at the defendant school during an inter-house rugby match. He sued for damages on two distinct bases: (1) an allegation that the school was negligent in failing to take reasonable care for his safety on the rugby field, by failing to coach or instruct him in proper tackling techniques (the rugby claim); and (2) an allegation that the school was negligent in (a) failing to inform or advise his father (i) of the inherent risk of serious injury in the game of rugby, (ii) of the consequent need for personal accident insurance, and (iii) that the school had not arranged such insurance for him; and (b) in default of such information or advice failing itself to ensure that he was covered by personal accident insurance (the insurance claim). The trial judge dismissed both claims ([1989] 1 All ER 272); the plaintiff appealed in respect of the insurance claim.

Held
The appeal would be dismissed.

O'Connor LJ:

'There is no dispute that had a personal accident policy been in position the plaintiff would have received the appropriate payment as a result of his injury. It is the plaintiff's case that he has suffered this loss as a result of the negligence of the school and that although it is pure economic loss it is recoverable.

Counsel for the plaintiff accepts that there is no duty on parents to take out personal accident insurance policies in favour of their children. He accepts that there is no general duty on schools to take out personal accident policies in favour of their pupils and quite plainly it is no part of a school's function to advise parents or anybody else on insurance matters.

The next matter which is of importance is that it is not suggested that the school was negligent in allowing the plaintiff to play rugby knowing that there was no personal accident policy in position. I am satisfied that the plaintiff's "insurance claim" cannot be brought within the scope of the duty owed by school to pupil arising out of the relationship which existed between them.

When one considers the duty owed by a school to its pupils one finds first of all the duties which the law imposes on all schools because they are schools. These duties are of general application whether the school be provided by the state, or privately, and regardless of whether it be fee-paying or free. Next one must look at the individual school to see whether it owes some additional duty to its pupils. On analysis such may be no more than a special standard of care to discharge the general duties, for example a school for the blind. The terms on which the school accepts pupils may show that it would be fair and reasonable to impose some additional duty on the school. Personal accident insurance is a very good example of such a term. If a school decides that all pupils are to be covered by personal accident insurance under a block policy taken out by the school and the school negligently fails to renew the policy, then in my

judgment an injured pupil would have a good claim against the school.

However, I can see no justification for the court to write in such a term for a period before the school has introduced it, whether by agreement with the parents or unilaterally.

It is said that knowledge reaching the school ... on the rugby injury/personal accident insurance topic put them under a duty ... to warn parents of the desirability of taking out personal accident insurance. I do not think that the facts support this contention.'

Waters v *Commissioner of Police of the Metropolis* [2000] 4 All ER 934 House of Lords (Lords Slynn of Hadley, Jauncey of Tullichettle, Clyde, Hutton and Millett)

• *Female officer – complaint – failure to respond*

Facts
The appellant female police officer alleged that she had been raped and buggered in her police residential accommodation by a fellow officer when they were both off duty. In these proceedings she alleged that her complaint had not been dealt with properly by her superiors, that they had allowed other officers to harass, victimise 'and otherwise oppress her' and that she had suffered psychiatric injury as a result. Her claim was struck out and her appeal was dismissed. Had these decisions been correct?

Held
They had not since the claim was not one which plainly and obviously had to fail.

Lord Slynn of Hadley:

'Two features of the claim need to be emphasised. In the first place there is no allegation of a conspiracy between the various police officers named to harm or fail to look after the appellant. In the second place the appellant does not rely simply on individual acts taken separately; she attaches importance to the cumulative effect of the acts particularly in regard to the causation of psychiatric injury which she alleges.

In the appellant's case before your Lordships some 89 allegations of hostile treatment are listed as taken from the statement of claim. … At the heart of her claim lies the belief that the other officers reviled her and failed to take care of her because she had broken the team rules by complaining of sexual acts by a fellow police officer. …

The principal claim raised in the action is one of negligence – the "employer" failed to exercise due care to look after "his employee". … Of course, the police constable does not have an ordinary contract of employment with the commissioner or with anyone else: he maintains his traditional status as a constable. Yet it is clear, or at the least arguable that duties analogous to those owed to an employee are owed to officers in the police service (see *White* v *Chief Constable of the South Yorkshire Police* [1999] 1 All ER 1, *Knightley* v *Johns* [1982] 1 All ER 851, *Costello* v *Chief Constable of Northumbria* [1999] 1 All ER 550.

The main question is thus whether it is plain and obvious that no duty of care can be owed to the appellant by the commissioner on the facts alleged here or that if there can be such a duty whether it is plain and obvious here that the facts cannot amount to a breach.

If an employer knows that acts being done by employees during their employment may cause physical or mental harm to a particular fellow employee and he does nothing to supervise or prevent such acts, when it is in his power to do so, it is clearly arguable that he may be in breach of his duty to that employee. It seems to me that he may also be in breach of that duty if he can foresee that such acts may happen and if they do, that physical or mental harm may be caused to an individual. I would accept (Evan LJ was prepared to assume without deciding) that if this sort of sexual assault is alleged

(whether it happened or not) and the officer persists in making complaints about it, it is arguable that it can be foreseen that some retaliatory steps may be taken against the woman and that she may suffer harm as a result. Even if this is not necessarily foreseeable at the beginning it may become foreseeable or indeed obvious to those in charge at various levels who are carrying out the commissioner's responsibilities that there is a risk of harm and that some protective steps should be taken.

The courts have recognised the need for an employer to take care of his employees quite apart from statutory requirements (*Spring* v *Guardian Assurance plc* [1994] 3 All ER 129 at 161). … This can be the position whether the foreseeable harm is caused to the mind or to the body of the employee: *Mount Isa Mines* v *Pusey* (1970) 125 CLR 383 at 404 per Windeyer J.

On the basis of these cases, subject to consideration of one overriding point, I do not find it possible to say (any more than Evans LJ was prepared to say) that this is a plain and obvious case that (a) no duty analogous to an employers duty can exist; (b) that the injury to the plaintiff was not foreseeable in the circumstances alleged and (c) that the acts alleged could not be the cause of the damage. As to the last of these whilst I accept that many of the individual items taken in isolation are the least very unlikely to have caused the illness alleged, the appellant's case puts much emphasis on the cumulative effect of what happened under the system as it existed.

That leaves the question on which the Court of Appeal decided against the appellant. Are there reasons of policy why such a claim should not be entertained by the court – or more correctly at this stage, is it plain and obvious that policy reasons preclude such a claim being taken to trial so that it should now be struck out? Put another way can it be said that it is not "fair, just and reasonable" to recognise a duty of care? (See *Caparo Industries plc* v *Dickman* [1990] 1 All ER 568).

The courts have accepted that the police may not be sued for negligence in respect

of their activities in the investigation and suppression of crime: *Elguzouli-Daf* v *Comr of Police of the Metropolis* [1995] 1 All ER 833. The Court of Appeal in particular took the view in the present case that the decisions of the House in *Hill* v *Chief Constable of West Yorkshire* [1988] 2 All ER 238 and *Calveley* v *Chief Constable of the Merseyside Police* [1989] 1 All ER 1025 precluded a duty of care for policy reasons.
...

I do not consider that either of these cases is conclusive against the appellant in the present case. It is true that one of her complaints is the failure to investigate the assault on her and that if taken alone would not constitute a viable cause of action. But the complaints she makes go much wider than this and she is in any event not suing as a member of the public but as someone in an "employment" relationship with the respondent. Even the failure to investigate is part of her complaint as to that. Entirely different factors to those considered in *Hill*'s case arise.

She is not as in *Calveley*'s case complaining of delays in the investigation or procedural irregularities. It does not seem to me that it is an answer here as it was in *Calveley*'s case to say that the appellant should proceed by way of judicial review. Here there is a need to investigate detailed allegations of fact. It has to be accepted of course that this detailed investigation would take time and that police officers would be taken off other duties to prepare the case and give evidence. But this is so whenever proceedings are brought against the police or which involve the police. Sometimes that has to be accepted. Here the allegations of the systematic failure to protect her are complex (and some pruning may be possible, indeed advantageous) but that in itself does not make the claims frivolous or vexatious or an abuse of the process of the court.

It has been said many times that the law of negligence develops incrementally so that the fact that there is no reported case succeeding against the police similar to the present one is not necessarily a sufficient reason for striking out.

It is very important to bear in mind what was said in *X and Ors (Minors)* v *Bedfordshire CC, M (A Minor)* v *Newham London BC, E (A Minor)* v *Dorset CC* [1995] 3 All ER 353, in *Barrett* v *Enfield London BC* [1999] 3 All ER 193, and in *W* v *Essex CC* [2000] 2 All ER 237 as to the need for caution in striking out on the basis of assumed fact in an area where the law is developing as it is in negligence in relation to public authorities if not specifically in relation to the police.

I would accordingly accept that the main claim against the commissioner for breach of personal duty (although the acts were done by those engaged in performing his duty) should not be struck out. The plaintiff's case on vicarious liability is more tenuous since it is difficult to see how many of the acts could have caused the psychiatric injury alleged. Contrary to what the Court of Appeal thought the appellant does allege malice so that the claim for misfeasance in a public office is not barred on the ground that malice is not alleged. I agree with the Court of Appeal that the difficulties of establishing intimidation as a separate tort may be considerable. I have come to the conclusion, however, that the facts which are needed to establish these claims will also feature in the negligence claim: the argument whether those facts establish any of the other claims should be relatively short. If the appellant fails on the main way she puts her case she seems at this stage unlikely to succeed on the others (though that is not inevitably so). If she succeeds on the main way she puts her claim she does not need the other ways.

Whilst not giving any indication either way as to whether the case is likely to succeed I hold that this is not a case which plainly and obviously must fail.'

Comment

For the ingredients of the tort of misfeasance in public office, see *Three Rivers District Council* v *Bank of England (No 3)* [2000] 3 All ER 1.

White v *Jones* [1995] 2 WLR 187 House of Lords (Lords Keith of Kinkel, Goff of Chieveley, Browne-Wilkinson, Mustill and Nolan)

• *Negligence – solicitor instructed to draw up will – duty to intended beneficiary*

Facts

A testator quarrelled with his two daughters and instructed his solicitors, the defendants, to prepare a will cutting his daughters out of his estate. After this was done the testator became reconciled with his daughters and instructed the defendants to prepare a fresh will leaving £9,000 to each daughter. The defendants did nothing for a month and then began preparation of the new will. They arranged to visit the testator one month later, but unfortunately the testator died three days before the meeting. The distribution of the estate was governed by the old will, so the daughters lost their bequests of £9,000 each. They sued the defendants, alleging that they had been negligent in the preparation of the new will and claimed £9,000 each by way of damages. The trial judge held that the defendants owed no duty of care to the plaintiffs and dismissed the action. The Court of Appeal approved *Ross* v *Caunters* [1979] 3 All ER 580 and allowed the plaintiffs' appeal.

Held (Lords Keith of Kinkel and Mustill dissenting)

The defendants' appeal would be dismissed since they owed the plaintiffs a duty of care and their negligence had effectively deprived the plaintiffs of the intended legacies.

Lord Goff of Chieveley:

'... an ordinary action in tortious negligence on the lines proposed by Sir Robert Megarry V-C in *Ross* v *Caunters* [1980] Ch 297 must, with the greatest respect, be regarded as inappropriate, because it does not meet any of the conceptual problems which have been raised. Furthermore ... the *Hedley*

Byrne & Co Ltd v *Heller & Partners Ltd* [1964] AC 465 principle cannot, in the absence of special circumstances, give rise on ordinary principles to an assumption of responsibility by the testator's solicitor towards an intended beneficiary. Even so it seems to me that it is open to your Lordships' House ... to fashion a remedy to fill a lacuna in the law and so prevent the injustice which would otherwise occur on the facts of cases such as the present. ... In my opinion, therefore, your Lordships' House should in cases such as these extend to the intended beneficiary a remedy under the *Hedley Byrne* principle by holding that the assumption of responsibility by the solicitor towards his client should be held in law to extend to the intended beneficiary who (as the solicitor can reasonably foresee) may, as a result of the solicitor's negligence, be deprived of his intended legacy in circumstances in which neither the testator nor his estate will have a remedy against the solicitor. Such liability will not of course arise in cases in which the defect in the will comes to light before the death of the testator, and the testator either leaves the will as it is or otherwise continues to exclude the previously intended beneficiary from the relevant benefit. I only wish to add that, with the benefit of experience during the 15 years in which *Ross* v *Caunters* has been regularly applied, we can say with some confidence that a direct remedy by the intended beneficiary against the solicitor appears to create no problems in practice. That is therefore the solution which I would recommend to your Lordships.'

Comment

Applied in *Carr-Glynn* v *Frearsons* [1998] 4 All ER 225 (defendant solicitors owed duty to plaintiff that testatrix's interest in property could pass to her); see also *Hooper* v *Fynmores* (2001) The Times 19 July (solicitors liable to disappointed intended beneficiary because they postponed visit to client in hospital to enable her to execute new will). It should be noted that lay will-writers also owe a duty of care to intended beneficiaries

(*Esterhuizen* v *Allied Dunbar Assurance plc* (1998) The Times 10 June) and that, in appropriate cases, before suing for negligence, a disappointed intended beneficiary should mitigate his or her loss by seeking rectification of the will: *Walker* v *Geo H Medlicott & Son* [1999] 1 All ER 685.

Distinguished in *Goodwill* v *British Pregnancy Advisory Service* [1996] 2 All ER 161 (no special relationship between the parties or voluntary assumption of responsibility).

Yuen Kun Yeu v *Attorney-General of Hong Kong* [1987] 3 WLR 776 Privy Council (Lords Keith of Kinkel, Templeman, Griffiths, Oliver of Aylmerton and Sir Robert Megarry)

• *Negligence – test for establishing whether duty of care exists*

Facts
The Commissioner of Deposit-taking Companies in Hong Kong had a wide statutory discretion as to the registration of deposit-taking businesses. The appellants made substantial deposits with a registered deposit-taking company: subsequently it went into liquidation and they lost their money. The appellants alleged negligence by the commissioner in the discharge of his functions and sought an award of damages.

Held
They should not succeed as there was no special relationship between the commissioner and the company, or between the commissioner and would-be depositors, capable of giving rise to a duty of care.

Lord Keith of Kinkel:

'In their Lordships' opinion the circumstance that the commissioner had, on the appellants' averments, cogent reason to suspect that the company's business was being carried on fraudulently and improvidently did not create a special relationship between the commissioner and the company of the nature described in the authorities. They are also of opinion that no special relationship existed between the commissioner and those unascertained members of the public who might in future become exposed to the risk of financial loss through depositing money with the company. Accordingly, their Lordships do not consider that the commissioner owed to the appellants any duty of care on the principle which formed the ratio of *Home Office* v *Dorset Yacht Co Ltd* [1970] 2 All ER 294. To hark back to Lord Atkin's words, there were not such close and direct relations between the commissioner and the appellants as to give rise to the duty of care desiderated.

The appellants, however, advanced an argument based on their averment of having relied on the registration of the company when they deposited their money with it. It was said that registration amounted to a seal of approval of the company, and that by registering the company and allowing the registration to stand the commissioner made a continuing representation that the company was creditworthy. In the light of the information in the commissioner's possession that representation was made negligently and led to the appellant's loss ... While the investing public might reasonably feel some confidence that the provisions of the ordinance as a whole went a long way to protect their interests, reliance on the fact of registration as a guarantee of the soundness of the particular company would be neither reasonable nor justifiable, nor should the commissioner reasonable be expected to know of such reliance, if it existed. Accordingly their Lordships are unable to accept the appellants' arguments about reliance as apt, in all the circumstances, to establish a special relationship between them and the commissioner such as to give rise to a duty of care.'

Comment
Followed in *Davis* v *Radcliffe* [1990] 1 WLR 821 and *Clough* v *Bussan* [1990] 1 All ER 431 (no particular duty owed by police to defendant motorist).

7　Negligence: Breach of the Duty

Airedale NHS Trust v Bland [1993] 2 WLR 316 House of Lords (Lords Keith of Kinkel, Goff of Chieveley, Lowry, Browne-Wilkinson and Mustill)

- *Withdrawal of treatment – breach of duty of care?*

Facts

When aged 17½ Anthony Bland was crushed in the 1989 Hillsborough football disaster. He had since then been in a persistent vegetative state, without hope of recovery or improvement of any kind. The plaintiffs now sought a declaration that they could lawfully discontinue all life-sustaining treatment.

Held

The declaration had been properly granted.

Lord Browne-Wilkinson:

'... this House in *F v West Berkshire Health Authority* [1989] 2 WLR 1025 developed and laid down a principle, based on concepts of necessity, under which a doctor can lawfully treat a patient who cannot consent to such treatment if it is in the best interests of the patient to receive such treatment. In my view, the correct answer to the present case depends on the extent of the right to continue lawfully to invade the bodily integrity of Anthony Bland without his consent. If in the circumstances they have no right to continue artificial feeding, they cannot be in breach of any duty by ceasing to provide such feeding.

What then is the extent of the right to treat Anthony Bland which can be deduced from *F v West Berkshire Health Authority*? Both Lord Brandon of Oakbrook and Lord Goff make it clear that the right to administer invasive medical care is wholly dependent upon such care being in the best interests of the patient ... Moreover, a doctor's decision whether invasive care is in the best interests of the patient falls to be assessed by reference to the test laid down in *Bolam v Friern Hospital Management Committee* [1957] 1 WLR 582, viz is the decision in accordance with a practice accepted at the time by a responsible body of medical opinion? ... In my judgment it must follow from this that, if there comes a stage where the responsible doctor comes to the reasonable conclusion (which accords with the views of a responsible body of medical opinion) that further continuance of an intrusive life support system is not in the best interests of the patient, he can no longer lawfully continue that life support system: to do so would constitute the crime of battery and the tort of trespass to the person. Therefore he cannot be in breach of any duty to maintain the patient's life. Therefore he is not guilty of murder by omission ...

Finally, the conclusion I have reached will appear to some to be almost irrational. How can it be lawful to allow a patient to die slowly, though painlessly, over a period of weeks from lack of food but unlawful to produce his immediate death by a lethal injection, thereby saving his family from yet another ordeal to add to the tragedy that has already struck them? I find it difficult to find a moral answer to that question. But it is undoubtedly the law and nothing I have said casts doubt on the proposition that the doing of a positive act with the intention of ending life is and remains murder.'

Comment

See also *Frenchay Healthcare NHS Trust v S* [1994] 2 All ER 403 (court should be reluctant to place those treating the patient in a position of having to carry out treatment which they considered to be contrary to the patient's best interests unless it had real doubt about the reliability, bona fides or correctness of the medical opinion in question) and *Practice Note* [1996] 4 All ER 766 (procedure for applications to court for sanction of withdrawal of treatment). See, too, *NHS Trust A v M* [2001] 1 All ER 801 (withdrawal of treatment of patient in permanent vegetative state did not infringe arts 2 and 3 of the European Convention for the Protection of Human Rights and Fundamental Freedoms) and *Re A (Children) (Conjoined Twins: Surgical Separation)* [2000] 4 All ER 961 where *Airedale* was distinguished.

Blyth v *Birmingham Waterworks Co* (1856) 11 Exch 781 Court of Exchequer (Alderson, Martin and Bramwell BB)

• *Negligence – frost of exceptional severity*

Facts
In pursuance of statutory powers, the defendants laid down water pipes. During 'one of the severest frosts on record', a plug failed to work correctly and a large quantity of water escaped into the plaintiff's house.

Held
On the facts, the defendants were not liable.

Alderson B:

'The case turns upon the question whether the facts proved show that the defendants were guilty of negligence. Negligence is the omission to do something which a reasonable man, guided upon those considerations which ordinarily regulate the conduct of human affairs, would do, or doing something which a prudent and reasonable man would not do. The defendants might have been liable for negligence, if, unintentionally, they omitted to do that which a reasonable person would have done, or did that

which a person taking reasonable precautions would not have done. A reasonable man would act with reference to the average circumstances of the temperature in ordinary years. The defendants had provided against such frosts as experience would have led men, acting prudently, to provide against; and they are not guilty of negligence, because their precautions proved insufficient against the effects of the extreme severity of the frost of 1855, which penetrated to a greater depth than any which ordinarily occurs south of the polar regions. Such a state of circumstances constitutes a contingency against which no reasonable man can provide. The result was an accident, for which the defendants cannot be held liable.'

Comment
In *Overseas Tankship (UK) Ltd* v *Morts Dock & Engineering Co Ltd, The Wagon Mound* [1961] 1 All ER 404 Viscount Simonds said that the Privy Council were there following and developing the law of negligence as laid down by Alderson B in this case.

Bolitho v *City and Hackney Health Authority* [1997] 4 All ER 771 House of Lords (Lords Browne-Wilkinson, Slynn of Hadley, Nolan, Hoffmann and Clyde)

• *Medical practitioner – test of negligence – proof of causation*

Facts
Patrick, a boy aged two, was readmitted to hospital under the care of Dr Horn and Dr Rodger. On the following day, at 12.40 and 2pm he experienced an episode. At about 2.30pm he collapsed and, as a result, he suffered a cardiac arrest which led to severe brain damage: he subsequently died. The defendants accepted that Dr Horn had been in breach of her duty of care in so far as she had not gone to see the boy, following each of the first two episodes, as a sister had asked her to do. By

the end of the trial it was common ground, first, that intubation so as to provide an air way in any event would have ensured that the respiratory failure which occured did not lead to cardiac arrest and, second, that such intubation would have had to be carried out, if at all, before the final catastrophic episode. The trial judge found that Dr Horn would not have intubated had she attended the boy, as requested, and that a responsible body of medical opinion supported her approach. He therefore dismissed the claim and the Court of Appeal dismissed an appeal against this decision.

Held
The further and final appeal would also be dismissed.

Lord Browne-Wilkinson:

'... the judge answered the first of his two questions by holding that Dr Horn would not herself have intubated if, contrary to the facts, she had attended.

As to the second of the judge's questions (ie whether any competent doctor should have intubated if he had attended Patrick at any time after 2pm), the judge had evidence from no less than eight medical experts, all of them distinguished. Five of them were called on behalf of Patrick and were all of the view that, at least after the second episode, any competent doctor would have intubated. Of these five, the judge was most impressed by Dr Heaf, a consultant paediatrician in respiratory medicine at the Royal Liverpool Children's Hospital ... On the other side, the defendants called three experts of all whom said that, on the symptoms presented by Patrick ... intubation would not have been appropriate. Of the defendants' experts, the judge found Dr Dinwiddie, a consultant paediatrician in respiratory diseases at the Great Ormond Street Hospital, most impressive. ...

Having made his findings of fact, the judge directed himself as to the law by reference to the speech of Lord Scarman in *Maynard* v *West Midlands Regional Health Authority* [1985] 1 All ER 635 at 639:

"... I have to say that a judge's 'preference' for one body of distinguished professional opinion to another also professionally distinguished is not sufficient to establish negligence in a practitioner whose actions have received the seal of approval of those whose opinions, truthfully expressed, honestly held, were not preferred. If this was the real reason for the judge's finding, he erred in law even though elsewhere in his judgment he stated the law correctly. For in the realm of diagnosis and treatment negligence is not established by preferring one *respectable* body of professional opinion to another. Failure to exercise the ordinary skill of a doctor (in the appropriate speciality, if he be a specialist) is necessary." (My emphasis.)

The judge held that the views of Dr Heaf and Dr Dinwiddie, though diametrically opposed, both represented a responsible body of professional opinion espoused by distinguished and truthful experts. Therefore, he held, Dr Horn, if she had attended and not intubated, would have come up to a proper level of skill and competence, ie the standard represented by Dr Dinwiddie's views. Accordingly, he held that it had not be proved that the admitted breach of duty by the defendants had caused the catastrophe with occurred to Patrick. ...

The Bolam test and causation
The locus classicus of the test for the standard of care required of a doctor or any other person professing some skill or competence is the direction to the jury given by McNair J in *Bolam* v *Friern Hospital Management Committee* [1957] 2 All ER 118 at 122:

"I myself would prefer to put it this way: a doctor is not guilty of negligence if he has acted in accordance with a practice accepted as proper by a responsible body of medical men skilled in that particular art ... Putting it the other way round, a doctor is not negligent, if he is acting in accordance with such a practice, merely because there is a body of opinion that takes a contrary view."

It was this test which Lord Scarman was repeating, in different words, in *Maynard*'s case in the passage by reference to which the judge directed himself. ...

Where, as in the present case, a breach of a duty of care is proved or admitted, the burden still lies on the plaintiff to prove that such breach caused the injury suffered (see *Bonnington Castings Ltd* v *Wardlaw* [1956] 1 All ER 615 and *Wilsher* v *Essex Area Health Authority* [1988] 1 All ER 871). In all cases, the primary question is one of fact: did the wrongful act cause the injury? But in cases where the breach of duty consists of an omission to do an act which ought to be done (eg the failure by a doctor to attend) that factual inquiry is, by definition, in the realms of hypothesis. The question is what would have happened if an event which by definition did not occur, had occured. In a case of non-attendance by a doctor, there may be cases in which there is a doubt as to which doctor would have attended if the duty had been fulfilled. But in this case there was no doubt: if the duty had been carried out it would have either been Dr Horn or Dr Rodger, the only two doctors at St Bartholomew's who had responsibility for Patrick and were on duty. Therefore in the present case, the first relevant question is "what would Dr Horn or Dr Rodger have done if they had attended?" As to Dr Horn, the judge accepted her evidence that she would not have intubated. By inference, although not expressly, the judge must have accepted that Dr Rodger also would not have intubated: as a senior house officer she would not have intubated without the approval of her senior registrar, Dr Horn.

Therefore the *Bolam* test had not part to play in determining the first question, viz what would have happened? Nor can I see any circumstances in which the *Bolam* test could be relevant to such a question.

However, in the present case, the answer to the question "what would have happened?" is not determinative of the issue of causation. At the trial the defendants accepted that if the professional standard of care required any doctor who attended to intubate Patrick, Patrick's claim must succeed. Dr Horn could not escape liability by proving that she would have failed to take the course which any competent doctor would have adopted. A defendant cannot escape liability by saying that the damage would have occurred in any event because he would have committed some other breach of duty thereafter. I have no doubt that this concession was rightly made by the defendants. But there is some difficulty in analysing why it was correct. ...

There were ... two questions for the judge to decide on causation: (1) What would Dr Horn have done, or authorised to be done, if she had attended Patrick? and (2) If she would not have intubated, would that have been negligent? The *Bolam* test has no relevance to the first of those questions but is central to the second.

There can be no doubt that, as the majority of the Court of Appeal held, the judge directed himself correctly in accordance with that approach ... the judge asked himself the right questions and answered them on the right basis. ...

My Lords, I agree ... that ... the court is not bound to hold that a defendant doctor escapes liability for negligent treatment or diagnosis just because he leads evidence from a number of medical experts who are genuinely of opinion that the defendant's treatment or diagnosis accorded with sound medical practice. In *Bolam*'s case [1957] 2 All ER 118 at 122 McNair J stated that the defendant had to have acted in accordance with the practice accepted as proper by a "*responsible* body of medical men" (my emphasis). Later he referred to "a standard of practice recognised as proper by a competent *reasonable* body of opinion" (see [1957] 2 All ER 118 at 122; my emphasis). Again, in the passage which I have cited from *Maynard*'s case, Lord Scarman refers to a "respectable" body of professional opinion. The use of these adjectives – responsible, reasonable and respectable – all show that the court has to be satisfied that the exponents of the body of opinion relied on can demonstrate that such opinion has a logical basis. In particular, in cases involving, as they so often do, the weighing of risks against benefits, the judge before accepting a body of opinion as being responsible, reasonable or respectable, will need to be satisfied that, in forming their views, the experts have directed their minds to the question of comparative risks and benefits and have reached a defensible conclusion on the matter. ...

I emphasise that, in my view, it will very seldom be right for a judge to reach the conclusion that views genuinely held by a competent medical expert are unreasonable. The assessment of medical risks and benefits is a matter of clinical judgment which a judge would not normally be able to make without expert evidence. As the quotation from Lord Scarman makes clear, it would be wrong to allow such assessment to deteriorate into seeking to persuade the judge to prefer one of two views both of which are capable of being logically supported. It is only where a judge can be satisfied that the body of expert opinion cannot be logically supported at all that such opinion will not provide the bench mark by reference to which the defendant's conduct falls to be assessed.

I turn to consider whether this is one of those rare cases. Like the Court of Appeal, in my judgment it plainly is not. ... when the evidence is looked at it is plainly not a case in which Dr Dinwiddie's views can be dismissed as illogical. ... it cannot be suggested that it was illogical for Dr Dinwiddie a most distinguished expert to favour running what, in his view, was a small risk of total respiratory collapse rather than to submit Patrick to the invasive procedure of intubation.'

Comment

For examples of cases where the court has found that professional opinion was not responsible, reasonable or respectable, see *Hucks* v *Cole* (1968) [1993] 4 Med LR 393 (failure to treat with penicillin) and *Edward Wong Finance Co Ltd* v *Johnson, Stokes & Master* [1984] AC 296 (completion of mortgage transaction in 'Hong Kong style').

See also *Shakoor* v *Situ* [2000] 4 All ER 181 (practitioner of traditionl Chinese herbal medicine found to have acted in accordance with standard of care appropriate to traditional Chinese herbal medicine as properly practised in accordance with standards required in United Kingdom and therefore had not been in breach of duty).

Bolton v *Stone* [1951] AC 850 House of Lords (Lords Porter, Normand, Oaksey, Reid and Radcliffe)

* *Negligence – injury from cricket ball*

Facts

The plaintiff was standing on the highway when she was hit by a cricket ball which had been struck from the defendant's adjoining cricket ground. The evidence showed that, in the many years that cricket had been played on the ground, only very occasionally had the ball been hit so far. The ball had travelled over 100 yards after being hit and had cleared a seven foot boundary fence. The plaintiff sued in, inter alia, negligence. In the House of Lords it was conceded that, in the circumstances, nuisance could not be established unless negligence was proved.

Held

The defendants were not negligent in failing to take steps to guard against such a small risk: such an injury would not have been anticipated by a reasonable man.

Lord Oaksey:

'An ordinary, careful man does not take precautions against every foreseeable risk. He can, of course, foresee the possibility of many risks, but life would be almost impossible if he were to attempt to take precautions against every risk which he can foresee. He takes precautions against risks which are reasonably likely to happen.'

Lord Reid:

'In the crowded conditions of modern life, even the most careful person cannot avoid creating some risks and accepting others. What a man must not do ... is to create a risk which is substantial.'

Comment
Distinguished in *Overseas Tankship (UK) Ltd v The Miller Steamship Co Pty Ltd (The Wagon Mound No 2)* [1966] 3 WLR 498. Applied in *Simms* v *Leigh Rugby Football Club Ltd* [1969] 2 All ER 923 (player's injury so improbable club not required to guard against it).

Condon v *Basi* [1985] 1 WLR 866
Court of Appeal (Sir John Donaldson MR, Stephen Brown LJ and Glidewell J)

• *Negligence – injury during football match*

Facts
The plaintiff and defendant were playing on opposite sides in a football match, and the defendant made a foul tackle on the plaintiff resulting in breaking the plaintiff's leg. The plaintiff claimed damages for negligence and assault.

Held
His claim should succeed. The duty of care between sports players is a duty to take reasonable care in the light of the circumstances in which they are playing. A player is negligent if he fails to exercise reasonable care *or* if he acts in a way to which another player cannot be expected to consent. On the facts of the case, there had been, in the words of the county court judge, 'serious and dangerous foul play which showed a reckless disregard of the plaintiff's safety'.

Sir John Donaldson MR:

'... if it is found by the tribunal of fact that the defendant failed to exercise that degree of care which was appropriate in all the circumstances, or that he acted in a way to which the plaintiff cannot be expected to have consented ... there is liability.'

Henderson v *Henry E Jenkins & Sons* [1969] 3 WLR 732 House of Lords (Viscount Dilhorne, Lords Reid, Guest, Donovan and Pearson)

• *Negligence – burden of proof*

Facts
While the respondents' five year old lorry was descending a steep hill, its brakes failed: the lorry struck and killed a van driver. A hole had developed in the brake fluid pipe, a very uncommon fault of which the lorry driver would have had no warning.

Held (Lord Guest and Viscount Dilhorne dissenting)
It was for the respondents to prove that, in all the circumstances which they knew or ought to have known, they took all proper steps to avoid danger. As they had failed to do this, the van driver's estate was entitled to damages.

Lord Pearson:

'... it seems to me clear, as a prima facie inference, that the accident must have been due to default of the respondents in respect of inspection or maintenance or both. Unless they had a satisfactory answer, sufficient to displace the inference, they should have been held liable.'

Comment
Applied in *Pearce* v *Round Oak Steel Works Ltd* [1969] 3 All ER 680 (plaintiff injured by machine in defendants' factory: burden on defendants to show had exercised reasonable care).

Luxmoore-May v *Messenger May Baverstock* [1990] 1 WLR 1009
Court of Appeal (Slade, Mann LJJ and Sir David Croom-Johnson)

• *Auctioneer – standard of care*

Facts

The plaintiffs owned two paintings of fox-hounds and they asked the defendant provincial auctioneers to look at them: their representative, Mrs Zarek, thought they were worth about £30 but took them away 'for research'. The defendants offered expert advice by a Mr Thomas, an independent contractor. He valued them at £30 to £50. Shortly before the sale, Mrs Zarek took the paintings to Christie's of London but they made no favourable comment about them. The paintings were sold at auction for £840: five months later they were sold at Sotheby's for £88,000: the plaintiffs sued for the difference.

Held

Their claim could not succeed as the defendants had not been guilty of negligence.

Slade LJ:

' ... I am of the opinion that the judge ... demanded too high a standard of skill on the part of the defendants and of Mr Thomas, in concluding that no competent valuer could have missed the signs of Stubbs [a noted 18th century sporting artist] potential. In my judgment, the question whether the foxhound pictures had Stubbs potential ... was one which competent valuers, and indeed competent dealers, could have held widely differing views. It has not been argued that a valuation of £30 to £40 would have been too low if these pictures were simply to be regarded as objects to be hung on a wall *without* Stubbs potential. For these reasons, I am of the opinion that negligence on the part of Mr Thomas has not been established, and accordingly that negligence on the part of the defendants would not have been established, even if Mrs Zarek, after taking Mr Thomas's advice, had taken no further advice in relation to the pictures.'

Comment

Applied: *Maynard* v *West Midlands Regional Health Authority* [1984] 1 WLR 634 (no liability since body of competent medical opinion thought defendants' acts reasonable).

McHale v *Watson* [1966] ALR 513 High Court of Australia (McTiernan ACJ, Kitto, Menzies and Owen JJ)

* *Negligence – standard of care*

Facts

The plaintiff girl was injured when a steel spike thrown by the defendant, a boy of 12, glanced off a post at which he was aiming and hit the plaintiff in the eye. The plaintiff had been standing about five feet to the left of the post.

Held

The defendant had not been negligent.

Kitto J:

'To expect a boy of that age to consider before throwing the spike whether the timber was hard or soft, to weigh the chances of being able to make the spike stick in the post and to foresee that it might glance off and hit the girl, would be, I think, to expect a degree of sense and circumspection which nature ordinarily withholds till life has become less rosy.'

Scott v *London & St Katherine Docks Co* (1865) 3 H & C 596 Court of Exchequer Chamber (Erle CJ, Crompton, Byles, Blackburn, Keating and Mellor JJ)

* *Negligence – res ipsa loquitur*

Facts

The plaintiff was passing the defendants' warehouse, where bags of sugar were being lowered by a crane, when he was struck and injured by a bag which apparently had fallen off the crane. The plaintiff relied on this fact alone as establishing negligence on the part of the defendants or their servants.

Held

There should be a new trial as there was evidence of negligence by the defendants' servants.

Erle CJ:

> 'The majority of the court have come to the following conclusion. There must be reasonable evidence of negligence, but, where the thing is shown to be under the management of the defendant, or his servants, and the accident is such as, in the ordinary course of things, does not happen if those who have the management of the machinery use proper care, it affords reasonable evidence, in the absence of explanation by the defendant, that the accident arose from want of care.'

Comment

Distinguished in *Stafford* v *Conti Commodity Services Ltd* [1981] 1 All ER 691 (investment decisions under plaintiff's, not defendants', management).

Sidaway v *Bethlem Royal Hospital Governors* [1985] AC 871 House of Lords (Lords Scarman, Diplock, Keith of Kinkel, Bridge of Harwich and Templeman)

• *Negligence – risk of misfortune*

Facts

The plaintiff underwent an operation on the spinal cord to relieve neck pain, and was told by the surgeon of the possibility of disturbing a nerve root and the consequences of that, but not of the possibility of danger to the spinal cord. As a result of the operation, the plaintiff was severely disabled. In the plaintiff's action for damage to her spinal cord, based on an alleged breach of duty to warn her of the risks involved, it was found that there was a 1 – 2 per cent risk of damage to nerve roots and an even lower percentage of risk of damage to the spinal cord.

Held (Lord Scarman dissenting)

The plaintiff's action would fail. The test was whether the surgeon had acted in accordance with a practice accepted at the time as proper by a responsible body of medical opinion.

Lord Bridge of Harwich:

> 'I can see no reasonable ground on which the judge could properly reject the conclusion to which the unchallenged medical evidence led in the application of the *Bolam* v *Friern Hosptial Management Committee* [1957] 2 All ER 118 test. The trial judge's assessment of the risk at 1 per cent or 2 per cent covered both nerve root and spinal cord damage and covered a spectrum of possible ill-effects 'ranging from the mild to the catastrophic'. In so far as it is possible and appropriate to measure such risks in percentage terms (some of the expert medical witnesses called expressed a marked and understandable reluctance to do so), the risk of damage to the spinal cord of such severity as the appellant in fact suffered was, it would appear, certainly less than 1 per cent. But there is no yardstick either in the judge's findings or in the evidence to measure what fraction of 1 per cent that risk represented. In these circumstances, the appellant's expert witness's agreement that the non-disclosure complained of accorded with a practice accepted as proper by a responsible body of neuro-surgical opinion afforded the respondents a complete defence to the appellant's claim.'

Ward v *Tesco Stores Ltd* [1976] 1 WLR 810 Court of Appeal (Megaw, Lawton and Ormrod LJJ)

• *Negligence – burden of proof*

Facts

The plaintiff was shopping in the defendants' supermarket when she slipped on some yoghurt which had been spilt on the floor. The evidence was that the floor was swept some six times a day and in addition, staff were instructed to deal promptly with spillages, which were a common occurence. The plaintiff was unable to say how long the yoghurt had been on the floor on the day she fell, but said that on a subsequent visit she had seen a spillage remain uncleared for some time. The plaintiff alleged the defendants were negligent in their maintenance of the floor.

Held (Ormrod LJ dissenting)
The plaintiff should succeed. She had made out a prima facie case which the defendant had not rebutted.

Megaw LJ:

'It is for the plaintiff to show that there has occurred an event which is unusual and which, in the absence of explanation, is more consistent with fault on the part of the defendants than the absence of fault; and to my mind the learned judge was wholly right in taking that view of the presence of this slippery liquid on the floor of the supermarket in the circumstances of this case: that is that the defendants knew or should have known that it was a not uncommon occurrence; and that if it should happen, and should not be promptly attended to, it created a serious risk that customers would fall and injure themselves. When the plaintiff has established that, the defendants can still escape from liability. They could escape from liability if they could show that the accident must have happened, or even on balance of probability would have been likely to have happened, irrespective of the existence of a proper and adequate system, in relation to the circumstances, to provide for the safety of customers. But, if the defendants wish to put forward such a case, it is for them to show that, on balance of probability, either by evidence or by inference from the evidence that is given or is not given, this accident would have been at least equally likely to have happened despite a proper system designed to give reasonable protection to customers. That, in this case, they wholly failed to do.'

Comment
See also *Bell v Department of Health and Social Security* (1989) The Times 13 June (defendant liable for plaintiff's slip on tea spilled on office floor).

Whitehouse v Jordan [1981] 1 WLR 246 House of Lords (Lords Wilberforce, Edmund-Davies, Fraser of Tullybelton, Russell of Killowen and Bridge of Harwich)

• *Negligence – error of judgment*

Facts
The defendant, a senior hospital registrar, delivered the plaintiff baby. The birth was a difficult one and the defendant decided to use forceps, but after pulling five or six times, he delivered the baby by Caesarean section. The prolonged use of the forceps resulted in brain damage to the plaintiff, who sued the defendant in negligence.

Held
Even if the defendant had pulled too hard and too long (which was not shown by the evidence to be the case), this did not here amount to legal negligence.

Lord Edmund-Davies:

'To say that a surgeon committed an error of clinical judgment is wholly ambiguous, for, while some such errors may be completely consistent with the due exercise of professional skill, other acts or omissions in the course of exercising "clinical judgment" may be so glaringly below proper standards as to make a finding of negligence inevitable. Indeed, I should have regarded this as a truism were it not that, despite the exposure of the "false antithesis" by Donaldson LJ in his dissenting judgment in the Court of Appeal, counsel for the defendants adhered to it before your Lordships. But doctors and surgeons fall into no special category, and, to avoid any future disputation of a similar kind, I would have it accepted that the true doctrine was enunciated, and by no means for the first time, by McNair J in *Bolam v Friern Hospital Management Committee* [1957] 1 WLR 582 at 586 in the following words:

" ... where you get a situation which involves the use of some special skill or competence, then the test as to whether there has been negligence or not is not the test of the man on the top of a Clapham omnibus because he has not got this special skill. The test is the standard of the ordinary skilled man exercising and professing to have that special skill."

If a surgeon fails to measure up to that standard in any respect ("clinical judgment" or otherwise), he has been negligent and should be so adjudged.'

Comment
Applied in *Clark* v *MacLennan* [1983] 1 All ER 416 (defendants liable for departure from general precautionary practice) and *Stafford* v *Conti Commodity Services Ltd* [1981] 1 All ER 691 (broker's error of judgment not necessarily negligence).

Wooldridge v *Sumner* [1963] 3 WLR 616 Court of Appeal (Sellers, Danckwerts and Diplock LJJ)

• *Negligence – injury to spectator*

Facts
The plaintiff, a photographer, was attending a horse show and was standing on the edge of the arena. One of the horses, owned by the defendant, suddenly panicked on one of the corners and began to gallop towards where the plaintiff was standing. In his attempt to move out of the way, the plaintiff was struck and injured by the horse.

Held
There had been no breach of duty by the defendant and the plaintiff's claim would fail.

Diplock LJ:

'A person attending a game or competition takes the risk of any damage caused to him by any act of a participant done in the course of and for the purposes of the game or competition, notwithstanding that such an act may involve an error of judgment or lapse of skill, unless the participant's conduct is such

as to evince a reckless disregard of the spectator's safety.

The spectator takes the risk because such an act involves no breach of the duty of care owed by the participant to him. He does not take the risk by virtue of the doctrine expressed or obscured by the maxim volenti non fit injuria. The maxim states a principle of estoppel applicable originally to a Roman citizen who consented to being sold as a slave. Although pleaded and argued below, it was only faintly relied on by counsel for the first defendant in this court. In my view, the maxim, in the absence of express contract, has no application to negligence simpliciter where the duty of care is based solely on proximity or 'neighbourship' in the Atkinian sense. The maxim in English law presupposes a tortious act by the defendant. The consent that is relevant is not consent to the risk of injury, but consent to the lack of reasonable care that may produce that risk and requires on the part of the plaintiff at the time at which he gives his consent full knowledge of the nature and extent of the risk that he ran. In *Dann* v *Hamilton* [1939] 1 KB 509, Asquith J expressed doubts whether the maxim ever could apply to license in advance a subsequent act of negligence, for if the consent precedes the act of negligence, the plaintiff cannot at that time have full knowledge of the extent as well as the nature of the risk which he will run. Asquith J, however, suggested that the maxim might, nevertheless, be applicable to cases where a dangerous physical condition had been brought about by the negligence of the defendant and the plaintiff with full knowledge of the existing danger elected to run the risk thereof. With the development of the law of negligence in the last twenty years, a more consistent explanation of this type of case is that the test of liability on the part of the person creating the dangerous physical condition is whether it was reasonably foreseeable by him that the defendant would so act in relation to it as to endanger himself. This is the principle which has been applied in the rescue cases (see *Cutler* v *United Dairies*

(London) Ltd [1933] 2 KB 297 and contrast *Haynes* v *Harwood* [1935] 1 KB 146) and the part of Asquith J's judgment in *Dann* v *Hamilton* dealing with the possible application of the maxim to the law of negligence was not approved by the Court of Appeal in *Ward* v *T E Hopkins & Son Ltd* [1959] 1 WLR 966. In the type of case envisaged by Asquith J, if I may adapt the words of Morris LJ in *Ward* v *Hopkins*, the plaintiff could not have agreed to run the risk that the defendant might be negligent, for the plaintiff would only play his part after the defendant had been negligent.'

Comment
Applied in *Nettleship* v *Weston* [1971] 3 WLR 370 (defendant must agree, expressly or impliedly, to waive any claim) and *White* v *Blackmore* [1972] 3 WLR 296 (volenti non fit injuria not available where spectator's injury arises from lack of reasonable safety precautions). See also *Wilks* v *The Cheltenham Home Guard Motor Cycle and Light Car Club* [1971] 1 WLR 668 (motorcycle scramble rider not liable for spectator's injury since no evidence of negligence and res ipsa loquitur not applicable).

8   Negligence: Causation

Allied Maples Group Ltd v Simmons & Simmons [1995] 1 WLR 1602
Court of Appeal (Stuart-Smith, Hobhouse and Millett LJJ)

- *Causation – loss of a chance*

Facts
The plaintiffs wished to purchase certain properties from G. Four of these properties could not be conveyed to the plaintiffs because there were conditions against alienation or planning consents which were personal to G's subsidiary, K Ltd, in which the properties were vested. The plaintiffs, on the advice of the defendant solicitors, acquired all the shares in K Ltd, intending to sell the unwanted properties of K and keep the four desired. However, some of the properties owned by K had liabilities which, after the acquisition, resulted in claims against K, and hence the plaintiffs. The plaintiffs sued the defendants to recover their losses. In the High Court it was held that the plaintiffs were entitled to succeed because if the defendants had given the advice on liability which they ought to have given, the plaintiffs would have taken steps to obtain a warranty from G or to protect themselves in some other way. The defendants appealed to the Court of Appeal.

Held
The appeal would be dismissed. Where the plaintiff's loss depends on the hypothetical action of a third party, the plaintiff can succeed if he shows that he had a substantial chance rather than a speculative one. He does not have to prove on the balance of probabilities that the third party would have acted so as to confer a benefit or avoid the risk to the plaintiff. If he proves as a matter of causation that he has a real or substantial chance as opposed to a speculative one, the evaluation of the chance is part of the assessment of the quantum of damage, the range lying somewhere between something that just qualifies as real or substantial on the one hand, and near certainty on the other.

Stuart-Smith LJ:

'In these circumstances, where the plaintiffs' loss depends upon the actions of an independent third party, it is necessary to consider as a matter of law what is necessary to establish as a matter of causation, and where causation ends and quantification of damage begins. (1) What has to be proved to establish a causal link between the negligence of the defendants and the loss sustained by the plaintiffs depends in the first instance on whether the negligence consists in some positive act or misfeasance, or an omission or non-feasance. In the former case, the question of causation is one of historical fact ... (2) If the defendant's negligence consists of an omission, for example ... to give proper ... advice, causation depends, not upon a question of historical fact, but on the answer to the hypothetical question, what would the plaintiff have done if the ... advice [had been] given. This can only be a matter of inference to be determined from all the circumstances ... Although the question is a hypothetical one, it is well established that the plaintiff must prove on the balance of probability that he would have taken action to obtain the benefit or avoid the risk. But again, if he does establish that, there is no discount because the balance is only just tipped in his favour ... (3) In many cases the plaintiff's loss depends on the hypothetical action of a third party, either in addition to action by

92

the plaintiff, as in this case, or independently of it. In such a case does the plaintiff have to prove on the balance of probability … that the third party would have acted so as to confer the benefit or avoid the risk to the plaintiff, or can the plaintiff succeed provided that he shows that he had a substantial chance rather than a speculative one, the evaluation of the substantial chance being a question of quantification of damages?'

Comment

The *Allied Maples* approach was adopted by Chadwick J in *Acton* v *Graham Pearce & Co* [1997] 3 All ER 909 and applied by the Court of Appeal in *Blue Circle Industries plc* v *Ministry of Defence* [1998] 3 All ER 385 (damages awarded for breach of statutory duty properly reflected lost chance to sell land concerned).

Baker v *Willoughby* [1970] 2 WLR 50 House of Lords (Viscount Dilhorne, Lords Reid, Guest, Donovan and Pearson)

- *Damages – subsequent further injury*

Facts

The plaintiff was knocked down by the defendant whilst crossing the road. The effect of the injuries was to reduce the movement in his left leg so that he could no longer carry on with his previous employment. Shortly afterwards, the plaintiff was shot in the leg by robbers and had to have his left leg amputated. What was the extent of the defendant's liability?

Held

The second injury was irrelevant for the purpose of assessing the damages to which the plaintiff was entitled in respect of the first injury.

Lord Reid:

'A man is not compensated for the physical injury; he is compensated for the loss which he suffers as a result of that injury. His loss

is not in having a staff leg; it is in his inability to lead a full life, his inability to enjoy those amenities which depend on freedom of movement and his inability to earn as much as he used to earn or could have earned if there had been no accident. In this case, the second injury did not diminish any of these. So why should it be regarded as having obliterated or superseded them?'

Comment

Doubted and not followed in *Jobling* v *Associated Dairies Ltd* [1981] 3 WLR 155.

Barnett v *Chelsea & Kensington Hospital Management Committee* [1968] 2 WLR 422 High Court (Nield J)

- *Negligence – cause of death*

Facts

After drinking tea, the plaintiff's husband went to the casualty department of the defendants' hospital complaining of stomach pains and vomiting. A doctor was contacted, but did not come to examine the husband and sent a message that he should go home to bed and call his own doctor. The plaintiff's husband died shortly after from arsenic poisoning.

Held

Although the doctor had been negligent in failing to examine the deceased, the defendants were not liable because this was not the cause of his death.

Nield J:

'It remains to consider whether it is shown that the deceased's death was caused by this negligence or whether, as the defendants have said, the deceased must have died in any event. In his concluding submission counsel for the plaintiff submitted that Dr Banerjee should have examined the deceased and, had he done so, he would have caused tests to be made which would have indicated the treatment required and that, since the defendants were at fault in these respects, therefore the onus of proof passed to the defendants to show that the appropriate treatment would have failed, and authorities were cited to me. I find myself unable to accept this argument and I am of the view that the onus of proof remains on the plaintiff ... However, were it otherwise and the onus did pass to the defendants, then I would find that they have discharged it.'

Comment
See also *Hotson* v *East Berkshire Area Health Authority* [1987] 3 WLR 232.

Galoo Ltd v *Bright Grahame Murray* [1994] 1 WLR 1360 Court of Appeal (Glidewell, Evans and Waite LJJ)

• *Negligence – causation*

Facts
It was contended, inter alia, that the defendant auditors had owed the plaintiff purchaser of shares in another company a duty of care when preparing accounts which, to their (the defendants') knowledge, were to be relied on by the plaintiffs in calculating the purchase price of the shares and were to be prepared for that specific purpose.

Held
The judge had been correct in refusing to strike out this part of the plaintiffs' claim.

Glidewell LJ:

'The distinction between the set of facts which it was held in *Morgan Crucible Co plc* v *Hill Samuel Bank Ltd* [1990] 3 All ER 330 would suffice to establish a duty of care owed by auditors from those facts which it was held in *Caparo Industries plc* v *Dickman* [1990] 1 All ER 568 would not have this effect is inevitably a fine one. In my judgment that distinction may be expressed as follows. Mere foreseeability that a potential bidder may rely on the audited accounts does not impose on the auditor a duty of care to the bidder, but if the auditor is expressly made aware that a particular identified bidder will rely on the audited accounts or other statements approved by the auditor, and intends that the bidder should so rely, the auditor will be under a duty of care to the bidder for the breach of which he may be liable.'

Comment
Distinguished in *Sasea Finance Ltd* v *KPMG* [2000] 1 All ER 676 (auditors' duty to 'blow the whistle').

See also *British Racing Drivers Club Ltd* v *Hextall Erskine & Co* [1996] 3 All ER 667 (solicitors' negligent advice effective cause of loss).

Hotson v *East Berkshire Area Health Authority* [1987] 3 WLR 232 House of Lords (Lords Bridge of Harwich, Brandon of Oakbrook, Mackay of Clashfern, Ackner and Goff of Chieveley)

• *Negligence – causation*

Facts
A boy aged 13, the plaintiff, injured his hip in a fall. He was taken to the defendants' hospital; the injury was not correctly diagnosed and he was sent home. Even if a correct diagnosis had been made, there was a 75 per cent risk that the boy's disability would have developed, but the medical staff's breach of duty had turned the risk into an inevitability.

Held
The boy was without a remedy.

Lord Ackner:

'... the plaintiff was not entitled to any damages in respect of the deformed hip because the judge had decided that this was not caused by the admitted breach by the authority of their duty of care but was caused ... when he fell some 12 feet from a rope on which he had been swinging.'

Comment
See also *Barnett* v *Chelsea & Kensington Hospital Management Committee* [1968] 2 WLR 422.

Jobling v *Associated Dairies Ltd*
[1981] 3 WLR 155 House of Lords (Lords Wilberforce, Edmund-Davies, Russell of Killowen, Keith of Kinkel and Bridge of Harwich)

• *Injury – subsequent further injury*

Facts
In 1973 the plaintiff slipped and fell in the course of his employment as a result of a breach of statutory duty by his employer, the defendants. His back was injured and in consequence his earning capacity was reduced by 50 per cent. In 1976 the plaintiff was found to be suffering from spondylotic myelopathy, a spinal disease which was unrelated to the accident but which made him totally unfit to work. The trial of his claim against the defendants took place in 1979.

Held
The defendants were not liable for any loss of earnings suffered by the plaintiff after the onset of the disease in 1976.

Lord Wilberforce:

"We do not live in a world governed by the pure common law and its logical rules. We live in a mixed world where a man is protected against injury and misfortune by a whole web of rules and dispositions with a number of timid legislative interventions. To attempt to compensate him on the basis of selected rules without regard to the whole must lead either to logical inconsistencies or to over or under-compensation. As my noble and learned friend Lord Edmund-Davies has pointed out, no account was taken in *Baker* v *Willoughby* [1970] 2 WLR 50 of the very real possibility that the plaintiff might obtain compensation from the Criminal Injuries Compensation Board. If

he did in fact obtain this compensation he would, on the ultimate decision, be over-compensated.

In the present case, and in other industrial injury cases, there seems to me no justification for disregarding the fact that the injured man's employer is insured (indeed since 1972 compulsorily insured) against liability to his employees. The state has decided, in other words, on a spreading of risk. There seems to me no more justification for disregarding the fact that the plaintiff (presumably; we have not been told otherwise) is entitled to sickness and invalidity benefit in respect of his myelopathy, the amount of which may depend on his contribution record, which in turn may have been affected by his accident. So we have no means of knowing whether the plaintiff would be over-compensated if he were, in addition, to receive the assessed damages from his employer, or whether he would be under-compensated if left to his benefit. It is not easy to accept a solution by which a partially incapacitated man becomes worse off in terms of damages and benefit through a greater degree of incapacity. Many other ingredients, of weight in either direction, may enter into individual cases. Without any satisfaction I draw from this the conclusion that no general, logical or universally fair rules can be stated which will cover, in a manner consistent with justice, cases of supervening events, whether due to tortious, partially tortious, non-culpable or wholly accidental events.

If rationalisation is needed, I am willing to accept the "vicissitudes" argument as the best available. I should be more firmly convinced of the merits of the conclusion if the whole pattern of benefits had been considered, in however general a way. The result of the present case may be lacking in precision and rational justification, but so long as we are content to live in a mansion of so many different architectures this is inevitable.'

Comment
Doubted and not followed: *Baker* v *Willoughby* [1970] 2 WLR 50.

Kay v Ayrshire and Arran Health Board [1987] 2 All ER 417 House of Lords (Lords Keith of Kinkel, Brandon of Oakbrook, Griffiths, Mackay of Clashfern and Ackner)

• *Negligence – causation*

Facts
A boy suffering from pneumococcal meningitis was negligently given an overdose of penicillin. After recovering from the meningitis he was found to be suffering from deafness. Expert evidence on behalf of the hospital was to the effect that there was no recorded case of a penicillin overdose having caused deafness, although it was a common sequela of meningitis.

Held
Where there were two competing causes of damage, the law could not presume that the tortious cause was responsible if it was not first proved that it was an accepted fact that the tortious cause was capable of causing or aggravating such damage. Accordingly, in the light of the evidence, the deafness had to be regarded as resulting solely from the meningitis and the boy's claim would therefore fail.

Lord Ackner:

'[the boy] can derive no assistance from your Lordships' decision in *McGhee* v *National Coal Board* [1973] 1 WLR 1. In *McGhee*'s case the absence of washing facilities was known to be a factor which increased the risk of dermatitis arising from the circumstances in which the pursuer worked. In this case, as previously stated, there is no evidence to incriminate the overdose of intrathecal penicillin. Moreover, if, contrary to the view which I have expressed, the decision in *McGhee*'s case can be used to transfer to the respondents the onus of establishing that the excessive injection of penicillin did not cause the deafness, then in my judgment they have discharged that onus.'

Comment
Distinguished: *McGhee* v *National Coal Board* [1973] 1 WLR 1 which was applied in *Page* v *Smith (No 2)* [1996] 3 All ER 272.

McGhee v National Coal Board [1973] 1 WLR 1 House of Lords (Lords Reid, Wilberforce, Simon of Glaisdale, Kilbrandon and Salmon)

• *Negligence – causation*

Facts
The respondent employers sent the appellant to clean out brick kilns, but they negligently failed to provide him with adequate washing facilities. In consequence, he cycled home, continuing to exert himself, covered in sweat and grime. He was found to be suffering from dermatitis caused by working conditions in the brick kilns, but his journeys home had added materially to the risk that he might develop the disease.

Held
The respondents were liable.

Lord Salmon:

'I would suggest that the true view is that, as a rule, when it is proved, on a balance of probabilities, that an employer has been negligent and that his negligence has materially increased the risk of his employee contracting an industrial disease, then he is liable in damages to that employee if he contracts the disease notwithstanding that the employer is not responsible for other factors which have materially contributed to the disease.

... In the circumstances of the present case, the possibility of a distinction existing between (a) having materially increased the risk of contracting the disease, and (b) having materially contributed to causing the disease may no doubt be a fruitful source of interesting academic discussions between students of philosophy. Such a distinction is, however, far too unreal to be recognised by the common law.'

Comment
Distinguished in *Kay* v *Ayrshire and Arran Health Board* [1987] 2 All ER 417. Applied in *Page* v *Smith (No 2)* [1996] 3 All ER 272.

Performance Cars Ltd v *Abraham*
[1961] 3 WLR 749 Court of Appeal (Lord Evershed MR, Harman and Donovan LJJ)

• *Negligence – successive torts*

Facts
The plaintiffs' car was damaged in an accident and the respraying of the lower part of its body was necessary as a result. Two weeks later, and before the car had been resprayed, it was involved in a collision with the defendant's car. The defendant admitted liability and respraying of the lower part of the car was again required. Could the plaintiffs recover the cost of this respraying from the defendant?

Held
No, because that damage did not flow from the defendant's wrongful act.

Lord Evershed MR:

'In my judgment in the present case the defendant should be taken to have injured a motor car that was already injured in certain respects, that is, in respect of the need for respraying; and the result is that to the extent of that need or injury the damage claimed did not flow from the defendant's wrongdoing. It may no doubt be unfortunate for the plaintiffs that the collisions took place in the order in which they did. Had the first collision been that brought about by the defendant and had they recovered the £75 now in question from him, they could not clearly have recovered the same sum again from the other wrongdoer. It is, however, in my view irrelevant (if unfortunate for the plaintiffs) that the judgment obtained against the other wrongdoer has turned out to be worthless.'

9   Negligence: Remoteness of Damage

Hughes v *Lord Advocate* [1963] 2
WLR 779 House of Lords (Lords
Reid, Jenkins, Morris of Borth-y-
Gest, Guest and Pearce)

• *Negligence – foreseeability of damage*

Facts
Post Office employees had opened a manhole
in order to carry out repairs on the highway.
A tent was placed over the open manhole and
there were paraffin lamps around the tent. The
entrance to the tent was blocked by a ladder
and a tarpaulin. In the absence of the employees, the plaintiff, aged ten, went into the tent
with a paraffin lamp. He fell and dropped the
lamp into the hole. An explosion resulted and
he was severely burned.

Held
The plaintiff's injuries were of the same kind
as those which were reasonably foreseeable
and thus not too remote: he could recover
damages for negligence.

Lord Pearce:

'The dangerous allurement was left
unguarded in a public highway in the heart
of Edinburgh. It was for the respondent to
show by evidence that, although this was a
public street, the presence of children there
was so little to be expected that a reasonable man might leave the allurement
unguarded. But in my opinion their evidence fell short of that ...

The defenders are therefore liable for all
the foreseeable consequences of their
neglect. When an accident is of a different
type and kind from anything that a defender
could have foreseen he is not liable for it ...
But to demand too great precision in the test

of foreseeability would be unfair to the
pursuer since the facets of misadventure are
innumerable ... In the case of an allurement
to children it is particularly hard to foresee
with precision the exact shape of the disaster
that will arise. The allurement in this case
was the combination of a red paraffin lamp,
a ladder, a partially closed tent, and a cav-
ernous hole within it, a setting well-fitted to
inspire some juvenile adventure that might
end in calamity. The obvious risks were
burning and conflagration and a fall. All
these in fact occurred, but unexpectedly the
mishandled lamp instead of causing an ordinary conflagration produced a violent explosion. Did the explosion create an accident
and damage of a different type from the misadventure and damage that could be foreseen? In my judgment it did not. The accident was but a variant of the foreseeable ...
No unforeseeable extraneous, initial occurrence fired the train. The children's entry
into the tent with the ladder, the descent into
the hole, the mishandling of the lamp, were
all foreseeable. The greater part of the path
to injury had thus been trodden, and the mishandled lamp was quite likely at that stage
to spill and cause a conflagration. Instead,
by some curious chance of combustion, it
exploded and no conflagration occurred, it
would seem, until after the explosion. There
was thus an unexpected manifestation of the
apprehended physical dangers. But it would
be, I think, too narrow a view to hold that
those who created the risk of fire are
excused from the liability for the damage
by fire, because it came by way of explosive combustion. The resulting damage,
though severe, was not greater than or different in kind from that which might have
been produced had the lamp spilled and produced a more normal conflagration in the
hole.'

Lord Reid:

'The cause of the accident – the lamp – was a known source of danger, but the way in which it behaved was unforeseeable. This does not absolve the defendant because the accident was caused by a known danger, but caused in a way which could not have been foreseen. That is no defence.'

Comment

Applied in *Bradford* v *Robinson Rentals Ltd* [1967] 1 WLR 337 (injury foreseeable in severe cold) and *Ogwo* v *Taylor* [1987] 3 WLR 1145. Distinguished in *Doughty* v *Turner Manufacturing Co Ltd* [1964] 2 WLR 240 (damage different kind from foreseeable splash).

Distinguished: *Glasgow Corporation* v *Muir* [1943] AC 448 (no reasonable person would have anticipated danger to children).

See also *Jolley* v *Sutton London Borough Council* [2000] 3 All ER 409.

Jolley v *Sutton London Borough Council* [2000] 3 All ER 409 House of Lords (Lords Browne-Wilkinson, Mackay of Clashfern, Steyn, Hoffmann and Hobhouse of Woodborough)

* *Occupier's liability – children – accident reasonably foreseeable*

Facts

The defendants left lying (for at least two years) a boat on their land outside some flats. The 14-year-old claimant and his friend decided to repair it. They jacked it up but, while they were at work, the boat fell on the claimant and caused him serious injuries. The defendants accepted that they had been negligent in failing to remove the boat but contended that the accident was not one that they could have reasonably foreseen. The Court of Appeal accepted this contention: the claimant appealed against this decision.

Held

The appeal would be allowed since the accident had been reasonably foreseeable.

Lord Hoffmann:

'The issue in this appeal is a very narrow one. The council admits that it was the occupier of the grassed area near the flats where the plaintiff lived, that plaintiff was allowed to play there and that he was accordingly a "visitor" upon its land within the meaning of the Occupiers' Liability Act 1957: see s1(2). The council therefore owed the plaintiff the "common duty of care" defined in s2(2) of the Act: ... By way of further explanation, s1(3) says that the relevant circumstances will include "the degree of care, and of want of care, which would ordinarily be look for in such a visitor" so that, for example, in proper cases " an occupier must be prepared for children to be less careful than adults".

It is also agreed that the plaintiff must show that the injury which he suffered fell within the scope of the council's duty and that in cases of physical injury, the scope of the duty is determined by whether or not the injury fell within a description which could be said to have been reasonably foreseeable. *Donoghue* v *Stevenson* [1932] AC 562 of course established the general principle that reasonable foreseeability of physical injury to another generates a duty of care. The further proposition that reasonable foreseeability also governs the question of whether the injury comes within the scope of that duty had to wait until *Overseas Tankship (UK) Ltd* v *Morts Dock and Engineering Co Ltd, The Wagon Mound (No 1)* [1961] 1 All ER 404 for authoritative recognition. Until then, there was a view that the determination of liability involved a two-stage process. The existence of a duty depended upon whether injury of some kind was foreseeable. Once such a duty had been established, the defendant was liable for any injury which had been "directly caused" by an act in breach of that duty, whether such injury was reasonably foreseeable or not. But the present law is that unless the injury is of a description which was reasonably foreseeable, it is (according to taste) "outside the scope of the duty" or "too remote".

It is also agreed that what must have been foreseen is not the precise injury which occurred but injury of a given description. The foreseeability is not as to the particulars but the genus. And the description is formulated by reference to the nature of the risk which ought to have been forseen. So, in *Hughes* v *Lord Advocate* [1963] 1 All ER 705 the foreseeable risk was that a child would be injured by falling in the hole or being burned by a lamp or by a combination of both. The House of Lords decided that the injury which actually materialised fell within this description, notwithstanding that it involved an unanticipated explosion of the lamp and consequent injuries of unexpected severity. Like my noble and learned friend Lord Steyn, I can see no inconsistency between anything said in *The Wagon Mound (No 1)* and the speech of Lord Reid in *Hughes'* case. The two cases were dealing with altogether different questions. In the former, it was agreed that damage by burning was not damage of a description which could reasonably be said to have been foreseeable. The plaintiffs argued that they were nevertheless entitled to recover by the two-stage process I have described. It was this argument which was rejected. *Hughes*'s case starts from the principle accepted in *The Wagon Mound (No 1)* and is concerned with whether the injury which happened was of a description which was reasonably foreseeable.

The short point in the present appeal is therefore whether the judge was right in saying in general terms that the risk was that children would "meddle with the boat at the risk of some physical injury" ... or whether the Court of Appal were right in saying that the only foreseeable risk was of "children who were drawn to the boat climbing upon it and being injured by the rotten planking giving way beneath them" ... Was the wider risk, which would include within its description the accident which actually happened, reasonably foreseeable?

My Lords, although this is in end the question of fact, the courts are not without guidance. "Reasonable foreseeable" is not a fixed point on the scale of probability. As Lord Reid explained in *The Wagon Mound (No 2), Overseas Tankship (UK) Ltd* v *Miller Steamship Co Pty Ltd* [1966] 2 All ER 709 at 718, other factors have to be considered in deciding whether a given probability of injury generates a duty to take steps to eliminate the risk. In that case, the matters which the Privy Council took into account were whether avoiding the risk would have involved the defendant in undue cost or required him to abstain from some otherwise reasonable activity. In *Bolton* v *Stone* [1951] 1 All ER 1078, there was a foreseeable risk that someone might one day be hit by a cricket ball but avoiding this risk would have required the club to incur very large expense or stop playing cricket. The House of Lords decided that the risk was not such that a reasonable man should have taken either of these steps to eliminate it. On the other hand, in *The Wagon Mound (No 2)*, the risk was caused by the fact that the defendant's ship had, without any need or excuse, discharged oil into Sydney Harbour. The risk of the oil catching fire would have been regarded as extremely small. But, said Lord Reid:

"It does not follow that, no matter what the circumstances may be, it is justifiable to neglect a risk of such a small magnitude. A reasonable man would only neglect such a risk if he had some valid reason for doing so: eg, that it would involve considerable expense to eliminate the risk. He would weigh the risk against the difficulty of eliminating it."

My Lords, in this calculation it seems to me that the concession by the council is of significance. The council admit that they should have removed the boat. True, they make this concession solely on the ground that there was a risk that children would suffer minor injuries if the rotten planking gave way beneath them. But the concession shows that if there were a wider risk, the council would have had to incur no additional expense to eliminate it. They would only have had to do what they admit they should have done anyway. On the principle as stated by Lord Reid, the wider risk would also fall within the scope of the council's duty unless it was different in kind from that which should have been foreseen (like the fire and pollution risks in *The Wagon Mound (No 1)*) and either wholly unforeseeable (as the fire risk was assumed to be in *The Wagon Mound (No 1)*) or so remote that it could be "brushed aside as far-fetched": see *The Wagon Mound (No 2)* [1966] 2 All ER 709 at 719 per Lord Reid. ...

In the present case, the rotten condition of the boat had a significance beyond the particular danger it created. It proclaimed the boat and its trailer as abandoned, res nullius, there for the taking, to make of them whatever use the rich fantasy life of children might suggest.

In the Court of Appeal, Lord Woolf MR ... observed that there seemed to be no case of which counsel were aware "where want of care on the part of a defendant was established but a plaintiff, who was a child, has failed to succeed because the circumstances of the accident were not foreseeable". I would suggest that this is for a combination of three reasons: first, because a finding or admission of want of care on the part of the defendant establishes that it would have cost the defendant no more trouble to avoid the injury which happened that he should in any case have taken; secondly, because in such circumstances the defendants will be liable for the materialisation of even relatively small risks of a different kind, and thirdly, because it has been repeatedly said in cases about children that their ingenuity in finding unexpected ways of doing mischief to themselves and others should never be underestimated. For those reasons, I think that the judge's broad description of the risk as being that children would "meddle with the boat at the risk of some physical injury" was the correct one to adopt on the facts of this case. The actual injury fell within that description and I would therefore allow the appeal.'

Knightley v *Johns* [1982] 1 WLR 349 Court of Appeal (Stephenson and Dunn LJJ and Sir David Cairns)

* *Negligence – remoteness of damage*

Facts
A serious road accident had occurred near the exit of a tunnel which carried one-way traffic. The accident had been caused by the negligence of the first defendant. The police inspector in charge at the scene realised that he had forgotten to close the tunnel to oncoming traffic. This was particularly important as there was a sharp bend in the middle of the tunnel which obscured the exit, as well as the site of the first defendant's accident, to drivers entering the tunnel. The police inspector ordered two officers on motor cycles to go back and close off the tunnel. The two officers, one of whom was the plaintiff, rode into the tunnel against the oncoming traffic. Near the tunnel entrance the plaintiff collided with a motorist who, on the facts, was held not to have been negligent. Both the inspector in giving the order and the plaintiff in obeying the order were acting contrary to Standing Orders. The plaintiff claimed damages from, inter alia, the first defendant.

Held
The inspector had been guilty of negligence and this had been the real cause of the plaintiff's injuries. It was also a new cause, disturbing and interrupting the sequence of events between the first defendant's accident and that of the plaintiff. The inspector (and his chief constable) were liable in respect of the plaintiff's injuries; the first defendant was not.

Stephenson LJ:

'In the long run the question is ... one of remoteness of damage, to be answered, as has so often been stated, not by the logic of philosophers but by the common sense of plain men ... In my judgment, too much happened here, too much went wrong, the chapter of accidents and mistakes was too long and varied, to impose on [the first defendant] liability for what happened to the plaintiff in discharging his duty as a police officer, although it would not have happened had not [the first defendant] negligently overturned his car. The ordinary course of things took an extraordinary course.'

Comment

See also *Hill* v *Chief Constable of West Yorkshire* [1989] AC 53.

Overseas Tankship (UK) Ltd v *Morts Dock & Engineering Co Ltd, The Wagon Mound (No 1)* [1961] 1 All ER 404 Privy Council (Viscount Simonds, Lords Reid, Radcliffe, Tucker and Morris of Borth-y-Gest)

• *Negligence – remoteness of damages*

Facts

Through the carelessness of the appellants' servants, a large quantity of bunkering oil was spilt into a bay while a vessel was discharging gasoline products and taking in oil. It was found as a fact that the appellants did not know, and could not reasonably have been expected to know, that the oil was capable of being set alight when spread on water. Molten metal falling from the respondents' wharf set fire to some cotton waste floating in the oil, which in turn ignited the oil itself and caused a serious fire. Considerable damage was done to the respondents' wharf and equipment.

Held

The appellants were not liable for the damage since they could not reasonably have foreseen it.

Viscount Simonds:

'It is a principle of civil liability, subject only to qualifications which have no present relevance, that a man must be considered to be responsible for the probable consequences of his act. To demand more of him is too harsh a rule; to demand less is to

ignore that civilised order requires the observance of a minimum standard of behaviour. This concept, applied to the slowly developing law of negligence, has led to a great variety of expressions which can, as it appears to their Lordships, be harmonised with little difficulty with the single exception of the so-called rule *Polemis*. For, if it is asked why a man should be responsible for the natural or necessary or probable consequences of his act (or any other similar description of them) the answer is that it is not because they are natural or necessary or probable, but because since they have this quality, it is judged by the standard of the reasonable man, that he ought to have foreseen them. Thus, it is that, over and over again, it has happened that in different judgments in the case and sometimes in a single judgment, liability for a consequence has been imposed on the ground that it was reasonably foreseeable, or alternatively on the ground that it was natural or necessary or probable. The two grounds have been treated as coterminous and so they largely are. But, where they are not, the question arises to which the wrong answer was given in *Polemis*. For, if some limitation must be imposed on the consequences for which the negligent actor is to be held responsible – and all are agreed that some limitation there must be – why should that test (reasonable foreseeability) be rejected which, since he is judged by what the reasonable man ought to foresee, corresponds with the common conscience of mankind and a test (the 'direct' consequence) be substituted which leads to nowhere but the never ending and insoluble problems of causation.'

Comment

Disapproved: *Re Polemis and Furness, Withy & Co Ltd* [1921] 3 KB 560.

Applied in *Doughty* v *Turner Manufacturing Co Ltd* [1964] 2 WLR 240.

Distinguished in *Overseas Tankship (UK) Ltd* v *The Miller Steamship Co Pty Ltd, The Wagon Mound (No 2)* [1966] 3 WLR 498 (arising from same spillage, fire damaged respondents' ships: damage not too remote).

See also *Jolley* v *Sutton London Borough Council* [2000] 3 All ER 409.

Scott **v** *Shepherd* (1773) 2 Wm Bl 892 Court of Common Pleas (De Grey CJ, Nares, Blackstone and Gould JJ)

- *Squib – chain of causation*

Facts

The defendant threw a lighted squib into a covered market: it fell on Yates's gingerbread stall and to save himself and the wares Willis picked it up and threw it across the market house. It landed on Ryal's stall and he, to save his goods, threw it away: it struck the plaintiff in the face, exploded and put out one of his eyes. The plaintiff sought damages for trespass and assault.

Held (Blackstone J dissenting)

His action would be successful.

Nares J:

'I am of opinion that trespass would well lie in the present case. The natural and probable consequence of the act done by the defendant was injury to somebody, and, therefore, the act was illegal at common law ... Being, therefore, unlawful, the defendant was liable to answer for the consequences, be the injury mediate or immediately ... malus animus is not necessary to constitute a trespass ... The principle I go on is ... that if the act in the first instance be unlawful, trespass will lie. Wherever, therefore, an act is unlawful at first, trespass will lie for the consequences of it ... I do not think it necessary, to maintain trespass, that the defendant should personally touch the plaintiff; if he does it by a mean it is sufficient. Qui facit per aliud facit per se. He is the person who, in the present case, gave the mischievous faculty to the squib. That mischievous faculty remained in it until the explosion. No new power of doing mischief was communicated to it by Willis or Ryal. It is like the case of a mad ox turned loose in a crowd. The person who turns him loose is answerable in trespass for whatever mischief he may do. The intermediate acts of Willis and Ryal will not purge the original tort in the defendant. But he who does the first wrong is answerable for all the consequential damages ...'

10 Contributory Negligence

Alliance & Leicester Building Society v Edgestop Ltd [1993] 1 WLR 1462 High Court (Mummery J)

- *Contributory negligence – availability of defence in action for deceit*

Facts

A private unlimited company of estate agents was sued by the plaintiff building society claiming that the estate agents were vicariously liable for the deceit of one of its former employees. The defendants pleaded contributory negligence. The question arose on a striking out application as to whether in law the defendants were entitled to plead such a defence to a claim in deceit. The master held that this was not possible: the defendants appealed.

Held

The appeal would be dismissed.

Mummery J:

'There is no decision precisely on the point whether contributory negligence could be a defence to a claim for deceit. In principle, however, the position, before and apart, from the [Law Reform (Contributory Negligence) Act 1945] is clear. The contributory negligence of a plaintiff suing in deceit could not be pleaded as a defence. There are at least three reasons for this. (1) At common law contributory negligence of a plaintiff is no defence in the case of an intentional tort. As Lord Lindley said in *Quinn* v *Leathem* [1901] AC 495 at 537: "The intention to injury the plaintiff negatives all excuses ..." ... Deceit is a tort intentionally committed. (2) At common law a successful plea of contributory negligence would have startling consequences in the context of deceit. Before and apart from the Act, contributory negligence of a plaintiff would defeat the plaintiff's entire claim. Apart from the case of property damage at sea, governed by s1 of the Maritime Conventions Act 1911, there was no power to apportion liability on the grounds of blameworthiness. If the plea of contributory negligence were available to a person against whom deceit was established he would escape all liability for his fraud. The result would be even more absurd and unjust than that in negligence cases where a plaintiff who had suffered serious damage, mainly as a result of the defendant's negligence, could recover nothing if he were partly to blame for the damage he had suffered. (3) That result would also have offended against the general principle stated by Jessel MR in *Redgrave* v *Hurd* (1881) 20 Ch D 1. He laid down general principles applicable in misrepresentation cases. Although that case was decided in the context of the equitable remedies of specific performance and rescission, his statements have been treated for over a century as applicable to claims for damages for misrepresentation. He said (at 13–14):

"Nothing can be plainer, I take it, on the authorities in equity than that the effect of false representation is not got rid of on the ground that the person to whom it was made had been guilty of negligence.".…

That, in my view, was the position before 1945. Has it been changed by the 1945 Act?
…

In my judgment, neither the 1945 Act nor any decision on it affects the general principles laid down by Jessel MR on the unavailability of the defence of negligence to an action for deceit. … In brief, a person liable for deceit, whether personally or vicariously, is not entitled as a matter of law to deny, by a plea of contributory negligence, that his deceit was the sole effective cause of the damage suffered by his victim. Nothing in the Act in principle or on authority entitles a person liable for deceit to plead contributory negligence.'

Comment

See also *Corporacion Nacional del Cobre de Chile* v *Sogemin Metals Ltd* [1997] 2 All ER 917 (defence of contributory negligence not available in an action based on bribery).

Fitzgerald v *Lane* [1989] AC 328 House of Lords (Lords Bridge of Harwich, Brandon of Oakbrook, Templeman, Ackner and Oliver of Aylmerton)

• *Contributory negligence – apportionment*

Facts

Although the lights were green to traffic and red against pedestrians, the plaintiff walked on to a pelican crossing. He was struck by the first defendant's car and thrown across the road where he was struck by the second defendant's car travelling in the opposite direction. As a result of these collisions he suffered multiple injuries.

Held

As the plaintiff's responsibility for his injuries had been at least as great as that of the defendants jointly, he was entitled to no more than 50 per cent of his claim, the amount awarded by the Court of Appeal.

Lord Ackner:

'*The correct approach to the determination of contributory negligence, apportionment and contribution*
It is axiomatic that, whether the plaintiff is suing one or more defendants for damages for personal injuries, the first question which the judge has to determine is whether

the plaintiff has established liability against one or other or all the defendants, ie that they, or one or more of them, were negligent (or in breach of statutory duty) and that that negligence (or breach of statutory duty) caused or materially contributed to his injuries. The next step, of course liability has been established, is to assess what is the total of the damage that the plaintiff has sustained as a result of the established negligence. It is only after these two decisions have been made that the next question arises, namely whether the defendant or defendants have established (for the onus is on them) that the plaintiff, by his own negligence, contributed to the damage which he suffered. If, and only if, contributory negligence is established does the court then have to decide, pursuant to s1 of the Law Reform (Contributory Negligence) Act 1945, to what extent it is just and equitable to reduce the damages which would otherwise be recoverable by the plaintiff, having regard to his "share in the responsibility for the damage".

All the decisions referred to above are made in the main action. Apportionment of liability in a case of contributory negligence between plaintiff and defendants must be kept separate from apportionment of *contribution between the defendants inter se*. Although the defendants are each liable to the plaintiff for the whole amount for which he has obtained judgment, the proportions in which, as between themselves, the defendants must meet the plaintiff's claim do not have any direct relationship to the extent to which the total damages have been reduced by the contributory negligence, although the facts of any given case may justify the proportions being the same.

Once the questions referred to above in the main action have been determined in favour of the plaintiff to the extent that he has obtained a judgment against two or more defendants, then and only then should the court focus its attention on the claims which may be made between those defendants for contribution pursuant to the Civil Liability (Contribution) Act 1978, re-enacting and extending the court's powers under s6 of the Law Reform (Married Women and Tortfeasors) Act 1935. In the contribution proceedings, whether or not they are heard during the trial of the main action or by separate proceedings, the court is concerned to discover what contribution is just and equitable, having regard to the responsibility between the tortfeasors inter se, for the damage which the plaintiff has been adjudged entitled to recover. That damage may, of course, have been subject to a reduction as a result of the decision in the main action that the plaintiff, by his own negligence, contributed to the damage which he sustained.

Thus, where the plaintiff successfully sues more than one defendant for damages for personal injuries and there is a claim between co-defendants for contribution, there are two distinct and different stages in the decision-making process, the one in the main action and the other in the contribution proceedings.'

11 Volenti Non Fit Injuria

Bowater v Rowley Regis Corporation [1944] KB 476 Court of Appeal (Scott, Goddard and du Parcq LJJ)

- *Negligence – volenti non fit injuria*

Facts
The plaintiff rubbish collector was provided by his employers, the defendants, with a horse and cart. He was ordered to take a horse which was known to be restive and to have run away on previous occasions. He protested, but eventually obeyed. The horse ran away and the plaintiff was thrown from the cart and injured.

Held
The plaintiff was entitled to damages as the defendants had been guilty of negligence. He had not been contributorily negligent and, as it was not part of his employment to manage unruly horses, he had not accepted the risk.

Goddard LJ:

'The maxim volenti non fit injuria is one which in the case of master and servant is to be applied with extreme caution. Indeed, I would say that it can hardly ever be applicable where the act to which the plaintiff is said to be "volens" arises out of his ordinary duty, unless the work for which the plaintiff is engaged is one in which danger is necessarily involved. Thus a man in an explosives factory must take the risk of an explosion occurring in spite of the observance and provision of all statutory regulations and safeguards. A horse-breaker must take the risk of being thrown or injured by a restive or unbroken horse; it is an ordinary risk of his employment. But a man whose occupation is not one of a nature inherently dangerous but who is asked or required to undertake a risky operation is in a different position. To rely on this doctrine the master must show that the workman undertook that the risk should be on him. It is not enough that, whether under protest or not, he obeyed an order or complied with a request which he might have declined as one which he was not bound either to obey or to comply with. It must be shown that he agreed that what risk there was should lie on him. I do not mean that it must necessarily be shown that he contracted to take the risk, as that would involve consideration, though a simple case of showing that a workman did take a risk upon himself would be that he was paid extra for so doing, and in some occupations "danger money" is often paid ...

For this maxim or doctrine to apply it must be shown that a servant who is asked or required to use dangerous plant is a volunteer in the fullest sense; that, knowing of the danger, he expressly or impliedly said that he would do the job at his own risk and not at that of his master. The evidence in this case fell far short of that and, in my opinion, the plaintiff was entitled to recover.'

Comment
Applied in *Merrington v Ironbridge Metal Works Ltd* [1952] 2 All ER 1101 (while fighting fire fireman neither sciens nor volens).

Morris v Murray [1991] 2 WLR 195 Court of Appeal (Fox, Stocker LJJ and Sir George Waller)

- *Volenti non fit injuria – aircraft joyride*

Facts
The plaintiff was a passenger in an aeroplane

which crashed because the pilot (Mr Murray) was drunk. The plaintiff had, in fact, been out drinking with the pilot, had driven to the airport with him and had assisted in the preparations for the flight. The plaintiff brought a claim against the estate of the deceased pilot claiming damages for personal injury. An autopsy on the pilot showed that he had consumed the equivalent of 17 whiskies. The trial judge gave judgment for the plaintiff; he held that the defence of volenti could not succeed, although he did reduce the damages payable by 20 per cent because of the plaintiff's contributory negligence in participating in this enterprise.

Held

The defendant's appeal would be allowed.

Fox LJ:

'In my opinion, on the evidence the plaintiff knew that he was going on a flight, he knew that he was going to be piloted by Mr Murray and he knew that Mr Murray had been drinking heavily that afternoon. The plaintiff's actions that afternoon, from leaving the Blue Boar to the take-off suggests that he was capable of understanding what he was doing. There is no clear evidence to the contrary. I think that he knew what he was doing and was capable of appreciating the risks. I do not overlook that the plaintiff's evidence was that, if he had been sober, he would not have gone on the flight. That is no doubt so but it does not establish that he was in fact incapable of understanding what he was doing that afternoon.

If he was capable of understanding what he was doing, then the fact is that he knowingly and willingly embarked on a flight with a drunken pilot. The flight served no useful purpose at all; there was no need or compulsion to join it. It was just entertainment. The plaintiff co-operated fully in the joint activity and did what he could to assist it. He agreed in evidence that he was anxious to start the engine and to fly. A clearer source of great danger could hardly be imagined. The sort of errors of judgment

which an intoxicated pilot may make are likely to have a disastrous result. The high probability was that Mr Murray was simply not fit to fly an aircraft. Nothing that happened on the flight itself suggests otherwise, from the take-off down wind to the violence of the manoeuvres of the plane in flight.

The situation seems to me to come exactly within Asquith J's example of the case where –

"the drunkenness of the driver at the material time is so extreme and so glaring that to accept a lift from him is like engaging in an intrinsically and obviously dangerous occupation ..."

(See *Dann* v *Hamilton* [1939] 1 KB 509 at 518.)

I think that in embarking on the flight the plaintiff had implicitly waived his rights in the event of injury consequent on Mr Murray's failure to fly with reasonable care.

The facts go far beyond *Dann* v *Hamilton, Nettleship* v *Weston* [1971] 2 QB 691 and *Slater* v *Clay Cross Co Ltd* [1956] 2 QB 264. It is much nearer to the dangerous experimenting with the detonators in *Imperical Chemical Industries Ltd* v *Shatwell* [1965] AC 656. I would conclude, therefore, that the plaintiff accepted the risks and implicitly discharged Mr Murray from liability from injury in relation to the flying of the plane.

The result, in my view, is that the maxim volenti non fit injuria does apply in this case. The judge appears to have been influenced by the fact that Mr Murray managed to get the plane airborne. He did, but the take-off down wind was irregular and the bizarre movements of the plane in flight must raise the greatest doubts whether he was in proper control of it. The judge thought that the case was analogous to *Owens* v *Brimmell* [1977] QB 859. But the volenti defence was not in issue in that case.

Considerations of policy do not lead me to any different conclusion. Volenti as a defence has, perhaps, been in retreat during this century, certainly in relation to master and servant cases. It might be said that the merits could be adequately dealt with by the application of the contributory negligence rules. The judge held that the plaintiff was only 20 per cent to blame (which seems to me to be too low) but if that were increased to 50 per cent, so that the plaintiff's damages were reduced by half, both sides would be substantially penalised for their conduct. It seems to me, however, that the wild irresponsibility of the venture is such that the law should not intervene to award damages and should leave the loss where it falls. Flying is intrinsically dangerous and flying with a drunken pilot is great folly. The situation is very different from what has arisen in motoring cases.

I should mention that the defence of volenti has been abrogated in relation to passengers in motor vehicles covered by comprehensive insurance (see s148 of the Road Traffic Act 1972). It is not suggested, however, that there is any similar enactment relating to aircraft and applicable to this case.'

Comment

See also *Pitts* v *Hunt* [1990] 3 WLR 542.

Pitts v *Hunt* [1990] 3 WLR 542
Court of Appeal (Dillon, Balcombe and Beldam LJJ)

• *Negligence – joint illegal enterprise*

Facts

The plaintiff was 18 and his friend Mark 16. Mark owned a motor cycle which he used as a trail bike, but he was not, as the plaintiff was aware, insured to use it on a road and he did not have a licence. After spending the evening drinking, they set off for home on Mark's bike with the plaintiff on the pillion. Encouraged by the plaintiff, Mark rode in a fast, reckless and hazardous manner, intending to frighten members of the public. They collided with a car; the plaintiff was severely injured and Mark (more than twice over the legal limit) was killed. The plaintiff claimed damages in negligence against, inter alia, Mark's personal representative. The judge held that the claim

was barred by the maxim ex turpi causa non oritur actio and public policy; he also decided that volenti non fit injuria would have defeated the claim, but for s148(3) of the Road Traffic Act 1972, and that in any case the plaintiff had been 100 per cent contributorily negligent. The plaintiff appealed.

Held

The appeal would be dismissed on grounds of public policy and the application of the maxim ex turpi causa non oritur actio and because the circumstances precluded the court from finding that Mark had owed the plaintiff a duty of care.

Beldam LJ:

'On the facts found by the judge in this case the plaintiff was playing a full and active part in encouraging the young rider to commit offences which, if a death other than that of the young rider himself had occurred, would have amounted to manslaughter. And not just manslaughter by gross negligence on the judge's findings. It would have been manslaugther by the commission of a dangerous act either done with the intention of frightening other road users or when both the plaintiff and the young rider were aware or but for self-induced intoxication would have been aware that it was likely to do so and nevertheless they went on and did the act regardless of the consequences. Thus on the findings made by the judge in this case I would hold that the plaintiff is precluded on grounds of public policy from recovering compensation for the injuries which he sustained in the course of the very serious offences in which he was participating.'

Dillon LJ:

'I feel unable to draw any valid distinction between the reckless riding of the motor cycle in the present case by the deceased boy, Hunt, and the plaintiff under the influence of drink, and the reckless driving of the cars, albeit stolen, in *Smith* v *Jenkins* and *Bondarenko* v *Sommers* (1968) 69 SR (NSW) 269. The words of Barwick CJ in *Smith* v *Jenkins* (1970) 119 CLR 397 at 399-400:

"The driving of the car by the appellant, the manner of which is the basis of the respondent's complaint, was in the circumstances as much a use of the car by the respondent as it was a use by the appellant. That use was their joint enterprise of the moment."

apply with equal force to the riding of the motor cycle in the present case. This is a case in which ... the plaintiff's action in truth arises directly ex turpi causa.'

Balcombe LJ:

'In a case of this kind I find the ritual incantation of the maxim ex turpi causa non oritur actio more likely to confuse than to illuminate. I prefer to adopt the approach of the majority of the High Court of Australia in the most recent of the several Australian cases to which we were referred, *Jackson* v *Harrison* (1978) 138 CLR 438. That is to consider that what would have been the cause of action had there been no joint illegal enterprise, that is the tort of negligence based on the breach of a duty of care owed by the deceased to the plaintiff, and then to consider whether the circumstances of the particular case are such as to preclude the existence of that cause of action ... I prefer to found my judgment on the simple basis that the circumstances of this particular case were such as to preclude the court from finding that the deceased owed a duty of care to the plaintiff.

I agree ... that s148(3) of the Road Traffic Act 1972 does not affect the position under this head ...

Counsel for the first defendant sought to persuade us that the application of the volenti doctrine is to extinguish liability and, if liability has already been extinguished, there is nothing on which s148(3) of the Road Traffic Act 1972 can bite. As Dillon LJ says, if this argument were to be accepted, it would mean that s148(3) could never apply to a normal case of volenti, although that was clearly its intention ... I agree that the effect of s148(3) is to exclude any defence of volenti which might otherwise be available. On this issue I agree with the judge below that Ewbank J's decision in *Ashton* v *Turner* [1981] QB 137 at 148 was incorrect ...

I agree that the judge's finding that the plaintiff was 100 per cent contributorily negligent is logically unsupportable and, to use his own words, "defies common sense". Such a finding is equivalent to saying that the plaintiff was solely responsible for his own injuries, which he clearly was not.'

Comment

See also *Revill* v *Newbery* [1996] 1 All ER 291 (duty of care owed to trespasser even though trespasser engaged in criminal activity). Section 148(3) of the Road Traffic Act 1972 has been replaced by s149 of the Road Traffic Act 1988 but its effect is unchanged.

12 Breach of Statutory Duty

Atkinson v *Newcastle Waterworks Co* (1877) 2 Ex D 441 Court of Appeal (Lord Cairns LC, Cockburn CJ and Brett LJ)

* *Breach of statutory duty – civil action*

Facts
The plaintiff's house, timber yard and saw mills caught fire and were burnt down. By statute, the defendants were obliged to supply water and keep the mains charged to a pre-scribed pressure: on the occasion in question they had failed to do so: for this the Act provided penalties.

Held
No action for damages lay for the defendants' breach of statutory duty.

Lord Cairns LC:

> 'The proposition a priori appears to be somewhat startling that a company supply-ing a town with water – although they are willing to be put under obligation to keep up the pressure, and to be subject to penalties if they fail to do so – should further be willing to assume, or that Parliament should think it necessary to subject them to liabil-ity to individual actions by any householder who could make out a case. In the one case they are merely under liability to penalties if they neglect to perform their duty, in the other case they are practically insurers, so far as water can produce safety from damage by fire. It is necessary to look at the provisions of s43 [of the Waterworks Clauses Act 1847]. Four cases are there specified, which cover all the duty imposed by the former sections, and for neglect of any one of these duties, there is a penalty of £10. For neglect of two of them, viz, to furnish to the town commissioners a suffi-cient supply of water for public purposes, and to furnish a supply of water to the owner or occupier, there is a further penalty of 40s a day, payable to every person who has paid or tendered the rate, for as long as such neglect or refusal continues after notice in writing has been given of the want of supply. It is not material to say, but it is pos-sible that it might be held that neglect or refusal to fix fire-plugs whould also subject the company to the 40s penalty. If so that penalty would be applicable in three cases out of the four. We have to consider why in some cases the penalty should go into the pocket of the individuals injured, and not in others. In the case of the obligation to keep the pipes charged, and allow all persons to use the water for the purpose of extinguish-ing fires, the provision is for the benefit of the public, and not of any individual spe-cially, and the guarantee for the perfor-mance of the obligation is the liability to the public penalty of £10.'

Cutler v *Wandsworth Stadium Ltd* [1949] AC 398 House of Lords (Lords Simonds, du Parcq, Normand, Morton of Henryton and Reid

* *Breach of statutory duty – civil action*

Facts
By statute, so long as a totalisator was in oper-ation, space had to be made available for bookmakers at dog racing tracks. A book-maker brought an action for an alleged breach of this obligation.

Held
As the statutory provision was intended to

benefit the public as opposed to bookmakers, a breach of it was a public and not a private wrong. The bookmaker therefore had no right of civil action against the occupier.

Lord Reid:

> 'The occupier is required to take such steps as are necessary to secure "that there is available for bookmakers space on the track where they can conveniently carry on book-making". This cannot mean that space must be provided on every occasion for as many bookmakers as wish to carry on business on that occasion. It cannot mean that, after the allotted space is fully occupied, an individual bookmaker who cannot find room there can demand further space where he can conveniently carry on business. The occupier must provide a space which is adequate in all the circumstances and which is in a convenient situation, but if he does that he has fulfilled his statutory obligation. He is not required by anything in the Act to find a place for each bookmaker who presents himself. If the Act does not give to an individual bookmaker a right to demand a place for himself, I find nothing to suggest that it gives him any other right enforceable by civil action. The sanction of prosecution appears to me to be appropriate and sufficient for the general obligation imposed by the sub-section.'

Comment

Applied in *Thornton* v *Kirklees Metropolitan Borough Council* [1979] 3 WLR 1 (damages awarded for housing authority's breach of duty), *Davis* v *Radcliffe* [1990] 1 WLR 821 and *X (Minors)* v *Bedfordshire County Council* [1995] 3 All ER 353.

See also *Phelps* v *Hillingdon London Borough Council* [2000] 4 All ER 504 where the House of Lords decided that a claim for breach of statutory duty could not succeed since there were alternative remedies (appeal procedures and judicial review) and it could be assumed that Parliament had not intended to create a statutory remedy by way of damages.

Goodes v *East Sussex County Council* [2000] 3 All ER 603 House of Lords (Lords Slynn of Hadley, Steyn, Hoffmann, Clyde and Hobhouse of Woodborough)

• *Duty to maintain highway – ice – highway authority's liability*

Facts

At about 7.10 am, when overtaking vehicles on the A267, the claimant's car skidded on ice on the road surface, left the road and he suffered severe injuries. A forecast of frost had been received by the defendant at 11.45 pm the previous evening. Pre-salting had been arranged, starting at 5.30 am, and the stretch of road where the accident occurred would have been treated within 15 minutes after its occurrence. Had the defendant highway authority been in breach of its duty, imposed by s41 of the Highways Act 1980, to maintain the road? The Court of Appeal answered this question in the affirmative. On the highway authority's appeal against this decision, the question arose whether s41 of the 1980 Act did indeed oblige the defendant to keep the highway free from ice.

Held

It did not and the appeal would therefore be allowed.

Lord Clyde:

> 'My Lords, I have no difficulty in holding that s41 of the Highways Act 1980 imposes an absolute duty on the highway authority. There is no hardship in so holding since the section has to be taken along with s58 which provides a defence that reasonable care has been taken by the authority. The scheme of the provisions is in its broad effect that the authority should be liable for damage caused by failure to take reasonable care to maintain a highway, but the injured party is not required to provide the failure to take reasonable care. It is for the authority to prove that it has exercised all reasonable

care. Such a reversal of the onus which would have been imposed on the plaintiff in an action for damages at common law is justifiable by the consideration that the plaintiff is not likely to know or be able readily to ascertain in what respects the authority has failed in its duty. All that the plaintiff will know is that there is a defect in the road which has caused him injury and it is reasonable to impose on the authority the burden of explaining that they had exercised all reasonable care and should not be found liable.

But the question in the case is precisely what is the meaning and scope of the absolute duty. The point is not immediately solved by the terms of the definition of s295 of the Highways Act 1959 because the ambiguous term "includes" is used. Maintenance certainly includes the work of repair and the taking of measures which will obviate the need to repair, to forestall the development of a defect in the road which will, if allowed to develop, require remedial action. The standard of maintenance is to be measured by considerations of safety. The obligation is to maintain the road so that it is safe for the passage of those entitled to use it. But the question still remains as to precisely what is the scope of that maintenance. It certainly requires that the highway be kept in a structurally sound condition. The question is whether, as the respondent claims, it extends also to the removal of ice which has formed on the surface of the road as a natural consequence of the weather. The appellant contends for a narrower construction which excludes the removal of ice, or indeed snow.

The matter is one of construction of the statutory language. I have come to the conclusion that the narrower construction is to be preferred. The obligation relates to the physical or structural condition of the highway. To use the words of Diplock LJ in *Burnside* v *Emerson* [1968] 3 All ER 741 at 744, in a passage quoted by Lord Denning MR in *Haydon* v *Kent CC* [1978] 2 All ER 97 at 103, the obligation is to keep the highway –

"in such good repair as renders it reasonably passable for the ordinary traffic of the neighbourhood at all seasons of the year without danger caused by its physical condition."

I can note quite briefly the reasons for the view which I have reached.

First, in the ordinary use of language I would not strictly describe the removal of ice from the surface of the road as maintaining the highway. By the highway is meant the stretch of land over which people may pass rather than the rights of passage which they may enjoy. The removal of ice may be a maintaining of the use of the highway or facilitating or easing the access which the highway provides, but it is not a maintaining of the highway itself. ...

Secondly, a consideration of the law relating to the maintenance and repair of highways up to the passing of the Highways Act 1959 supports the adoption of the narrower construction. ...

Thirdly, I find some assistance in the meaning attributed to the word "maintain" in s25(1) of the Factories Act 1937. That section provided that "All floors ... shall be of sound construction and properly maintained". Of course the context and the precise phraseology are different, but the purpose of securing the safety of a factory floor may be comparable with the purpose of securing a safe highway. In *Latimer* v *AEC Ltd* [1953] 2 All ER 449 the plaintiff slipped due to the presence of a film of oil on the surface of the floor. Lord Reid observed:

"The question, then, is whether s25(1) applies to things which are not part of the floor, but whose presence on it is a source of danger. If s25 stood alone, I would say that it did not. No doubt the section is one dealing with safety, but, even so, keeping the surface of a floor free from dangerous material does not appear to me to come within the scope of maintaining the floor."

Fourthly, if, as I have held, the duty imposed upon the authority is an absolute one, then it would seem appropriate not to adopt any wider construction of the scope of the duty than is necessary. To hold that they suddenly become in breach of duty in respect of all their highways wherever snow falls or ice forms on them so as to create a danger and they correspondingly become no longer in breach when perhaps a few hours later on a rise of temperature the snow or ice dissolves and the road is again safe seems to me to be bordering on the absurd. Of course if the matter was one of an action for damage, s58 might avail to provide a defence in such a case. But while that section may mitigate the effect of the absolute nature of the duty under s44 it does not determine the scope of that obligation. It seems to me that some at least of the problems to which snow and ice on highways may give rise are intended to be met by s150 [Duty to remove snow, soil, etc, from highway], but that section does not assist the plaintiff in the present case. ...

It might be thought that there should be a liability upon a highway authority ... for damages in the event of injury occurring through a failure to take sufficient measures to preserve the safety of the highways under conditions of ice and snow. But there is no remedy there available at common law and if the statute is construed in the way I have preferred there is no remedy under the statute. Attempts to achieve such a result by construction seem to me to involve a straining of the statutory language beyond what it can reasonably bear. If a remedy, with the financial consequences which it may involve, is desired, that is a matter for Parliament.'

Comment
Their Lordships disapproved *Haydon* v *Kent County Council* [1978] 2 All ER 97 and *Cross* v *Kirklees Metropolitan Borough Council* [1998] 1 All ER 564.

Issa v Hackney London Borough Council [1997] 1 All ER 999 Court of Appeal (Nourse, Saville and Brooke LJJ)

• *Statutory nuisance – premises prejudicial to health – criminal offence – civil liability*

Facts
When the plaintiff boys were aged nine and seven their parents, with whom they lived, were granted a joint tenancy of a property owned by the defendants. Four years later, it having been found that the premises were severely affected with condensation and associated mould growth and were prejudicial to health and therefore a statutory nuisance, the defendants pleaded guilty to an offence under the Public Health Act 1936. They were fined £500 and the boys' father was awarded compensation and costs. The defendants complied with an order for the nuisance to be abated. Subsequently, the plaintiffs (suing by their father as next friend) claimed damages for illhealth allegedly suffered as a result of the condition of the premises.

Held
Their action could not succeed.

Nourse LJ:

'In summary, [counsel for the defendants] submits that Pt III of the 1936 Act is a selfcontained code dealing with the abatement of statutory nuisances, and that there is no ground for construing it so as to incorporate the creation of a civil cause of action. He adds that, since this is not a case where the only method of enforcement provided by the Act is prosecution for the criminal offence of failure to perform the statutory obligation, the principles stated by Lord Diplock in *Lonrho Ltd* v *Shell Petroleum Co Ltd (No 2)* [1981] 2 All ER 456 do not come into play.

In my judgment, [these] submissions ... are correct.'

Comment

Brooke LJ observed that s4 of the Defective Premises Act 1972, as interpreted by the courts, did not assist people in the position of the present plaintiffs. Part III of the Public Health Act 1936 has been replaced by Pt III of the Environmental Protection Act 1990.

Kane v *New Forest District Council* [2001] 3 All ER 914

See Chapter 6.

Lonrho Ltd v *Shell Petroleum Co Ltd* [1981] 3 WLR 33 House of Lords (Lords Diplock, Edmund-Davies, Keith of Kinkel, Scarman and Bridge of Harwich)

* *Breach of statutory duty – civil liability – conspiracy*

Facts

Lonrho owned an oil pipeline from Beira to Umtali and Shell and BP used it. After the government of Southern Rhodesia made a unilateral declaration of independence, UDI, by statute the United Kingdom prohibited the supply of oil to Rhodesia, as it then was. As a result, the pipeline ceased to be used and Lonrho lost its profits from it. Lonrho alleged that, before UDI, Shell and BP had assured the illegal Rhodesian regime that it would continue to be supplied with oil and that this had influenced the decision to declare independence and prolonged the period during which the pipeline would be out of use.

Held

Contravention of the sanctions order did not give Lonrho a right to recover in tort any loss caused by it. Further, Lonrho could not claim in conspiracy as any agreement to contravene the sanctions would have been to further the commercial interests of Shell and BP, not to injure Lonrho.

Lord Diplock:

'The sanctions order ... creates a statutory prohibition on the doing of certain classes of acts and provides the means of enforcing the prohibition by prosecution for a criminal offence which is subject to heavy penalties including imprisonment. So one starts with the presumption laid down originally by Lord Tenterden CJ in *Doe d Bishop of Rochester* v *Bridges* (1831) 1 B & Ad 847, where he spoke of the "general rule" that "where an Act creates an obligation, and enforces the performance in a specified manner ... that performance cannot be enforced in any other manner", a statement that has frequently been cited with approval ever since, including on several occasions in speeches in this House. Where the only manner of enforcing performance for which the Act provides is prosecution for the criminal offence of failure to perform the statutory obligation or for contravening the statutory prohibition which the Act creates, there are two classes of exception to this general rule.

The first is where on the true construction of the Act is apparent that the obligation or prohibition was imposed for the benefit or protection of a particular class of individuals, as in the case of the Factories Acts and similar legislation.

... The second exception is where the statute creates a public right (ie a right to be enjoyed by all those of Her Majesty's subjects who wish to avail themselves of it) and a particular member of the public suffers what Brett J in *Benjamin* v *Storr* (1874) LR 9 CP 400 described as "particular, direct and substantial" damage "other and different from that which was common to all the rest of the public".

... My Lords, it has been the unanimous opinion of the arbitrators with the concurrence of the umpire, of Parker J and of each of the three members of the Court of Appeal that the sanctions orders made pursuant to the Southern Rhodesia Act 1965 fell within neither of these two exceptions. Clearly they were not within the first category of exception. They were not imposed for the *benefit* or *protection* of a particular class of individuals who were engaged in supplying or delivering crude oil or petroleum products to Southern Rhodesia. They were intended to put an end to such transactions. Equally plainly they did not create any public right to be enjoyed by all those of Her Majesty's subjects who wished to avail themselves of it. On the contrary, what they did was to withdraw a previously existing right of citizens of, and companies incorporated in, the United Kingdom to trade with Southern Rhodesia in crude oil and petroleum products.

... I can see no ground on which contraventions by Shell and BP of the sanctions orders, though not amounting to any breach of their contract with Lonrho, nevertheless constituted a tort for which Lonrho could recover in a civil suit any loss caused to them by such contraventions ...

The civil tort of conspiracy to injure the plaintiff's commercial interests where that is the predominant purpose of the agreement between the defendants and of the acts done in execution of it which caused damage to the plaintiff must I think be accepted by this House as too well-established to be discarded, however anomalous it may seem today. It was applied by this House eighty years ago in *Quinn* v *Leathem* [1901] AC 495, and accepted as good law in *Crofter Hand Woven Harris Tweed Co Ltd* v *Veitch* [1942] AC 435 at 439, where it was made clear that injury to the plaintiff and not the self-interest of the defendants must be the predominant purpose of the agreement in execution of which the damage-causing acts were done. ...

This House, in my view, has an unfettered choice whether to confine the civil action of conspiracy to the narrow field to which alone it has an established claim or whether to extend this already anomalous tort beyond those narrow limits that are all that common sense and the application of the legal logic of the decided cases require.

My Lords, my choice is unhesitatingly the same as that of Parker J and all three members of the Court of Appeal. I am against extending the scope of the civil tort of conspiracy beyond acts done in execution of an agreement entered into by two or more persons for the purpose not of protecting their own interests but of injuring the interests of the plaintiff.'

Comment

Applied in *RCA Corp* v *Pollard* [1982] 3 WLR 1007 and *Mid Kent Holdings plc* v *General Utilities plc* [1996] 3 All ER 132. Explained in *Lonrho plc* v *Fayed* [1991] 3 WLR 188. See also *Issa* v *Hackney London Borough Council* [1997] 1 All ER 999 and *Michaels* v *Taylor Woodrow Development Ltd* [2000] 4 All ER 645 where Laddie J said that where wrongful and damaging acts committed by a defendant alone do not give rise to a cause of action, the commission of those acts by two or more defendants in concert do not give rise to a cause of action either, save in exceptional circumstances of which conspiracies to injure are one, and possibly the only, example.

Olotu v *Home Office* [1997] 1 All ER 385 Court of Appeal (Lord Bingham of Cornhill CJ, Auld and Mummery LJJ)

• *Breach of statutory duty – liability of Crown Prosecution Service*

Facts

After being committed in custody for trial in the Crown Court, the plaintiff, inter alia, sued the Crown Prosecution Service (CPS) claiming damages for breach of its statutory duty (under reg 6(1) of the Prosecution of Offences Act (Custody Time Limits) Regulations 1987) to bring her before the court before the expiry of the custody time limit so that she might be granted bail.

Held

The claim would be struck out.

Lord Bingham of Cornhill CJ:

'The issue is whether the statutory duty

imposed on the CPS is a public law duty only, or whether it gives rise to a private law right enforceable by a person injured by breach of such duty and so entitled to recover compensation.

Although novel in the present context, this is a familiar question and there was no issue between the parties as to the principles to be applied. They are to be found in *Hague v Deputy Governor of Parkhurst Prison, Weldon v Home Office* [1991] 3 All ER 733 at 741–742, 747 and 750–752 and *X and Others (Minors) v Bedfordshire CC, M (A Minor) v Newham London BC, E (A Minor) v Dorset CC* [1995] 3 All ER 353 at 364–365. We must study the relevant provisions of the statute and the regulations in order to determine whether Parliament and the Secretary of State intended that anyone injured by failure of the CPS to perform its statutory duty should enjoy a private law right of action sounding in damages. In seeking to understand the intention of Parliament and the Secretary of State, regard must be paid to the object and scope of the provisions, the class (if any) intended to be protected by them, and the means of redress open to a member of such a class if the statutory duty is not performed.'

Mummery LJ:

'There is no allegation of malice, of misfeasance in a public office, or of negligence, on the part of the CPS. The claim is starkly pleaded as one of strict liability for damages for breach of a duty imposed by statute.

It is a question of available remedies. The plaintiff was undoubtedly entitled to remedies in the criminal proceedings (bail) and in judicial review proceedings. The issue is whether she is entitled to an additional remedy against the CPS by way of a civil law claim for damages. It is common

ground that it is not enough for the plaintiff simply to show that she has suffered damage in consequence of a breach of duty imposed by statute. The court must be satisfied that, on the true construction of the relevant statutory provisions, a right of action for damages has been created by Parliament. ...

As this case concerns the liberty of the subject, it requires the fullest and most anxious consideration. I am, however, unable to accept [counsel for the plaintiff's] submission that a claim for damages lies against the CPS for breach of statutory duty. The statute and the regulations are silent on damages. There are strong indicators against the implied creation of a statutory tort of strict liability in a case such as this: the availability to the plaintiff of other remedies both in the criminal proceedings (bail) and in public law proceedings (habeas corpus and mandamus); the absence of any indication in s22 of the [Prosecution of Offences Act 1985] that the Secretary of State had power to make regulations conferring a private right of action on accused persons; and considerations of the kind relied on by the Court of Appeal in *Elguzouli-Daf v Comr of Police of the Metropolis, McBrearty v Ministry of Defence* [1995] 1 All ER 833 in concluding that, in the absence of voluntary assumption of responsibility to a particular defendant in criminal proceedings, there is no general duty of care owed by the CPS at common law in the conduct of its prosecution of a defendant and that the CPS is immune from actions for negligence.'

Comment
Distinguished in *R v Governor of Brockhill Prison, ex parte Evans (No 2)* [2000] 4 All ER 15 (prisoner held beyond release date entitled to damages for false imprisonment).

13 Employers' Liability

Coltman v Bibby Tankers Ltd, The Derbyshire [1987] 3 WLR 1181 House of Lords (Lords Keith of Kinkel, Roskill, Griffiths, Oliver of Aylmerton and Goff of Chieveley)

• *Employers' liability – defective equipment*

Facts

A 90,000 ton bulk carrier owned by the defendants sank off the coast of Japan with the loss of all hands. The plaintiffs, personal representatives of a crew member, alleged that the ship had been unseaworthy because of defects in its hull and that the ship was defective 'equipment' within s1 of the Employer's Liability (Defective Equipment) Act 1969.

Held

The ship was 'equipment' in this sense, regardless of its size. Accordingly, where a seaman suffered in consequence of the unseaworthiness of a ship its owner was liable in negligence for that injury or loss of life.

Lord Oliver:

'My Lords, it is common ground that the 1969 Act was introduced with a view to rectifying what was felt to be the possible hardship to an employee resulting from the decision of this House in *Davie v New Merton Board Mills Ltd* [1959] 2 WLR 331. In that case an employee was injured by a defective drift supplied to him by his employers for the purpose of his work. The defect resulted from a fault in manufacture but the article had been purchased by the employers without knowledge of the defect from a reputable supplier and without any negligence on their part. It was held that the employ-

ers' duty was only to take reasonable care to provide a reasonably safe tool and that that duty had been discharged by purchasing from a reputable source an article whose latent defect they had no means of discovering. Thus the action against them failed although judgment was recovered against the manufacturer. Clearly this opened the door to the possibility that an employee required to work with, on or in equipment furnished by his employer and injured as a result of some negligent failure in design or manufacture might find himself without remedy in a case where the manufacturer and the employer were, to use the words of Viscount Simonds, "divided in time and space by decades and continents" so that the person actually responsible was no longer traceable or, perhaps, was insolvent or had ceased to carry on business ... Parliament accordingly met this by imposing on employers a vicarious liability and providing, in a case where injury was due to a defect caused by the fault of the third party, that the employer should, regardless of his own conduct, be liable to his employee as if he had been responsible for the defect, leaving it to him to pursue against the third party such remedies as he might have whether original or by way of contribution.'

General Cleaning Contractors Ltd v Christmas [1953] 2 WLR 6 House of Lords (Earl Jowitt, Lords Oaksey, Reid and Tucker)

• *Employers' liability – safe system of working*

Facts

The plaintiff, a window-cleaner for twenty

years, was employed as such by the defendants. In cleaning sash windows, he followed the usual practice of standing on the outside sill and cleaning first the top half: this was then pushed up so as to leave just enough hand-hold while cleaning the bottom half. On one occasion the sash fell shut, dislodging the plaintiff's hand and causing him to fall. He sued his employers in negligence.

Held

The plaintiff's claim would succeed. The method of cleaning windows, although customary, was known to be dangerous and the employers were under a duty to devise a safer system.

Lord Reid:

> 'It is the duty of the employer to consider the situation, to devise a suitable system, to instruct his men what they must do, and to supply any implements that may be required such as in this case wedges or objects to be put on the window sill to prevent the window from closing. No doubt, he cannot be certain that his men will do as they are told when they are working alone. But, if he does all that is reasonable to ensure that his safety system is operated, he will have done what he is bound to do. In this case the appellants do not appear to have done anything as they thought they were entitled to leave the taking of precautions to the discretion of each of their men. In this I think that they were in fault, and I think that this accident need not have happened if the appellants had done as I hold they ought to have done.'

Comment

Applied in *Pape* v *Cumbria County Council* [1992] 3 All ER 211.

Mulcahy v *Ministry of Defence*
[1996] 2 All ER 758

See Chapter 6.

Pape v *Cumbria County Council*
[1992] ICR 132 High Court (Waite J)

• *Employer's liability – duty to warn of dangers*

Facts

The plaintiff aged 57 was employed as a part-time cleaner by the defendants and was required to use various detergents and chemical cleaning products in the course of her employment. The defendants supplied the plaintiff with gloves, which she used occasionally, but they did not warn her of the dangers of irritant dermatitis from sustained exposure of skin to cleaning products. The plaintiff later began to suffer from irritated skin on her hands and wrists, which developed into acute dermatitis affecting her entire skin, and she claimed damages for personal injuries.

Held

Her action would be successful as the defendants had been under a duty to warn her of the dangers and, as no attempt had been made to give her any such warning, the defendants had been in breach of their duty of care.

Waite J:

> [Counsel] are both satisfied that there is no English authority precisely on this point. I do not think there is any difficulty about tackling this case from first principles. The question to be answered here is the same as the question that was exposed by the House of Lords in *General Cleaning Contractors Ltd* v *Christmas* [1953] AC 180 at 193, namely, reading from the speech of Lord Reid, the following:
>
> > "… whether it is the duty of the appellants to instruct their servants what precautions they ought to take, and to take reasonable steps to see that those instructions are carried out."
>
> The House held in that case in the context of a claim against a window cleaning company that it had a duty not only to provide a safe system of work but to instruct employees in the use of it. The answer to that question

was Yes. So it is in my judgment in the present case. The dangers of dermatitis or acute eczema from the sustained exposure of unprotected skin to chemical cleansing agents is well known, well enough known to make it the duty of a reasonable employer to appreciate the risks it presents to members of his cleaning staff but at the same time not so well known as to make it obvious to his staff without any necessity for warning or instruction.

There was a duty on the defendants to warn their cleaners of the dangers of handling chemical cleaning materials with unprotected hands and to instruct them as to the need to wear gloves at all times. It is common ground that no such warning or instruction was given and that is sufficient to place the defendants in breach of their duty of care. Since that is enough to establish liability I think it undesirable that I should attempt to answer the question, to which any reply would perforce be obiter in the present case, as to whether the placing of rubber gloves in the cleaning cupboard with a facility for replacement on demand was sufficient to discharge the defendants' further duty of care to ensure that any warning and instruction had it been given was observed and carried out ...

It remains to deal with damages. Counsel have already been able to agree a formula for the assessment of special damages ...

subject to only one outstanding issue, namely the multiplier to be applied to the figure which is the already agreed multiplicand for lost future earnings ... The plaintiff enjoyed her work and apart from her eczema is in basic good health. She might reasonably have expected had it not been for the defendants' breach of duty to carry on working for someone, even if retired from the defendants' employment at 60, in a job for which there always seems to be a demand whatever the fortunes of the economy as a whole. All in all I consider that the multiplier of five would be appropriate.

As for general damages, pain and suffering and loss of amenity, counsel are once again agreed that there is no reported decision on facts sufficiently similar to provide an analogy for the instant case. Dealing with the matter at large, therefore, and remembering this is a case where the plaintiff's pain, embarrassment and discomfort were of a severe order when at their height and her symptoms will to some extent at least as regards her hands remain with her for ever, I have decided an appropriate figure to award under this head would be £22,000.'

Comment

The ordinary principles of employers' liability apply to claims for psychiatric, or physical, injury or illness arising from the stress of the work: *Hatton* v *Sutherland* [2002] 2 All ER 1

14 Product Liability

Grant v *Australian Knitting Mills Ltd* [1936] AC 85 Privy Council (Lords Hailsham LC, Blanesburgh, Macmillan, Wright and Sir Lancelot Sanderson)

Negligence – liability of manufacturer

Facts

The plaintiff contracted a skin disease after wearing underpants manufactured by the defendants. The disease was due to an excess of chemical left in the garment during manufacture.

Held

The defendants were liable to the plaintiff in tort under the principle of *Donoghue (or McAlister) v Stevenson* [1932] AC 562.

Lord Wright:

'The presence of the deleterious chemical in the pants, due to negligence in manufacture, was a hidden and latent defect, just as much as were the remains of the snail in the opaque bottle : it could not be detected by any examination that could reasonably be made. Nothing happened between the making of the garments and their being worn to change their condition. The garments were made by the manufacturers for the purpose of being worn exactly as they were worn in fact by the appellant: it was not contemplated that they should be first washed. It is immaterial that the appellant has a claim in contract against the retailers, because that is a quite independent cause of action, based on different considerations, even though the damage may be the same. Equally irrelevant is any question of liability between the retailers and the manufacturers on the contract of sale between them. The tort liability is independent of any question of contract.

It was argued, but not perhaps very strongly, that *Donoghue*'s case was a case of food or drink to be consumed internally, whereas the pants here were to be worn externally. No distinction, however, can be logically drawn for this purpose between a noxious thing taken internally and a noxious thing applied externally: the garments were made to be worn next the skin: indeed Lord Atkin specifically puts as examples of what is covered by the principle he is enunciating things operating externally, such as "an ointment, a soap, a cleaning fluid, or cleaning powder" ... The decision in *Donoghue*'s case did not depend on the bottle being stoppered and sealed; the essential point in this regard was that the article should reach the consumer or user subject to the same defect as it had when it left the manufacturer. That this was true of the garments is in their Lordships' opinion beyond question. At most there might in other cases be a greater difficulty of proof of that fact.'

Comment

The defendants were also liable under the Australian equivalent of what is now the Sale of Goods Act 1979.

15 Occupiers' Liability

Billings (AC) & Sons Ltd v *Riden*

[1957] 3 WLR 496 House of Lords
(Viscount Simonds, Lords Reid,
Cohen, Keith of Avonholm and
Somervell of Harrow)

- *Occupier's liability – independent contractor*

Facts

The appellants had been employed by the occupier of a house to reconstruct the front pathway. In the course of carrying out this work, they laid a foundation of stones, bordered by a muddy area. On this was laid a plank which, for the time being, was the only means of access to the house. This plank passed alongside some railings which guarded it from a sunken basement next door. The appellants removed these railings also. One night the respondent, a lawful visitor to the premises, fell into the basement and was injured. She claimed against the appellants.

Held

The appellants, who were independent contractors of the occupier, owed a duty to take reasonable care for the safety of visitors. They had been in breach of this duty as they had made the route to the house unsafe: they were therefore liable. However, the respondent's damages would be reduced by 50 per cent for contributory negligence: she knew the path was dangerous, but refused assistance and did not have a torch, despite the fact that it was dark.

Lord Reid:

'In my opinion, the appellants were under a duty to all persons who might be expected lawfully to visit the house, and that duty was the ordinary duty to take such care as in all the circumstances of the case was reasonable to ensure that visitors were not exposed to danger by their actions. It was argued that, even so, that duty was adequately discharged in all cases by giving warning of the danger and that, if a visitor in full knowledge of the danger chose to incur it, she did so at her own risk and the contractor cannot be held liable. I do not agree. There may be many cases in which warning is an adequate discharge of the duty. There may be another safe and reasonably convenient access only a short distance away, or the situation may be such that with knowledge of the danger the visitor can easily and safely avoid it. But there are other cases where that is not so. Let me take the example of a doctor called to an urgent case in a house the only access to which has unnecessarily been made dangerous by a contractor. It cannot be right that he should be entitled to say to the doctor: "Now I have shown you the danger and if you choose to go on you do so at your own risk".

I do not think there is anything new in what I have just said. The principle was at least adumbrated a century ago in *Clayards* v *Dethick & Davis* (1848) 12 QB 439. A cab proprietor had stables in a mews from which the only road to the street was a long narrow passage. The Commissioners of Sewers employed the defendants to open a trench along the passage and gave notice to the occupiers of stables in the mews that the trench would be open for a day or two and that they must put up with it; the notice advised them to get other stables. The part of the passage not excavated was obstructed by earth and gravel thrown out from the trench. The cab proprietor safely led out one of his horses but the next fell into the trench owing to the earth and gravel giving way.

The danger was obvious and there was evidence that a warning had been given, but the case was left to a jury and the cab proprietor succeeded. …

The only cases brought to our notice which are inconsistent with what I have said are *Malone* v *Laskey* [1907] 2 KB 141 and *Ball* v *London County Council* [1949] 1 All ER 1056. In *Malone*'s case, a contractor had put up a water tank insecurely and it fell on the caretaker's wife and injured her. *Heaven* v *Pender* (1883) 11 QBD 503 was cited, but not *Clayards* v *Dethick*. The case, so far as relating to negligence, was decided against the plaintiff on the simple but, in my view, erroneous ground that, as the contractor was not the occupier and there was no contractual relationship between him and the plaintiff, he owed no duty of care to her. In *Ball*'s case, *Malone*'s case was followed as being binding on the Court of Appeal, and it is to be noted that there were other grounds which might also have been fatal to the plaintiff's case. … In my judgment, *Malone*'s case ought to be overruled in so far as it dealt with negligence.'

Comment

For the position where the plaintiff is injured because of a defect in the premises themselves, see the Occupiers' Liability Act 1957. See also *Hunter* v *Canary Wharf Ltd* [1997] 2 All ER 426.

British Railways Board v *Herrington* [1972] 2 WLR 537
House of Lords (Lords Reid, Morris of Borth-y-Gest, Wilberforce, Pearson and Diplock)

• *Negligence – duty owed to trespasser*

Facts

The respondent, a six year old boy, was playing in a field beside which ran the appellants' railway line. The fence between the field and the line was in a bad state of repair and in fact people often broke through it to cross the railway line. Some weeks before the appellants had been told of the presence of children on the line. The respondent passed through the fence and was severely injured by the electrified rail.

Held

The appellants owed the respondent a duty of common humanity and, although he had been a trespasser, he was entitled to recover damages.

Lord Reid:

'So the question whether an occupier is liable in respect of an accident to a trespasser on his land would depend on whether a conscientious humane man with his knowledge, skill and resources could reasonably have been expected to have done or refrained from doing before the accident something which would have avoided it. If he knew before the accident that there was a substantial probability that trespassers would come, I think that most people would regard as culpable failure to give any thought to their safety. He might often reasonably think, weighing the seriousness of the danger and the degree of likelihood of trespassers coming against the burden he would have to incur in preventing their entry or making his premises safe, or curtailing his own activities on his land, that he could not fairly be expected to do anything. But, if he could at small trouble and expense take some effective action, again I think that most people would think it inhumane and culpable not to do that. If some such principle is adopted, there will no longer be any need to strive to imply a fictitious licence. It would follow that an impecunious occupier with little assistance at hand would often be excused from doing something which a large organisation with ample staff would be expected to do.'

Lord Morris of Borth-y-Gest:

'The duty that lay on the appellants was a limited one. There was no duty to ensure that no trespasser could enter on the land. And, certainly, an occupier owes no duty to make his land fit for trespassers to trespass in. Nor need he make surveys of his land in order to decide whether dangers exist of which he is unaware. The general law remains that one who trespasses does so at his peril. But, in the present case, there were a number of special circumstances: (a) the place where the fence was faulty was near to a public path and public ground; (b) a child might easily pass through the fence; (c) if a child did pass through and go on to the track, he would be in grave danger of death or serious bodily harm; (d) a child might not realise the risk involved in touching the live rail or being in a place where a train might pass at speed. Because of these circumstances (all of them well known and obvious) there was, in my view, a duty which, while not amounting to the duty of care which an occupier owes to a visitor, would be a duty to take such steps as common sense or common humanity would dictate; they would be steps calculated to exclude or to warn or otherwise within reasonable and practicable limits to reduce or avert danger.'

Lord Diplock:

'I would then seek to summarise the characteristics of an occupier's duty to trespassers ... First, the duty does not arise until the occupier has actual knowledge either of the presence of the trespasser on his land or of facts which make it likely that the trespasser will come on to his land; and has also actual knowledge of facts as to the condition of his land or of activities carried out on it which are likely to cause personal injury to a trespasser who is unaware of the danger. He is under no duty to the trespasser to make any enquiry or inspection to ascertain whether or not such facts do exist. His liability does not arise until he actually knows of them.

Secondly, once the occupier has actual knowledge of such facts, his own failure to appreciate the likelihood of the trespasser's presence or the risk to him involved, does not absolve the occupier from his duty to the trespasser if a reasonable man possessed of the actual knowledge of the occupier would recognise that likelihood and that risk.

Thirdly, the duty when it arises is limited to taking reasonable steps to enable the trespasser to avoid the danger. Where the likely trespasser is a child too young to understand or heed a written or a previous oral warning, this may involve providing reasonable physical obstacles to keep the child away from the danger.

Fourthly, the relevant likelihood to be considered is of the trespasser's presence at the actual time and place of danger to him. The degree of likelihood needed to give rise to the duty cannot, I think be more closely defined than as being such as would compel a man of ordinary humane feelings to take some steps to mitigate the risk of injury to the trespasser to which the particular danger exposes him. It will thus depend on all the circumstances of the case: the permanent or intermittent character of the danger; the severity of the injuries which it is likely to cause; in the case of children, the attractiveness to them of that which constitutes the dangerous object or condition of the land; the expense involved in giving effective warning of it to the kind of trespasser likely to be injured, in relation to the occupier's resources in money or in labour.'

Comment
Distinguished: *Edwards* v *Railway Executive* [1952] AC 737.

Not followed: *Addie (R) & Sons (Collieries) Ltd* v *Dumbreck* [1929] AC 358.

Applied in *Pannett* v *P McGuinness & Co Ltd* [1972] 3 WLR 386 (duty to take reasonable steps for safety of child trespassers) and *Harris* v *Birkenhead Corporation* [1976] 1 All ER 341. See also *Revill* v *Newbery* [1996] 1 All ER 291.

Ferguson v *Welsh* [1987] 1 WLR 1553 House of Lords (Lords Keith of Kinkel, Brandon of Oakbrook, Griffiths, Oliver of Aylmerton and Goff of Chieveley)

• *Occupier's liability – duty to contractor's employee*

Facts

As part of a council's sheltered housing scheme, it was necessary to demolish a building and Spence's tender for this aspect of the work was accepted on condition, amongst others, that the council's approval be obtained before subcontractors were employed on the site. Without obtaining such approval, Spence subcontracted the work to the Welsh brothers and, as they adopted an unsafe system of work, the appellant, their employee, was injured. The judge held that the Welsh brothers were liable and the Court of Appeal ordered a new trial against Spence. Were the council also liable?

Held

No, because the appellant had been unable to show that the council knew or ought to have known that Spence would subcontract the work without authority to persons who would employ an unsafe system of work. The council had not been in breach of the common duty of care owed to visitors under s2(2) of the Occupiers' Liability Act 1957 or the ordinary common law duty of care.

Lord Keith of Kinkel:

'It would not ordinarily be reasonable to expect an occupier of premises having engaged a contractor whom he has reasonable grounds for regarding as competent, to supervise the contractor's activities in order to ensure that he was discharging his duty to his employees to observe a safe system of work. In special circumstances, on the other hand, where the occupier knows or has reason to suspect that the contractor is using an unsafe system of work, it might well be

reasonable for the occupier to take steps to see that the system was made safe.

The crux of the present case therefore, is whether the council knew or had reason to suspect that Mr Spence, in contravention of the terms of his contract, was bringing in cowboy operators who would proceed to demolish the building in a thoroughly unsafe way. The thrust of the affidavit evidence admitted by the Court of Appeal was that Mr Spence had long been in the habit of sub-contracting his demolition work to persons who proceeded to execute it by the unsafe method of working from the bottom up. If the evidence went the length of indicating that the council knew or ought to have known that this was Mr Spence's usual practice, there would be much to be said for the view that they should be liable to Mr Ferguson. No responsible council should countenance the unsafe working methods of cowboy operators. It should be clearly foreseeable that such methods exposed the employees of such operators to very serious dangers. It is entirely reasonable that a council occupying premises where demolition work is to be executed should take steps to see that the work is carried out by reputable and careful contractors. Here, however, the council did contract with Mr Spence subject to the condition that subcontracting without their consent was prohibited. The fresh evidence sought to be adduced by Mr Ferguson does not go the length of supporting any inference that the council or their responsible officers knew or ought to have known that Mr Spence was likely to contravene this prohibition.'

Harris v *Birkenhead Corporation* [1976] 1 WLR 279 Court of Appeal (Megaw, Lawton and Ormrod LJJ)

• *Negligence – unoccupied house – occupation or control – child trespasser*

Facts

The defendants acquired X's house by compulsory purchase order which stated that within a specified time they would enter and take possession. X vacated the house, but did not inform the defendants of the date of her departure. The defendants knew that property in the area was likely to be vandalised if left vacant and although they generally boarded up empty houses, they did not do so to X's house. The house was left empty by the defendants for three months, during which time it was ruined by vandals. The plaintiff, aged four and a half, wandered into the house from a nearby playground and was severely injured when she fell from a window.

Held
The defendants were occupiers of the premises and liable because they had been in breach of their duty to the plaintiff.

Ormrod LJ:

'The only question on the first part of this case is whether the corporation is properly regarded in law as a person occupying or in control of the premises in which the accident happened... there is, in my judgment, only one possible answer to that question. They were at all material times the persons with the right to control that property. It would have been almost absurd to suggest that, in the circumstances of this case, the second defendant [the previous owner] could have been expected by the law to go to expense in securing these premises against the damage which was inevitable and was bound to happen to them immediately or very soon after the tenant had vacated them. In those circumstances it would be a disastrous injustice to her to hold her liable for this appalling accident.'

Lawton LJ:

'... a man cannot claim that he has no knowledge when he has shut his eyes to the obvious.'

Comment
Applied: *British Railways Board* v *Herrington* [1972] 1 All ER 749. See also *Revill* v *Newbery* [1996] 1 All ER 291.

McAuley v Bristol City Council
[1992] 1 All ER 749 Court of Appeal (Neill and Ralph Gibson LJJ)

• *Landlord's duty under Defective Premises Act 1972*

Facts
The plaintiff and her husband were weekly tenants of a house owned by the defendants. The tenancy agreement required the defendants to keep the structure and exterior of the property in good repair while the plaintiffs were required to keep the premises, including the garden, in a clean and orderly condition. Under condition 6(c) of the agreement the plaintiffs were required to give the defendants access 'for any purpose which may from time to time be required ...' The plaintiff fell and sustained injury because a concrete garden step was unstable and, in an action for damages, she alleged, inter alia, that the defendants had been in breach of the duty of care imposed by s4(1) of the Defective Premises Act 1972.

Held
Her action would be successful.

Ralph Gibson LJ:

'Section 4(1) [of the 1972 Act] applies where the landlord is under an obligation to repair. A duty of care is imposed upon the landlord, assuming proof of knowledge or means of knowledge under subs(2) in respect of a "relevant defect", that is to say a defect which constitutes a failure to carry out the repairing obligation. Subsection (4) extends the basis of liability by treating the landlord as being under an obligation to repair, when in fact he is not. The extension is made when the landlord is given a right to enter "to carry out any description of maintenance or repair" but the extension of liability is not general. The landlord, when he is given a right to enter to carry out "any description of maintenance or repair" is to be treated as if he were under an obligation to the tenant "for that description of maintenance or repair", not all and any description of maintenance or repair.

Thus, in this case, assuming that there was no actual obligation, contractual or statutory, to repair the garden step, the plaintiff, to succeed under s4, must show that the defect in the garden step was a "relevant defect", ie that it was a defect in the state of the premises which constituted a failure by the council to carry out repair of a description for which the council had a right to enter the premises.

There is, I think, no warrant for a wide construction of the words of the section. They apply to all landlords, and not merely to local authorities, and can operate so as to impose a substantial burden upon a landlord in respect of premises under the immediate control of the tenant and in respect of which the landlord has assumed no contractual obligation.

Condition 6(c) applies to "any purpose which may from time to time be required by the council"; it does not say "for any purpose for which the council may be required to enter". I do not accept that the right of entry is limited to entry for the purpose of discharging the obligations of the council. The words are not, I think, perfectly drafted but the meaning seems to me to be clear, namely "any purpose for which from time to time entry may be required by the council" ...

In imposing the obligations stated in s4 of the 1972 Act where there is no obligation to repair, whether contractual or statutory, Parliament required proof of a tenancy which "expressly or impliedly gives the landlord the right to enter the premises to carry out any description of maintenance or repair". If such a right is proved, the landlord is, if the other conditions are satisfied, to be treated as under an obligation to the tenant for that description of repair. Parliament thus legislated by reference to the common law. If the common law says that the right to repair is implied, the statute imposes the obligation. The provisions apply to any tenancy agreement. The fact that, for this purpose, it would suit the tenants very well to have implied against them a right in favour of the landlord enforceable against the tenants does not, in my judgment, enable the court to imply such a right in circumstances where it could not properly do so upon the relevant principles ...

The decisive question in this case, therefore, is whether the court can properly hold that the council impliedly reserved a right against the tenant to carry out repair to the garden ... After some hesitation, I have reached the conclusion that the necessary reservation should be implied in restricted terms. The defect in the step exposed the tenants and visitors to the premises to the risk of injury. In this case ... the basis of the agreement was that the premises would be kept in reasonable and habitable condition and that, apart from interior decorative work and work to keep the garden in a clean and orderly condition, the work would be done by the council. The council had expressly reserved the right to enter "for any purpose for which from time to time entry may be required", if I have correctly construed the term, and the agreement did not expressly identify those purposes. If there should be a defect in the garden which exposed the tenants and lawful visitors to the premises to significant risk of injury, then I think that, to give business efficacy to the agreement ... a right should be implied in the council to carry out repairs for the removal of that risk of injury. A reasonable tenant could not sensibly object to such a right. If the council became aware of a dangerous defect in the steps of a steep garden, as in this case, and asked the tenant for access to repair it, in the interest of all persons who might be expected to be affected by the defect, the court could, in my judgment, properly require the tenant to allow such access upon the basis of an implied right in the council to do the work. So limited, I would hold that the implied right to enter to do the necessary repair was proved and the [defendants'] appeal should be dismissed.'

Comment

In *Lee* v *Leeds City Council* (2002) The Times

29 January the Court of Appeal said that where the defect which had caused the injury in respect of which a claim was made under s4 of the Defective Premises Act 1972 was not a defect arising from want of repair, it could not be a 'relevant defect' for the purposes of the section.

Ogwo v *Taylor* [1987] 3 WLR 1145 House of Lords (Lords Mackay of Clashfern LC, Bridge of Harwich, Elwyn-Jones, Templeman and Ackner)

• *Negligence – duty of care to fireman*

Facts

The defendant negligently set the roof of his house on fire whilst trying to burn off old paintwork on the eaves and guttering with a blow-lamp. The plaintiff, a fireman, came to put out the fire and whilst doing so he entered the loft of the house with a water hose. The intense heat in the confined loftspace caused much steam and afterwards the plaintiff discovered that he had suffered severe steam burns. The question was whether the defendant was liable for the plaintiff's burns, and whether a person who negligently starts a fire owes a duty of care to the firemen who come to put it out.

Held

The plaintiff should succeed as the defendant had been in breach of his duty of care.

Lord Bridge:

'Of course, I accept that not everybody, whether professional fireman or layman, who is injured in a fire negligently started will *necessarily* recover damages from the tortfeasor. The chain of causation between the negligence and the injury must be established by the plaintiff and may be broken in a number of ways. The most obvious would be where the plaintiff's injuries were sustained by his foolhardy exposure to an unnecessary risk either of his own volition

or acting under the orders of a senior fire officer. But, subject to this, I can see no basis of principle which would justify denying a remedy in damages against the tortfeasor responsible for starting a fire to a professional fireman doing no more and no less than his proper duty and acting with skill and efficiency in fighting an ordinary fire who is injured by one of the risks to which the particular circumstances of the fire give rise. Fire out of control is inherently dangerous. If not brought under control, it may, in most urban situations, cause untold damage to property and possible danger to life. The duty of professional firemen is to use their best endeavours to extinguish fires and it is obvious that, even making full use of all their skills, training and specialist equipment, they will sometimes be exposed to unavoidable risks of injury, whether the fire is described as "ordinary" or "exceptional". If they are not to be met by the doctrine of volenti, which would be utterly repugnant to our contemporary notions of justice, I can see no reason whatever why they should be held at a disadvantage as compared to the layman entitled to invoke the principle of the so-called "rescue" cases.

Counsel for the defendant suggested it would be anomalous that a fireman should recover damages for injuries sustained in fighting a fire caused by negligence when his colleague who suffers similar injuries in fighting another fire of which the cause is unknown has no such remedy. If this be an anomaly, it is one which is common to most, if not all, injuries sustained by accident and is inevitable under a system which requires proof of fault as the basis of liability. The existence of the suggested anomaly is the strongest argument advanced by those who support the introduction of a "no fault" system of compensation. But it has no special application to the case of firemen.

At the end of the day I am happy to find my views in full accord with those expressed in the latest authority directly in point, which is the decision at first instance of Woolf J in *Salmon* v *Seafarer Restaurants Ltd*.'

Comment

Approved: *Salmon* v *Seafarer Restaurants Ltd* [1983] 1 WLR 1264 (occupier owes fireman duty of care under s2 of the Occupiers' Liability Act 1957 but entitled to expect fireman to exercise skills ordinarily shown by a fireman). As to fire brigade's duty to a property owner, see *Capital and Counties plc* v *Hampshire County Council* [1997] 2 All ER 865.

Revill v *Newbery* [1996] 1 All ER 291 Court of Appeal (Neill, Evans and Millett LJJ)

- *Occupiers' liability – duty of care owed to a trespasser*

Facts

At about 2am the plaintiff attempted to break into a brick shed on the defendant's allotment where he was sleeping to guard his property. The defendant loaded a shotgun, poked the barrel through a small hole in the door, and fired and hit the plaintiff at a range of around five feet. The plaintiff pleaded guilty to the relevant criminal offences, and claimed against the defendant under s1 Occupiers' Liability Act 1984 and for negligence. At first instance the plaintiff succeeded, the judge rejecting the defences of ex turpi causa non oritur actio, accident and self-defence but finding that the plaintiff was two-thirds to blame. The defendant appealed.

Held

The appeal would be dismissed.

Neill LJ:

'*The law*

In this court the claim for damages for trespass to the person was not pursued. It is therefore unnecessary to consider further the statement of Lord Denning MR in *Letang* v *Cooper* [1964] 2 All ER 929 that actions for trespass to the person should be confined to cases where the injuries had been intentionally inflicted. In the present case, as the judge pointed out, it was not argued that Mr

Newbery "ever intended to hit anyone with the shot either at any time or on this particular occasion".

I turn therefore to the principles of law which are relevant to the claims based on s1 of the [Occupiers' Liability Act 1984] and on negligence at common law. ...

The effect of the decision of the House of Lords in *British Railways Board* v *Herrington* [1972] 1 All ER 749 was that it became possible for a plaintiff, even though he was a trespasser, to recover in negligence. But the precise nature of the duty owed to a trespasser gave rise to controversy and in 1984 Parliament intervened. ...

I must next consider the nature of the duty owed under s1 of the 1984 Act in a case such as the present. I shall postpone any consideration of the defence of ex turpi cause until later.

The words in s1(1)(a) of the 1984 Act "by reason of any danger due to ... things done or omitted to be done on [the premises]" are very similar to the words used in s1(1) of the Occupiers' Liability Act 1957 to regulate the duty owed by an occupier of premises to visitors "in respect of dangers due ... to things done or omitted to be done on [the premises]". ...

I have come to the conclusion ... that the better view is that the duty imposed by s1 of the 1984 Act is a duty imposed on an occupier as occupier. Section 1 is concerned with the safety of the premises and with dangers due to things done or omitted to be done on the premises. In considering whether Mr Newbery is liable on the facts of this case, the fact that he was the occupier is irrelevant. Accordingly, in my view it is necessary to consider the possible liability of Mr Newbery in the same way as one would have examined the liability of a third person, for example a friend of Mr Newbery who was staying in the hut, if that third person had fired the shot.

On the other hand, the provisions of s1 of the 1984 Act are very helpful in defining the scope of the duty owed at common law to an intruder who comes on premises in the middle of the night. Indeed, though I have reached my conclusion by a longer route than the judge, I agree with him that on the facts of this case the question of liability at common law is to be determined on the same lines as if one were considering a breach of duty under s1. Accordingly, in considering whether a duty was owed to Mr Revill, one can follow the guidance given in s1(3) of the 1984 Act; and in defining the duty of care one can adopt the formula set out in s1(4), namely a duty "to take such care as is reasonable in all the circumstances of the case to see that [the trespasser] does not suffer injury on the premises by reason of the danger concerned".

I shall consider later the application of the common law duty to the facts of this case. Before I do so, however, I must consider the relevance of the defence of ex turpi causa and also whether Mr Revill's criminal conduct makes it possible for the court to assess the relevant standard of care.

The maxim ex turpi causa non oritur action can be roughly translated as meaning that no cause of action may be founded upon an immoral or illegal act. The application of the maxim was considered by the Court of Appeal in *Pitts v Hunt* [1990] 3 All ER 344. ...

For the purposes of the present judgment I do not find it necessary to consider further the joint criminal enterprise cases or the application of the doctrine of ex turpi causa in other areas of the law of tort. It is sufficient for me to confine my attention to the liability of someone in the position of Mr Newbery towards an intruding burglar. It seems to me to be clear that, by enacting s1 of the 1984 Act, Parliament has decided that an occupier cannot treat a burglar as an outlaw and has defined the scope of the duty owed to him. As I have already indicated, a person rather than an occupier owes a similar duty to an intruder such as Mr Revill. ...

I am satisfied that the liability of someone in the position of Mr Newbery is to be determined by applying a test similar to that set out in s1(4) of the 1984 Act. There is in my view no room for a two-stage determination whereby the court considers first whether there has been a breach of duty and then considers whether notwithstanding a breach

the plaintiff is barred from recovering by reason of the fact that he was engaged in crime. It is to be noted that the defence of volenti is dealt with specifically in s1(6).

I therefore propose to examine the question of Mr Newbery's liability in the present case by applying principles of law similar to those set out in s1 of the 1984 Act.

The liability of Mr Newbery ...
I turn therefore to the question posed by s1(3)(b) of the 1984 Act. I consider that this question is also relevant when liability at common law is being examined. Did Mr Newbery know or have reasonable grounds to believe that Mr Revill was in the vicinity of the danger or that he might come into the vicinity of the danger? The danger was the gun which was about to be discharged.

Each case must depend on its own facts. There may well be cases where in order to frighten a burglar away a gun is discharged in the air and the burglar is injured because unexpectedly he is on the roof. That, however, is not the case. I have carefully considered what weight should be given to the fact that Mr Newbery thought that the intruder was at the window rather than at the door. I have come to the conclusion, however, that the judge was entitled to treat the discharge of the gun not merely as a warning shot but as a shot which was likely to strike anyone who was in the vicinity of the door. Although the intruder may have been at the window, a person in Mr Newbery's position could reasonably have anticipated that if the window were shuttered, as it was, the intruder might move to the door. The hole through which the gun was discharged was at body height and, as I understand it, the gun was fired more or less horizontally.

It is right to emphasise, as did the judge, that Mr Newbery certainly did not intend to hit Mr Revill. Nevertheless, I am satisfied that on the facts of this case the judge was entitled to find that Mr Revill was a person to whom Mr Newbery owed *some* duty and that Mr Newbery was in breach of that duty. The finding of a substantial proportion of contributiory negligence [two-thirds] was more than justified.'

16 Private Nuisance

Adams v *Ursell* [1913] 1 Ch 269
High Court (Swinfen Eady J)

* *Nuisance – smells*

Facts
Using 'the most approved appliances', the defendant established a fried fish shop in a working-class district but next to the plaintiff's house which was rather superior.

Held
The plaintiff was entitled to an injunction to restrain the nuisance caused by odour and vapour from the defendant's premises.

Swinfen Eady J:

> 'It does not follow that because a fried fish shop is a nuisance in one place it is a nuisance in another.'

Davey v *Harrow Corporation* [1957] 2 WLR 941 Court of Appeal (Lord Goddard CJ, Jenkins and Morris LJJ)

* *Nuisance – roots of trees*

Facts
Roots of the defendants' trees penetrated into the plaintiff's land and caused subsidence to his house.

Held
The defendants were liable and it was immaterial whether the trees were planted or self-sown.

Lord Goddard CJ:

> ' .. it must be taken to be established law that, if trees encroach whether by branches or roots and cause damage, an action for nuisance will lie.'

Comment
Approved in *Leakey* v *National Trust for Places of Historic Interest or Natural Beauty* [1980] 2 WLR 265.

See also *Delaware Mansions Ltd* v *Westminster City Council* [2001] 4 All ER 737 (roots a continuing nuisance of which defendant knew or ought to have known: reasonable remedial expenditure recoverable).

Hunter v *Canary Wharf Ltd*; *Hunter* v *London Docklands Development Corp* [1997] 2 All ER 426 House of Lords (Lords Goff of Chieveley, Lloyd of Berwick, Hoffmann, Cooke of Thorndon and Hope of Craighead)

* *Private nuisance – interference with television reception – dust from road construction – right to sue*

Facts
In the first action, the plaintiffs sought redress for interference with television reception by Canary Wharf Tower, a building 250 metres high and over 50 metres square, erected on land developed by the defendants. In the second, the plaintiffs claimed damages in respect of damage caused by what they alleged were excessive amounts of dust created by the construction by the defendants of the 1,800 metres long Limehouse Link Road. The plaintiffs lived in areas affected by the interference or dust. Preliminary issues of law to reach the House of Lords in the first action were: (1) whether interference with television reception is capable of constituting an actionable nuisance, and (2) whether it is

necessary to have an interest in property to claim in private nuisance and, if so, what interest in property will satisfy this requirement. In the second action, at this stage only question (2) arose.

Held

The answers were: (1) in the absence of an easement, more was required than the mere presence of a neighbouring building, and (2) (Lord Cooke of Thorndon dissenting) a right to the land, greater than that of a mere licensee, was an essential element.

Lord Goff of Chieveley:

'Interference with television signals
I turn first to consider the question whether interference with television signals may give rise to an action in private nuisance. This question was first considered over 30 years ago by Buckley J in *Bridlington Relay Ltd* v *Yorkshire Electricity Board* [1965] 1 All ER 264. That case was concerned not with interference caused by the presence of a building, but with electrical interference caused by the activities of the defendant electricity board. Buckley J held that such interference did not constitute a legal nuisance, because it was interference with a purely recreational facility, as opposed to interference with the health or physical comfort or well-being of the plaintiffs. He did not however rule out the possibility that ability to receive television signals free from interference might one day be recognised as "so important a part of an ordinary householder's enjoyment of his property that such interference should be regarded as a legal nuisance" (see [1965] 1 All ER 264 at 271). ... Certainly [today] it can be asserted with force that for many people television transcends the function of mere entertainment, and in particular that for the aged, the lonely and the bedridden it must provide a great distraction and relief from the circumscribed nature of their lives. ... the present case is to be distinguished from the *Bridlington Relay* case, in which the problem was caused not just by the presence of a neighbouring building but by electrical interfer-

ence resulting from the defendant electricity board's activities.

As a general rule, a man is entitled to build on his own land, though nowadays this right is inevitably subject to our system of planning controls. Moreover, as a general rule, a man's right to build on his land is not restricted by the fact that the presence of the building may of itself interfere with his neighbour's enjoyment of his land. The building may spoil his neighbour's view (see *A-G (ex rel Gray's Inn Society)* v *Doughty* (1752) 2 Ves Sen 453 and *Fishmongers' Co* v *East India Co* (1752) 1 Dick 164; in the absence of an easement, it may restrict the flow of air onto his neighbour's land (see *Bland* v *Moseley* (1587) 9 Co Rep 58a, cited in *Aldred's Case* (1610) 9 Co Rep 57b, and *Chastey* v *Ackland* [1895] 2 Ch 389); and, again in the absence of an easement, it may take away light from his neighbour's windows (*Dalton* v *Henry Angus & Co, Comrs of HM Works and Public Buildings* v *Henry Angus & Co* (1881) 6 App Cas 740 at 794–795, 823, per Lord Selborne LC and Lord Blackburn): nevertheless his neighbour generally cannot complain of the presence of the building, though this may seriously detract from the enjoyment of his land. As Lindley LJ said in *Chastey* v *Ackland* [1895] 2 Ch 389 at 402 (a case concerned with interference with the flow of air):

> "... speaking generally, apart from long enjoyment, or some grant or agreement, no one has a right to prevent his neighbour from building on his own land, although the consequence may be to diminish or alter the flow of air over it on to land adjoining. So to diminish a flow of air is not actionable as a nuisance."

From this it follows that, in the absence of an easement, more is required than the mere presence of a neighbouring building to give rise to an actionable private nuisance. Indeed, for an action in private nuisance to lie in respect of interference with the plaintiff's enjoyment of his land, it will generally arise from something emanating from the defendant's land. Such an emanation may take many forms – noise, dirt, fumes, a noxious smell, vibrations, and suchlike. Occasionally, activities on the defendant's land are in themselves so offensive to neighbours as to constitute an actionable nuisance, as in *Thompson-Schwab* v *Costaki* [1956] 1 All ER 652, where the sight of prostitutes and their clients entering and leaving neighbouring premises were held to fall into that category. Such cases must, however, be relatively rare. ...

In the result, I find myself to be in agreement on this point with Pill LJ, who delivered the judgment of the Court of Appeal ([1996] 1 All ER 482 at 490), when he expressed the opinion that no action lay in private nuisance for interference with television caused by the mere presence of a building. ...

Right to sue in private nuisance
I turn next to the question of the right to sue in private nuisance. In the two cases now under appeal before your Lordship's House, one of which relates to interference with television signals and the other to the generation of dust from the construction of a road, the plaintiffs consist in each case of a substantial group of local people. Moreover, they are not restricted to householders who have the exclusive right to possess the places where they live, whether as freeholders or tenants, or even as licensees. They include people with whom householders share their homes, for example as wives or husbands or partners, or as children or other relatives. All of these people are claiming damages in private nuisance, by reason of interference with their television viewing or by reason of excessive dust. ...

Since the tort of nuisance is a tort directed against the plaintiff's enjoyment of his rights over land, an action of private nuisance will usually be brought by the person in actual possession of the land affected, either as the freeholder or tenant of the land in question, or even as a licensee with exclusive possession of the land (see *Newcastle-under-Lyme Corp* v *Wolstanton Ltd* [1946] 2 All ER 447 at 455–456 per Evershed J); though a reversioner may sue in respect of

a nuisance of a sufficiently permanent character to damage his reversion. It was however established in *Foster* v *Warblington UDC* [1906] 1 KB 648 that, since jus tertii is not a defence to an action of nuisance, a person who is in exclusive possession of land may sue even though he cannot prove title to it. That case was concerned with a nuisance caused by the discharge of sewage by the defendant council into certain oyster beds. The plaintiff was an oyster merchant who had for many years been in occupation of the oyster beds which had been artificially constructed on the foreshore, which belonged to the lord of the manor. The plaintiff excluded everybody from the oyster beds, and nobody interfered with his occupation of the oyster beds or his removal and sale of oysters from them. It was held by the Court of Appeal that he could sue the defendant council in nuisance, notwithstanding that he could not prove his title. ...

Subject to this exception, however, it has for many years been regarded as settled law that a person who has no right in the land cannot sue in private nuisance. For this proposition, it is usual to cite the decision of the Court of Appeal in *Malone* v *Laskey* [1907] 2 KB 141. In that case, the manager of a company resided in a house as a licensee of the company which employed him. The plaintiff was the manager's wife who lived with her husband in the house. She was injured when a bracket fell from a wall in the house. She claimed damages from the defendants in nuisance and negligence, her claim in nuisance being founded upon an allegation, accepted by the jury, that the fall of the bracket had been caused by vibrations from an engine operating on the defendants' adjoining premises. The Court of Appeal held that she was unable to succeed in her claim in nuisance. ... I should add that an alternative claim by the plaintiff in negligence also failed, though that claim would have succeeded today (see *A C Billings & Sons Ltd* v *Riden* [1957] 3 All ER 1. ...

It follows that, on the authorities as they stand, an action in private nuisance will only lie at the suit of a person who has a right to the land affected. Ordinarily, such a person can only sue if he has the right to exclusive possession of the land, such as a freeholder or tenant in possession, or even a licensee with exclusive possession. Exceptionally however, as *Foster* v *Warblington UDC* shows, this category may include a person in actual possession who has no right to be there; and in any event a reversioner can sue in so far [as] his reversionary interest is affected. But a mere licensee on the land has no right to sue. ...

It was suggested in the course of argument that at least the spouse of a husband or wife, who for example as freeholder or tenant, had exclusive possession of the matrimonial home should be entitled to sue in private nuisance. ...

But I do see how a spouse who has no interest in the matrimonial home has, simply by virtue of his or her cohabiting in the matrimonial home with his or her wife or husband whose freehold or leasehold property it is, a right to sue. No distinction can sensibly be drawn between such spouses and other cohabitees in the home, such as children, or grandparents. Nor do I see any great disadvantage flowing from this state of affairs. If a nuisance should occur, then the spouse who has an interest in the property can bring the necessary proceedings to bring the nuisance to an end, and can recover any damages in respect of the discomfort or inconvenience caused by the nuisance. ...

For all these reasons, I can see no good reason to depart from the law on this topic as established in the authorities. I would therefore hold that *Khorasandjian* v *Bush* [1993] 3 All ER 669 must be overruled in so far as it holds that a mere licensee can sue in private nuisance ...'

Comment

In *Khorasandjian* v *Bush* the Court of Appeal decided (a) the court had jurisdiction in private nuisance to grant an injunction restraining persistent harassment by unwanted telephone calls, (b) the jurisdiction could be exercised notwithstanding that the parties were not married and had never cohabited or

that the recipient of the calls had no proprietary interest, either freehold or leasehold, in the premises where the calls were received, and (c) the inconvenience and annoyance to the recipient caused by such calls constituted an actionable interference with the ordinary and reasonable use and enjoyment of property and could be restrained quia timet without further proof or damage. As Lord Goff of Chieveley observed in *Hunter*, a tort of harassment has now received statutory recognition in the Protection from Harassment Act 1997.

Hunter was applied in *Hussain* v *Lancaster City Council* [1999] 4 All ER 125 (defendant not liable in nuisance or negligence for racial and other harassment suffered by tenants from other tenants on its estate), but *Hussain* was distinguished in *Lippiatt* v *South Gloucestershire Council* [1999] 4 All ER 149 (defendant could be liable in nuisance for allowing travellers to occupy its land from where they allegedly trespassed on plaintiffs' adjoining land and caused damage).

A 'tolerated trespasser' has a sufficient interest to support an action for nuisance: *Pemberton* v *Southwark London Borough Council* [2000] 3 All ER 924.

See also *Southwark London Borough Council* v *Mills* [1999] 4 All ER 449 (ordinary use of residential premises incapable of amounting to nuisance).

Kennaway v *Thompson* [1980] 3 WLR 361 Court of Appeal (Lawton and Waller LJJ and Sir David Cairns)

• *Nuisance – private against public interest*

Facts

The plaintiff built a house on land where the defendant club organised motor boat races and water skiing. When she began to build, she felt that the club's activities would not interfere with her enjoyment of her new house, but those activities developed and boats became more powerful and noisy.

Held

Despite the public interest in the club's activities, an injunction would be granted restricting the club's racing and the noise level of boats at other times.

Lawton J:

'The principles enunciated in *Shelfer*'s case, which is binding on us, have been applied time and time again during the past 85 years. The only case which raises a doubt about the application of the *Shelfer* principles to all cases is *Miller* v *Jackson* [1977] 3 WLR 20, a decision of this court. The majority, Geoffrey Lane and Cumming-Bruce LJJ, Lord Denning MR dissenting, adjudged that the activities of an old-established cricket club which had been going for over seventy years, had been a nuisance to the plaintiffs by reason of cricket balls landing on their garden. The question then was whether the plaintiffs should be granted an injunction. Geoffrey Lane LJ was of the opinion that one should be granted. Lord Denning MR and Cumming-Bruce LJ though otherwise. Lord Denning MR said that the public interest should prevail over the private interest. Cumming-Bruce LJ stated that a factor to be taken into account when exercising the judicial discretion whether to grant an injunction was that the plaintiffs had bought their house knowing that it was next to the cricket ground. He thought that there were special circumstances which should inhibit a court of equity from granting the injunction claimed. The statement of Lord Denning MR that the public interest should prevail over the private interest runs counter to the principles enunciated in *Shelfer*'s case and does not accord with the reason of Cumming-Bruce LJ for refusing an injunction. We are of the opinion that there is nothing in *Miller* v *Jackson*, binding on us, which qualifies what was decided in *Shelfer*. Any decisions before *Shelfer*'s case (and there were some at first instance as counsel for the defendants pointed out) which give support for the proposition that the public interest should prevail over the private interest must be read subject to the decision in *Shelfer*'s case.

It follows that the plaintiff was entitled to an injunction .. But she was only entitled to an injunction restraining the club from activities which caused a nuisance, and not all of their activities did.'

Comment

Distinguished in *Tetley* v *Chitty* [1986] 1 All ER 663 (go-karting a nuisance and plaintiff granted an injunction to stop it and damages).

Applied: *Shelfer* v *City of London Electric Lighting Co Ltd* [1895] 1 Ch 287.

Leakey v *National Trust for Places of Historic Interest or Natural Beauty* [1980] 2 WLR 65 Court of Appeal (Megaw, Shaw and Cumming-Bruce LJJ)

* *Nuisance – natural process*

Facts

The defendants owned and occupied a parcel of land consisting of a conical shaped hill 'Burrow Hump' next to the plaintiffs' houses which were situated effectively at the base of the hill being separated from it only by a narrow strip of land. The hill was composed of keaper marl which made it prone to cracking and slipping. In the past weathering had caused soil slides onto the plaintiffs' property. After the long drought in 1976, a large crack appeared. The plaintiffs notified the defendants of this and the defendants, having taken legal advice, refused to act. A large slide of earth onto the plaintiffs' property then occurred, the soil in fact reaching the plaintiffs' houses. The plaintiffs sued for a mandatory injunction to get it removed. Pursuant to this, the defendants spent £2,000 removing the material. The action then proceeded to trial and before O'Connor J the plaintiffs succeeded in establishing nuisance. Between the first instance decision and the Court of Appeal hearing, the defendants spent a further £4,000 on protective works. The purpose of the appeal was to establish whether the case of

Goldman v *Hargrave* [1966] 3 WLR 513 represented the law of England.

Held
1. There is a general duty imposed on occupiers in relation to hazards occurring on their land whether natural or man-made. A person on whose land a natural hazard develops which threatens to encroach on another's land must do all that is reasonable to prevent it;
2. this was properly described as a claim in nuisance;
3. the defendants were liable for nominal damages.

Megaw LJ:

'In my judgment, there is, in the scope of the duty as explained in *Goldman* v *Hargrave*, a removal, or at least a powerful amelioration, of the injustice which might otherwise be caused in such a case by the recognition of the duty of care. Because of that limitation on the scope of the duty, I would say that, as a matter of policy, the law ought to recognise such a duty of care.

This leads on to the question of the scope of the duty. This is discussed, and the nature and extent of the duty is explained, in the judgment in *Goldman* v *Hargrave*. The duty is a duty to do that which is reasonable in all the circumstances, and no more than what, if anything, is reasonable, to prevent or minimise the known risk of damage or injury to one's neighbour or to his property. The considerations with which the law is familiar are all to be taken into account in deciding whether there has been a breach of duty, and, if so, what that breach is, and whether it is causative of the damage in respect of which the claim is made. Thus, there will fall to be considered the extent of the risk. What, so far as reasonably can be foreseen, are the chances that anything untoward will happen or that any damage will be caused? What is to be foreseen as to the possible extent of the damage if the risk becomes a reality? Is it practicable to prevent, or to minimise, the happening of any damage? If it is practicable, how simple or how difficult are the measures which could be taken, how much and how lengthy work do they involve, and what is the probable cost of such works? Was there sufficient time for preventive action to have been taken, by persons acting reasonably in relation to the known risk, between the time when it became known to, or should have been realised by, the defendant, and the time when the damage occurred? Factors such as these, so far as they apply in a particular case, fall to be weighed in deciding whether the defendant's duty of care requires, or required, him to do anything, and, if so, what.'

Comment
Applied: *Goldman* v *Hargrave* [1966] 3 WLR 513 and *Sedleigh-Denfield* v *O'Callagan* [1940] AC 880.

Approved: *Davey* v *Harrow Corporation* [1957] 2 WLR 941.

Distinguished: *Rylands* v *Fletcher* (1868) LR 3 HL 330.

Overruled: *Giles* v *Walker* (1890) 24 QBD 656 and *Pontardawe Rural District Council* v *Moore-Gwyn* [1929] 1 Ch 656.

Applied in *Home Brewery plc* v *William Davis & Co (Loughborough) Ltd* [1987] 2 WLR 117 (percolation of water from higher to lower land) and *Bradburn* v *Lindsay* [1983] 2 All ER 408 (right of support and treatment to prevent spread of dry rot).

In *Marcic* v *Thames Water Utilities Ltd* [2002] 2 All ER 55 the Court of Appeal decided that the failure of a water company to take any steps to remedy the discharge of sewerage onto the claimant's land constituted a nuisance at common law for which the water company was liable in damages. Their Lordship also concluded that the claimant's right to respect for his home under art 8 of the European Convention for the Protection of Human Rights and Fundamental Freedoms and his right to peaceful enjoyment of his possessions under art 1 of Protocol 1 to the Convention had been infringed.

See also *Holbeck Hall Hotel Ltd* v *Scarborough Borough Council* [2000] 2 All

ER 705 (defendant council owned and occupied the land between claimant's cliff-top hotel and the sea: land slips occurred in 1982 and 1986 and massive slip in 1993: last slip caused collapse of hotel's seaward wing and rest had to be demolished: defendant not liable since defendant's duty to take care to avoid damage which it ought to have foreseen without further geological investigation and 1993 damage was greater than anything foreseen or foreseeable without such investigation) and *Rees* v *Skerrett* (2001) The Times 18 June (person demolishing house in terrace under duty to take reasonable steps to weatherproof neighbour's exposed wall).

17 Public Nuisance

Gillingham Borough Council v Medway (Chatham) Dock Co Ltd
[1993] QB 343 High Court
(Buckley J)

- *Public nuisance – effect of planning permission*

Facts
The defendants were lessees of a port. The plaintiffs alleged that the use of the roads around the port at night by numerous heavy goods vehicles (HGVs) constituted a public nuisance. The evidence established that in 1988 there were approximately 750 HGV 'movements' every night and that the sleep and comfort of the residents in the vicinity of the port were disturbed. The defendants conceded that these conditions constituted a substantial interference with the residents' enjoyment of their property up to June 1990 and that, subject to defences, enough residents were affected to constitute a public nuisance. However the defendants argued that they had been given planning permission to operate a commercial port, that such a port could operate viably only on a 24-hour basis, that no limits had been placed on the volume of traffic in the vicinity when they had been granted planning permission and that their estimate of the likely throughput of traffic had been remarkably accurate.

Held
The plaintiffs' action would not succeed.

Buckley J:

'Parliament has set up a statutory framework and delegated the task of balancing the interests of the community against those of individuals and of holding the scales between individuals to the local planning authority. There is the right to object to any proposed grant, provision for appeals and inquiries, and ultimately the minister decides. There is the added safeguard of judicial review. If a planning authority grants permission for a particular construction or use in its area it is almost certain that some local inhabitants will be prejudiced in the quiet enjoyment of their properties. Can they defeat the scheme simply by bringing an action in nuisance? If not, why not? It has been said, no doubt correctly, that planning permission is not a licence to commit nuisance and that a planning authority has no jurisdiction to authorise nuisance. However, a planning authority can, through its development plans and decisions, alter the character of a neighbourhood. That may have the effect of rendering innocent activities which, prior to the change, would have been an actionable nuisance (see *Allen v Gulf Oil Refining Ltd* [1980] QB 156 at 174–175 per Cumming-Bruce LJ, referred to in the speech of Lord Wilberforce [1981] AC 1001 at 1013–1014)).

The point arises in this case. Prior to January 1984 Medway and Bridge roads had been relatively quiet residential roads. True, they led to the old Naval Dockyard but that did not generate many HGVs and probably none at night. For obvious reasons sites for naval bases were not chosen for their land communications. It seems to me that I must judge the present claim in nuisance by reference to the present character of the neighbourhood pursuant to the planning permission for use of the dockyard as a commercial port. Thus, these roads are now in the neighbourhood of and lead immediately to a commercial port which operates 24 hours per day. In those circumstances I hold that the undoubted disturbance to the residents is not actionable. ...

I do not believe that my views are inconsistent with cases such as *Halsey* v *Esso Petroleum Co Ltd* [1961] 1 WLR 683 or *Attorney-General* v *PYA Quarries Ltd* [1957] 2 QB 169. There may well have been planning permission for the activities in question in those cases. Certainly there was in the *PYA Quarries* case, but the complaints there related to unreasonable uses. The depot and the quarry in those cases could have been operated commercially in accordance with the planning permission without causing the damage or disturbance complained of.

In short, where planning consent is given for a development or change of use, the question of nuisance will thereafter fall to be decided by reference to a neighbourhood with that development or use and not as it was previously.'

Comment

See also *Hunter* v *Canary Wharf Ltd* [1997] 2 All ER 426 and *Wandsworth London Borough Council* v *Railtrack plc* (2001) The Times 2 August (droppings from pigeons on railway bridge fell on pavement: bridge owner liable in public nuisance).

Thomas v *National Union of Mineworkers (South Wales Area)* [1985] 2 WLR 1081 High Court (Scott J)

• *Nuisance – obstruction of highway*

Facts

During a strike, the plaintiffs decided to return to work, but 60-70 pickets outside the colliery gates sought to deter them by using abusive and violent language. The plaintiffs sought interlocutory injunctions.

Held

On the facts, and in the light of the relevant law, the injunctions would not be granted.

Scott J:

'The working miners are entitled to use the highway for the purpose of entering and leaving their respective places of work. In the exercise of that right they are at present having to suffer the presence and behaviour of the pickets and demonstrators. The law has long recognised that unreasonable interference with the rights of others is actionable in tort ... It is, however, not every act of interference with the enjoyment by an individual of his property rights that will be actionable in nuisance. The law must strike a balance between conflicting rights and interests ...

Nuisance is strictly concerned with, and may be regarded as confined to, activity which unduly interferes with the use or enjoyment of land or of easements. But there is no reason why the law should not protect on a similar basis the enjoyment of other rights. All citizens have the right to use the public highway. Suppose an individual were persistently to follow another on a public highway, making rude gestures or remarks in order to annoy or vex. If continuance of such conduct were threatened no one can doubt but that a civil court would, at the suit of the victim, restrain by an injunction the continuance of the conduct. The tort might be described as a species of private nuisance, namely unreasonable inference with the victim's rights to use the highway. But the label for the tort does not, in my view, matter.

In the present case, the working miners have the right to use the highway for the purpose of going to work. They are, in my judgment, entitled under the general law to exercise that right without unreasonable harassment by others. Unreasonable harassment of them in their exercise of that right would, in my judgment, be tortious.

A decision whether in this, or in any other similar case, the presence or conduct of pickets represents a tortious interference with the right of those who wish to go to work to do so without harassment must depend on the particular circumstances of the particular case. The balance to which I have earlier referred must be struck between the rights of those going to work and the rights of the pickets.'

Comment
As to the right to engage in peaceful picketing, see s220 of the Trade Union and Labour Relations (Consolidation) Act 1992.

18 The Rule in *Rylands* v *Fletcher*

Cambridge Water Co Ltd v *Eastern Counties Leather plc* [1994] 2 WLR 53 House of Lords (Lords Templeman, Goff of Chieveley, Jauncey of Tullichettle, Lowry and Woolf)

- *Need for foreseeability of damage*

Facts

The defendants used a chlorinated solvent at their tannery which was situated some 1.3 miles from the plaintiff's borehole where water was abstracted for domestic purposes. This water became unfit for human consumption by solvent contamination when the solvent seeped into the ground below the defendants' premises and then percolated into the borehole. The plaintiffs brought an action in, inter alia, *Rylands*. In the High Court this action was dismissed on the grounds that the defendants had not made a non-natural user of their land, which was situated in an industrial village. On appeal, the Court of Appeal declined to determine the matter on the basis of *Rylands* but imposed liability on other grounds. The defendants appealed.

Held

Foreseeability of harm of the relevant type by the defendants was required to recover damages under the rule in *Rylands* v *Fletcher* (and also in nuisance). Contrary to the finding at first instance, the defendants had made a non-natural use of their land. However, on the facts of the case the contamination was not foreseeable and the appeal would be allowed.

Lord Goff, with whose speech the other Law Lords agreed, also briefly considered the meaning of the phrase 'natural use of the land', and doubted whether the storage of substantial quantities of chemicals on industrial premises could ever be a natural user. Lord Goff pointed out that now foreseeability of damage was an essential ingredient of the tort, courts might feel less inclined to extend the concept of natural use to circumstances such as those in the present case.

Lord Goff of Chieveley:

Foreseeability of damage under the rule in Rylands *v* Fletcher

'I start with the judgment of Blackburn J in *Fletcher* v *Rylands* (1866) LR 1 Ex 265 itself. His celebrated statement of the law is to be found at pp279–280, where he said:

> "We think that the true rule of law is, that the person who for his own purposes brings on his lands and collects and keeps there anything likely to do mischief if it escapes, must keep it in at his peril, and, if he does not do so, is prima facie answerable for all the damage which is the natural consequence of its escape. He can excuse himself by showing that the escape was owing to the plaintiff's default; or perhaps that the escape was the consequence of vis major, or the act of God; but as nothing of this sort exists here, it is unnecessary to inquire what excuse would be sufficient. The general rule, as above stated, seems on principle just. The person whose grass or corn is eaten down by the escaping cattle of his neighbour, or whose mine is flooded by the water from his neighbour's reservoir, or whose cellar is invaded by the filth of his neighbour's privy, or whose habitation is made unhealthy by the fumes and noisome vapours of his neighbour's alkali works, is damnified without any fault of his own; and it seems but reasonable and just that the neighbour, who has brought something on his own property which was

not naturally there, harmless to others so long as it is confined to his own property, but which he knows to be mischievous if it gets on his neighbour's, should be obliged to make good the damage which ensues if he does not succeed in confining it to his own property. But for his act in bringing it there no mischief could have accrued, and it seems but just that he should at his peril keep it there so that no mischief may accrue, or answer for the natural and anticipated consequences. And upon authority, this we think is established to be the law whether the things so brought be beasts, or water, or filth, or stenches."

In that passage, Blackburn J spoke of "anything *likely* to do mischief if it escapes"; and later he spoke of something "which he *knows* to be mischievous if it gets on his neighbour's [property]", and the liability to "answer for the natural *and anticipated* consequences". Furthermore, time and again he spoke of the strict liability imposed upon the defendant as being that he must keep the thing in at his peril; and, when referring to liability in actions for damage occasioned by animals, he referred, at p282, to the established principle that "it is quite immaterial whether the escape is by negligence or not". The general tenor of his statement of principle is therefore that knowledge, or at least foreseeability of the risk, is a prerequisite of the recovery of damages under the principle; but that the principle is one of strict liability in the sense that the defendant may be held liable notwithstanding that he has exercised all due care to prevent the escape from occurring.

There are however early authorities in which foreseeability of damage does not appear to have been regarded as necessary: see, eg, *Humphries* v *Cousins* (1877) 2 CPD 239. Moreover, it was submitted by Mr Ashworth for CWC that the requirement of foreseeability of damage was negatived in two particular cases, the decision of the Court of Appeal in *West* v *Bristol Tramways Co* [1908] 2 KB 14, and the decision of this House in *Rainham Chemical Works Ltd* v *Belvedere Fish Guano Co* [1921] 2 AC 465.

In *West* v *Bristol Tramways Co* the defendant tramway company was held liable for damage to the plaintiff's plants and shrubs in his nursery garden adjoining a road where the defendant's tramline ran, the damage being caused by fumes from creosoted wooden blocks laid by the defendants between the rails of the tramline. The defendants were so held liable under the rule in *Rylands* v *Fletcher*, notwithstanding that they were exonerated from negligence, having no knowledge of the possibility of such damage; indeed the evidence was that creosoted wood had been in use for several years as wood paving, and no mischief had ever been known to arise from it. The argument that no liability arose in such circumstances under the rule in *Rylands* v *Fletcher* was given short shrift, both in the Divisional Court and in the Court of Appeal. For the Divisional Court, it was enough that the creosote had been found to be dangerous by the jury, Phillimore J holding that creosote was like the wild animals in the old cases. The Court of Appeal did not call upon the plaintiffs, and dismissed the appeal in unreserved judgments. Lord Alverstone CJ relied upon a passage from *Garrett on the Law of Nuisances*, 2nd ed (1897), p129, and rejected a contention by the defendant that, in the case of non-natural use of land, the defendant will not be liable unless the thing introduced onto the land was, to the knowledge of the defendant, likely to escape and cause damage. It was however suggested, both by Lord Alverstone CJ (with whom Sir Gorell Barnes P agreed) and by Farwell LJ that, by analogy with cases concerning liability for animals, the defendant might escape liability if he could show that, according to the common experience of mankind, the thing introduced onto the land had proved not to be dangerous.

The *Rainham Chemical* case [1921] 2 AC 465 arose out of a catastrophic explosion at a factory involved in the manufacture of high explosive during the First World War, with considerable loss of life and damage to neighbouring property. It was held that the company carrying on the business at the premises was liable for the damage to neighbouring property under the rule in *Rylands* v *Fletcher*; but the great question in the case, at least so far as the appellate courts were concerned, was whether two individuals, who were shareholders in and directors of the company, could be held personally responsible on the same principle.

However, this House dismissed their appeal on a point of some technicality, viz that their Lordships could not satisfy themselves that the two individuals had sufficiently divested themselves of the occupation of the premises, so as to substitute the occupation of the company in the place of their own – notwithstanding that the company itself was also in occupation: see [1921] 2 AC 465, 478-479, per Lord Buckmaster; pp480, 483-484, per Lord Sumner; p491, per Lord Parmoor; and pp492, 493-494, per Lord Carson.

I feel bound to say that these two cases provide a very fragile base for any firm conclusion that foreseeability of damage has been authoritatively rejected as a prerequisite of the recovery of damages under the rule in *Rylands* v *Fletcher*. Certainly, the point was not considered by this House in the *Rainham Chemical* case. In my opinion, the matter is open for consideration by your Lordships in the present case, and, despite recent dicta to the contrary (see, eg *Leakey* v *National Trust for Places of Historic Interest or Natural Beauty* [1980] QB 485, 519, per Megaw LJ), should be considered as a matter of principle. Little guidance can be derived from either of the two cases in question, save that it seems to have been assumed that the strict liability arising under the rule precluded reliance by the plaintiff on lack of knowledge or the means of knowledge of the relevant danger.

The point is one on which academic opinion appears to be divided: cf *Salmond & Heuston on the Law of Torts*, 20th ed (1992), pp324-325, which favours the prerequisite of foreseeability, and *Clerk & Lindsell on Torts*, 16th ed (1989), p1429, para 25.09, which takes a different view. However, quite apart from the indications to be derived from the judgment of Blackburn J in *Fletcher* v *Rylands*, LR 1 Ex 265 itself, to

which I have already referred, the historical connection with the law of nuisance must now be regarded as pointing towards the conclusion that foreseeability of damage is a prerequisite of the recovery of damages under the rule. I have already referred to the fact that Blackburn J himself did not regard his statement of principle as having broken new ground; furthermore, Professor Newark has convincingly shown that the rule in *Rylands* v *Fletcher* was essentially concerned with an extension of the law of nuisance to cases of isolated escape. Accordingly since, following the observations of Lord Reid when delivering the advice of the Privy Council in *The Wagon Mound (No 2)* [1967] 1 AC 617, 640, the recovery of damages in private nuisance depends on foreseeability by the defendant of the relevant type of damage, it would appear logical to extend the same requirement to liability under the rule in *Rylands* v *Fletcher*.

Natural use of land

I turn to the question whether the use by ECL of its land in the present case constituted a natural use, with the result that ECL cannot be held liable under the rule in *Rylands* v *Fletcher*. In view of my conclusion on the issue of foreseeability, I can deal with this point shortly.

The judge held that it was a natural use. He said:

"In my judgment, in considering whether the storage of organochlorines as an adjunct to a manufacturing process is a non-natural use of land, I must consider whether that storage created special risks for adjacent occupiers and whether the activity was for the general benefit of the community. It seems to me inevitable that I must consider the magnitude of the storage and the geographical area in which it takes place in answering the question. Sawston is properly described as an industrial village, and the creation of employment is clearly for the benefit of that community. I do not believe that I can enter upon an assessment of the point on a scale of desirability that the manufacture of wash leathers comes, and I content myself with holdings that this storage in this place is a natural use of land."

It is commonplace that this particular exception to liability under the rule has developed and changed over the years. It seems clear that, in *Fletcher* v *Rylands*, LR 1 Ex 265 itself, Blackburn J's statement of the law was limited to things which are brought by the defendant onto his land, and so did not apply to things that were naturally upon the land. Furthermore, it is doubtful whether in the House of Lords in the same case Lord Cairns, to whom we owe the expression "non-natural use" of the land, was intending to expand the concept of natural use beyond that envisaged by Blackburn J. Even so, the law has long since departed from any such simple idea, redolent of a different age; and, at least since the advice of the Privy Council delivered by Lord Moulton in *Rickards* v *Lothian* [1913] AC 263, 280, natural use has been extended to embrace the ordinary use of land. I ask to be forgiven if I again quote Lord Moulton's statement of the law which has lain at the heart of the subsequent development of this exception:

> "It is not every use to which land is put that brings into play at that principle. It must be some special use bringing with it increased danger to others, and must not merely be the ordinary use of the land or such a use as is proper for the general benefit of the community."

Rickards v *Lothian* itself was concerned with a use of a domestic kind, viz the overflow of water from a basin whose runaway had become blocked. But over the years the concept of natural use, in the sense of ordinary use, has been extended to embrace a wide variety of uses, including not only domestic uses but also recreational uses and even some industrial uses.

It is obvious that the expression "ordinary use of the land" in Lord Moulton's statement of the law is one which is lacking in precision. There are some writers who welcome the flexibility which has thus been introduced into this branch of the law, on the ground that it enables judges to mould and adapt the principle of strict liability to the changing needs of society; whereas others regret the perceived absence of principle in so vague a concept, and fear that the whole idea of strict liability may as a result be undermined. A particular doubt is introduced by Lord Moulton's alternative criterion – "or such a use as is proper for the general benefit of the community". If these words are understood to refer to a local community, they can be given some content as intended to refer to such matters as, for example, the provision of services; indeed the same idea can, without too much difficulty, be extended to, for example, the provision of services to industrial premises, as in a business park or an industrial estate. But if the words are extended to embrace the wider interests of the local community or the general benefit of the community at large, it is difficult to see how the exception can be kept within reasonable bounds. A notable extension was considered in your Lordships' House in *Read* v *J Lyons & Co Ltd* [1947] AC 156, 169-170, per Viscount Simon, and p174, per Lord Macmillan, where it was suggested that, in time of war, the manufacture of explosives might be held to constitute a natural use of land, apparently on the basis that, in a country in which the greater part of the population was involved in the war effort, many otherwise exceptional uses might become "ordinary" for the duration of the war. It is however unnecessary to consider so wide an extension as that in a case such as the present. Even so, we can see the introduction of another extension in the present case, when the judge invoked the creation of employment as clearly for the benefit of the local community, viz "the industrial village" at Sawston. I myself, however, do not feel able to accept that the creation of employment as such, even in a small industrial complex, is sufficient of itself to establish a particular use as constituting a natural or ordinary use of land.

Fortunately, I do not think it is necessary for the purposes of the present case to attempt any redefinition of the concept of natural or ordinary use. This is because I am satisfied that the storage of chemicals in substantial quantities, and their use in the manner employed at ECL's premises, cannot fall within the exception. ... Indeed I feel bound to say that the storage of substantial quantities of chemicals on industrial premises should be regarded as an almost classic case of non-natural use; and I find it very difficult to think that it should be thought objectionable to impose strict liability for damage caused in the event of their escape. It may well be that, now that it is recognised that foreseeability of harm of the relevant type is a prerequisite of liability in damages under the rule, the courts may feel less pressure to extend the concept of natural use to circumstances such as those in the present case; and in due course it may become easier to control this exception, and to ensure that it has a more recognisable basis of principle. For these reasons, I would not hold that ECL should be exempt from liability on the basis of the exception of natural use.

However, for the reasons I have already given, I would allow ECL's appeal with costs before your Lordships' House and in the courts below.'

Rylands v *Fletcher* (1868) LR 3 HL 330 House of Lords (Lords Cairns LC and Cranworth)

• *Escape of dangerous things*

Facts

The plaintiff built a colliery on his land. One shaft was extended to join up with some old shafts which had been excavated under land adjacent to the plaintiff's. Using competent but, on this occasion, negligent independent contractors, the defendants constructed a reservoir on nearby land under which some of the old mine shafts were situated. When they filled the reservoir, the water entered the old shafts and, by that route, flooded the plaintiff's mine. The defendants themselves had not been negligent.

Held

The defendants were liable for the damage caused. Their Lordships approved the judgment of Blackburn J in the Court of Exchequer Chamber in which he said:

'The question of law, therefore, arises: What is the liability which the law casts upon a person who, like the defendants, lawfully brings on his land something which, though harmless while it remains there, will naturally do mischief if it escape out of his land? It is agreed on all hands that he must take care to keep in that which he has brought on the land, and keep it there in order that it may not escape and damage his neighbour's, but the question arises whether the duty which the law casts upon him under such circumstances is an absolute duty to keep it in at his peril, or is, as the majority of the Court of Exchequer have thought, merely a duty to take all reasonable and prudent precautions in order to keep it in, but no more. If the first be the law, the person who has brought on his land and kept there something dangerous, and failed to keep it in, is responsible for all the natural consequences of its escape. If the second be the limit of his duty, he would not be answerable except on proof of negligence, and consequently would not be answerable for escape arising from any latent defect which ordinary prudence and skill could not detect. ...

We think that the true rule of law is that the person who, for his own purposes, brings on his land, and collects and keeps there anything likely to do mischief if it escapes, must keep it in at his peril, and, if he does not do so, he is prima facie answerable for all the damage which is the natural consequence of its escape. He can excuse himself by showing that the escape was owing to the plaintiff's default, or, perhaps, that the escape was the consequence of vis major, or the act of God; but, as nothing of this sort exists here, it is unnecessary to inquire what excuse would be sufficient. The general rule, as above stated, seems on principle just. The person whose grass or corn is eaten down by the escaped cattle of his neighbour, or whose mine is flooded by the water from his neighbour's reservoir, or whose cellar is invaded by the filth of his neighbour's privy, or whose habitation is made unhealthy by the fumes and noisome vapours of his neighbour's alkali works, is damnified without any fault of his own; and it seems but reasonable and just that the neighbour who has brought something on his own property which was not naturally there, harmless to others so long as it is confined to his own property, but which he knows will be mischievous if he gets on his neighbour's, should be obliged to make good the damage which ensues if he does not succeed in confining it to his own property. But for his act in bringing it there no mischief could have accrued, and it seems but just that he should at his peril keep it there, so that no mischief may accrue, or answer for the natural and anticipated consequences. On authority this, we think, is established to be the law, whether the thing so brought be beasts or water, or filth or stenches.'

Lord Cairns LC:

'... if the defendants, not stopping at the natural use of their close [land], had desired to use it for any purpose which I may term a non-natural use, for the purpose of introducing into the close that which, in its natural condition, was not in or upon it ... then it appears to me that that which the defendants were doing they were doing at their own peril.'

Comment

Approved in *Leakey* v *National Trust for Places of Historic Interest or Natural Beauty* [1980] 2 WLR 65.

Distinguished in *Noble* v *Harrison* [1926] 2 KB 332 (tree not a dangerous thing) and *Green* v *Chelsea Waterworks Co* (1894) 70 LT 547 (burst water main). See also *Cambridge Water Co Ltd* v *Eastern Counties Leather plc* [1994] 2 WLR 53.

19 Fire

Emanuel (H & N) Ltd v ***Greater London Council*** [1971] 2 All ER 835 Court of Appeal (Lord Denning MR, Edmund-Davies and Phillimore LJJ)

- *Escape of fire – act of third party*

Facts
An arrangement was made whereby a firm of independent contractors, engaged by the Ministry of Works, would remove two wartime bungalows and all materials and rubbish from a site owned by the defendant council. The contractors started a fire to burn unwanted materials. Sparks blew on to the plaintiffs' property and the resulting fire caused damage.

Held
The council as occupier was liable for the escape of fire caused by the negligence of anyone other than a stranger. The contractors were on the land with the council's leave, and although the contractors were forbidden by the terms of their contract from starting fires on the land, the council could reasonably have anticipated that they might start a fire.

Lord Denning MR:

'I turn to consider the law. After considering the cases, it is my opinion that the occupier of a house or land is liable for the escape of fire which is due to the negligence not only of his servants, but also of his independent contractors and of his guests, and of anyone who is there with his leave or licence. The only circumstances when the occupier is not liable for the negligence is when it is the negligence of a stranger. It was so held in a case in the Year Books 570 years ago, *Beaulieu* v *Finglam* (1401) YB 2 Hen 4 ... The occupier is, therefore, liable for the neg-

ligence of an independent contractor, such as the man who comes in to repair the pipes and uses a blowlamp: see *Balfour* v *Barty-King* [1957] 1 All ER 156; and of a guest who negligently drops a lighted match: see *Boulcott Golf Club Inc* v *Engelbrecht* [1945] NZLR 556. The occupier is liable because he is the occupier and responsible in that capacity for those who come by his leave and licence: see *Sturge* v *Hackett* [1963] 3 All ER 166.

But the occupier is not liable for the escape of fire which is not due to the negligence of anyone. Sir John Holt himself said in *Tuberville* v *Stampe* (1697) 1 Ld Raym 264 that if a man is properly burning up weeds or stubble and, owing to an unforeseen wind-storm, without negligence, the fire is carried into his neighbour's ground, he is not liable. Again, if a haystack is properly built at a safe distance, and yet bursts into flames by spontaneous combustion, without negligence, the occupier is not liable. That is to be inferred from *Vaughan* v *Menlove* (1837) 3 Bing NC 468. So also if a fire starts without negligence owing to an unknown defect in the electric wiring: *Collingwood* v *Home and Colonial Stores Ltd* [1936] 3 All ER 200; or a spark leaps out of the fireplace without negligence: *Sochacki* v *Sas* [1947] 1 All ER 344. All those cases are covered, if not by the common law, at any rate by the Fire Prevention (Metropolis) Act 1774, which covers all cases where a fire begins or spreads by accident without negligence. But that Act does not cover a fire which begins or is spread by negligence: see *Filliter* v *Phippard* (1847) 11 QBD 347, *Musgrove* v *Pandelis* [1919] 2 KB 43 and *Goldman* v *Hargrave* [1966] 2 All ER 989.

Nevertheless, as I have said earlier, the occupier is not liable if the outbreak of fire is due to the negligence of a "stranger". But who is a "stranger" for this purpose?

I think a "stranger" is anyone who in lighting a fire or allowing it to escape acts contrary to anything which the occupier could anticipate that he would do: such as the person in *Rickards* v *Lothian* [1913] AC 263. Even if it is a man whom you have allowed or invited into your house, nevertheless, if his conduct in lighting a fire is so alien to your invitation that he should qua the fire be regarded as a trespasser, he is a "stranger". Such as the man in Scrutton LJ's well-known illustration:

> "When you invite a person into your house to use the staircase you do not invite him to slide down the banisters ..."
>
> ...

There has been much discussion about the exact legal basis of liability for fire. The liability of the occupier can be said to be a strict liability in this sense that he is liable for the negligence not only of his servants but also of independent contractors and, indeed, of anyone except a "stranger". By the same token it can be said to be a "vicarious liability", because he is liable for the defaults of others as well as his own. It can also be said to be a liability under the principle of *Rylands* v *Fletcher*, because fire is undoubtedly a dangerous thing which is likely to do damage if it escapes. But I do not think it necessary to put it into any one of these three categories. It goes back to the time when no such categories were thought of. Suffice it to say that the extent of the liability is now well defined as I have stated it. The occupier is liable for the escape of fire which is due to the negligence of anyone other than a stranger.'

Comment

Applied, inter alia: *Balfour* v *Barty-King* [1957] 2 WLR 84 and *Wheat* v *E Lacon & Co Ltd* [1966] 2 WLR 581.

20 Animals

Curtis v *Betts* [1990] 1 WLR 459
Court of Appeal (Slade, Nourse and Stuart-Smith LJJ)

* *Dangerous dog – liability*

Facts
The plaintiff, aged 10, had known the defendants' bull mastiff Max since it was a puppy and he was very friendly with it. When the dog was being loaded into the back of the defendants' Land Rover, the boy called its name and approached it. Although the dog was on a lead held by the first defendant, it leapt at the plaintiff and bit him on the face: the plaintiff had been in no way to blame.

Held
The plaintiff was entitled to damages as the requirements of s2(2)(a)(b) and (c) of the Animals Act 1971 had been satisfied.

Stuart-Smith LJ:

'Like Slade and Nourse LJJ and others before me, I have not found s2(2) of the Animals Act 1971 easy to construe ...

Paragraph (a) is concerned with the type of damage that it is foreseeable that the animal may cause. It may be of two types: the first is of a kind that the animal unless restrained, is likely to cause; the second is if it is likely to be severe. In each case the question relates to the animal in question ... I can see no reason for ... limiting the plain words of the paragraph. Moreover, it seems to me to be contrary to the decision of this court in *Cummings* v *Granger* [1976] 3 WLR 842 ... At the time of this incident Max was a big dog: he weighed about 10 stone and he had big teeth and a large mouth ... if he did bite anyone the damage was likely to be severe.

Paragraph (b) presents more difficulty. Here again there are two limbs to the subsection. The first deals with what may for convenience be called permanent characteristics, the second, temporary characteristics. Dogs are not normally fierce or prone to attack humans; a dog which has a propensity to do this at all times and in all places and without discrimination as to persons would clearly fall within the first limb. One that is only aggressive in particular circumstances, for example when guarding its territory or, if a bitch, when it had a litter of pups, will come within the second limb. In the present case the judge concluded that Max fell within the second limb. He said that he was –

"satisfied on the balance of probabilities that the defendants knew of the tendency of these dogs to be what one may term fierce, when protecting the boundaries of what they considered their territory, which expression may have included the rear of the Land Rover" ...

In my judgment the judge correctly directed himself on this aspect of the matter ... he was ... justified in concluding that the place and circumstances of the attack were within the ambit of the dog protecting its territory ... Counsel for the defendants did not seek to challenge the judge's finding that the defendants knew of Max's propensity to be fierce in defence of his territory; but he submitted that this did not extend to knowledge of such a propensity with regard to the place and circumstances of the attack. But counsel for the defendants realistically accepted that this submission was dependent on the last. If the judge was justified in holding, as in my view he was, that the attack was part and parcel of defence of territory, then it seems to me to follow that the characteristic of the dog to act as it did at the place and in the circumstances of the attack were within the ambit of the defendants' knowledge and para (c) was satisfied.

I would only add this. In my view it is desirable, when judges have to decide cases under this subsection, that they should consider each part of the subsection in turn and satisfy themselves that the plaintiff has made out his case on one or other of the limbs of each part.'

Wallace v *Newton* [1982] 1 WLR 375 High Court (Park J)

• *Animals – violent horse*

Facts

The plaintiff was a groom employed by the defendant to care for several horses. One of the horses, named 'Lord Justice', was known to have a nervous and unpredictable temperament. One day while the plaintiff was attempting to load the horse into a horse box it became violent and uncontrollable and jumped forward, crushing the plaintiff's arm against the breast bar. The plaintiff sued the defendant for damages for breach of duty under (inter alia) s2(2) of the Animals Act 1971.

Held

The plaintiff was entitled to damages.

Park J:

'Under s2(2)(a) of the Animals Act 1971 the plaintiff has to establish first that the damage which she suffered was of a kind which Lord Justice was likely to cause, and on this part of the case there is no dispute. Under s2(2)(b) the plaintiff has to establish that the likelihood of the damage was due to characteristics of Lord Justice which were not normally found in horses. The question is whether the words "characteristics which are not normally found in horses" have to be interpreted as meaning that Lord Justice must be shown to have had a vicious tendency to injure people by attacking them or

whether the words have to be given their ordinary natural meaning, that is that Lord Justice had characteristics of a kind not usually found in horses. If the plaintiff has to establish that her injuries were due to Lord Justice's vicious tendency to injure people, then her claim would fail. He was not, as the plaintiff herself agreed, a vicious horse or a dangerous horse in the way in which the defendant understood that word. On the other hand, if she has to establish that her injuries were due to a characteristic of Lord Justice which was unusual in a horse, then she would establish this limb of her case. I think this is the meaning to be given to the words in s2(2)(b).

On the evidence I am satisfied that, certainly during the period that the plaintiff had Lord Justice in her charge, the horse was unpredictable and unreliable in his behaviour, and in that way he was, as the plaintiff said, dangerous. The injury to her arm was due to this characteristic, which is not normally found in a horse. So, in my judgment, the plaintiff has established the second limb of her case.

Under s2(2)(c) the plaintiff has to prove that these characteristics were known to the defendant, as Lord Justice's keeper, or at any time known to a person who at that time had charge of Lord Justice as the defendant's servant. I have no doubt at all that Tom Read [the head man in charge of the defendant's horses] well knew about Lord Justice's unpredictability and unreliability and because of that knowledge he very properly warned the plaintiff about the horse. The defendant says that she knew nothing of the incident a week before the plaintiff's accident and of the consequent change of procedure. I am sure that her evidence is honest, but ... to me it is inconceivable that Tom Read did not tell her everything about Lord Justice and in particular about the incident which occurred a week before the accident. I think that the defendant at the material time knew as much about the horse as Tom Read.

For these reasons I am satisfied that the defendant is liable to the plaintiff under the provisions of s2(2) of the Act.'

Comment

There is nothing in the 1971 Act to prevent one keeper suing another keeper, in appropriate circumstances: *Flack* v *Hudson* (2000) The Times 22 November.

21 Defamation

Berkoff v Burchill [1996] 4 All ER 1008 Court of Appeal (Neill, Millett and Phillips LJJ)

• *Libel – words capable of being defamatory – 'hideously ugly'*

Facts
The plaintiff actor, director and writer was well known for his work on stage, screen and television. It was alleged that words used in articles written by the first defendant and published by the second defendant in the *Sunday Times* conveyed the meaning that the plaintiff was hideously ugly. Were these words capable of being defamatory?

Held (Millett LJ dissenting)
They were.

Neill LJ:

'No order has been made as to the mode of trial in this case. One must therefore proceed on the basis that the action is likely to be tried, if at all, with a jury. The question of fact: libel or no libel, is a matter for the jury. But the court has jurisdiction to rule that as a matter of law words are incapable of being defamatory. ...

I am not aware of any entirely satisfactory definition of the word "defamatory". It may be convenient, however, to collect together some of the definitions which have been used and approved in the past. ...

It will be seen from this collection of definitions that words may be defamatory, even though they neither impute disgraceful conduct to the plaintiff nor any lack of skill or efficiency in the conduct of his trade or business or professional activity, if they hold him up to contempt, scorn or ridicule or tend to exclude him from society. On the other hand, insults which do not diminish a man's standing among other people do not found an action for libel or slander. The exact borderline may often be difficult to define. ...

It is trite law that the meaning of words in a libel action is determined by the reaction of the ordinary reader and not by the intention of the publisher, but the perceived intention of the publisher may colour the meaning. In the present case it would, in my view, be open to a jury to conclude that in the context the remarks about Mr Berkoff gave the impression that he was not merely physically unattractive in appearance but actually repulsive. It seems to me that to say this of someone in the public eye who makes his living, in part at least, as an actor, is capable of lowering his standing in the estimation of the public and of making him an object of ridicule.

I confess that I have found this to be a far from easy case, but in the end I am satisfied that it would be wrong to decide this preliminary issue in a way which would withdraw the matter completely from the consideration of a jury.'

Phillips J:

'Where the issue is whether words have damaged a plaintiff's reputation by exposing him to ridicule, that question cannot be answered simply by considering whether the natural and ordinary meaning of the words used is defamatory per se. The question has to be considered in the light of the actual words used and the circumstance in which they are used. There are many ways of indicating that a person is hideously ugly, ranging from a simple statement of opinion to that effect, which I feel could never be defamatory, to words plainly intended to convey that message by way of ridicule. The words used in this case fall into the latter category. Whether they have exposed the plaintiff to ridicule to the extent that his reputation has been damaged must be answered by the jury.'

Derbyshire County Council v *Times Newspapers Ltd* [1993] 2 WLR 449 House of Lords (Lords Keith of Kinkel, Griffiths, Goff of Chieveley, Browne-Wilkinson and Woolf)

• *Local authorities – actions for libel*

Facts
The Sunday Times, one of the defendants' newspapers, published articles questioning the propriety of certain investments involving the plaintiffs' superannuation fund. The preliminary point arose as to whether the plaintiff council could maintain an action for libel for any words which reflected upon it as the county council for Derbyshire in relation to its governmental and administrative functions in Derbyshire, including its statutory responsibility for the investment and control of the superannuation fund.

Held
A local authority cannot maintain an action for defamation in respect of its governing reputation.

Lord Keith of Kinkel:

'The authorities ... clearly establish that a trading corporation is entitled to sue in respect of defamatory matters which can be seen as having a tendency to damage it in the way of its business. Examples are those that go to credit such as might deter banks from lending to it, or to the conditions experienced by its employees, which might impede the recruitment of the best qualified workers, or make people reluctant to deal with it. *South Hetton Coal Co Ltd* v *North-Eastern News Association Ltd* [1894] 1 QB 133 would appear to be an instance of the latter kind, and not ... an authority for the

view that a trading corporation can sue for something that does not affect it adversely in the way of its business ... Similar considerations can no doubt be advanced in connection with the position of a local authority. Defamatory statements might make it more difficult to borrow or to attract suitable staff and thus affect adversely the efficient carrying out of its functions.

There are, however, features of a local authority which may be regarded as distinguishing it from other types of corporation, whether trading or non-trading. The most important of these features is that it is a governmental body. Further, it is a democratically elected body, the electoral process nowadays being conducted almost exclusively on party political lines. It is of the highest public importance that a democratically elected governmental body, or indeed any governmental body, should be open to uninhibited public criticism. The threat of a civil action for defamation must inevitably have an inhibiting effect on freedom of speech ...

It is of some significance to observe that a number of departments of central government in the United Kingdom are statutorily created corporations, including the Secretaries of State for Defence, Education and Science, Energy, Environment and Social Services. If a local authority can sue for libel there would appear to be no reason in logic for holding that any of these departments (apart from two which are made corporations only for the purposes of holding land) were not also entitled to sue. But as is shown by the decision in *A-G* v *Guardian Newspapers Ltd (No 2)* [1988] 2 WLR 805, a case concerned with confidentiality, there are rights available to private citizens which institutions of central government are not in a position to exercise unless they can show that it is [in] the public interest to do so. The same applies, in my opinion, to local authorities. In both cases I regard it as right for this House to lay down that not only is there no public interest favouring the right of organs of government, whether central or local, to sue for libel, but that it is contrary to the public interest that they should have it. It is contrary to the public interest because to admit such actions would place an undesirable fetter on freedom of speech ...

In the case of a local authority temporarily under the control of one political party or another it is difficult to say that the local authority as such has any reputation of its own. Reputation in the eyes of the public is more likely to attach itself to the controlling political party, and with a change in that party the reputation itself will change. A publication attacking the activities of the authority will necessarily be an attack on the body of councillors which represents the controlling party, or on the executives who carry on the day-to-day management of its affairs. If the individual reputation of any of these is wrongly impaired by the publication any of these can himself bring proceedings for defamation. Further, it is open to the controlling body to defend itself by public utterances and in debate in the council chamber.

The conclusion must be, in my opinion, that under the common law of England a local authority does not have the right to maintain an action of damages for defamation. That was the conclusion reached by the Court of Appeal, which did so principally by reference to art 10 of the European Convention on Human Rights ... , to which the United Kingdom has adhered but which has not been enacted into domestic law.

My Lords, I have reached my conclusion upon the common law of England without finding any need to rely upon the European convention. Lord Goff of Chieveley in *A-G v Guardian Newspapers Ltd (No 2)* expressed the opinion that in the field of freedom of speech there was no difference in principle between English law on the subject and art 10 of the convention. I agree, and can only add that I find it satisfactory to be able to conclude that the common law of England is consistent with the obligations assumed by the Crown under the treaty in this particular field ... It follows that *Bognor Regis UDC v Campion* [1972] 2 WLR 983 was wrongly decided and should be overruled.'

Comment

Applied in *Goldsmith* v *Bhoyrul* [1997] 4 All ER 268 (political party – here the Referendum Party, a company limited by guarantee – cannot sue for defamation, although individual candidates, officials or other persons connected with the party may do so).

Holley v *Smyth* [1998] 1 All ER 853 Court of Appeal (Staughton, Auld LJJ and Sir Christopher Slade)

• *Defamation – threatened libel – interlocutory injunction*

Facts

Believing that the plaintiff had been guilty of disreputable conduct in a financial transaction, the defendant sent the plaintiff's solicitors two draft press releases containing this allegation. The plaintiff sought an interlocutory injunction to restrain publication of the releases and the defendant made clear that he intended to justify his assertions if he was allowed to publish the releases and was subsequently sued for defamation. The injunction was granted: the defendant appealed.

Held

The injunction would be discharged.

Auld LJ:

'In my judgment, the authorities establish the following propositions. The courts' power to grant interlocutory relief to restrain a libel is discretionary ... but it is a discretion that must be exercised with great caution.

The discretion to grant such relief is guided by the statutory constraint in s37(1) of the Supreme Court Act 1981 that it should be exercised only where "it appears to the court to be just and convenient to do so".

Where there is a defence or claim of justification the discretion is further guided by the rule in *Bonnard* v *Perryman* [1891] 2 Ch 269 that it is not normally just or convenient to grant relief unless the plaintiff has proved that the libel is plainly untrue.

There is no jurisprudential basis for confining the *Bonnard* v *Perryman* rule or its rigour to threatened publication by the media. ...

There may be exceptions to the general rule, but neither the would-be libeller's motive nor the manner in which he threatens publication nor the potential damage to the plaintiff is normally a basis for making an exception. ... I can see no basis for regarding the potential damage to the [plaintiff] here as of such an exceptional nature or gravity to take the case outside the general rule.

Accordingly, I am of the view that [the judge's] reasons for the exercise of his discretion to grant relief were wrong and that the circumstances of this case do not justify the court in regarding it as an exception to the application of the general rule. If [the defendant's] allegations are true, he is entitled to publish them, or to threaten to publish them, regardless of his motive or of the damage such publication would or may do to the plaintiffs. Unless it can be shown at this interlocutory stage that they are plainly untrue, the scheme of the law is that he should not normally be deprived in the meantime of an entitlement which he may subsequently establish. If he succeeds in doing so, his motive continues to be irrelevant, if he fails then the law will require him to compensate the plaintiffs and his motive may be punished by an award of aggravated damages (see *Rookes* v *Barnard* [1964] 1 All ER 367 at 407 per Lord Devlin). ...

In my view, on the material before the court, none of those matters would entitle it to conclude, differently from [the judge], that [the defendant's] threatened publication is plainly untrue.'

Loutchansky v *Times Newspapers Ltd* [2001] 4 All ER 115 Court of Appeal (Thorpe and Brooke LJJ, Sir Martin Nourse)

• *Libel – qualified privilege – matters not known at time of publication*

Facts

In an action for libel, the defendants sought permission to amend their defence of qualified privilege by adding matters which were not known to them at the time of publication of the newspaper articles which had given rise to the proceedings. They asserted that they were entitled to rely on facts of which they had been unaware at the material time in support of their contention that they were under a duty, in the public interest, to publish the matters of which complaint was made. Gray J refused permission to make the amendments and the defendants appealed against this decision.

Held

The appeal would be dismissed.

Brooke LJ:

'The House of Lords has ruled in *Reynolds* v *Times Newspapers Ltd* [1999] 4 All ER 609 ... that the media do not have an unfettered right to publish what they believe to be in the public interest. Some discipline has to be introduced, in order to give appropriate effect to the interests recognised as legitimate by art 10(2) [of the European Convention for the Protection of Human Rights and Fundamental Freedoms]. This discipline involves the court examining the occasion of a publication, and not the circumstances as they might have appeared to the publishers weeks or months later if they had waited to make further inquiries, or waited to see if further facts came to light. If they were to be taken to have that additional opportunity, they would by the same token have more time to seek out the complainant and obtain his version of events. It would then be likely that what they then published would be different from what they in fact published, and it is what they in fact published which is the subject of Mr Loutchansky's complaint.'

Comment

In *Loutchansky* v *Times Newspapers Ltd (No 2)* [2002] 1 All ER 652 the Court of Appeal made points as follows:

1. When deciding whether there was a duty to publish defamatory words to the world at large, the relevant interest was that of the public in a modern democracy in free expression and, more particularly, in the promotion of a free and vigorous press to keep the public informed. The corresponding duty on the journalist and his editor was to act responsibly.
2. Where it was known that archive material was or might be defamatory, the attachment of an appropriate notice warning against treating it as the truth would normally remove any sting from the material.
3. Where information is published on the Internet, for the purposes of s4A of the Limitation Act 1980 each individual publication of it (as opposed to just the first) has its own limitation period.
4. The summary disposal procedure under s8 of the Defamation Act 1996 is also available in a suitable case for disposing of quantum alone once liability has been determined or admitted.

In *Baldwin* v *Rusbridger* (2001) The Times 23 July the Court of Appeal concluded that there are powerful considerations of public policy against extending the law to give journalists qualified privilege for attacks in their newspapers upon those who had criticised them in court.

Mahon v *Rahn (No 2)* [2000] 4 All ER 41

See Chapter 31.

Rantzen v *Mirror Group Newspapers (1986) Ltd* [1993] 3 WLR 953 Court of Appeal (Neill, Roch and Staughton LJJ)

• *Libel – damages – excessive award – court's power to order a new trial or substitute another award – guidelines*

Facts

The plaintiff was a well-known television presenter and the founder and chairperson of the 'Childline', charity for sexually abused children. She sued the defendants in libel in respect of four articles in *The People* newspaper which she claimed bore the meaning that her activities on behalf of sexually abused children were insincere and hypocritical as she had protected a known abuser of children. The defendants pleaded justification and fair comment, but the jury found for the plaintiff and awarded her £250,000 damages. The defendants appealed, seeking a reduction in damages under s8 of the Courts and Legal Services Act 1990 and RSC O.59 r11(4) (see now r52(10)(3) of the Civil Procedure Rules), and in the light of art 10 of the European Convention for the Protection of Human Rights and Fundamental Freedoms.

Held

An award of £110,000 would be substituted for the jury's award.

Neill LJ:

'Counsel for Miss Rantzen submitted that there was no reason to depart from the former practice which had been reaffirmed by the Court of Appeal … in *Sutcliffe* v *Pressdram Ltd* [1990] 1 All ER 269 [where] Lord Donaldson MR collected together some of the formulations which had been used to identify the test which had to be satisfied before the Court of Appeal could grant a new trial. These formulations included: (1) "the damages are so excessive that no twelve men could reasonably have given them" (see *Praed* v *Graham* (1889) 24 QBD 53 at 55 per Lord Esher MR) … In the reports there are many other passages to the same effect. …

On behalf of the defendants, however, it was submitted that s8 of the [Courts and Legal Services Act 1990] now empowers the court to intervene more readily and to apply a less stringent test. Counsel contended that s8 was enacted to address the concern which was widely felt that awards of damages in libel actions had become unreasonable. The new power conferred by s8 of the 1990 Act, and by the rule made under it, was clearly designed to be exercisable whenever an award of damages was considered by the Court of Appeal to be "excessive". It was no longer necessary or appropriate to use the barrier against interference which the earlier formulations had erected. ...

As we explain later ... it is necessary to examine the powers of the court to order a new trial and to substitute a fresh award in accordance with s8(2) of the 1990 Act and O.59 r11(4), in the light of the guidance recently given by the House to Lords as to the relationship between the common law and art 10 of the convention and also in the light of the guidance as to the proper scope of art 10 given by the European Court of Human Rights in Strasbourg. ...

It is always to be remembered that the convention is not part of English domestic law and therefore the courts have no power to enforce convention rights directly. ...

Where freedom of expression is at stake, however, recent authorities lend support for the proposition that art 10 has a wider role and can properly be regarded as an articulation of some of the principles underlying the common law. ...

How then should the Court of Appeal interpret its power to order a new trial on the ground that the damages awarded by the jury were excessive? How is the word "excessive" in s8(1) of the 1990 Act to be interpreted?

After careful consideration we have come to the conclusion that we must interpret our power so as to give proper weight to the guidance given by the House of Lords and by the court in Strasbourg. In particular we should take account of the following passage in Lord Goff's speech in *A-G v Guardian Newspapers Ltd (No 2)* [1988] 3 All ER 545 at 660, [1990] 1 AC 109 at 283–284:

"The exercise of the right to freedom of expression under art 10 may e subject to restrictions (as are prescribed by law and are necessary in a democratic society) in relation to certain prescribed matters which include 'the interests of national security' and 'preventing the disclosure of information received in confidence'. It is established in the jurisprudence of the European Court of Human Rights that the word 'necessary' in this context implies the existence of a pressing social need, and that interference with freedom of expression should be no more than is proportionate to the legitimate aim pursued. I have no reason to believe that English law, as applied in the courts, leads to any different conclusion."

If one applies these words it seems to us that the grant of an almost limitless discretion to a jury fails to provide a satisfactory measurement for deciding what is "necessary in a democratic society" or "justified by a pressing social need". We consider therefore that the common law if properly understood requires the courts to subject large awards of damages to a more searching scrutiny that has been customary in the past. It follows that what has been regarded as the barrier against intervention should be lowered. The question becomes: could a reasonable jury have thought that this award was necessary to compensate the plaintiff and to re-establish his reputation?

We must turn shortly to consider the award of damages in the present case. Before doing so, however, we should express our conclusions as to what further guidance, if any, can be given to a jury by the judge in his summing up. ...

The matter can be approached in three stages: (a) references to other jury awards in defamation cases; (b) references to (what we may call) s8 awards by the Court of Appeal in defamation cases; (c) references to conventional awards in personal injury actions.

We are not persuaded that at the present time it would be right to allow references to be made to awards by juries in previous cases. Until very recently it had been the practice to give juries other than minimal guidance as to how they should approach the task of awarding damages and in these circumstances previous awards cannot be regarded as establishing a norm or standard to which reference can be made in the future.

Awards made by the Court of Appeal in the exercise of its powers under s8 of the 1990 Act and O.59 r11(4) stand on a different footing. It seems to us that it must have been the intention of the framers of the 1990 Act that over a period of time the awards made by the Court of Appeal would provide a corpus to which reference could be made in subsequent cases. Any risk of overcitation would have to be controlled by the trial judge, but to prevent reference to such awards would seem to us to conflict with the principle that restrictions on freedom of expression should be "prescribed by law". The decisions of the Court of Appeal could be relied upon as establishing the prescribed norm.

We come therefore to the most difficult aspect of the matter, the possibility of references to awards in personal injury cases. ... We have come to the conclusion ... that there is no satisfactory way in which the conventional awards in actions for damages for personal injuries can be used to provide guidance for an award in an action for defamation. Despite ... submissions to the contrary, it seems to us that damages for defamation are intended at least in part as a vindication of the plaintiff to the public. This element of the damages was recognised by Lord Hailsham LC in *Cassell & Co Ltd v Broome* [1972] 1 All ER 801 at 824. We therefore feel bound to reject the proposal that the jury should be referred to awards made in actions involving serious personal injuries.

It is to be hoped that in the course of time a series of decisions of the Court of Appeal will establish some standards as to what are, in the terms of s8 of the 1990 Act, "proper" awards. In the meantime the jury should be invited to consider the purchasing power of any award which they may make. In addition they should be asked to ensure that any award they make is proportionate to the damage which the plaintiff has suffered and is a sum which it is necessary to award him to provide adequate compensation and to re-establish his reputation.

We return to the facts of the present case.

A very substantial award was clearly justified ... The jury were entitled to conclude that the publication of the article and its aftermath were a terrible ordeal for Miss Rantzen. But, as has been pointed out, Miss Rantzen still has an extremely successful career as a television presenter. She is a distinguished and highly respected figure in the world of broadcasting. Her work in combating child abuse has achieved wide acclaim. We have therefore been driven to the conclusion that the court has power to, and should, intervene. Judged by any objective standards of reasonable compensation or necessity or proportionality the award of £250,000 was excessive.'

Comment

The whole question of damages for defamation received further consideration by the Court of Appeal in *John* v *MGN Ltd* [1996] 2 All ER 35. Elton John had been awarded £75,000 and £275,000 by way of compensatory and exemplary damages respectively and these jury awards were reduced, on appeal, to £25,000 and £50,000. In delivering the judgment of the court Sir Thomas Bingham MR said that the time had come when judges, and counsel, could draw to the attention of juries the level of awards in personal injury cases: it was

'offensive to public opinion ... that a defamation plaintiff should recover damages for injury to reputation greater, perhaps by a significant factor, than if that same plaintiff had been rendered a helpless cripple or an insensate vegetable.'

As to exemplary damages, his Lordship said that the question was whether the sum awarded for compensatory damages was sufficient to punish the defendant newspaper and to deter it, or other national newspapers of a similar character, from such conduct in future.

See also *Thompson* v *Commissioner of Police of the Metropolis* [1997] 2 All ER 762 and *Kiam* v *MGN Ltd* [2002] 2 All ER 219 (Court of Appeal will not interfere with jury's libel damages award unless it regards award as substantially exceeding highest jury could reasonably have thought necessary) and *Grobbelaar* v *News Group Newspapers Ltd* [2001] 2 All ER 437 (jury's verdict set aside since it represented miscarriage of justice).

Waple v *Surrey County Council*
[1998] 1 All ER 624 Court of Appeal (Nourse, Brooke LJJ and Sir Brian Neill)

• *Absolute privilege – judicial proceedings – response to request for information following service of contribution notice*

Facts
The plaintiff and her husband were the adoptive parents of a boy and, problems having arisen between the boy and his adopters, the defendant council placed the boy with foster parents. The husband having declined to supply the council with details of his means, the council served on him a contribution notice requiring him to contribute to the boy's maintenance. In response to inquiries made by the adoptive parents' solicitor as to the decision to remove the boy from them, the council's solicitor wrote a letter which allegedly defamed the plaintiff. In proceedings for defamation, the judge decided that the letter had been written on an occasion of absolute privilege. The plaintiff appealed against this decision.

Held
The appeal would be allowed.

Brooke LJ:

'The judge described the events which followed the service of the contribution notice in the present case as "legal proceedings of a sort", but it will be seen that if the local authority reaches agreement with the parent as to the quantum and the arrangements for paying his or her contribution, there will be no need to involve a court so long as the parent keeps up the agreed payments.

The modern rules about absolute privilege extend the privilege to statements made in the course of judicial or quasi-judicial proceedings, and statements contained in documents made in such proceedings. It has been settled for over 100 years that the courts should be very slow to extend the scope of this privilege: see *Royal Aquarium and Summer and Winter Garden Society Ltd* v *Parkinson* [1892] 1 QB 431 at 451 when Lopes LJ rationalised the width of the privilege by reference to the requirement of public policy to ensure freedom of speech in a context in which it was essential that such freedom of speech should exist, "and with the knowledge that Courts of Justice are presided over by those who from their high character are not likely to abuse the privilege, and who have the power and ought to have the will to check any abuse of it by those who appear before them".

It is instructive to consider the policy given by the courts from time to time when fixing or refixing the limits of this type of absolute privilege. In *Watson* v *M'Ewan, Watson* v *Jones* [1905] AC 480 the House of Lords extended the scope of the privilege to statements made by a witness to the client and solicitor in preparing a case for trial. ...

In *Lincoln* v *Daniels* [1961] 3 All ER 740, [1962] 1 QB 237 this court ruled that communications sent to the Secretary of the Bar Council alleging professional misconduct by a barrister did not attract absolute privilege, since they were not a step in an inquiry before an Inn of Court. Devlin LJ accepted that this was a matter of form rather than substance ... He had identified three categories of the absolute privilege which covers proceedings in or before a court of justice. The first covers what is said in court and the second covers everything that is done from the inception of the proceedings onwards, such as the pleadings:

"The third category is the most difficult of the three to define. It is based on the authority of *Watson* v *M'Ewan* ([1905] AC 480), in which the House of Lords held that the privilege attaching to evidence which a witness gave coram judice extended to the prerecognition or proof of that evidence taken by a solicitor. It is immaterial whether the proof is or is not taken in the course of proceedings. In *Beresford* v *White* ((1914) 30 TLR 591), the privilege was held to attach to what was said in the course of an interview by a solicitor with a person who might or might not be in a position to be a witness on behalf of his client in contemplated proceedings." (See [1961] 3 All ER 740 at 749–750.)

Devlin LJ went on to say that it was obvious that unless there were a category of this sort the absolute privilege granted for matters said and done coram judice might be rendered illusory (see [1961] 3 All ER 740 at 751). He did not treat the principle enunciated by Lord Halsbury LC in *Watson* v *M'Ewan* as necessarily limited to the proofs of witnesses. He thought it might well cover, for example, instructions given by a party to his solicitor, going beyond matters to which the party could himself depose, for the preparation of a statement of claim or like document. In considering later authorities, he said that these showed that the connection between the two things – the evidence and the precognition, the document and the draft, the actuality that is undeniably privileged and the foreshadowing of it – must be reasonably close (see [1961] 3 All ER 740 at 752). ...

Devlin LJ considered, therefore, that in this third category of cases the privilege

should be extended only to situations where it was strictly necessary to do so in order to protect those who were to participate in the proceedings from a flank attack. ...

The judge ... said that it could not be doubted that the privilege from suit of those engaged in the preparation for, or conduct of, litigation of whatever nature was far reaching. This does not, however, in my judgment, resolve the issue which arises in the present case since as Devlin LJ pointed out in *Lincoln* v *Daniels,* it is the form, not the substance with which the court is traditionally concerned in cases of this type, and I have already observed that the mere fact that a contribution notice is served does not inevitably mean that relevant proceedings will ever start in a court of justice any more than the writing of a letter before action inevitably has that effect. ...

In my judgment, it is not open to us ... to extend the scope of the absolute privilege granted to statements made in connection with judicial proceedings to the statement made in [the council's solicitor's] letter. ... This is the kind of exchange in which solicitors acting for a public authority often involve themselves, and although in the ordinary way their letters would attract qualified privilege, I can see no warrant for extending the scope of absolute privilege to cover a communication of this type. It is not the type of communication embraced in Devlin LJ's third category in *Lincoln* v *Daniels.*

22 Trespass to the Person

Meering v Grahame-White Aviation Co Ltd (1919) 122 LT 44 Court of Appeal (Atkin, Duke and Warrington LJJ)

• *False imprisonment – person under police influence*

Facts

In an action for false imprisonment it appeared that an infant, the plaintiff, who was employed in an aviation works, was suspected of stealing a keg of varnish. He complied with a request to go to the offices of his employers, the defendants, and to remain in the waiting room. Two of the company's police, who had accompanied him to the offices, stayed in the neighbourhood, and the plaintiff agreed to wait there on being told that he was wanted to give evidence in connection with certain thefts. The defendants argued that the plaintiff had not been detained in the waiting room as he was free to go when and where he liked.

Held

This argument would fail: from the moment the plaintiff came under the influence of the police he was no longer a free person.

Atkin LJ:

'It appears to me that a person could be imprisoned without his knowing it. I think a person can be imprisoned while he is asleep, while he is in a state of drunkenness, while he is unconscious, and while he is a lunatic. Those are cases where it seems to me that the person might properly complain if he were imprisoned, though the imprisonment began and ceased while he was in that state. Of course, the damages might be diminished and would be affected by the

question whether he was conscious of it or not. So a man might in fact, to my mind, be imprisoned by having the key of a door turned against him so that he is imprisoned in a room in fact although he does not know that the key has been turned. It may be that he is being detained in that room by persons who are anxious to make him believe that he is not in fact being imprisoned, and at the same time his captors outside that room may be boasting to persons that he is imprisoned, and it seems to me that if we were to take this case as an instance supposing it could be proved that Prudence had said while the plaintiff was waiting: "I have got him detained there waiting for the detective to come in and take him to prison" – it appears to me that that would be evidence of imprisonment. It is quite unnecessary to go on to show that in fact the man knew that he was imprisoned. If a man can be imprisoned by having the key turned upon him without his knowledge, so he can be imprisoned if, instead of a lock and key or bolts and bars, he is prevented from, in fact, exercising his liberty by guards and warders or policemen. They serve the same purpose. Therefore it appears to me to be a question of fact. It is true that in all cases of imprisonment so far as the law of civil liberty is concerned that "stone walls do not a prison make", in the sense that they are not the only form of imprisonment, but any restraint within defined bounds which is a restraint in fact may be an imprisonment.'

Comment

Atkin LJ's words were approved by the House of Lords in *Murray* v *Ministry of Defence* [1988] 2 All ER 521 where their Lordships confirmed that (a) where a person is unaware that he has been falsely imprisoned and has suffered no harm he would normally receive only nominal damages, and (b) false imprisonment is actionable without proof of special damage.

Tuberville v *Savage* (1699) 1 Mod Rep 3 Court of King's Bench (Kelynge CJ, Twiden, Moreton and Rainsford JJ)

• *Assault by word of mouth?*

Facts
The defendant said 'If it were not Assize time, I would not take such language from you'. It was Assize time – were these words an assault?

Held
They were not.

> 'The declaration of the defendant was that he would not assault him, the judges being in town; and the *intention* as well as the *act* makes an assault. Therefore, if one strike another upon the hand or arm ... in discourse it is no assault; but if one, intending to assault, strike at another and miss him, this is an assault; so, if he hold up his hand against another in a threatening manner and say nothing, it is an assault.'

Comment
In *R* v *Ireland* [1997] 4 All ER 225 the House of Lords decided that the making of silent telephone calls which caused psychiatric injury to the victim was capable of amounting to an assault in law under s47 of the Offences against the Person Act 1861 where the calls caused the victim to apprehend an immediate application of force. Furthermore, an offence of inflicting grievous bodily harm under s20 of the 1861 Act could be committed even though no physical violence was applied directly or indirectly to the body of the victim. Lord Hope of Craighead said:

> 'The important question ... is whether the

making of a series of silent telephone calls can amount in law to an assault. There is no clear guidance on this point either in the statute or in the authorities. On the one hand in *Meade's and Belt's Case* (1823) 1 Lew CC 184 Holroyd J said that no words or singing can amount to an assault. On the other hand in *R* v *Wilson* [1955] 1 All ER 744 at 745 Lord Goddard CJ said that the appellant's words, "Get out the knives" would itself be an assault.'

Their Lordships here affirmed the decision of the Court of Appeal ([1997] 1 All ER 112) where Swinton Thomas LJ cited *Tuberville* v *Savage* as an illustration of the principle that putting a person in fear may amount to an assault.

The publication of press articles calculated to incite racial hatred of an individual can amount to harassment under the Protection from Harassment Act 1997: *Thomas* v *News Group Newspapers Ltd* (2001) The Times 25 July. The test of harassment is objective: *R* v *Colohan* (2001) The Times 14 June (mental illness of offender not a defence).

Wilson v *Pringle* [1987] QB 237 Court of Appeal (O'Connor, Croom-Johnson and Balcombe LJJ)

• *Trespass to the person – hostility*

Facts
The defendant and plaintiff were both schoolboys. The defendant jumped on the plaintiff whilst playing around and caused the plaintiff to sustain injury. The plaintiff claimed damages for battery. The plaintiff claimed that as the defendant had admitted jumping on the plaintiff there could be no defence.

Held
The defendant also had to show hostility on the part of the defendant. The question of hostility was a question of fact and therefore the case should be remitted for trial.

Croom-Johnson LJ:

'In our view … in a battery there must be an intentional touching or contact in one form or another of the plaintiff by the defendant. That touching must be proved to be a hostile touching.'

23 Trespass to Land

Bernstein of Leigh (Lord) v Skyviews & General Ltd [1977] 3 WLR 136 High Court (Griffiths J)

Facts

The defendants flew over the plaintiff's property for the purpose of taking aerial photographs of the plaintiff's country house which they then offered to sell him. The plaintiff claimed damages, alleging that by entering airspace above his property the defendants were guilty of trespass or were guilty of an actionable invasion of the plaintiff's right to privacy by taking the photographs without his consent.

Held

The action would fail since the rights of a landowner in the air space above his land are restricted to such heights as is necessary for the ordinary use and enjoyment of his land and the structures upon it, and the defendant's flight was hundreds of feet above the ground. Apart from common law, the defendants were protected by s40(1) of the Civil Aviation Act 1949, which exempted certain flights by aircraft from actions in trespass or nuisance. The taking of photographs cannot of itself make an act a trespass.

Griffiths J:

'I can find no support in authority for the view that a landowner's rights in the air space above his property extend to an unlimited height ... The problem is to balance the rights of an owner to enjoy the use of his land against the rights of the general public to take advantage of all that science now offers in the use of air space. This balance is in my judgment best struck in our present society by restricting the rights of an owner in the air space above his land to such height as is necessary for the ordinary use and enjoyment of his land and the structures on it, and declaring that above that height he has no greater rights in the air space than any other member of the public.'

Hickman v Maisey [1900] 1 QB 752 Court of Appeal (Collins, Romer and A L Smith LJJ)

• *Trespass on the highway*

Facts

The defendant, a 'racing tout', used a highway which ran across the plaintiff's land for the purpose of watching P's horses in training and using the information thereby obtained for the purposes of his business. The effect was to depreciate the value of P's land as a place for the training of race horses.

Held

The defendant was liable for trespass as his use of the highway was unreasonable.

A L Smith LJ:

'The question is ... what is the lawful use of a highway? Many authorities show ... that prima facie the right of the public is to pass and repass along the highway ... but I quite agree with Lord Esher MR in *Harrison v Duke of Rutland* [1893] 1 QB 142 that though it is a slight extension of the rule as previously stated namely that, though highways are dedicated prima facie for the purpose of passage 'things are done upon them by everybody which are recognised as being rightly done and as constituting a reasonable and usual mode of using the highway ... I cannot agree that in this case the defendant was using the highway in an ordinary and reasonable manner. I do not agree with the defendant's argument that the intention and object of the defendant in going upon the highway cannot be taken into account in determining whether he was using it in a lawful manner. His intention and object are all important.'

24 Deceit

Downs v Chappell [1996] 3 All ER 344 Court of Appeal (Butler-Sloss, Roch and Hobhouse LJJ)

• *Deceit – negligence – measure of damages*

Facts

In 1988 the plaintiffs bought a bookshop from the first defendant for £120,000. The sale particulars represented that, in 1987, the business had a turnover of approximately £109,000 and a gross profit of £33,500. When the plaintiff asked for independent verification of these figures, at the first defendant's request the second defendant accountants told the plaintiffs that the 1987 figures were approximately £110,000 and £34,000 respectively. Turnover and profit having fallen short of these figures, the plaintiffs eventually sold the business for less than £60,000 having previously (in March 1990) refused two offers of £76,000. The plaintiffs claimed damages in deceit and negligence against the first and second defendants respectively.

Held

Since it had been proved that the plaintiffs had been caused to buy the business by the defendants' representations, their action would be successful. They would be awarded £44,000 by way of damages.

Hobhouse LJ:

'Causation and the assessment of damages is a matter of fact. In a misrepresentation case, where the plaintiff would not have entered into the transaction, he is entitled to recover all the losses he has suffered, both capital and income, down to the date that he discovers that he had been misled and he has

an opportunity to avoid further loss. The diminution in value test will normally be inappropriate. Where what is bought is a business, the losses made in the business are prima facie recoverable, as is the reduction in the value of the business and its premises. Foreseeable market fluctuations are not too remote and should be taken into account either way in the relevant account. ... No distinction is to be made as between the plaintiffs and either of the defendants. The plaintiffs have proved that the torts of both of the defendants have caused them loss and that their loss is substantial. The plaintiffs' loss must be assessed as at March 1990 when they had an informed opportunity to sell at £76,000. Their recoverable damages are accordingly £44,000. Judgment should be entered for the plaintiffs against each of the defendants for that sum of damages.'

Comment

See also *South Australia Asset Management Corp v York Montague Ltd* [1996] 3 All ER 365 and *Smith New Court Securities Ltd v Scrimgeour Vickers (Asset Management) Ltd* [1996] 4 All ER 769 (*Downs v Chappell* overruled as to assessment of damages).

Smith New Court Securities Ltd v Scrimgeour Vickers (Asset Management) Ltd [1996] 4 All ER 769 House of Lords (Lords Browne-Wilkinson, Keith of Kinkel, Mustill, Slynn of Hadley and Steyn)

• *Fraudulent misrepresentation – share purchase – measure of damages*

Facts

The plaintiffs' purchase of shares in Ferranti having been induced by the defendants' fraudulent misrepresentation and a previous unrelated fraud on Ferranti having been discovered after the shares had been purchased but before the plaintiffs sold them, the question arose as to how the plaintiffs' damages were to be assessed. The discovery of the unrelated fraud led to a dramatic fall in the value of Ferranti shares.

Held

The plaintiffs were entitled to the difference between the amount that they paid for the shares and the amount which they received on their sale.

Lord Browne-Wilkinson:

'The damage issue which is the subject-matter of the appeal raises for decision for the first time in your Lordships' House the question of the correct measure of damages where a plaintiff has acquired property in reliance on a fraudulent misrepresentation made by the defendant. ...

In sum, in my judgment the following principles apply in assessing the damages payable where the plaintiff has been induced by a fraudulent misrepresentation to buy property.

(1) The defendant is bound to make reparation for all the damage directly flowing from the transaction.

(2) Although such damage need not have been foreseeable, it must have been directly caused by the transaction.

(3) In assessing such damage, the plaintiff is entitled to recover by way of damages the full price paid by him, but he must give credit for any benefits which he has received as a result of the transaction.

(4) As a general rule, the benefits received by him include the market value of the property acquired as at the date of acquisition; but such general rule is not to be inflexibly applied where to do so would prevent him obtaining full compensation for the wrong suffered.

(5) Although the circumstances in which the general rule should not apply cannot be comprehensively stated, it will normally not apply where either (a) the misrepresentation has continued to operate after the date of the acquisition of the asset so as to induce the plaintiff to retain the asset or (b) the circumstances of the case are such that the plaintiff is, by reason of the fraud, locked into the property.

(6) In addition, the plaintiff is entitled to recover consequential losses caused by the transaction.

(7) The plaintiff must take all reasonable steps to mitigate his loss once he has discovered the fraud.

Before seeking to apply those principles to the present case, there are two points I must make. First, in *Downs* v *Chappell* [1996] 3 All ER 344 at 361 Hobhouse LJ, having quantified the recoverable damage very much along the lines that I have suggested, sought to cross-check his result by looking to see what the value of the business would have been if the misrepresentations had been true and then comparing that value to the contract price. Whilst Hobhouse LJ accepted that this was not the correct measure of damages, he was seeking to check that the plaintiff was not being compensated for a general fall in market prices (for which the defendant was not accountable) rather than for the wrong done to him by the defendant. In my view, such a cross-check is not likely to be helpful and is conducive to overelaboration both in the evidence and in argument. Second, in *Royscot Trust Ltd* v *Rogerson* [1991] 3 All ER 294 the *Doyle* v *Olby (Ironmongers) Ltd* [1969] 2 All ER 119 measure of damages was adopted in assessing damages for innocent misrepresentation under the Misrepresentation Act 1967. I express no view on the correctness of that decision.

How then do those principles apply in the present case? First, there is no doubt that the total loss incurred by [the plaintiffs] was caused by the [defendants'] fraud, unless it can be said that [the plaintiffs'] own decision to retain the shares until after the revelation of the [unrelated] fraud was a causative factor. The [unrelated] fraud had been committed before [the plaintiffs] acquired the shares ... Unknown to everybody, on that date the shares were already pregnant with disaster. Accordingly, when pursuant to the [defendants'] fraud, [the plaintiffs] acquired the Ferranti shares they were induced to purchase a flawed asset. This is not a case of the difficult kind that can arise where the depreciation in the asset acquired between the date of acquisition and the date of realisation may be due to factors affecting the market which have occurred after the date of the defendant's fraud. In the present case the loss was incurred by reason of the purchasing of the shares which were pregnant with the loss and that purchase was caused by the [defendants'] fraud.

Can it be said that the loss flowed not from [the plaintiffs'] acquisition but from [the plaintiffs'] decision to retain the shares? In my judgment it cannot. The judge found that the shares were acquired as a market making risk and at a price which [the plaintiffs] would only have paid for an acquisition as a market making risk. As such, [the plaintiffs] could not dispose of them on [the purchase date] otherwise than at a loss. [The plaintiffs] were in a special sense locked into the shares having bought them for a purpose and at a price which precluded them from sensibly disposing of them. It was not alleged or found that [the plaintiffs] acted unreasonably in retaining the shares for as long as they did or in realising them in the manner in which they did.'

Comment

Lord Browne-Wilkinson said that *Doyle* had correctly established points as follows: (i) the measure of damages where a contract has been induced by fraudulent misrepresentation is reparation for all the actual damage directly flowing from (ie caused by) entering into the transaction; (ii) in assessing such damages it is not an inflexible rule that the plaintiff must bring into account the value as at the transaction date of the asset acquired: there can be no circumstances in which it is proper to require a defendant only to bring into account the actual proceeds of the asset provided that he has acted reasonably in retaining it; (iii) damages for deceit are not limited to those which were reasonably foreseeable; and (iv) the damages recoverable can include consequential loss suffered by reason of having acquired the asset.

25 Malicious Falsehood

Joyce v Sengupta [1993] 1 WLR 337
Court of Appeal (Sir Donald Nicholls
V-C, Butler-Sloss LJ and Sir Michael
Kerr)

- *Malicious falsehood – choice of action
– damages*

Facts
In an article on the front page of the defendants' newspaper it was alleged that the plaintiff was, inter alia, 'the thief who stole Princess Anne's intimate letters'. As legal aid is not available for defamation proceedings, the plaintiff sought damages for malicious falsehood, proceedings which could and did attract legal aid. The judge struck out the statement of claim as an abuse of the process of the court: the plaintiff appealed.

Held
The appeal would be allowed.

Sir Donald Nicholls V-C:

'Before turning to the issues raised by the appeal I should comment briefly on the difference between defamation and malicious falsehood. The remedy provided by the law for words which injure a person's reputation is defamation. Words may also injure a person without damaging his reputation. An example would be a claim that the seller of goods or land is not the true owner. Another example would be a false assertion that a person has closed down his business. Such claims would not necessarily damage the reputation of those concerned. The remedy provided for this is malicious falsehood, sometimes called injurious falsehood or trade libel. This cause of action embraces particular types of malicious falsehood such as slander of title and slander of goods, but it is not confined to those headings.

Falsity is an essential ingredient of this tort. The plaintiff must establish the untruth of the statement of which he complains. Malice is another essential ingredient. A genuine dispute about the ownership of goods or land should not of itself be actionable. So a person who acted in good faith is not liable. Further, since the object of this cause of action is to provide a person with a remedy for a false statement made maliciously which has caused him damage, at common law proof of financial loss was another essential ingredient. The rigour of this requirement was relaxed by statute. I shall have to return to the question of damages at a later stage. For present purposes it is sufficient to note that if a plaintiff establishes that the defendant maliciously made a false statement which has caused him financial damage, or in respect of which he is relieved from proving damage by the Defamation Act 1952, the law gives him a remedy. The false statement may also be defamatory, or it may not. As already mentioned, it need not be defamatory. Conversely, the fact that the statement is defamatory does not exclude a cause of action for malicious falsehood, although the law will ensure that a plaintiff does not recover damages twice over for the same loss.

Abuse of process: (1) no right to trial by jury
It is as plain as a pikestaff that, had legal aid been available for libel, this action would have been a straightforward defamation action. In an action for malicious falsehood the plaintiff has to take on the burden of proving that the words were false and that in publishing them the defendant was actuated by malice. It would make no sense for Miss Joyce to take on this burden. If this had been

169

a defamation action she would not have to prove malice, and if the newspaper wished to put in issue the truth of the defamatory assertions it would have to plead and prove justification as a defence.

One consequence of this action being a claim for malicious falsehood and not defamation is that there is no absolute right to a trial by jury ... Against this background counsel submitted that the present action should be struck out by the court as an abuse of process because it is based on a secondary tort which deprives the defendants of their absolute right to have a jury trial. This right is a legitimate juridical advantage they would have had if the plaintiff had relied on the primary tort. By a "secondary tort" was meant a tort which would not be relied upon save for the plaintiff's need to secure a collateral purpose unrelated to the merits of her claim.

I am not able to accept this submission. The concept of a legitimate juridical advantage has been taken from the field of conflict of laws where an issue arises over the country in which a dispute between the parties should be determined. The issue there concerns which of two countries, with their different laws and legal systems, would be the more appropriate forum.

I can see no place for that concept in wholly domestic proceedings. English law has marked out causes of action on which plaintiffs may rely. Many causes of action overlap. On one set of facts a plaintiff may have more than one cause of action against a defendant. He may have a cause of action in tort and also for breach of contract. This is an everyday occurrence ... I have never heard it suggested before that a plaintiff is not entitled to ... take full advantage of the various remedies English law provides for the wrong of which he complains. I have never heard it suggested that he must pursue the most appropriate remedy, and if he does not do so he is at risk of having his proceedings struck out as a misuse of the court's procedures. In my view those suggestions are as unfounded as they are novel ...

Abuse of process: (2) "economic lunacy" and legal aid

[Counsel for the defendants'] second submission was as bold as his first. He submitted that another reason why this action is an abuse is that only nominal damages, or at best modest damages of a few hundred pounds, will be recoverable by the plaintiff. The amount she stands to obtain is wholly out of line with the costs each side will incur. In practice the defendants will never recover their costs even if they are successful in defending the actions and even if they make a payment into court of an amount in excess of any damages awarded at the trial. [Counsel] submitted that, so far as the plaintiff is concerned, the action is "economic lunacy", given that any damages awarded to her will be swallowed up by the Legal Aid Board's charge over them as property recovered in the proceedings. Public funds are being used to support the plaintiff in a wholly uneconomic way.

With all respect to counsel, this is a hopeless submission. I shall consider later the question of damages. For the moment let me assume that the defendants are correct in submitting that the plaintiff is unlikely to recover more than a few hundred pounds in damages. I shall make that assumption although I am not to be taken as indorsing it. Even so I do not see how it follows that this action should be struck out as an abuse. The plaintiff's main purpose in bringing this action is to clear her name. If she wins, she will succeed in doing so. Compared with a libel action, the amount of damages she may recover in malicious falsehood may be small, but there is no reason why she should not be entitled to pursue such a claim. I see no justification for the court stopping her action. The defendants, it must be borne in mind, are resisting her claim in its entirety. The prospect that they are unlikely to recoup their costs even if their defence is wholly successful is an unfortunate fact of everyday life for many defendants when sued by legally aided plaintiffs.

The reality here is that the defendants are

unhappy that the plaintiff has obtained legal aid to pursue the action. They fear if this action is permitted to proceed, the flood-gates will be opened. The Legal Aid Board will be flooded with applications for legal aid to pursue claims for malicious falsehood against newspapers. Newspapers will be faced with the prospect, not intended by Parliament, of legally aided plaintiffs pursuing claims against them founded on defamatory articles.

As to these fears, it is vital to keep in mind that the decision on whether or not to grant legal aid has been entrusted by Parliament to the Legal Aid Board, not the court. Parliament has prescribed a framework of limitations and conditions but the Legal Aid Board retains a discretion. A person whose financial resources make him eligible for legal aid must satisfy the board that he has reasonable grounds for taking, defending or being a party to the proceedings ...

Abuse of process: (3) the action is bound to fail
The defendant's third submission was that the action is incapable of success and should be struck out summarily. The jurisdiction the defendants invoke here is well established. The court will not permit an action to go to trial if plainly and obviously it cannot succeed. But when exercising this jurisdiction the court is careful not to conduct a summary trial on affidavit evidence without the benefit of discovery of documents and cross-examination of witnesses on disputed questions of fact. If there is an issue or dispute that ought to be tried, the action must go to trial ...

So far as the statement of claim is concerned I am satisfied that, although open to criticism here and there, it does disclose the essentials of a cause of action for malicious falsehood. It is susceptible to a request for further particulars in some respects, but the omissions are not so serious or incapable of being made good that the defendants will be embarrassed in the conduct of their defence ...

Damages
I turn to the points raised regarding damages. The plaintiff claims, first, that she suffered financial loss in consequence of the ... article. Having regard to the nature and prominence of the assertions in the article, her chances of finding work in any employment requiring trust and confidence have been diminished. Secondly, she relies on s3 of the Defamation Act 1952 ... She alleges that the article was likely to cause pecuniary damage to her by seriously prejudicing her opportunity to obtain other employment requiring trust and confidence.

On this interlocutory appeal it would be wholly inappropriate for us to attempt to go into the detail of the evidence which may properly be called in support of these claims. Suffice to say, on the first claim the plaintiff will need to give particulars of the financial loss she claims to have suffered sufficient to ensure that the defendants will not be taken by surprise by any evidence she may adduce on the amount of her loss.

As to the second claim, this is an allegation of general damage. In support of this claim the plaintiff cannot adduce evidence of actual loss ... I do not accept, however, that in consequence the award under this head must necessarily be nominal only ... The whole purpose of s3 was to give the plaintiff a remedy in malicious falsehood despite the difficulty of proving actual loss. A plaintiff is seldom able to call witnesses to say they ceased to deal with him because of some slander that had come to their ears. In consequence actions for malicious falsehood had become extremely rare ... Section 3 was enacted to right this injustice. The section would fail in its purpose if, whenever relied on, it could lead only to an award of nominal damages.

Damages for distress and injury to feelings
The plaintiff claims, thirdly, that as a consequence of the article she suffered anxiety, distress and injury to her feelings. [Counsel] submitted that this third head of damages is irrecoverable as a matter of law and should be struck out. [Counsel for the plaintiff] contended that, although at common law proof of pecuniary damage was an essential ingredient of the tort, once pecuniary loss is

established, or a claim under s3 is made out, a plaintiff is entitled to recover his whole loss. If he suffered mental distress, the law will include an award of damages under this head also.

The point seems never to have been decided ... it is well settled that at common law proof of "special damage" is an essential ingredient in this cause of action. At common law if such damage is not established the action will fail ...

[The] state of the authorities suggests that damages for anxiety and distress are not recoverable for malicious falsehood. If that is the law it could lead to a manifestly unsatisfactory and unjust result in some cases. Take the example I gave earlier of a person who maliciously spreads rumours that his competitor's business has closed down. Or the rumour might be that the business is in financial difficulty and that a receiver will soon be appointed. The owner of the business suffers severe financial loss. Further, because of the effect the rumours are having on his business he is worried beyond measure about his livelihood and his family's future. He suffers acute anxiety and distress. Can it be right that the law is unable to give him any recompense for this suffering against the person whose malice caused it? Although injury to feelings alone will not found a cause of action in malicious falsehood, ought not the law to take such injury into account when it is connected with financial damage inflicted by the falsehood? ...

The point bristles with problems, not all of which were explored in argument. One possibility is that in an action for malicious falsehood damages are limited to financial loss. That would mark out a clear boundary, but it would suffer from the drawback of

failing to do justice in the type of case I have mentioned. I instinctively recoil from the notion that in no circumstances can an injured plaintiff obtain recompense from a defendant for understandable distress caused by a false statement made maliciously. However, once it is accepted there are circumstances in which non-pecuniary loss, or some types of non-pecuniary loss, can be recovered in a malicious falsehood action, it becomes extremely difficult to define those circumstances or those types of loss in a coherent manner. It would be going too far to hold that all non-pecuniary loss suffered by a plaintiff is recoverable in a malicious falsehood action, because that would include injury to reputation at large. The history of malicious falsehood as a cause of action shows it was not designed to provide a remedy for such injury: the remedy for such loss is an action for defamation in which, incidentally, damages for injury to feelings may be included in a general award of damages ...

My conclusion is that, on the limited argument addressed to us, it would be undesirable to decide this point. It is an important point of law but only a minor point in the present application. The pleading should be left as it stands and, if need be, this issue can be pursued further at the trial.'

Comment

In *Khodaparast* v *Shad* [2000] 1 All ER 545 the Court of Appeal said that once a claimant is entitled to sue for malicious falsehood, a species of defamation, whether on proof of special damage or by reason of s3 of the Defamation Act 1952, there is no reason in principle why he should not recover aggravated damages for injury to feelings.

26 Passing Off

Clark v Associated Newspapers Ltd
[1998] 1 All ER 959 High Court
(Lightman J)

- *Passing off – false attribution of authorship*

Facts
The defendant's newspaper, the *Evening Standard,* was publishing articles written by a Mr Peter Bradshaw which were parodies of the diaries of the plaintiff Member of Parliament which were still enjoying substantial sales. The plaintiff contended that the articles were in such a form that a substantial number of the newspaper's readers attributed them to his authorship. He brought an action under s84 of the Copyright, Designs and Patents Act 1988 (false attribution of work) and in passing off, seeking an injunction to restrain publication of the articles.

Held
The injunction would be granted.

Lightman J:

'(a) *Passing off*...
In summary, the plaintiff has a substantial reputation as a diarist and his identity as author of the articles would plainly be of importance to readers of the *Evening Standard* in deciding whether to read the articles. This, as it seems to me, is reflected in the choice of format adopted, and most particularly in the design of the heading, which is calculated to exploit the public recognition enjoyed by the plaintiff as author of the diaries and the public interest which any diary written by the plaintiff may be expected to generate. The consequent identification of the plaintiff as author is not sufficiently neutralised to prevent a substantial number of readers being deceived. ...

There can be no doubt that for the defendant falsely to attribute the articles to the plaintiff can cause serious damage to the plaintiff: his reputation and goodwill as an author is placed at risk and so accordingly are the prospective sales of his published works and the market value of the publishing rights and other rights to exploit his works. The plaintiff must be entitled to an injunction to restrain the defendant from continuing its present course of conduct. The question raised is whether there is a probability that he has suffered more than nominal damage. In the light of the evidence before me, I am satisfied that I can and should find that he has suffered such damage and that the plaintiff is entitled to an inquiry as to damages.

(b) *Section 84*
In my judgment (as I have already held) the headings of the articles contain a clear and unequivocal false statement attributing their authorship to the plaintiff, and the vice of this statement is not cured by the various "counter-messages" relied on by the defendant. I would be minded to accept that ... the effect of such a false statement can be neutralised by an express contradiction, but ... it has to be as bold, precise and compelling as the false statement ... and in this case the contradiction lacks the required prominence and is less likely to get home to the readers, as is confirmed (if confirmation is necessary) by the evidence in this case.

The plaintiff is accordingly entitled to relief in respect of the commission of the statutory tort.'

Comment
Two specific points made by Lightman J are

173

worthy of note. First, for the common law tort of passing off to be established, a complainant must establish either actual damage or the likelihood of damage. False attribution of authorship (the statutory tort), most particularly to an author with an established reputation, is calculated to place his reputation and goodwill at risk of substantial damage and indeed to cause damage and damage may be presumed. Second, his Lordship's judgment should not be seen as a bar to the publication of parodies. Where the line is to be drawn between what does and what does not constitute false attribution of authorship is a question of judgment, and often a difficult question on which minds may differ. In this case in respect of the format which it adopted in the fully understandable aim of achieving the maximum impact on readers, the defendant made an honest and understandable error of judgment: the articles fell on the wrong side of the line. The vice lay in the format of the articles. The defendant could however continue to publish parodies of the diaries so long as there was no attribution of authorship to the plaintiff and it was made sufficiently clear that Mr Bradshaw, and not the plaintiff, was the author.

Reckitt & Colman Products Ltd v *Borden Inc* [1990] 1 WLR 491
House of Lords (Lords Bridge of Harwich, Brandon of Oakbrook, Oliver of Aylmerton, Goff of Chieveley and Jauncey of Tullichettle)

• *Passing off – plastic lemon container*

Facts
Effectively, the plaintiffs were the only company marketing in the United Kingdom lemon juice ('Jif') in lemon-like plastic containers, but the defendants adopted a similar approach. The plaintiffs sought an injunction to restrain the defendants from passing off their lemon juice as that of the plaintiffs by

use of a get-up deceptively similar to that used by the plaintiffs. The trial judge found that although a careful shopper would conclude that the defendants' 'lemon' was not that of the plaintiffs, since it was merely a question of reading the label, nevertheless the evidence conclusively established that the introduction of the defendants lemons was bound to result in many shoppers purchasing them in the belief that they were purchasing the plaintiffs' well-known and liked lemons, since the crucial point of reference for a shopper who wished to purchase one of the plaintiffs' lemons was the lemon shape itself and no attention was paid to the label. Accordingly, he granted the injunction and his decision was upheld by the Court of Appeal. The defendants appealed.

Held
The appeal would be dismissed

Lord Oliver of Aylmerton:

'In the end, the question comes down not to whether the [plaintiffs] are entitled to a monopoly in the sale of lemon juice in natural-size lemon-shaped containers but whether the [defendants], in deliberately adopting, out of all the many possible shapes of container, a container having the most immediately striking feature of the [plaintiffs'] get-up, have taken sufficient steps to distinguish their product from that of the [plaintiffs] ... the trial judge was satisfied of the fact that a substantial part of the purchasing public requires specifically Jif lemon juice, associates it with the lemon-shape, lemon-size container which is the dominant characteristic of the get-up and pays little or no attention to the label. It is no answer to say that the diversion of trade which he was satisfied would take place would be of relatively short duration, since the public would ultimately become educated to the fact that there were two brands of lemon juice marketed in such containers and would then be likely to pay more attention to the labels to be sure that they got the brand which they required. His finding was that the diversion would be likely to run into millions of units. It inevitably follows from these findings that the [defendants] have not in fact sufficiently and effectively distinguished their goods from those of the [plaintiffs] and it is not for the [plaintiffs] or for the court to suggest what more they should do .... In the light of the trial judge's finding, I see no escape from the proposition that the [plaintiffs] were entitled to the injunction which they obtained in the form in which it was granted.'

27 The Economic Torts

Lonrho plc v Fayed [1991] 3 WLR
188 House of Lords (Lords Bridge of
Harwich, Brandon of Oakwood,
Templeman, Goff of Chieveley and
Jauncey of Tullichettle)

* *Tort of conspiracy – ingredients*

Facts

There was a bitter dispute in relation to the
take-over of House of Fraser plc, the owner
of Harrods. While the plaintiffs' bid to purchase House of Fraser had been referred to the
Monopolies and Mergers Commission
(MMC) and they were the subject of an undertaking not to purchase any more shares in that
company, the defendants made a bid for
House of Fraser which was not referred to the
MMC. The plaintiffs alleged that the defendants had influenced the decision of the
Secretary of State not to refer the defendants'
bid to MMC by fraudulent misrepresentations
made about themselves which deprived the
plaintiffs of the opportunity to bid for the
company and claimed that the defendants had
thereby committed, inter alia, the torts of
wrongful interference with the plaintiffs' trade
or business and conspiracy to injure. The
judge struck out the claim: the plaintiffs
appealed and the Court of Appeal allowed the
appeal in relation to unlawful interference but
dismissed it in relation to conspiracy. The
parties appealed and cross-appealed.

Held

As the two causes of action stood or fell
together, the case should proceed to trial.

Lord Bridge of Harwich:

'It was ... accepted in the Court of Appeal
that the statement of claim had not alleged

that the predominant purpose of the alleged
conspiracy was to injure Lonrho and that
accordingly the Court of Appeal were bound
by their own decision in *Metall und Rohstoff
AG v Donaldson Lufkin & Jenrette Inc*
[1989] 3 WLR 563 to hold that the pleaded
cause of action in conspiracy could not
succeed ...

It will be convenient to consider first the
clear-cut issue of law which arises on the
cross-appeal. In the *Metall* case the Court
of Appeal interpreted the decision of this
House in *Lonrho Ltd v Shell Petroleum Co
Ltd* [1981] 3 WLR 33 as holding it to be an
essential ingredient in the civil tort of conspiracy to establish that the predominant
purpose of the conspirators was to injure the
plaintiff irrespective of whether the means
they used to effect that purpose were lawful
or unlawful ...

In *Rookes* v *Barnard* [1964] 2 WLR 269
Lord Devlin said:

"There are, as is well known, two sorts of
conspiracies, the *Quinn* v *Leathem*
([1901] AC 495) type which employs
only lawful means but aims at an unlawful end, and the type which employs
unlawful means."

Of these two types of tortious conspiracy
the *Quinn* v *Leathem* type, where no unlawful means are used, is now regarded as an
anomaly for the reasons so clearly explained
by Lord Diplock in *Lonrho Ltd* v *Shell
Petroleum Co Ltd* ...

Where conspirators act with the predominant purpose of injuring the plaintiff and in
fact inflict damage on him, but do nothing
which would have been actionable if done
by an individual acting alone, it is in the fact
of their concerted action for that illegitimate
purpose that the law, however anomalous it
may now seem, finds a sufficient ground to

condemn their action as illegal and tortious. But when conspirators intentionally injure the plaintiff and use unlawful means to do so, it is no defence for them to show that their primary purpose was to further or protect their own interests; it is sufficient to make their action tortious that the means used were unlawful.

Did the House in *Lonrho Ltd v Shell Petroleum Co Ltd* depart from this reasoning and lay down for the first time a new principle that a plaintiff, seeking to establish the tort of conspiracy to injure, must in every case prove that the intention to injure him was the predominant purpose of the defendants, whether the means used were lawful or unlawful? ...

My Lords, I am quite unable to accept that Lord Diplock or the other members of the Appellate Committee concurring with him, of whom I was one, intended the decision in *Lonrho Ltd v Shell Petroleum Co Ltd* to effect, sub silentio, such a significant change in the law as it had been previously understood. The House ... had never been invited to take such a step. Moreover, to do so would have been directly contrary to the view of Lord Denning MR expressed in the judgment which the House was affirming and inconsistent with the dicta in what Lord Diplock described as "Viscount Simon LC's now classic speech in *Crofter Hand Woven Harris Tweed Co Ltd v Veitch* [1942] AC 435 at 439". I would overrule the *Metall* case in this respect.

It follows from this conclusion that Lonrho's acceptance that the pleaded intention on the part of the defendants to cause injury to Lonrho was not the predominant purpose of their alleged unlawful action is not necessarily fatal to the pleaded cause of action in conspiracy and therefore affords no separate ground for striking out that part of the pleading. If the defendants fail to establish that Lonrho's primary pleading asserting the tort of interference with business by unlawful means should be struck out, they are in no stronger position in relation to the pleaded cause of action in conspiracy. It is not, I think, necessary for present purposes to consider whether the

pleaded conspiracy adds anything of substance or raises any significantly different issues from those on which the rest of the pleading depends. At this interlocutory stage it is sufficient to say that the two pleaded causes of action must stand or fall together. Either both should be struck out or both should go to trial ... I have reached the conclusion that it would be inappropriate to strike out the statement of claim and that the case must accordingly proceed to trial ...

I would emphasise that the only question of law which, in my opinion, it is appropriate for the House to decide at this stage is that involved in overruling the *Metall* case. The facts pleaded in the statement of claim are strongly disputed. When the facts have been found at trial they may or may not give rise to important questions of law requiring resolution, but for the present purposes it suffices to say that the appellants fail to demonstrate that Lonrho's claim is obviously doomed to fail. Nothing in this opinion should be understood as saying any more than that.'

Lumley v *Gye* (1853) 2 E & B 216
Court of Queen's Bench (Coleridge, Erle, Wightman and Crompton JJ)

• *Procurement of breach of contract*

Facts
The plaintiff, the lessee and manager of the Queen's Theatre, claimed damages from the defendant for causing Johanna Wagner to break a contract by which she had undertaken to perform at the plaintiff's theatre for a specified time.

Held (Coleridge J dissenting)
His action would be successful.

Crompton J:

'Whatever may have been the origin or foundation of the law as to enticing of servants, and whether it be, as contended by the plaintiff, an instance and branch of a wider rule, or, as contended by the defendant, an anomaly and an exception from the general rule of law on such subjects, it must now be considered clear law that a person who wrongfully and maliciously, or, which is the same thing, with notice, interrupts the relation subsisting between master and servant by procuring the servant to depart from the master's service, or by harbouring and keeping him as servant after he has quitted it and during the time stipulated for as the period of service, whereby the master is injured, commits a wrongful act for which he is responsible at law. I think that the rule applies wherever the wrongful interruption operates to prevent the service during the time for which the parties have contracted that the service shall continue, and I think that the relation of master and servant subsists, sufficiently for the purpose of such action, during the time for which there is in existence a binding contract of hiring and service between the parties. I think that it is a fanciful and technical and unjust distinction to say that they not having actually entered into the service, or that the service is not actually continuing, can make any difference.'

Comment

In *Torquay Hotel Co Ltd* v *Cousins* [1969] 1 All ER 522 Lord Denning MR said that the principle of *Lumley* v *Gye* extends not only to inducing a breach of contract, but also to preventing the performance of it.

28 Remedies

Allen v *Bloomsbury Health Authority* [1993] 1 All ER 651 High Court (Brooke J)

- *Unwanted pregnancy – assessment of damages*

Facts

After divorcing her husband, the plaintiff mother of two children aged 10 and 11 underwent a sterilisation operation at the defendants' hospital. The defendants failed to notice that she was four weeks pregnant by her then partner, whom she had no wish to marry, and by the time that the pregnancy was diagnosed the plaintiff felt that it was too late to have a termination. Had the pregnancy been diagnosed at the time of the operation the plaintiff would have had an abortion. She feared that the foetus would have been damaged by the operation, but she gave birth to a healthy daughter (Faye). The defendants admitted liability and the only issue was as to the quantum of damages.

Held

The plaintiff would be awarded damages totalling £96,631 consisting of general damages (Mrs Allen's future loss of earnings till Faye is 11, child-minding costs when Fay is 11 to 14, cost of maintaining Faye till she is 18 and Mrs Allen's pain and suffering and loss of amenity, together with interest) and special damages, together with interest.

Brooke J:

'Although a claim of this type has not yet been considered by the House of Lords, the principles on which damages are to be awarded have been considered a number of times by the Court of Appeal, and I was referred to all the leading cases which have been decided in the last seven years. I derive from these cases the following principles which should guide me when I consider Mrs Allen's claim.

(1) If a doctor fails to act towards his patient with the standard of care reasonably to be expected of him, and as a foreseeable result of the doctor's breach of duty a child is born whose potential for life would have been lawfully terminated but for the doctor's negligence, the law entitles the mother to recover damages for the foreseeable loss and damage she suffers in consequence of the doctor's negligence (see *Emeh v Kensington and Chelsea and Westminster Area Health Authority* [1984] 3 All ER 1044).

(2) A plaintiff mother is entitled to recover general damages (and any associated financial special damage) for the discomfort and pain associated with the continuation of her pregnancy and the delivery of her child, although she must set off against this claim a sum in respect of the benefit of avoiding the pain and suffering and associated financial loss which would have resulted from the termination of her pregnancy under general anaesthetic, since in the events which have happened she has not had to undergo that operation (see *Emeh*'s case [1984] 3 All ER 1044 at 1056 per Purchas LJ, *Thake v Maurice* [1986] 1 All ER 497 at 508 per Kerr LJ, *Gardiner v Mountfield* (1989) 5 BMLR 1 at 5–6 per Scott Baker J).

(3) She is also entitled to damages for economic loss quite unassociated with her own physical injury which falls into two main categories: (i) the financial loss she suffers because when the unwanted baby is born she has a growing child to feed, clothe, house, educate and care for until the child becomes an adult; (ii) the financial loss she

179

suffers because she has lost or may lose earnings or incur other expense because of her obligations towards her child which she would have sought to avoid (see *Emeh*'s case [1984] 3 All ER 1044 at 1053, 1056 per Slade and Purchas LJJ respectively; adopted and applied by the Court of Appeal in *Thake* v *Maurice* [1986] 1 All ER 497.

(4) Although the law recognises that it is foreseeable that if an unwanted child is born following a doctor's negligence a mother may suffer wear and tear and tiredness in bringing up a healthy child, the claim for general damages she might otherwise have had on this account is generally set off against and extinguished by the benefit of bringing a healthy child into the world and seeing one's child grow up to maturity (see *Thake* v *Maurice* [1986] 1 All ER 497 at 508 per Kerr LJ).

(5) However, the law is willing to recognise a claim for general damages in respect of the foreseeable additional anxiety, stress and burden involved in bringing up a handicapped child, which is not treated as being extinguished by any countervailing benefit, although this head of damages is different in kind from the typical claim for anxiety and stress associated with and flowing from an injured plaintiff's own personal injuries (see *Emeh*'s case [1984] 3 All ER 1044 at 1052 per Waller LJ) ...

For my purpose I am content to assume that the Court of Appeal has recognised that in the unique circumstances surrounding the breach of a doctor's duty to a pregnant woman (or a woman who may become pregnant against her wishes) she should be entitled to recover damages for the two quite distinct foreseeable heads of loss which I identified when I was analysing the principles which should guide me in this case. The first, a claim for damages for personal injuries during the period leading up to the delivery of the child, is a claim which is comparable to, though different from, a claim for damages for personal injuries resulting from the infliction of a traumatic injury to a plaintiff by a negligent defendant. The second, a claim for the economic loss involved in the expense of losing paid employment and the obligation of having to pay for the upkeep and care of an unwanted child, is a totally different type of claim, although it may in turn be associated with a different type of claim for damages for the loss of amenity associated with bringing up a handicapped child ...

One important issue does, however, arise for my decision. This relates to the principles by which the financial cost of bringing up the unwanted child is to be measured. By definition the mother has decided in this class of case that she did not want to have another baby, and in many cases she could not afford to have another baby without considerable hardship to herself and/or the other members of her family. The baby, for its part, did not choose to be born and has no claim itself for the cost of being reared (see *McKay* v *Essex Area Health Authority* [1982] 2 All ER 771).

Should the tortfeasor whose negligence has "caused" the baby's "wrongful birth" be compelled to pay the "reasonable" costs of its upkeep? If so, how should those costs be measured, given that it is of the essence of the tortfeasor's negligence that the cost of upkeep is being borne by a mother who looked to him to exercise reasonable care in preventing her from incurring it? Alternatively, should the tortfeasor merely have to pay what is "necessary", whatever that word means in this context? Is it "necessary" for a child to have extra music lessons or to go on school trips or to go away for holidays or to be able to buy books and equipment for his interests and hobbies like his school contemporaries? If the test is necessity, how does a judge measure necessity without descending to the criteria adopted by the old poor law guardians or the modern curators of the social fund? ...

It will be evident that there is not yet any clear guidance from the Court of Appeal about the basis on which the future cost of maintaining the unplanned child should be assessed ...

In my judgment in this type of case defendants are liable to pay for all such expenses as may be reasonably incurred for the education and upkeep for the unplanned child, having regard to all the circumstances of the case and, in particular, to his condition in life and his reasonable requirements at the time the expenditure is incurred.

Before I leave this consideration of the legal principles which I should apply when qualifying Mrs Allen's claim, I remind myself that the Court of Appeal has made it clear that I should exclude all the considerations which moral philosophers or theologians might regard as relevant when I compute the figure which I consider appropriate for the cost of Faye's care ...

If an unplanned child is borne after a failure by a hospital doctor to exercise the standard of care reasonably to be expected of him and the child's parents have sent all their other children to expensive private boarding schools for the whole of their education then it appears to me that as the law now stands a very substantial claim for the cost of private education of a healthy child of a reasonably wealthy family might have to be met from the funds of the health authority responsible for the doctor's negligence. However, if this is regarded as inappropriate on policy grounds it is, as Waller LJ pointed out in *Emeh*'s case, for Parliament, not the courts to determine policy questions: judges at first instance, at any rate, can do no more than try to identify and apply principles approved by the higher courts unless and until Parliament intervenes.'

Comment
In *Walkin* v *South Manchester Health Authority* [1995] 4 All ER 132 Auld LJ said that Brooke J's suggestion that an unwanted pregnancy creates two different causes of action according to the nature of the damages claimed is not supported by the authorities nor by his own analysis of them. Postnatal economic loss may be unassociated with 'physical injury' in the sense that it stems from the cost of rearing a child rather than any disability in pregnancy or birth, but it is not associated with the cause of both, namely the unwanted pregnancy giving rise to the birth of a child. In Auld LJ's view, claims in such circumstances for prenatal pain and suffering and postnatal economic costs arise out of the same cause of action.

Arthur v Anker [1996] 3 All ER 783
Court of Appeal (Sir Thomas Bingham MR, Neill and Hirst LJJ)

• *Wrongful interference with goods – distress damage feasant*

Facts
A private car park could only be used by permission, express or implied, of certain leaseholders. In order to deter unauthorised use, the leaseholders displayed a 'polite notice' warning that unauthorised vehicles would be towed away at their owners' risk and expense. Since this notice was ineffective, the leaseholders engaged Armtrac Security Services (Armtrac) to protect the land. Armtrac erected readily visible 'Warning' notices at the entrance and elsewhere on the site in terms as follows:

'WHEELCLAMPING AND REMOVAL OF VEHICLES IN OPERATION
Vehicles failing to comply or left without authority will be wheelclamped and a release fee of £40 charged (in the case of Health Authorities £30). Vehicles causing an obstruction or damage or left for an unreasonable length of time may be towed away and held at the company's pound in Truro. A release fee of £90 plus storage costs will be charged. For release contact ARMTRAC SECURITY [and a telephone number was given].'

Knowing that it was a private car park and appreciating the effect of the notices, the plaintiff parked his car on the land, without authority, at about 1.45pm. The defendant, an Armtrac employee, clamped it. On his return, the plaintiff refused to pay the £40. He telephoned his wife and she arrived in a pick-up truck which she parked in the car park. The defendant tried (unsuccessfully) to clamp that vehicle too: the wife assaulted and abused him. During the night the plaintiff removed his car together with the clamps and padlocks. The plaintiff husband and wife claimed compensation and exemplary and aggravated damages (including loss of earnings) for malicious falsehood and tortious interference with their car. The defendant pleaded in defence that the plaintiff had wrongfully trespassed on the car park by parking his car there; that he had been entitled to immobilise the vehicle and to demand £40 as reasonable costs of the distraint; and that, further or alternatively, the plaintiff, having seen the notices, had consented to the immobilisation of the car and could not now complain of it. The defendant counterclaimed for the value of the clamps and padlocks which had been taken by the plaintiff and not returned, and also for damages for the assault by the plaintiff wife. The trial judge dismissed the plaintiffs' claims and gave the defendant judgment for £660 on his counterclaim (£480 for two wheelclamps, £80 for two padlocks and £100 for the plaintiff wife's assault). The plaintiffs appealed.

Held

The appeal would be dismissed.

Sit Thomas Bingham MR:

'The judge treated [the defendant], representing Armtrac, as the agent of the leaseholders ... he was clearly right to do so. ... In argument, as in the county court, [the defendant's] defence of distress damage feasant was addressed before his defence of consent. But I think it may be convenient to consider these topics in the reverse order.

Consent or volenti

In *Smith* v *Baker & Sons* [1891] AC 325 at 360 Lord Herschell said:

"It was said that the maxim, 'Volenti non fit injuria', applied, and effectually precluded the plaintiff from recovering. The maxim is founded on good sense and justice. One who has invited or assented to an act being done towards him cannot, when he suffers from it, complain of it as a wrong." ...

But the counsel [for the plaintiff] argued

that the demand for payment amounted to blackmail and that the commission of this crime negated the effect of [the plaintiff's] consent. I give my reasons below for concluding that [the defendant's] requirement of payment as a condition of de-clamping the vehicle did not amount to blackmail. It is enough at this point to say that by voluntarily accepting the risk that his car might be clamped [the plaintiff] also, in my view, accepted the risk that the car would remain clamped until he paid the reasonable cost of clamping and de-clamping. He consented not only to the otherwise tortious act of clamping the car, but also to the otherwise tortious action of detaining the car until payment. I would not accept that the clamper could exact any unreasonable or exorbitant charge for releasing the car, and the court would be very slow to find implied acceptance of such a charge. The same would be true if the warning were not of clamping or towing away, but of conduct by or on behalf of the landowner which would cause damage to the car. Nor may the clamper justify detention of the car after the owner has indicated willingness to comply with the condition for release: the clamper cannot justify any delay in releasing the car after the owner offers to pay, and there must be means for the owner to communicate his offer. But those situations did not arise here. The judge held that the de-clamping fee was reasonable. The contrary had not been argued. In my view the judge was right to hold that [the plaintiff] impliedly consented to what occurred, and he cannot now complain of it. ...

Distress damage feasant

The application of this ancient remedy to animals was abrogated by s7(1) of the [Animals Act 1971], which substituted a new procedure for detaining trespassing livestock. But the terms of that subsection do not suggest that any wider application of the remedy has been affected, and historically the remedy has been recognised in relation not only to animate things, but also to inanimate objects such as fishing equipment (*Reynell* v *Champernoon* (1631) Cro

Car 228), grain and straw (*Williams* v *Ladner* (1798) 8 Term Rep 72), and a railway locomotive (*Ambergate, Nottingham and Boston and Eastern Junction Rly Co* v *Midland Rly Co* (1853) 2 E & B 793). It is common ground in the present case that the remedy survives and is in principle capable of applying to inanimate objects. It is, however, plain that application of the remedy to facts such as the present is remote from anything which could ever have been contemplated by those who developed the remedy (the same could also, of course, be said of *Ambergate*); that if the remedy were in principle applicable, it would apply to a party who genuinely did not know that he was trespassing and had received no notice that his car might be clamped; and that that application of the remedy in such circumstances would be unlikely to promote social harmony between the clamper and the clamped. I do not for my part feel constrained to undertake heroic surgery to seek to apply this medieval remedy to twentieth century facts such as we have here. ...

It is plain that physical damage to the land or anything on it is not necessary to found a claim to distrain damage feasant. But I do not think a mere technical trespass, mere unlawful presence on the land without more, is enough. Actual damage would be shown in the party is entitled to the use of the land were denied, or obstructed in, the use of it (see *Williams* v *Ladner* (1798) 8 Term Rep 72). Thus, if any of the leaseholders, or any of the leaseholders' licensees (including suppliers seeking to make deliveries), were unable to use the car park, or prevented from unloading, by a trespassing car, that would amount to actual damage. But there is no evidence and no finding of any such evidence in the present case. ...

On the facts of the present case, I reach a conclusion different from that of the judge. Even if it be accepted that a landowner may in some circumstances distrain damage feasant a car parked without permission on his land, he can only do so to recover compensation for actual damage he has suffered. The leaseholders here are not found to have suffered any actual damage; they have no claim to be compensated; and what [the defendant] claimed as their agent was not compensation.

Crime

We were referred to two English criminal cases arising out of private wheelclamping: *Stear* v *Scott* [1992] RTR 226 and *Lloyd* v *DPP* [1992] 1 All ER 982. In both cases the defendants had knowingly parked on private land despite warnings that cars so parked would be clamped. In both cases the cars were clamped, and in both the defendants removed the clamps, damaging the clamp or the padlock which secured it. Both defendants were convicted under s1(1) of the Criminal Damage Act 1971 of causing damage without lawful excuse, both appealed and both appeals failed. Neither court found it necessary to review the civil law rights of a landowner in this situation. The cases are authority for the proposition –

"that, at any rate as a general rule, if a motorist parks his car without permission on another person's property knowing that by doing so he runs the risk of it being clamped, he has no right to damage or destroy the clamp. If he does so he will be guilty of a criminal offence." (See *Lloyd* v *DPP* [1992] 1 All ER 982 at 992.)

This would appear to make clear that [the plaintiffs] were not, on any showing, entitled to convert the clamps and padlocks belonging to [the defendant]. On this basis [the defendant] was entitled to judgment on his counterclaim in any event. ...

If my conclusion on consent is correct, [the defendant] did have reasonable grounds for demanding payment and was entitled to reinforce his demand by his threat to keep the car clamped until he was paid. But even if my conclusion on consent is wrong, he plainly believed that he had reasonable grounds to demand payment and to keep the car clamped until he was paid. He was not, even arguably, guilty of blackmail. ...

Conclusion

Since the judge was right on the first, consent, issue, the appeal from his decision must be dismissed. ...'

Comment

Neill LJ said that, pending some control introduced by Parliament, matters such as arose here can be satisfactorily dealt with by means of clearly worded notices and by the application of the doctrine of volenti. His Lordship noted that this doctrine has been preserved in relation to trespassers by s1(6) of the Occupiers' Liability Act 1984.

See also *Vine* v *Waltham Forest London Borough Council* [2000] 4 All ER 169 where Roch LJ said: 'The act of clamping the wheel of another person's car, even when that car is trespassing, is an act of trespass to that other person's property unless it can be shown that the owner of the car has consented to, or willingly assumed, the risk of his car being clamped.'

British Transport Commission v *Gourley* [1956] 2 WLR 41 House of Lords (Earl Jowitt, Lords Goddard, Reid, Radcliffe, Tucker, Keith of Avonholm and Somervell of Harrow)

* *Damages – loss of earnings – income tax*

Facts

The plaintiff was injured as a result of the defendant's negligence. The trial judge awarded him £37,720 damages in respect of loss of earnings (actual and prospective) paying no regard to the tax and surtax he would have had to pay if he had not been injured. This tax would have reduced the earnings award to £6,695.

Held (Lord Keith of Avonholm dissenting)

The judge ought to have taken the tax position into account. The award in respect of lost earnings should be reduced to £6,695.

Comment

In *Daish* v *Wanton* [1972] 1 All ER 25, Stephenson LJ said: 'We have to consider *Gourley*'s case in first computing the plain-

tiff's actual net loss of earnings and *Parry* v *Cleaver* [1969] 1 All ER 555 in then considering whether any particular gain or benefit is to be deducted against net loss.' In *Deeny* v *Gooda Walker Ltd (No 2)* [1996] 1 All ER 933 it was accepted that the *Gourley* principle does not apply where the award of damages is itself a taxable receipt.

Clunis v *Camden and Islington Health Authority* [1998] 3 All ER 180 Court of Appeal (Beldam, Potter LJJ and Bracewell J)

* *Health authority – negligence – plaintiff guilty of manslaughter*

Facts

The plaintiff was discharged from a mental hospital and moved into the defendant's area: the defendant was under a statutory duty to provide after-care services for him. The plaintiff stabbed a Mr Zito to death and he pleaded guilty to manslaughter on grounds of diminished responsibility. When the plaintiff sued for damages, alleging negligence in the after-care provisions, the defendant sought to have the claim struck out on the ground, inter alia, that it was based on the plaintiff's own illegal act.

Held

The defendant's application would be successful.

Beldam LJ:

'The rule stated by Lord Mansfield CJ in *Holman* v *Johnson* (1775) 1 Cowp 341 at 343 was a rule of public policy that: "No court will lend its aid to a man who founds his cause of action upon an illegal or an immoral act." The question in that case arose on a claim for goods sold and delivered, but Lord Mansfield CJ did not confine his principles to such cases.

We do not consider that the public policy that the court will not lend its aid to a litigant who relies on his own criminal or immoral act is confined to particular causes of action. Although [counsel for the plaintiff] asserted that in the present case the plaintiff's cause of action did not depend upon proof that he had been guilty of manslaughter, the claim against the defendant authority is founded on the assertion that the manslaughter of Mr Zito was the kind of act which [the defendant's employee] ought reasonably to have foreseen and that breaches of duty by the defendant authority caused the plaintiff to kill Mr Zito. Further the foundation of the injury, loss and damage alleged is that, having been convicted of manslaughter, the plaintiff will in consequence be detained under the Mental Health Act 1983 for longer than he otherwise would have been. In our view the plaintiff's claim does arise out of and depend upon proof of his commission of a criminal offence. But whether a claim brought is founded in contract or in tort, public policy only requires the court to deny its assistance to a plaintiff seeking to enforce a cause of action if he was implicated in the illegality and in putting forward his case he seeks to rely upon the illegal acts. As Best CJ said in *Adamson* v *Jarvis* (1827) 4 Bing 66 at 72–73:

> "From the inclination of the Court in this last case, and from the concluding part of Lord Kenyon's judgment in *Merryweather* v *Nixon* (1799) 8 Term Rep 186, 101 ER 1337), and from reason, justice, and sound policy, the rule that wrongdoers cannot have redress or contribution against each other is confined to cases where the person seeking redress must be presumed to have known that he was doing an unlawful act."

The restriction of the operation of the policy to cases in which the person seeking redress must be presumed to have known that he was doing an unlawful act was confirmed in *Burrows* v *Rhodes* [1899] 1 QB 816. In that case the court had to decide whether the plaintiff could recover damages for deceit after he had been duped by the defendants into joining in a military expedition led by one of the defendants into the Transvaal (the Jameson raid) and who, had he known of the

purpose for which he was joining the expedition, would have been guilty of an offence under the Foreign Enlistment Act 1870. The defendants had argued that his action should be dismissed as his case was founded on an illegal act. The court rejected the argument because the plaintiff himself was innocent, had not been convicted and did not have the necessary intention to be involved in the commission of the offence. ...

The plaintiff in this case, though his responsibility is in law reduced, must in Best CJ's words be presumed to have known that he was doing an unlawful act. The only case cited to us to suggest that the court would entertain a claim to recover damages based on a plaintiff's conviction of a criminal offence knowingly committed is *Meah* v *McCreamer* [1985] 1 All ER 367. In that case the plaintiff, who had suffered a head injury in a road accident, was held to be entitled to damages which arose from his subsequent conviction of two offences of rape. Subsequently, in *Meah* v *McCreamer (No 2)* [1986] 1 All ER 943, he was held not to be entitled to a claim as damages sums he had been ordered to pay in compensation to the victims of the rapes. At the first hearing the judge, Woolf J, recorded that it had not been argued on behalf of the defendant that the plaintiff was not entitled to be compensated for having committed the crimes and was entitled to receive substantial damages in respect of that claim (see [1985] 1 All ER 367 at 371). At the second hearing it was argued that it would be contrary to public policy for the plaintiff to be indemnified in respect of the consequences of his crimes (see [1986] 1 All ER 943 at 950). Basing himself on the judgment of Lord Denning MR in *Gray* v *Barr (Prudential Assurance Co Ltd, third party)* [1971] 2 All ER 949 at 956–957, Woolf J held that public policy "would be a further ground for holding that the plaintiff is not entitled to be indemnified for his criminal attacks on the two ladies concerned" (see [1986] 1 All ER 943 at 951).

Whilst any decision of that judge must be given the greatest weight, we do not consider that, in the absence of argument on the issue of public policy, his decision in *Meah v McCreamer* can be regarded as authoritative on this issue.

In *Gray v Barr* a defendant who had shot and killed the plaintiff's husband in circumstances amounting to manslaughter, though acquitted of the criminal offence, was held to be precluded from claiming indemnity under a policy of insurance. Lord Denning MR ([1971] 2 All ER 949 at 956) emphasised that in manslaughter of every kind there must be a guilty mind. He held that if the defendant's conduct was wilful and culpable he was not entitled to recover.

In the present case we consider the defendant has made out its plea that the plaintiff's claim is essentially based on his illegal act of manslaughter; he must be taken to have known what he was doing and that it was wrong, notwithstanding that the degree of his culpability was reduced by reason of mental disorder. The court ought not to allow itself to be made an instrument to enforce obligations alleged to arise out of the plaintiff's own criminal act ...'

Comment

As to the plaintiff's claim that statutory obligations gave rise to a common law duty of care, see the comment on *Stovin v Wise* [1996] 3 All ER 801.

Hunt v Severs [1994] 2 All ER 385 House of Lords (Lords Keith of Kinkel, Bridge of Harwich, Jauncey of Tullichettle, Browne-Wilkinson and Nolan)

• *Plaintiff cared for by the tortfeasor – whether value of these services and travelling expenses recoverable*

Facts

In 1985, the plaintiff, riding on the pillion of a motorcycle driven by the defendant, suffered severe injuries in a road accident. The defendant's liability in negligence was never in dispute. After the plaintiff's discharge from

hospital in 1987 the parties lived together; they married in 1990. As a result of her injuries, the plaintiff had no chance of being employed and future complications were a possibility: she had a life expectancy of 25 years. In arriving at his award for future cost of care and future loss of earnings, the judge took a multiplier of 14, discounting £1 pa at 4.5 per cent. The damages included amounts for services rendered and to be rendered by the defendant in caring for the plaintiff and his travelling expenses in visiting the plaintiff in hospital.

Held

The judge's decision as to the multiplier would not be disturbed as the multiplier of 15, as substituted by the Court of Appeal, could not be seen as demonstrably giving a more accurate assessment. However, the award in respect of the defendant's travelling expenses and past and future care could not be allowed.

Lord Bridge of Harwich:

'Included in the award of special damages was a sum of £4,429 representing the defendant's travelling expenses incurred in visiting the plaintiff while she was in hospital and a sum of £17,000 representing the value of the past services rendered by the defendant in caring for the plaintiff when she was at home. Included in the award for future loss was a sum of £60,000 representing the estimated value of the services which would be rendered by the defendant in caring for the plaintiff in future. ...

Three issues arose for decision. The first relates to the award in respect of the defendant's travelling expenses, the second to that in respect of his past and future care of the plaintiff, the third to the Court of Appeal's increase in the judge's award. The first two issues are theoretically distinct, but I propose to address them together. There is no dispute that the defendant's visits to the plaintiff in hospital made a valuable and important contribution to her general wellbeing and were calculated to assist her recovery from the devastating consequences of the accident. But for the fact that the defendant was himself the tortfeasor, the propriety of the award under this head would be no more open to question than the award for his services as a voluntary carer. Accordingly, it seems to me that both these issues must depend upon the same considerations of principle. ...

The starting point for any inquiry into the measure of damages which an injured plaintiff is entitled to recover is the recognition that damages in the tort of negligence are purely compensatory. He should recover from the tortfeasor no more and no less than he has lost. Difficult questions may arise when the plaintiff's injuries attract benefits from third parties. According to their nature these may or may not be taken into account as reducing the tortfeasor's liability. The two well-established categories of receipt which are to be ignored in assessing damages are the fruits of insurance which the plaintiff himself has provided against the contingency causing his injuries (which may or may not lead to a claim by the insurer as subrogated to the rights of the plaintiff) and the fruits of the benevolence of third parties motivated by sympathy for the plaintiff's misfortune. The policy considerations which underlie these two apparent exceptions to the rule against double recovery are, I think, well understood: see, for example, *Parry v Cleaver* [1970] AC 1 at 14 and *Hussain v New Taplow Paper Mills Ltd* [1988] AC 514 at 528. But I find it difficult to see what considerations of public policy can justify a requirement that the tortfeasor himself should compensate the plaintiff twice over for the self same loss. If the loss in question is a direct pecuniary loss (eg loss of wages) *Hussain*'s case is clear authority that the defendant employer, as the tortfeasor who makes good the loss either voluntarily or contractually, thereby mitigates his liability in damages pro tanto. ...

The law with respect to the services of a third party who provides voluntary care for a tortiously injured plaintiff has developed somewhat erratically in England. The voluntary carer has no cause of action of his own against the tortfeasor. The justice of allowing the injured plaintiff to recover the value of the services so that he may compensate the voluntary carer has been generally recognised, but there has been difficulty in articulating a consistent juridical principle to justify this result. ...

I accept that the basis of a plaintiff's claim for damages may consist in his need for services but I cannot accept that the question from what source that need has been met is irrelevant. If an injured plaintiff is treated in hospital as a private patient he is entitled to recover the cost of that treatment. But if he receives free treatment under the National Health Service, his need has been met without cost to him and he cannot claim the cost of the treatment from the tortfeasor. So it cannot, I think, be right to say that in all cases the plaintiff's loss is "for the purpose of damages ... the proper and reasonable cost of supplying [his] needs" [per Megaw LJ in *Donnelly v Joyce* [1974] QB 454].

... in both England and Scotland the law now ensures that an injured plaintiff may recover the reasonable value of gratuitous services rendered to him by way of voluntary care by a member of his family. Differences between the English common law route and the Scottish statutory route to this conclusion are, I think, rarely likely to be of practical importance, since in most cases the sum recovered will simply ... swell the family income. But it is nevertheless important to recognise that the underlying rationale of the English law, as all the cases before *Donnelly v Joyce* demonstrate, is to enable the voluntary carer to receive proper recompense for his or her services and I would think it appropriate for the House to take the opportunity so far as possible to bring the law of the two countries into accord by adopting the view of Lord Denning MR in *Cunningham v Harrison* [1973] QB 942 that in England the injured plaintiff who recovers damages under this head should hold them on trust for the voluntary carer.

By concentrating on the plaintiff's need and the plaintiff's loss as the basis of an award in respect of voluntary care received by the plaintiff, the reasoning in *Donnelly v*

Joyce diverts attention from the award's central objective of compensating the voluntary carer. Once this is recognised it becomes evident that there can be no ground in public policy or otherwise for requiring the tortfeasor to pay to the plaintiff, in respect of the services which he himself has rendered, a sum of money which the plaintiff must then repay to him. If the present case had been brought in Scotland and the claim in respect of the tortfeasor's services made in reliance on [the statute], it would have been immediately obvious that such a claim was not sustainable. ...

I turn to the separate issue relating to the appropriate multiplier to be applied in relation to the several elements of the plaintiff's future loss. ...

The assessment of damages is not and never can be an exact science. There are too many imponderables. For this reason, the courts have been traditionally mistrustful of reliance on actuarial tables as the primary basis of calculation, approving their use only as a check on assessments arrived at by the familiar conventional methods. ... We are told by counsel that the practice has changed in recent years and that actuarial tables tend to figure more prominently in the evidence on which courts rely. This may well be so. But before a judge's assessment of the appropriate multiplier for future loss, which he has arrived at by the conventional method of assessment and which is not attacked as being wrong in principle, can properly be adjusted by an appellate court by reference to actuarial calculations, it is essential, in my judgment, that the particular calculation relied on should be precisely in point and should be seen as demonstrably giving a more accurate assessment than the figure used by the judge. ...

I can find no fault in the trial judge's decision to take a multiplier of 14 and apply it, subject to the various adjustments he made, in arriving at his award for both the future cost of care and the future loss of earnings. The use of a discount rate of 4.5 per cent was not and is not disputed. The judge had due regard to the full present value of £1 pa for 25 years discounted at that rate, but decided,

as I think rightly, to take a slightly lower figure which he found to be in line with a spread of multipliers in comparable cases. I do not, with respect, think that the reasoning of the Court of Appeal entitled them to substitute a multiplier of 15 by rounding up the figure taken from the discount table.

I would accordingly allow the appeal, set aside the Court of Appeal's order and vary the trial judge's order by reducing the principal award by £81,429 ...'

Comment
As to the assessment of damages for personal injury, see *Wells* v *Wells* [1998] 3 All ER 481 and *Heil* v *Rankin* [2000] 3 All ER 138. See also the Damages Act 1996 and *Hardwick* v *Hudson* [1999] 3 All ER 426 (plaintiff's damages could not include wife's help with managerial responsibilities).

Hussain v *New Taplow Paper Mills Ltd* [1988] 2 WLR 266 House of Lords (Lords Bridge of Harwich, Havers, Ackner, Oliver of Aylmerton and Goff of Chieveley)

• *Damages – deduction of sickness benefit*

Facts
The appellant sustained an injury in the course of his employment by the respondents which necessitated the amputation of his left arm below the elbow. Under his contract of employment, he received full pay for 13 weeks and thereafter 50 per cent of his pre-accident earnings by way of long-term sickness benefit payable under an insurance scheme run by the defendants who had covered this liability by means of an insurance policy entirely at their own expense. Under the plaintiff's contract of employment such long-term benefit was a continuation of earnings and taxable: there was no evidence that his wages would have been any higher if the defendants had not operated the insurance scheme.

Held

The benefit should be brought into account and deducted from the damages awarded to the plaintiff for pre-trial and future loss of earnings.

Lord Bridge of Harwich:

'Counsel for the plaintiff seeks to apply by analogy a principle said to be established by *Parry* v *Cleaver* [1969] 2 WLR 821 in support of the argument that all payments to an employee enjoying the benefit of the defendants' permanent health insurance scheme are effectively in the nature of the fruits of insurance accruing to the benefit of the employee in consideration of the contributions he has made by his work for the defendants prior to incapacity. Much emphasis was laid on the long-term nature of the scheme payments to which the plaintiff has become entitled and it was submitted that they are strictly comparable to a disability pension. Both these arguments fall to the ground, as it seems to me, in the light of the concession rightly made at an early stage that the nature of payments under the scheme is unaffected by the duration of the incapacity which determines the period for which payments will continue to be made. The question whether the scheme payments are or are not deductible in assessing damages for loss of earnings must be answered in the same way whether, after the first 13 weeks of incapacity, the payments fall to be made for a few weeks or for the rest of an employee's working life. Looking at the payments made under the scheme by the defendants in the first weeks after the expiry of the period of 13 weeks of continuous incapacity, they seem to me indistinguishable in character from the sick pay which the employee receives during the first 13 weeks. They are payable under a term of the employee's contract by the defendants to the employee qua employee as a partial substitute for earnings and are the very antithesis of a pension, which is payable only after employment ceases. The fact that the defendants happen to have insured their liability to meet these contractual commitments as they arise cannot affect the issue in any way.'

Comment

Distinguished in *McCamley* v *Cammell Laird Shipbuilders Ltd* [1990] 1 All ER 854.

See also the Social Security (Recovery of Benefits) Act 1997 and *Wisely* v *John Fulton (Plumbers) Ltd* [2000] 2 All ER 545.

Kuddus v *Chief Constable of Leicestershire Constabulary* [2001] 3 All ER 193 House of Lords (Lords Slynn of Hadley, Mackay of Clashfern, Nicholls of Birkenhead, Hutton and Scott of Foscote)

- *Misfeasance in public office – availability of exemplary damages*

Facts

A police constable having forged the appellant's signature on a written statement withdrawing the appellant's complaint of theft of his property, the respondent Chief Constable admitted that the forgery and the constable's conduct amounted to the tort of misfeasance in public office. The respondent accepted that the appellant had a viable claim for aggravated damages, but the appellant's claim for exemplary damages had been struck out.

Held

The claim for exemplary damages should not have been struck out.

Lord Slynn of Hadley:

'The parties agree that an award of exemplary damages may be made in appropriate cases in English law even though, being punitive in nature, such an award is inconsistent with the principle that damages are intended to be compensatory. As the law now stands that agreement in my view is well founded.

In *Rookes* v *Barnard* [1964] 1 All ER 367 Lord Devlin, with whom on this point other members of the House agreed, having considered early cases concluded:

"These authorities clearly justified the use of the exemplary principle; and for my part I should not wish, even if I felt at liberty to do so, to diminish its use in this type of case where it serves a valuable purpose in restraining the arbitrary and outrageous use of executive power.'

Having reviewed further cases he said:

"These authorities convince me of two things. First, that your Lordships could not without a complete disregard of precedent, and indeed of statute, now arrive at a determination that refused altogether to recognise the exemplary principle. Secondly, that there are certain categories of cases in which an award of exemplary damages can serve a useful purpose in vindicating the strength of the law, and thus affording a practical justification for admitting into the civil law a principle which ought logically to belong to the criminal. I propose to state what these two categories are; and I propose also to state three general considerations which, in my opinion, should always be borne in mind when awards of exemplary damages are being made. I am well aware that what I am about to say will, if accepted, impose limits not hitherto expressed on such awards and that there is powerful, though not compelling, authority for allowing them a wider range. I shall not therefore conclude what I have to say on the general principles of law without returning to the authorities and making it clear to what extent I have rejected the guidance which they may be said to afford. The first category is oppressive, arbitrary of unconstitutional action by the servants of the government. I should not extend this category, – I say this with particular reference to the facts of this case, – to oppressive action by private corporations or individuals. Where one man is more powerful than another, it is inevitable that he will try to use his power to gain his ends; and if his power is much greater than the other's, he might perhaps be said to be using it oppressively. If he uses his power illegally, he must of course pay for his illegality in the ordinary way; but he is not to be punished simply because he is the more powerful. In the case of the government it is different, for the servants of the government are also the servants of the people and the use of their power must always be subordinate to their duty of service ... Cases in the second category are those in which the defendant's conduct has been calculated by him to make a profit for himself which may well exceed the compensation payable to the plaintiff."

Lord Devlin also referred to a third category in which exemplary damages are expressly authorised by statute which it is not necessary to consider in the present case.

It is equally accepted by the parties that exemplary damages are not precluded by the fact that aggravated damages may be awarded though it is clear that before the decision of the House in *Rookes* v *Barnard* the distinction between the two was not fully appreciated. ...

Lord Devlin stressed that a judge should not allow a case for exemplary damages to be left to the jury unless he is satisfied that it can be brought within the categories he had specified and that a claimant can only recover exemplary damages if he is "the victim of the punishable behaviour". The means of the parties are material to the assessment of exemplary damages. "Everything which aggravates or mitigates the defendant's conduct is relevant".

It seems to me that there is nothing in Lord Devlin's analysis which requires that in addition to a claim falling within one of the two categories it should also constitute a cause of action which had before 1964 been accepted as grounding a claim for exemplary damages.

In *AB* v *South West Water Services Ltd* [1993] 1 All ER 609 ... it was said that the combined effect of *Rookes* v *Barnard* and *Cassell & Co Ltd* v *Broome* [1972] 1 All ER 801 was that the claim must be "in respect of a cause of action for which prior to 1964 such an award had been made". ...

I share Bingham MR's view (in the *AB* case) that it is not easy to be sure whether the House in *Cassell & Co Ltd* v *Broome* ruled that the "pre-1964 test" had to be satisfied but that is the core of the question on this appeal ... although I well understand the approach of the Court of Appeal in the *AB* case, I do not consider that the House is bound by a clear or unequivocal decision in *Cassell & Co Ltd* v *Broome* to hold that the power to award exemplary damages is limited to cases where it can be shown that the cause of action had been recognised before 1964 as justifying an award of exemplary damages. It is certainly not bound by anything said by Lord Devlin in what is after all the basic statement of the law. I do not consider that in principle it should be so limited. In any event ... I do not think that courts should be required to undertake a trawl of the authorities in order to decipher whether awards of damages for misfeasance pre-1964 might have included an award for exemplary damages. ...

There are obviously strong views as to whether exemplary damages should or should not ever be awarded. It has not been contended in this case that your Lordships should hold that in principle they can never be awarded. In my view therefore the starting point is that the two decisions of the House already accept that exemplary damages may be awarded in some cases. The task of the House in the present appeal is to say whether it is arguable that they can, and if the facts are established should, be awarded in the present case for the tort of misfeasance in public office. In Lord Devlin's speech in *Rookes* v *Barnard* it seems to me that it is the features of the behaviour rather than the cause of action which must be looked at in order to decide whether the facts fall into the first category. In *Cassell & Co Ltd* v *Broome* Lord Diplock was also recognising that the task of the judge was to decide whether the facts brought the case into one of the categories.

So on the present appeal the question is whether the exemplary damages claimed are on the basis of facts which if established fall within the first category. For the purpose of the strike-out application, it is accepted that they do so fall. The claim is not excluded because it is shown that a case on the basis of misfeasance in a public office had been decided before 1964. I would therefore allow the appeal. The claim for exemplary damages should not have been struck out on the basis argued before the House.

Comment

Overruled: *AB* v *South West Water Services Ltd* [1993] 1 All ER 609.

McCamley v *Cammell Laird Shipbuilders Ltd* [1990] 1 WLR 963 Court of Appeal (O'Connor, Croom-Johnson and Balcombe LJJ)

• *Damages – deduction of insurance moneys*

Facts

The defendant employers admitted liability for the serious injuries suffered by the plaintiff in the course of his employment and the judge awarded £387,790 by way of damages. The defendants ('the insured') had a personal accident group insurance policy for the benefit of their employees ('the insured persons'). The plaintiff had not contributed to this policy and, before his accident, he had not been aware of it. He received £45,630 under the policy and also attendance and mobility allowances: were these sums, or any of them, to be taken into account in assessing damages?

Held

The allowances were deductible but the payment under the policy would be disregarded.

O'Connor LJ:

' ... the payment to the plaintiff was a payment by way of benevolence, even though the mechanics required the use of an insurance policy. The payment was not an ex gratia act where the accident had already happened, but the whole idea of the policy, covering all the many employees ... was clearly to make the benefit payable as an act of benevolence whenever a qualifying injury took place. It was a lump sum payable regardless of fault or whether the employers or anyone else were liable, and it was not a method of advancing sick pay covered by a contractual scheme such as existed in *Hussain* v *New Taplow Paper Mills Ltd* [1988] 2 WLR 266 ... That the arrangement was made before the accident is immaterial. The act of benevolence was to happen contingently on an event and was prepared for in advance. To refer to Lord Bridge's speech in *Hussain*'s case this payment was one analogous to "one of the two classic exceptions" to the rule that there should be no double recovery.

The point was well made on behalf of the plaintiff that this sum was not to be payable in respect of any particular head of damage suffered by him and was not an advance in respect of anything at all. To say that does not mean that in an appropriate case there may not be a general payment or an advance to cover a number of different heads of damage. The importance in the present case is that the sum was quantified before there had been an accident at all and when it could not have been foreseen what damages might be sustained when one did take place.'

Comment

Followed: *Hodgson* v *Trapp* [1988] 3 WLR 1281.

Distinguished: *Hussain* v *New Taplow Paper Mills Ltd* [1988] 2 WLR 266.

As to the deduction of social security benefits from tort damages, see now the Social Security (Recovery of Benefits) Act 1997.

Nykredit Mortgage Bank plc v Edward Erdman Group Ltd (No 2)

[1998] 1 All ER 305 House of Lords (Lords Goff of Chieveley, Jauncey of Tullichettle, Slynn of Hadley, Nicholls of Birkenhead and Hoffmann)

• *Negligent valuation – damages – date from which interest runs*

Facts

On 2 March 1990, in response to instructions from the plaintiff bank, the defendants negligently valued certain property at £3.5m. Ten days later the plaintiffs advanced £2.45m on the security of the property: the borrower defaulted immediately. Had the plaintiffs known the property's true value, they would not have lent the money: a fall in the property market after the valuation date greatly increased their loss. The property was sold in February 1993 for £345,000. The House of Lords decided ([1996] 3 All ER 365) that damages were limited to the amount of the overvaluation at the valuation date (agreed by the parties to be £1.4m) and that no account should be taken of the property market's fall. The question now arose as to what interest should be awarded upon the damages in the light of s35A(1) of the Supreme Court Act 1981.

Held

Interest was payable from the date on which the cause of action arose, ie the date on which the plaintiffs actually suffered the loss attributable to the defendants' breach of duty.

Lord Nicholls of Birkenhead:

'As every law student knows, causes of action for breach of contract and in tort arise at different times. In cases of breach of contract the cause of action arises at the date of the breach of contract. In cases in tort the cause of action arises, not when the culpable conduct occurs, but when the plaintiff first sustains damage. Thus the question which has to be addressed is what is meant by "damage" in the context of claims for loss which is purely financial (or economic, as it is sometimes described). ...

Take first a simple case which gives rise to difficulty. A purchaser buys a house which has been negligently overvalued or which is subject to a local land charge not noticed by the purchaser's solicitor. Had he known the true position the purchaser would not have bought. In such a case the purchaser's cause of action in tort accrues when he completes the purchase. He suffers actual damage by parting with his money and receiving in exchange property worth less than the price he paid.

In the ordinary way the purchaser in this example will not know of the negligence of his valuer or solicitor when completing the purchase. Despite this his cause of action arises at the date of completion ...

More difficult is the case where, as a result of negligent advice, property is acquired as security. In one sense the lender undoubtedly suffers detriment when the loan transaction is completed. He parts with his money, which he would not have done had he been properly advised. In another sense he may suffer no loss at that stage because often there will be no certainty he will actually lose any of his money: the borrower may not default. Financial loss is possible, but not certain. Indeed, it may not even be likely. Further, in some cases, and depending on the facts, even if the borrower does default the overvalued security may still be sufficient.

When, then, does the lender first sustain measurable, relevant loss? The first step in answering this question is to identify the relevant measure of loss. It is axiomatic that in assessing loss caused by the defendant's negligence the basic measure is the comparison between (a) what the plaintiff's position would have been if the defendant had fulfilled his duty of care and (b) the plaintiff's actual position. Frequently, but not always, the plaintiff would not have entered into the relevant transaction had the defendant fulfilled his duty of care and advised the plaintiff, for instance, of the true value of the property. When this is so, a professional negligence claim calls for a comparison between the plaintiff's position had he not entered into the transaction in question and his position under the transaction. That is the basic comparison. Thus, typically in the case of a negligent valuation of an intended loan security, the basic comparison called for is between (a) the amount of money lent by the plaintiff, which he would still have had in the absence of the loan transaction, plus interest at a proper rate, and (b) the

value of the rights acquired, namely the borrower's covenant and the true value of the overvalued property.

However, for the reasons spelled out by my noble and learned friend Lord Hoffmann in the substantive judgments in this case ([1996] 3 All ER 365), a defendant valuer is not liable for all the consequences which flow from the lender entering into the transaction. He is not even liable for all the foreseeable consequences. He is not liable for consequences which would have arisen even if the advice had been correct. He is not liable for these because they are the consequences of risks the lender would have taken upon himself if the valuation advice had been sound. As such they are not within the scope of the duty owed to the lender by the valuer.

For what, then, is the valuer liable? The valuer is liable for the adverse consequences, flowing from entering into the transaction, which are attributable to the deficiency in the valuation. This principle of liability, easier to formulate than to apply, has next to be translated into practical terms. As to this, the basic comparison remains in point, as the means of identifying whether the lender has suffered any loss in consequence of entering into the transaction. If he has not, then currently he has no cause of action against the valuer. The deficiency in security has, in practice, caused him no damage. However, if the basic comparison throws up a loss, then it is necessary to inquire further and see what part of the loss is the consquence of the deficiency in the security.

Typically, the answer to this further inquiry will correspond with the amount of the loss as shown by the basic comparison, for the lender would not have entered into the transaction had he been properly advised, but limited to the extent of the overvaluation. This was the measure applied in the present case. Nykredit suffered a loss, including unpaid interest, of over £3m. Of this loss the amount attributable to Erdman's incorrect valuation was £1.4m, being the extent of the overvaluation.

... for the cause of action to arise only

when the lender realises his security would be a highly unattractive proposition. It would mean that, however obvious it may be that the lender will not recover his money, he cannot start proceedings. ... I can see no necessity for the law to travel the commercially unrealistic road. ... An alternative, less extreme possibility is that the cause of action does not arise until the lender becomes entitled to have recourse to the security. I am not attracted by this, as a proposition of law. This suggestion involves the proposition that until then, as a matter of law, the lender can never suffer loss, and the lender can never issue his writ, whatever the circumstances. That does not seem right to me. This proposition, like the date of realisation submission, loses sight of the starting-point: that the lender would not have entered into the transaction had the valuer given proper advice. If the basic comparison shows a loss at an earlier stage, why should the lender have to wait until the borrower defaults before issuing his writ against the negligent valuer? There may be good reason why the lender wishes to start proceedings without delay.

I recognise that in practice the basic comparison may well not reveal a loss so long as the borrower's covenant is performing satisfactorily. For this reason there is little risk of a lender finding his action statute-barred before he needs to resort to the deficient security. But it would be unwise to elevate this practical consideration into a rigid proposition of law. ...

In the present case the borrower's covenant was worthless. The borrower defaulted at once, and the amount lent (£2.45m) at all times exceeded the true value of the property (£2.1m). Thus the cause of action arose at the time of the transaction (12 March 1990) or thereabouts. By December 1990 the bank had sustained its full allowable loss of £1.4m. I would award simple interest on that amount from 12 December 1990 until judgment at the agreed rate of 0.4 per cent above LIBOR (London Inter-bank Offered Rate).'

Comment
Presumably December 1990 was the time at which the parties agreed the amount of the full allowable loss.

The general rule as to the measure of damages for a negligent valuation is that the valuer is liable for the difference between the market value without the defects and the property's value with the defects as at the date of the plaintiff's purchase: *Gardner* v *Marsh & Parsons* [1997] 3 All ER 871.

In *IM Properties plc* v *Cape & Dalgleish* [1998] 3 All ER 203 the Court of Appeal decided that s35A(1) of the 1981 Act only confers power to award interest on any part payment of a debt or damages by the defendant made during the currency of the proceedings: the court does not have power to award interest on any sums paid prior to the commencement of proceedings or by a third party.

Parry v *Cleaver* [1969] 2 WLR 821 House of Lords (Lords Reid, Morris of Borth-y-Gest, Pearce, Wilberforce and Pearson)

* *Damages – deductions*

Facts
The appellant police constable was injured, as a result of the respondent's negligence, whilst he was directing traffic. In the following year he was discharged from the force and granted a police ill-health award for life.

Held (Lords Morris of Borth-y-Gest and Pearson dissenting)
In computing damages, the ill-health award was not deductible in assessing the amount payable for loss of earnings, although it would have to be brought into account in respect of his loss of retirement pension.

Lord Reid:

'It would be revolting to the ordinary man's sense of justice, and therefore contrary to public policy, that the sufferer should have his damages reduced so that he would gain nothing from the benevolence of his friends or relations or of the public at large, and that the only gainer would be the wrongdoer. We do not have to decide in this case whether these considerations also apply to public benevolence in the shape of various unconvenanted benefits from the welfare state, but it may be thought that Parliament did not intend them to be for the benefit of the wrongdoer.

As regards moneys coming to the plaintiff under a contract of insurance, I think that the real and substantial reason for disregarding them is that the plaintiff has bought them and that it would be unjust and unreasonable to hold that the money which he prudently spent on premiums and the benefit from it should enure to the benefit of the tortfeasor. Here again I think that the explanation that this is too remote is artificial and unreal. Why should the plaintiff be left worse off than if he had never insured? In that case he would have got the benefit of the premium money; if he had not spent it he would have had it in his possession at the time of the accident grossed up at compound interest ... Then I ask – why should it make any difference that he insured by arrangement with his employer rather than with an insurance company? In the course of the argument the distinction came down to be as narrow as this: if the employer says nothing or merely advises the man to insure and he does so, then the insurance money will not be deductible; but if the employer makes it a term of the contract of employment that he shall insure himself and he does so, then the insurance money will be deductible. There must be something wrong with an argument which drives us to so unreasonable a conclusion. ...

I can deal very shortly with the facts of the present case. The appellant ... had to be discharged from the force on 30 June 1964. In October 1964, he was able to obtain employment as a clerk. His wage as a constable was £21 18s 3d per week out of which he contributed £1 3s 1d under the Police Pensions Regulations 1962. Under these regulations there is no pension fund but no point is made of that; it is agreed that the case is to be treated as if there had been a fund to which he had contributed that sum, the remainder necessary to pay the benefits under the regulations being paid by the authority. As a result of his discharge he receives under the regulations an ill-health pension of £3 18s 4d per week for life. If he had served his full time as a constable he would have received a retirement pension of £686 per annum. In his new employment he received between £13 and £14 per week.

So by having to leave the police force the appellant lost two things: first, the wage which he would actually have received until his retirement from the police force if he had not been injured, ie his gross wage of £21 18s 3d minus the sum which would have been retained as a contribution £1 3s 1d; and secondly, the opportunity, by continuing to serve and to make this contribution to obtain his full retirement pension. On the other hand, he gained two things, the wage which he received as a clerk, which must admittedly be set-off against the wage he lost, and the ill-health pension. The main question in the case is whether this pension must be brought into account, and ... I am of opinion that it must not. That is the position up to the retiring age from the police force. Thereafter the position is different.

For a time after retirement from the police force he would still have been able to work at other employment, so allowance must be made for that. As regards police pension his loss after reaching police retiring age would be the difference between the full pension which he would have received if he had served his full time and his ill-health pension. It has been asked why his ill-health pension is to be brought into account at this point if not brought into account for the earlier period. The answer is that in the earlier period we are not comparing like with like. He lost wages but he gained something different in kind, a pension. But with regard to the period after retirement we are comparing like with like. Both the ill-health pension and the full retirement pension are the products of the same insurance scheme; his loss in the later period is caused by his having been deprived of the opportunity to continue in insurance so as to swell the ultimate product of that insurance from an ill-health to a retirement pension. There is no question as regards that period of a loss of one kind and a gain of a different kind.'

Comment

See also *Hunt* v *Severs* [1994] 2 All ER 385 and *Hussain* v *New Taplow Paper Mills Ltd* [1988] 2 WLR 266. *Parry* v *Cleaver* has been applied in, inter alia, *Cunningham* v *Harrison* [1973] 3 All ER 463 (ex gratia payments by employers not deductible from damages for future loss of earnings), *Dews* v *National Coal Board* [1987] 2 All ER 545 (no loss of pension so unpaid contributions to a pension fund not recoverable) and *Smoker* v *London Fire and Civil Defence Authority* [1991] 2 WLR 1052.

In *Longden* v *British Coal Corp* [1998] 1 All ER 289 Lord Hope of Craighead explained that the effect of *Parry* v *Cleaver* and *Smoker* v *London Fire and Civil Defence Authority* [1991] 2 All ER 449 is that incapacity and disability pensions fall outside the general rule that prima facie all receipts due to the accident must be set against losses claimed to have arisen because of the accident. The only reason why incapacity and disability pension payments received after the normal retirement age must be brought into account in computing the claim for loss of pension after that age is that the claim at this stage is for loss of pension, so one cannot properly calculate the loss of pension arising in this period without taking into account receipts of the same character arising in the same period. Therefore, in the case which was then before their Lordships, the plaintiff was required to set against his claim for the loss of the retirement pension an appropriate portion of the lump sum which he had received on his retirement on the ground of incapacity.

Smoker v London Fire and Civil Defence Authority; Wood v British Coal Corp [1991] 2 WLR 1052
House of Lords (Lords Mackay of Clachfern LC, Bridge of Harwich, Brandon of Oakbrook, Templeman and Lowry)

* *Damages – pension deductible?*

Facts

In the first case, the plaintiff fireman was disabled and his employers were liable in respect of his injuries. In relation to his claim for loss of earnings, the question arose whether there should be deducted from the amount of damages the amount that he had received by way of ill-health and injury pension and gratuity under a compulsory pension scheme to which he had contributed 10.75 per cent of his wages and his employer twice that amount.

The same question as to deductibility from loss of earnings damages arose in the second case where the injured former employee had received an incapacity retirement pension under a scheme to which he had contributed 5.14 per cent of his pay and the employer a like amount.

Held

In neither case were the pensions deductible.

Lord Templeman:

'The [former employers] claim that there has been a change of circumstance in that it can be shown that *Parry* v *Cleaver* [1970] AC 1 introduced uncertainty in the law and that since 1970 there has been a clear trend at common law against double recovery. But *Parry* v *Cleaver* established clearly that pension benefits are not deductible and that double recovery is not involved. The cases on which the appellants rely are mainly those in which the courts have decided that payments which correspond to wages must be taken into account when assessing loss of wages. Thus unemployment benefit (*Nabi* v *British Leyland* [1980] 1 All ER 667), family income supplement (*Gaskill* v *Preston* [1981] 3 All ER 427), supplementary benefit (*Lincoln* v *Hayman* [1982] 2 All ER 819), payments under job release schemes and student maintenance grants are statutory wages which reduce the loss of contractual wages resulting from the tort. In *Hussain* v *New Taplow Paper Mills Ltd* [1988] 1 All ER 541 at 547 the plaintiff was entitled to receive full-scale pay over 13 weeks and thereafter half his pre-accident earnings, and the House held that these payments were deductible because, in the words of Lord Bridge of Harwich:

" ... it has always been assumed as axiomatic that an employee who receives under the terms of his contract of employment either the whole or part of his salary or wages during a period when he is incapacitated for work cannot claim damages for a loss which he has not sustained ..." ...

I can find nothing in the authorities which casts doubt over the effect or logic of this House in *Parry* v *Cleaver*.

The appellants relied on s22 of the Social Security Act 1989 and Sch 4 to that Act. These provisions direct that social security benefits shall not be deducted in the assessment of damages for tort but that the tortfeasor shall repay to the state out of the damages thus assessed the amount of the social security benefits provided by the state for the benefit of the victim. These provisions, far from assisting the appellants, only demonstrate that Parliament is quite capable of legislating in this field but has not legislated to reduce the damages payable to the tortfeasor.'

Comment
Applied: *Parry* v *Cleaver* [1970] AC 1. In *Longden* v *British Coal Corp* [1998] 1 All ER 289 Lord Hope of Craighead explained that the effect of *Parry* v *Cleaver* and *Smoker* v *London Fire and Civil Defence Authority* is that incapacity and disability pensions fall outside the general rule that prima facie all receipts due to the accident must be set against losses claimed to have arisen because of the accident. The only reason why incapacity and

disability pension payments received after the normal retirement age must be brought into account in computing the claim for loss of pension after that age is that the claim at this stage is for loss of pension, so one cannot properly calculate the loss of pension arising in this period without taking into account receipts of the same character arising in the same period. Therefore, in the case which was then before their Lordships, the plaintiff was required to set against his claim for the loss of the retirement pension an appropriate portion of the lump sum which he had received on his retirement on the ground of incapacity.

Social Security Act 1989: see now the Social Security (Recovery of Benefits) Act 1997.

South Australia Asset Management Corp v *York Montague Ltd; United Bank of Kuwait plc* v *Prudential Property Services Ltd; Nykredit Mortgage Bank plc* v *Edward Erdman Group Ltd* [1996] 3 All ER 365 House of Lords (Lords Goff of Chieveley, Jauncey of Tullichettle, Slynn of Hadley, Nicholls of Birkenhead and Hoffmann)

• *Negligent valuation – measure of damages*

Facts
All three appeals raised a common question of principle: What is the extent of the liability of a valuer who has provided a lender with a negligent overvaluation of the property offered as security for a loan? The facts had two common features: first, if the lender had known the true value of the property, he would not have lent; second, a fall in the property market after the date of the valuation greatly increased the loss which the lender eventually suffered.

Held

The correct approach to the assessment of damages was to ascertain what element of the loss suffered as a result of the transaction going ahead was attributable to the inaccuracy of the information by comparing the valuation negligently provided and the correct property value at the time of the valuation, ie the figure which a reasonable valuer, using the information available at the relevant time, would have put forward as the amount which the property was most likely to fetch if sold on the open market. The valuer would not be liable for the amount of the lender's loss attributable to the fall in the property market.

Lord Hoffmann:

'The measure of damages in an action for breach of a duty to take care to provide accurate information must ... be distinguished from the measure of damages for breach of a warranty that the information is accurate. In the case of breach of a duty of care, the measure of damages is the loss attributable to the inaccuracy of the information which the plaintiff has suffered by reason of having entered into the transaction on the assumption that the information was correct. One therefore compares the loss he has actually suffered, with what his position would have been if he had not entered into the transaction and asks what element of this loss is attributable to the inaccuracy of the information. In the case of a warranty, one compares the plaintiff's position as a result of entering into the transaction with what it would have been if the information had been accurate. Both measures are concerned with the consequences of the inaccuracy of the information, but the tort measure is the extent to which the plaintiff is worse off because the information was wrong, whereas the warranty measure is the extent to which he would have been better off if the information had been right. ...

The distinction between the "no-transaction" and "successful transaction" cases is, of course, quite irrelevant to the scope of the duty of care. In either case, the valuer is responsible for the loss suffered by the lender in consequence of having lent upon an inaccurate valuation. When it comes to calculating the lender's loss, however, the distinction has a certain pragmatic truth. I say this only because, in practice, the alternative transaction which a defendant is most likely to be able to establish is that the lender would have lent a lesser amount to the same borrower on the same security. If this was not the case, it will not ordinarily be easy for the valuer to prove what else the lender would have done with his money. But in principle there is no reason why the valuer should not be entitled to prove that the lender has suffered no loss, because he would have used his money in some altogether different, but equally disastrous venture. Likewise the lender is entitled to prove that, even though he would not have lent to that borrower on that security, he would have done something more advantageous than keep his money on deposit: a possibility contemplated by Lord Lowry in *Swingcastle Ltd* v *Alastair Gibson (A Firm)* [1991] 2 All ER 353 at 365. Every transaction induced by negligent valuation is a "no-transaction" case, in the sense that ex hypothesi the transaction which actually happened would not have happened. A "successful transaction" in the sense in which that expression [was] used by the Court of Appeal (meaning a disastrous transaction which would have been somewhat less disastrous if the lender had known the true value of the property) is only the most common example of a case in which the court finds that, on the balance of probability, some other transaction would have happened instead. The distinction is not based on any principle and should, in my view, be abandoned. ...

Before I come to the facts of the individual cases, I most notice an argument advanced by the defendants concerning the calculation of damages. They say that the damage falling within the scope of the duty should not be the loss which flows from the valuation having been in excess of the true value, but should be limited to the excess over the highest valuation which would not have been negligent. This seems to me to confuse the standard of care with the question of the damage which falls within the scope of the duty. The valuer is not liable unless he is negligent. In deciding whether or not he has been negligent, the court must bear in mind that valuation is seldom an exact science and that within a band of figures valuers may differ without one of them being negligent. But once the valuer has been found to have been negligent, the loss for which he is responsible is that which has been caused by the valuation being wrong. For this purpose the court must for a view as to what a correct valuation would have been. This means the figure which it considers most likely that a reasonable valuer, using the information available at the relevant date, would have put forward as the amount which the property was most likely to fetch if sold upon the open market. While it is true that there would have been a range of figures which the reasonable valuer might have put forward, the figure most likely to have been put forward would have been the mean figure of that range. There is no basis for calculating damages upon the basis that it would have been a figure at one or other extreme of the range. Either of these would have been less likely than the mean ...'

Comment

See also *Downs v Chappell* [1996] 3 All ER 344 and *Patel v Hooper & Jackson* [1999] 1 All ER 992 (damages in respect of defendants' negligent valuation of property subsequently purchased by plaintiffs).

In *Platform Home Loans Ltd v Oyston Shipways Ltd* [1999] 1 All ER 833 the House of Lords affirmed that where there has been a negligent valuation, the amount of the overvaluation is the amount of damages recoverable by the person who lends money on the strength of the valuation. However, where the lender has been contributorily negligent, the appropriate reduction is made from his overall loss, where such loss exceeds the amount of the overvaluation. As Lord Millett explained, where the lender's negligence has caused or contributed directly to the overvaluation, it may be appropriate to apply the reduction to

the amount of the overvaluation as well as to the overall loss. Where, however, the lender's imprudence was partly responsible for the overall loss but did not cause or contribute to the overvaluation, it is the overall loss alone which should be reduced, possibly but not necessarily leading to a consequential reduction in the damages.

Thompson v Commissioner of Police of the Metropolis; Hsu v Commissioner of Police of the Metropolis [1997] 2 All ER 762 Court of Appeal (Lord Woolf MR, Auld LJ and Sir Brian Neill)

• *Police – unlawful conduct – level of damages*

Facts

Miss Thompson was lawfully arrested but considerable and unnecessary force was used to place her in a cell. She was charged with assaulting a police officer in the execution of his duty but seven months after the arrest she was acquitted. She claimed damages for false imprisonment and malicious prosecution and the jury awarded her £1,500 compensatory damages and £50,000 exemplary damages.

Mr Hsu was physically and racially abused after three police officers had tried to force their way into his house. Apart from physical injuries, he suffered from depression and post-traumatic distress. In his action for wrongful arrest, false imprisonment and assault the jury awarded him £20,000 compensatory damages (including aggravated damages) and £200,000 exemplary damages.

The commissioner appealed against these awards.

Held

As to compensatory damages, Miss Thompson's award would be increased to £20,000 but Mr Hsu's would not be disturbed. Although the court itself would have awarded Miss Thompson £25,000 by way of exemplary damages, it would not interfere with the jury's decision. The total amount awarded to Mr Hsu would be reduced to £35,000 and to that extent the commissioner's appeal would be allowed.

Lord Woolf MR:

'In a number of recent cases members of the public have been awarded very large sums of exemplary damages by juries against the Commissioner of Police of the Metropolis for unlawful conduct towards them by the police. As a result these two appeals have been brought by the commissioner. The intention is to clarify the directions which a judge should include in a summing up to assist the jury as to the amount of damages, particularly exemplary damages, which it is appropriate for them to award a plaintiff who is successful in this type of action. As similar appeals are pending any guidance given by us on this subject should influence the outcome of those appeals in addition to providing guidance for the future. ...

The Court of Appeal plays a significant role in regulating the amount of damages awarded by first instance courts by issuing guidelines.

... there are only two situations in which the Court of Appeal can normally interfere with an award of damages by a jury. The first is where the jury's award is totally disproportionate to the subject matter of the award or is otherwise wholly erroneous. ... The second situation is where the summing up is defective in a way which constitutes a misdirection unless the misdirection does not result in any miscarriage of justice. In general litigants are entitled to have an adequate direction given to the jury as to the issues which the jury have to decide, the principles of law which are relevant to those issues, an indication of the respective cases of the parties on those issues and, when appropriate, the effect in law of evidence which has been given. This general approach applies equally to issues as to damages as it does to issues as to liability. ...

The position [of appellate courts] was fundamentally changed in 1990 by s8 of the Courts and Legal Services Act 1990 and RSC O.59 r11(4), which gave the Court of Appeal jurisdiction where it had "power to order a new trial on the ground that damages awarded by a jury are excessive or inadequate ... [to] substitute for the sum awarded by the jury such sum as appears to the Court to be proper". The effect that this section had in relation to damages in actions for defamation was considered in *Rantzen* v *Mirror Group Newspapers (1986) Ltd* [1993] 4 All ER 975 ... Once s8 of 1990 Act has been given an interpretation as to one category of cases that interpretation must apply across the board. It is difficult to see how the same words can have different meanings depending upon the type of action to which they are being applied. ...

The guidance that should be given

While there is no formula which is appropriate for all cases and the precise form of a summing up is very much a matter within the discretion of the trial judge, it is suggested that in many cases it will be convenient to include in a summing up on the issue of damages additional directions on the following lines. As we mention later in this judgment we think it may often be wise to take the jury's verdict on liability before they receive directions as to quantum.

(1) It should be explained to the jury that if they find in the plaintiff's favour the only remedy which they have power to grant is an award of damages. Save in exceptional situations such damages are only awarded as compensation and are intended to compensate the plaintiff for any injury or damage which he has suffered. They are not intended to punish the defendant.

(2) As the law stands at present compensatory damages are of two types. (a) ordinary damages which we would suggest should be described as basic, and (b) aggravated damages. Aggravated damages can only be awarded where they are claimed by the plaintiff and where there are aggravating features about the defendant's conduct which justify the award of aggravated damages. (We would add that in the rare case where special damages are claimed in respect of some specific pecuniary loss this claim should be explained separately).

(3) The jury should be told that the basic damages will depend on the circumstances and the degree of harm suffered by the plaintiff. But they should be provided with an appropriate bracket to use as a starting point. The judge will be responsible for determining the bracket, and we envisage that in the ordinary way the judge will have heard submissions on the matter from counsel in the absence of the jury. ...

(4) In a straightforward case of wrongful arrest and imprisonment or malicious prosecution the jury should be informed of the approximate figure to be taken as the correct starting point for basic damages for the actual loss of liberty or for the wrongful prosecution, and also given an approximate ceiling figure. It should be explained that these are no more than guideline figures based on the judge's experioence and on the awards in other cases and the actual figure is one on which they must decide.

(5) In a straightforward case of wrongful arrest and imprisonment the starting point is likely to be about £500 for the first hour during which the plaintiff has been deprived of his or her liberty. After the first hour an additional sum is to be awarded, but that sum should be on a reducing scale so as to keep the damages proportionate with those payable in personal injury cases and because the plaintiff is entitled to have a higher rate of compensation for the initial shock of being arrested. As a guideline we consider, for example, that a plaintiff who has been wrongly kept in custody for 24 hours should for this alone normally be regarded as entitled to an award of about £3,000. For subsequent days the daily rate will be on a progressively reducing scale. ...

(6) In the case of malicious prosecution the figure should start at about £2,000 and for prosecution continuing for as long as two years, the case being taken to the Crown Court, an award of about £10,000 could be appropriate. If a malicious prosecution results in a conviction which is only set aside on an appeal this will justify a larger award to reflect the longer period during which the plaintiff has been in peril and has been caused distress.

(7) The figures which we have identified so far are provided to assist the judge in determining the bracket within which the jury should be invited to place their award. We appreciate, however, that circumstances can vary dramatically from case to case and that these and the subsequent figures which we provide are not intended to be applied in a mechanistic manner.

(8) If the case is one in which aggravated damages are claimed and could be appropriately awarded, the nature of aggravated damages should be explained to the jury. Such damages can be awarded where there are aggravating features about the case which would result in the plaintiff not receiving sufficient compensation for the injury suffered if the award were restricted to a basic award. Aggravating features can include humiliating circumstances at the time of arrest or any conduct of those responsible for the arrest or the prosecution which shows that they had behaved in a high-handed, insulting, malicious or oppressive manner either in relation to the arrest or imprisonment or in conducting the prosecution. Aggravating features can also include the way the litigation and trial are conducted. ...

(9) The juryshould then be told that if they consider the case is one for the award of damages other than basic damages then they should usually make a separate award for each category. (This is contrary to the present practice but in our view will result in greater transparency as to the make up of the award.)

(10) We consider that where it is appropriate to award aggravated damages the figure is unlikely to be less than £1,000. We do not think it is possible to indicate a precise arithmetical relationship between basic damages and aggravated damages because the circumstances will vary from case to case. In the ordinary way, however, we would not expect the aggravated damages to be as much as twice the basic damages except perhaps where, on the particular facts, the basic damages are modest.

(11) It should be strongly emphasised to the jury that the total figure for basic and

aggravated damages should not exceed what they consider is fair compensation for the injury which the plaintiff has suffered. It should also be explained that if aggravated damages are awarded such damages, though compensatory and not intended as a punishment, will in fact contain a penal element as far as the defendant is concerned.

(12) Finally the jury should be told in a case where exemplary damages are claimed and the judge considers that there is evidence to support such a claim that though it is not normally possible to award damages with the *object* of punishing the defendant, exceptionally this is possible where there has been conduct, including oppressive or arbitrary behaviour, by police officers which deserves the exceptional remedy of exemplary damages. It should be explained to the jury: (a) that if the jury are awarding aggravated damages these damages will have already provided compensation for the injury suffered by the plaintiff as a result of the oppressive and insulting behaviour of the police officer and, inevitably, a measure of punishment from the defendant's point of view; (b) that exemplary damages should be awarded if, but only if, they consider that the compensation awarded by way of basic and aggravated damages is in the circumstances an inadequate punishment for the defendants; (c) that an award of exemplary damages is in effect a windfall for the plaintiff and, where damages will be payable out of police funds, the sum awarded may not be available to be expended by the police in a way which would benefit the public (this guidance would not be appropriate if the claim were to be met by insurers); and (d) that the sum awarded by way of exemplary damages should be sufficient to mark the jury's disapproval of the oppressive or arbitrary behaviour but should be no more than is required for this purpose.

(13) Where exemplary damages are appropriate they are unlikely to be less than £5,000. Otherwise the case is probably not one which justifies an award of exemplary damages at all. In this class of action the conduct must be particularly deserving of condemnation for an award of as much as

£25,000 to be justified and the figure of £50,000 should be regarded as the absolute maximum, involving directly officers of at least the rank of superintendent.

(14) In an appropriate case the jury should also be told that even though the plaintiff succeeds on liability any improper conduct of which they find him guilty can reduce or even eliminate any away of aggravated or exemplary damages if the jury consider that this conduct caused or contributed to the behaviour complained of.

The figures given will of course require adjusting in the future for inflation. We appreciate that the guideline figures depart from the figures frequently awarded by juries at the present time. However they are designed to establish some relationship between the figures awarded in this area and those awarded for personal injuries. In giving guidance for aggravated damages we have attached importance to the fact that they are intended to be compensatory and not punitive although the same circumstances may justify punishment.

In the case of exemplary damages we have taken into account the fact that the action is normally brought against the chief officer of police and the damages are paid out of police funds for what is usually a vicarious liability for the acts of his officers in relation to which he is a joint tortfeasor (see now s88 of the Police Act 1996). In these circumstances it appears to us wholly inappropriate to take into account the means of the individual officers except where the action is brought against the individual tortfeasor. This would raise a complication in the event of the chief officer seeking an indemnity or contribution as to his liability from a member of his force. It is our view if this situation does arise it should be resolved by the court exercising its power under s2(1) or (2) of the Civil Liability (Contribution) Act 1978 to order that the exemplary damages should not be reimbursed in full or at all if they are disproportionate to the officer's means.

In deciding upon what should be treated as the upper limits for exemplary damages we have selected a figure which is sufficiently substantial to make it clear that there has been conduct of a nature which warrants serious civil punishment and indicates the jury's vigorous disapproval of what has occurred but at the same time recognises that the plaintiff is the recipient of a windfall in relation to exemplary damages. As punishment is the primary objective in this class of case it is more difficult to tie the amount of exemplary damages to the award of compensatory damages, including aggravated. However, in many cases it could prove a useful check subject to the upper limits we have identified if it is accepted that it will be unusual for the exemplary damages to produce a result of more than three times the basic damages being awarded (as the total of the basic aggravated and exemplary damages) except again where the basic damages are modest.

[Counsel for the commissioner] submitted that the jury should be invited to take into account the disciplinary procedures which are available as against the officers when considering whether the case is one which warrants the award of exemplary damages. In our view, this should only be done where there is clear evidence that such proceedings are intended to be taken in the event of liability being established and that there is at least a strong possibility of the proceedings succeeding.

We are also not in favour of plaintiffs' non-co-operation with the complaints procedure reducing an award of damages. It is highly desirable that complainants should co-operate in disciplinary investigations but they are not legally obliged to do so. If they are not sufficiently public spirited to do so, this cannot be held against them in law so as to reduce the amount payable when assessing the compensation to which they are entitled. Exemplary damages are awarded so as to punish the defendant. We have already referred to the circumstances in which the existence of disciplinary proceedings is relevant in determining whether to make any award of exemplary damages. If the jury decide an award is necessary then the amount is assessed on a consideration of the conduct for which the defendants are responsible which makes the award of exemplary damages appropriate. The plaintiff's conduct is here relevant only if it was a cause of the offending behaviour.

Where a false defence is persisted in this can justify an increase in the aggravated or exemplary damages ... but as this will almost invariably be the consequence of an unsuccessful defence, the guidance as to figures we have given takes this into account. If a malicious prosecution results in a conviction which is only set aside on an appeal this would justify a larger award.

In many cases it will be convenient for the jury's verdict on liability to be taken before they receive directions as to quantum.

The correctness of the awards in these cases
In the case of Mr Hsu: the award of £20,000 as compensation including aggravated damages is not a figure with which the court would interfere. Beside the physical injuries he sustained, the consequences for Mr Hsu have been more serious than they would otherwise have been because of his underlying condition. It is in relation to the exemplary damages that the appeal obviously must succeed because of the approach already indicated. There was unprovoked violence in connection with an arrest which took place at Mr Hsu's home. There were a number of officers involved. However, the whole incident was over in a matter of hours and there is already an award of aggravated damages which has to be taken into account. The figure we regard as appropriate is £15,000. So Mr Hsu recovers £35,000 in total. This should suffice to demonstrate publicly the strongest disapproval of what occurred and make it clear to the commissioner and his force that conduct of this nature will not be tolerated by the courts.

In the case of Miss Thompson ... [we] regard it as preferable for us to set out our assessment under each head. ... we ... consider the compensatory damages in this case of £1,500 totally out of line. We bear in mind this lady's initial arrest was lawful but we consider for the subsequent unlawful conduct continuing for seven months we would award £10,000 plus a like sum of aggravated damages and £25,000 exemplary damages (total £45,000). This is marginally less than the total award of the jury but when considering whether to allow the appeal we are concerned with the total award. We will not therefore allow the commissioner's appeal as the jury retain a margin of appreciation so this court will not intervene unless the difference as to amount is greater than this.

As to other appeals which are awaiting determination, we draw the parties' attention to the arrangements which can now be made by this court for assistance by way of alternative dispute resolution. We would hope that the guidance we have provided should enable the appeals to be settled without difficulty by the parties themselves, but if they are not we would hope that the parties would seek the assistance of ADR from the court before proceeding with the appeals. If they do not this may be an appropriate matter to be considered when determining the order for costs which should be made.'

Comment
See also *John* v *MGN Ltd* [1996] 2 All ER 35.

Wood v *British Coal Corp* see *Smoker* v *London Fire and Civil Defence Authority*

29 Miscellaneous Defences and Limitation

Byrne v Hall Pain & Foster [1999] 2 All ER 400 Court of Appeal (Simon Brown, Otton and Schiemann LJJ)

- *Negligence – surveyor's report – accrual of cause of action*

Facts
The plaintiffs proposed to purchase a flat and on 2 June 1988 the defendant surveyors submitted a written report as to its condition. Relying on the report, the plaintiffs exchanged contracts for the flat's purchase on 8 July and completion took place on 22 July. Subsequently, defects in the flat became apparent and on 18 July 1994 the plaintiffs issued proceedings, alleging negligence in the preparation of the report. Were the proceedings statute-barred, by virtue of s2 of the Limitation Act 1980?

Held
They were so barred.

Otton LJ:

'... the critical question arose as to when their cause of action arose. There can be little doubt that the negligent act or omission occurred on the occasion of the inspection on 2 June 1998. The plaintiffs were informed of the valuation shortly afterwards. The communication of the valuation to the plaintiffs still did not amount to a tort. Their cause of action arose when they acted on it and thereby suffered damage. This occurred, in my judgment, when they signed and then exchanged contracts. For all intents and purposes they were irrevocably bound to complete the purchase whenever that event took place, whether immediately after exchange or at the date agreed between them. From the moment that they exchanged the plaintiffs acquired an interest in the property (it matters not for the purposes of this case whether this was technically an equitable rather than a legal interest). They acquired an immediate and binding obligation to insure the property.

None of the remote events which might have led to rescission of the contract of sale, or completion not to take place, occurred. Thus completion was only a formality. Both the seller and the plaintiffs could have held the other to the deal and enforced their rights by a suit for specific performance. On exchange they acquired a lease which was worth less than they were led to believe by the report and upon the strength of which they agreed to purchase.'

Dobbie v Medway Health Authority [1994] 4 All ER 450 Court of Appeal (Sir Thomas Bingham MR, Beldam and Steyn LJJ)

- *Limitation period for personal injury – date of plaintiff's knowledge*

Facts
In 1973 the plaintiff was admitted to hospital for the removal of a lump from her breast. During the operation, the surgeon considered the lump to be cancerous and performed a mastectomy. Subsequent examination showed that the growth was benign. In 1988 the plaintiff heard of a similar case and realised, for the first time, that her breast need not have been removed until the lump had to be exam-

ined and found to be malignant. In 1989 she issued proceedings in negligence. The defendant contended that the claim was time-barred under s11(4)(b) and s14(1) of the Limitation Act 1980 as the time limit for actions for personal injuries was three years from the date of knowledge of the person injured which was defined as the date on which the plaintiff first had knowledge (a) that the injury was significant and (b) that it was attributable in whole or part to the act or omission which was alleged to constitute negligence. At first instance it was held that the action was statute-barred. The plaintiff appealed.

Held

The appeal would be dismissed.

Sir Thomas Bingham MR:

'The 1980 Act, ss11 and 14 ...
This special limitation regime applies to claims (such as the present) based in negligence for damages for personal injuries. It plainly modifies the ordinary rule (expressed in s11(4)(a)) that time runs from the accrual of the cause of action.

The effect of ss11(4)(b) and 14(1)(a) is to postpone the running of time until the claimant has knowledge of the personal injury on which he seeks to found his claim. That is "the injury in question". The word "knowledge" should be given its natural meaning (see *Davis* v *Ministry of Defence* (1985) The Times 7 August). As Lord Donaldson of Lymington MR said in *Halford* v *Brookes* [1991] 3 All ER 559 at 573:

> "In this context 'knowledge' clearly does not mean 'know for certain and beyond possibility of contradiction'. It does, however, mean 'know with sufficient confidence to justify embarking on the preliminaries to the issue of a writ, such as submitting a claim to the proposed defendant, taking legal and other advice and collecting evidence."

This test is not in my judgment hard to apply. It involves ascertaining the personal injury on which the claim is founded and asking when a claimant knew of it. In the case of an insidious disease or a delayed result of a surgical mishap, this knowledge may come well after the suffering of the disease or the performance of the surgery. But, more usually, the claimant knows that he has suffered personal injury as soon or almost as soon as he does so.

Time does not begin to run against a claimant until he knows that the personal injury on which he founds his claim is significant within the definition in s14(2). That gives rise to no issue in this appeal.

The effect of ss11(4)(b) and 14(1)(b) is to postpone the running of time until the claimant has knowledge that the personal injury on which he founds his claim was wholly or partly attributable to the act or omission of the defendant on which his claim in negligence is founded. "Attributable to" was construed by May LJ in *Davis* v *Ministry of Defence* to mean "capable of being attributed to" and not "caused by", and I see no reason to question that conclusion. It cannot plausibly be suggested that the words "act or omission" import any requirement that such act or omission should be actionable or tortious, since that would stultify the closing words of s14(1) and would moreover flout the recommendation on which the legislation was admittedly founded. In *Wilkinson* v *Ancliff (BLT) Ltd* [1986] 3 All ER 427 at 436 reference was made to a submission of counsel based on the use of the words "acts or omission" rather than conduct in s14(1)(b). I do not understand the court to have accepted that submission. But it is customary in discussing tortious liability to refer to acts and omissions, and I do not think the meaning of s14(1)(b) would be any different had the reference been to conduct. Time starts to run against the claimant when he knows that the personal injury on which he founds his claim is capable of being attributed to something done or not done by the defendant whom he wishes to sue. This condition is not satisfied where a man knows that he has a disabling cough or shortness of breath but does not know that his injured condition has anything to do with his working conditions, even though he has no inkling that his employer may have been at fault.

Authority on ss11 and 14

Reference should be made to two recent decisions of this court in which these sections have been considered.

The first case was *Nash* v *Eli Lilly & Co* [1993] 4 All ER 383. In that case a number of plaintiffs claimed damages based on side-effects suffered as a result of taking the drug Opren. Under the heading "Significant injury" the court accepted as valid a distinction between an expected, or accepted, side-effect and an injurious and unacceptable consequence of taking a drug (see [1993] 4 All ER 383 at 391). In considering attributability, the court held ([1993] 4 All ER 383 at 398):

> "It was not, in our judgment, the intention of Parliament to require for the purposes of s11 and s14 of the Act proof of knowledge of the terms in which it will be alleged that the act or omission of the defendants constituted negligence or breach of duty. What is required is knowledge of the essence of the act or omission to which the jury is attributable."

In *Broadley* v *Guy Clapham & Co* [1994] 4 All ER 439 the plaintiff suffered nerve palsy in her left leg, resulting in foot drop, following an operation on her knee. Balcombe LJ held that the plaintiff's claim was statute-barred because she had, more than the prescribed period before the issue of proceedings, known that the operation had been carried out in such a way that something had gone wrong, causing injury to her foot, or alternatively that the operation had been carried out in such a way as to damage a nerve, thereby causing foot drop. Leggatt LJ, agreeing with Balcombe and Hoffmann LJJ, held that the plaintiff had, on the facts, had constructive knowledge since she had had specific knowledge, soon after the operation, of an act or omission which might amount to negligence as would have enabled her to investigate it timeously. He said (at 447):

> "It is plain from the concluding words of s14(1) that 'knowledge that any acts or omissions did or did not, as a matter of law, involve negligence' is irrelevant. In

my judgment the only function of the words 'which is alleged to constitute negligence' is to point to the relevant act or omission to which the injury was attributable."

Hoffmann LJ rejected a submission that the plaintiff must know that the defendant's act or omission was capable of being attributed to some fault on his part, and said (at 448):

> "I think [counsel] was right when he said that the words 'which is alleged to constitute negligence, nuisance or breach of duty' serve to *identify* the facts of which the plaintiff must have knowledge without implying that he should know that they constitute a breach of rule, whether of law or some other code of behaviour. Section 14(1)(b) requires that one should look at the way the plaintiff puts his case, distil what he is complaining about and ask whether he had, in broad terms, knowledge of the facts on which that complaint is based." (Hoffmann LJ's emphasis.)

These decisions are, I think, consistent with and supportive of the construction of the statutory language set out above, subject to one possible qualification. The requirement that the injury of which a plaintiff has knowledge should be "significant" is, in my view, directed solely to the quantum of the injury and not to the plaintiff's evaluation of its cause, nature or usualness. Time does not run against a plaintiff, even if he is aware of the injury, if he would reasonably have considered it insufficiently serious to justify proceedings against an acquiescent and creditworthy defendant, if (in other words) he would reasonably have accepted it as a fact of life or not worth bothering about. It is otherwise if the injury is reasonably to be considered as sufficiently serious within the statutory definition: time then runs (subject to the requirement of attributability) even if the plaintiff believes the injury to be normal or properly caused. ...

The present case: ss11 and 14 ...

I am in complete agreement with the judge's conclusion. The personal injury on which the plaintiff seeks to found her claim is the removal of her breast and the psychological and physical harm which followed. She knew of this injury within hours, days or months of the operation and she, at all times, reasonably considered it to be significant. She knew from the beginning that this personal injury was capable of being attributed to, or more bluntly was the clear and direct result of, an act or omission of the health authority. What she did not appreciate until later was that the health authority's act or omission was (arguably) negligent or blameworthy. But her want of that knowledge did not stop time beginning to run. ...

The exercise of discretion: s33 ...
The judge did not consider it equitable to allow the action to proceed. He held that the evidence would be less cogent than if the action had been brought timeously, that the health authority would be prejudiced on the issue of consent, that the plaintiff should reasonably have taken advice sooner and that the time had come when the surgeon should not have to meet this complaint.

I approach this aspect on the basis that the plaintiff is a grievously injured woman who has suffered much and whose claim, if allowed to proceed, might prove to be very strong. But the delay in this case, after the date of actual knowledge, is very lengthy indeed. The plaintiff could have taken advice and issued proceedings years before she did. Sympathetic though anyone reading these paper must be to the plaintiff, it would in my judgment (as in that of the judge) be unfair to require the health authority to face this claim arising out of events which took place so long ago.'

Comment
See also *Forbes* v *Wandsworth Health Authority* [1996] 4 All ER 881 where the Court of Appeal said that where a plaintiff expected that an operation would be successful and it was not, with the result that he sustained a major injury (leg amputated), a reasonable man would take advice reasonably promptly if he was minded to make a claim and if he did not, he would be fixed with constructive knowledge of the matters set out in s14(1) of the 1980 Act.

30 Torts to Chattels

Parker v British Airways Board
[1982] 1 QB 1004 Court of Appeal
(Eveleigh, Donaldson LJJ and Sir
David Cairns)

- *Finders keepers?*

Facts
A passenger found a gold bracelet in the
British Airways executive lounge at
Heathrow. He handed it to an employee,
asking that it should be returned to him if it
was not claimed. The owner never claimed the
bracelet; the airline sold it and kept the proceeds; the passenger sued for its value.

Held
He was entitled to succeed.

Donaldson LJ:

'Mr Parker was not a trespasser in the executive lounge and, in taking the bracelet into
his care and control, he was acting with
obvious honesty. Prima facie, therefore, he
had a full finder's right and obligations. He
in fact discharged those obligations by
handing the bracelet to an official of British
Airways, although he could equally have
done so by handing the bracelet to the police
or in other ways such as informing the
police of the find and himself caring for the
bracelet.

Mr Parker's prima facie entitlement to a
finder's rights was not displaced in favour
of an employer or principal. There is no evidence that he was in the executive lounge in
the course of any employment or agency
and, if he was, the finding of the bracelet
was quite clearly collateral thereto. The
position would have been otherwise in the
case of most or perhaps all of British
Airways' employees.

British Airways, for their part, cannot
assert any title to the bracelet based on the
rights of an occupier over chattels attached
to a building. The bracelet was lying loose
on the floor. Their claim must, on my view
of the law, be based on a manifest intention
to exercise control over the lounge and all
things which might be in it. The evidence is
that they claimed the right to decide who
should and who should not be permitted to
enter and use the lounge, but their control
was in general exercised on the basis of
classes or categories of user and the availability of the lounge in the light of the need
to clean and maintain it. I do not doubt that
they also claimed the right to exclude individual undesirables, such as drunks, and
specific types of chattels such as guns and
bombs. But this control has no real relevance to a manifest intention to assert
custody and control over lost articles. There
was no evidence that they searched for such
articles regularly or at all.

Evidence was given of staff instructions
which govern the action to be taken by
employees of British Airways if they found
lost articles or lost chattels were handed to
them. But these instructions were not published to users of the lounge and in any
event I think that they were intended to do
no more than instruct the staff on how they
were to act in the course of their employment.

It was suggested in argument that in some
circumstances the intention of the occupier
to assert control over articles lost on his
premises speaks for itself. I think that this
is right. If a bank manager saw fit to show
me round a vault containing safe deposit
boxes and I found a gold bracelet on the
floor, I should have no doubt that the bank
had a better title than I, and the reason is the
manifest intention to exercise a very high

degree of control. At the other extreme is the park to which the public has unrestricted access during daylight hours. During those hours there is no manifest intention to exercise any such control. In between these extremes are the forecourts of petrol filling stations, unfenced front gardens of private houses, the public parts of shops and supermarkets as part of an almost infinite variety of land, premises and circumstances.

This lounge is in the middle band and in my judgment, on the evidence available, there was no sufficient manifestation of any intention to exercise control over lost property before it was found such as would give British Airways a right superior to that of Mr Parker or indeed any right over the bracelet. As the true owner has never come forward, it is a case of "finders keepers".'

Comment

Applied: *Armory* v *Delamirie* (1722) 5 Stra 505 (boy finder entitled to jewel of 'finest water'), *Bridges* v *Hawkesworth* (1851) 21 LJQB 75 (finder entitled to bank notes found in shop) and *Kowal* v *Ellis* (1977) 76 DLR (3d) 546 (finder entitled to abandoned pump).

Parker was applied in *Waverley Borough Council* v *Fletcher* [1995] 4 All ER 756 (council had superior right to brooch found in its park by unauthorised – and therefore trespassing – digger) and Auld LJ restated the two main principles as follows:

'(1) Where an article is found in or attached to land, as between the owner or lawful possessor of the land and the finder of the article, the owner or lawful possessor of the land has the better title.

(2) Where an article is found unattached on land, as between the two, the owner or lawful possessor of the land has a better title only if he exercised such manifest control over the land as to indicate an intention to control the land and anything that might be found on it.'

See also *Costello* v *Chief Constable of Derbyshire Constabulary* [2001] 3 All ER 150 (save so far as legislation otherwise provides, possession means the same thing and is entitled to the same legal protection whether or not it has been obtained lawfully or by theft or by other unlawful means).

31 Malicious Prosecution

Mahon v Rahn (No 2) [2000] 4 All ER 41 Court of Appeal (Brooke, Mantell and Laws LJJ)

- *Libel – document sent to financial regulator – malicious prosecution – prosecutors*

Facts

When the Securities Association (TSA), predecessor of the Securities and Futures Authority, was conducting inquiries into the claimants' firm of stockbrokers, it sought information from the defendant bankers. The defendants supplied certain information to TSA and sent a copy of their letter to the Serious Fraud Office (SFO). The SFO brought criminal charges against the claimants, but the prosecutions collapsed. The claimants sought damages for libel and malicious prosecution.

Held

Their claims could not succeed. As to the libel claim, the defendants' letter had been published on an occasion of absolute privilege. In relation to the claim for malicious prosecution, there was no real prospect that the claimants could prove that the defendants should properly be regarded as prosecutors.

Brooke LJ:

'It is well known that statements made in the course of judicial proceedings attract absolute privilege. In *Royal Aquarium and Summer and Winter Garden Society Ltd* v *Parkinson* [1892] 1 QB 431 at 451, Lopes LJ stated the general rule in these terms:

"The authorities establish beyond all question this ... that no action of libel or slander lies, whether against judges, counsel, witnesses, or parties, for words written or spoken in the course of any proceeding before any Court recognised by law, and this though the words written or spoken were written or spoken maliciously, without any justification or excuse, and from personal ill-will and anger against the person defamed."

In the *Royal Aquarium* case Fry LJ suggested in his judgment ... that absolute privilege applied only to proceedings in courts of law. This suggested restriction has not withstood the tests of time ...

During the course of the next hundred years the protection of absolute privilege has been extended to "tribunals exercising functions equivalent to those of an established court of justice" (see *O'Connor* v *Waldron* [1935] AC 76 at 81, per Lord Atkin). The specialist textbooks give examples of cases which fall on either side of the line. Most notably, absolute privilege has been found to attach to the proceedings of disciplinary tribunals established by professional bodies (see *Addis* v *Crocker* [1960] 2 All ER 629 (solicitors) and *Lincoln* v *Daniels* [1961] 3 All ER 740 (barristers)). In *Trapp* v *Mackie* [1979] 1 All ER 489 the House of Lords took the opportunity of identifying the criteria which must be applied when determining whether proceedings of a tribunal are protected by absolute privilege.

Lord Diplock, with whose speech the other members of the House agreed, suggested the following four matters which fell to be considered in this context: (1) under what authority the tribunal acts; (2) the nature of the question into which it is its duty to inquire; (3) the procedure adopted by it in carrying out the inquiry; and (4) the legal consequences of the conclusion reached by the tribunal as a result of the inquiry ...

On the facts of that case, which related to proceedings at a local inquiry held before a commissioner appointed by the Secretary of State to inquire into the dismissal of a school headmaster, Lord Diplock identified ten characteristics which the proceedings before that tribunal shared with courts of justice ... He made it clear that he was not suggesting that the presence of any one of these characteristics, taken in isolation, would suffice to attract absolute privilege or that the absence of any one of them would be fatal to the existence of such privilege. He contented himself by saying that "the cumulative effect of the ten characteristics that [he had] listed [were] more than enough to justify" the respondent's entitlement to absolute privilege before that tribunal.

Whether the privilege extends beyond the preparation of witness statements to the initial complaint which triggers off the proceedings in question is a different question to which I must turn in due course. It is now appropriate, however, to consider the functions of TSA and its rules and practices at the time of the events with which this action is concerned. ...

Given the power of the preliminary hearings officer to direct that a hearing should be in public, if a request is made to that effect, I do not consider that the general rule that proceedings should be in private should disentitle its proceedings from attracting absolute privilege if they would otherwise qualify for it. ...

I am completely satisfied that the proceedings before a TSA Authorisation Tribunal were such as to attract absolute privilege. I have already explained why I consider that they satisfy three of Lord Diplock's four tests in *Trapp*'s case. In the light of the power of the preliminary hearings officer to override the rules if he considered it just to do so I can see nothing in its procedure to disqualify it from attracting absolute privilege. Those who drafted its rules clearly intended them to be as close to the rules of a court of justice as was compatible with the need to provide a procedure which was reasonably swift and which was not overburdened with costly pre-hearing processes. The rule-makers were at pains to balance the requirements of justice (hence the creation of the overriding power) with the need to establish procedures which avoided the well-known problems which beset civil ligation in relation to the discovery process. ...

I now turn to the question whether the absolute privilege which I would accord to the proceedings themselves also attaches to a communication like the TSA letter. There could probably never be a case which illustrated more vividly the competing considerations of public policy which the court is required to resolve in a situation like this. ...

Important though the investigation of crime undoubtedly is, I have not found it possible to make a logical distinction between the situation in which a criminal investigator seeks evidence to support a criminal charge and a situation in which a financial regulator seeks evidence to put before a tribunal to the effect that someone is not a fit and proper person to conduct investment business. It appears to me ... that the flow of information to financial regulators might be seriously impeded if its informants feared that they might be harassed by libel proceedings, and if it was impeded in this way the purposes of Pt I of the Financial Services Act 1986, of protecting the public from unfit investment advisers, would be put at risk. For these reasons I would allow the defendants' appeal on the first issue and hold that the TSA letter was published on an occasion which attracted absolute privilege. ...

I turn now to consider the second issue which arises on this appeal. The claimants' case against the bank for malicious prosecution ...

In *Martin* v *Watson* [1995] 3 All ER 559 the facts were relatively simply. Mr Martin and Mrs Watson lived next door to each other in Orpington. Relations between them (and their respective spouses) had been acrimonious for many years. On 12 July 1988 Mrs Watson called the police to her home. She said that Mr Martin had indecently exposed himself to her, standing on a ladder in his garden. After discussing the matter with the police, she decided not to give them a formal statement. On 20 July 1989 she called the police again and made a similar complaint. Another officer saw her the following day and took a full witness statement from her. She said she was prepared to attend court and give evidence about the contents of her statement. On 27 July a police officer obtained a warrant for Mr Martin's arrest. On 7 August Mrs Watson called in the police again and made a further complaint. This time the police arrested Mr Martin and took him to the police station where he was interviewed and bailed to attend court the next day on a charge related to the event of 20 July 1989. He duly did so, but the Crown Prosecution Service (CPS) offered no evidence, and he was discharged. History does not relate why the CPS took this course.

In due course Mr Martin sued Mrs Watson for damages for malicious prosecution. It appears that at the trial of this action Mrs Watson told the judge that after the incident in July 1988 Mr Martin had acted in a similar fashion on a number of subsequent occasions. The judge clearly did not believe her. In July 1992 he awarded Mr Martin £3,500 as damages for malicious prosecution. The Court of Appeal, by a 2–1 majority, set aside this judgment on the ground that Mrs Watson did not prosecute him in the sense of setting the law in motion against him on a criminal charge. The majority of the court relied on the fact that it was a police officer and not Mrs Watson who had signed the charge sheet in the police station.

The House of Lords restored the original judgment. Lord Keith of Kinkel, with whom the other members of the House agreed, acknowledged that there was no English authority on the topic. ...

On the totality of the evidence I consider that the claimants have no real prospect of showing that anyone other than the SFO was the prosecutor. It was conducting wide investigations and exercising its own independent discretion as a skilled organisation set up to handle prosecutions involving serious fraud. This is no a case in which it would be reasonable to let the matter go forward, as the judge suggested, through the process of discovery and oral evidence at a trial, because there is already before the court ample evidence of the SFO's role in the matter. It has not been suggested that the claimants themselves would be able to adduce any further evidence in relation to the internal workings of the SFO in connection with this investigation. For these reasons I would allow the defendants' appeal on this point.'

Comment

See also *Taylor* v *Serious Fraud Office* [1998] 4 All ER 801 (relevant statements made during fraud investigation enjoy absolute immunity) and *Gregory* v *Portsmouth City Council* [2000] 1 All ER 560 (malicious prosecution does not extend to domestic disciplinary proceedings).

Malz v *Rosen* [1966] 1 WLR 1008
High Court (Diplock LJ)

• *Private citizen a prosecutor?*

Facts

An altercation having occurred over the parking of cars, the defendant gave a police sergeant an honest and accurate account of the incident. The sergeant said that the plaintiff had committed an offence and the defendant agreed to prefer a charge against the plaintiff and give evidence. After giving a written statement, the defendant signed a charge of using insulting behaviour. Although it had been intended that the prosecution would be conducted by a police officer, the plaintiff having instructed a solicitor the police instructed a solicitor and counsel. The plaintiff was acquitted and he sued for malicious prosecution.

Held

Although the defendant had been the prosecutor, he had had reasonable and probable cause for the prosecution and the plaintiff's action therefore failed.

Diplock LJ:

'It was needless to say, never intended or thought by anyone that the defendant would conduct or have the actual conduct of the prosecution at the magistrates' court. The original intention of the police was that one of the police officers would conduct it, but on ... the day fixed for the hearing, the plaintiff appeared by his solicitor and the matter was adjourned. In the result at the adjourned hearing the prosecution was represented by a solicitor and counsel who were instructed by the Metropolitan Police.

... I accept that the defendant was in the position of prosecutor and that, therefore, if it can be shown that he brought the accusation without reasonable or probable cause and with malice, an action for malicious prosecution will lie against him. I am, however, quite clear ... that, if an ordinary private citizen such as the defendant goes to the police and having given them an accurate and honest account of circumstances which have occurred, is told by a responsible police officer that according to those facts, an offence has been committed, and is asked by the police officer whether he is prepared to prefer a charge, then, if the ordinary citizen accepts that advice, there is no doubt that in law he has reasonable and probable cause for the prosecution. In saying that, I am adopting what Viscount Simonds said in *Glinski* v *McIver* [1962] 2 WLR 832 in relation to a charge brought on the advice of counsel or of a competent legal adviser.'

Law Update 2003 edition – due March 2003

An annual review of the most recent developments in specific legal subject areas, useful for law students at degree and professional levels, others with law elements in their courses and also practitioners seeking a quick update.

Published around March every year, the Law Update summarises the major legal developments during the course of the previous year. In conjunction with Old Bailey Press textbooks it gives the student a significant advantage when revising for examinations.

Contents

Administrative Law • Civil and Criminal Procedure • Commercial Law • Company Law • Conflict of Laws • Constitutional Law • Contract Law • Conveyancing • Criminal Law • Criminology • English and European Legal Systems • Equity and Trusts • European Union Law • Evidence • Family Law • Jurisprudence • Land Law • Law of International Trade • Public International Law • Revenue Law • Succession • Tort

For further information on contents or to place an order, please contact:

Mail Order
Old Bailey Press
at Holborn College
Woolwich Road
Charlton
London
SE7 8LN

Telephone No: 020 7381 7407
Fax No: 020 7386 0952
Website: www.oldbaileypress.co.uk

ISBN 1 85836 477 9
Soft cover 246 x 175 mm
450 pages approx
£10.95
Due March 2003

Unannotated Cracknell's Statutes for use in Examinations

New Editions of Cracknell's Statutes

£11.95 due 2002

Cracknell's Statutes provide a comprehensive series of essential statutory provisions for each subject. Amendments are consolidated, avoiding the need to cross-refer to amending legislation. Unannotated, they are suitable for use in examinations, and provide the precise wording of vital Acts of Parliament for the diligent student.

Commercial Law ISBN: 1 85836 472 8	**European Community Legislation** ISBN: 1 85836 470 1
Conflict of Laws ISBN: 1 85836 473 6	**Family Law** ISBN: 1 85836 471 X
Criminal Law ISBN: 1 85836 474 4	**Public International Law** ISBN: 1 85836 476 0

Employment Law
ISBN: 1 85836 475 2

For further information on contents or to place an order, please contact:

Mail Order
Old Bailey Press
at Holborn College
Woolwich Road
Charlton
London
SE7 8LN

Telephone No: 020 7381 7407
Fax No: 020 7386 0952
Website: www.oldbaileypress.co.uk

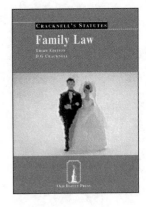

Suggested Solutions to Past Examination Questions 2000–2001

The Suggested Solutions series provides examples of full answers to the questions regularly set by examiners. Each suggested solution has been broken down into three stages: general comment, skeleton solution and suggested solution. The examination questions included within the text are taken from past examination papers set by the London University. The full opinion answers will undoubtedly assist you with your research and further your understanding and appreciation of the subject in question.

Only £6.95 Due December 2002

Constitutional Law
ISBN: 1 85836 478 7

Criminal Law
ISBN: 1 85836 479 5

English Legal System
ISBN: 1 85836 482 5

Elements of the Law of Contract
ISBN: 1 85836 480 9

Jurisprudence and Legal Theory
ISBN: 1 85836 484 1

Land Law
ISBN: 1 85836 481 7

Law of Tort
ISBN: 1 85836 483 3

For further information on contents or to place an order, please contact:

Mail Order
Old Bailey Press
at Holborn College
Woolwich Road
Charlton
London
SE7 8LN

Telephone No: 020 7381 7407
Fax No: 020 7386 0952
Website: www.oldbaileypress.co.uk

Old Bailey Press

The Old Bailey Press integrated student law library is tailor-made to help you at every stage of your studies from the preliminaries of each subject through to the final examination. The series of Textbooks, Revision WorkBooks, 150 Leading Cases and Cracknell's Statutes are interrelated to provide you with a comprehensive set of study materials.

You can buy Old Bailey Press books from your University Bookshop, your local Bookshop, direct using this form, or you can order a free catalogue of our titles from the address shown overleaf.

The following subjects each have a Textbook, 150 Leading Cases/Casebook, Revision WorkBook and Cracknell's Statutes unless otherwise stated.

Administrative Law
Commercial Law
Company Law
Conflict of Laws
Constitutional Law
Conveyancing (Textbook and 150 Leading Cases)
Criminal Law
Criminology (Textbook and Sourcebook)
Employment Law (Textbook and Cracknell's Statutes)
English and European Legal Systems
Equity and Trusts
Evidence
Family Law
Jurisprudence: The Philosophy of Law (Textbook, Sourcebook and
    Revision WorkBook)
Land: The Law of Real Property
Law of International Trade
Law of the European Union
Legal Skills and System
    (Textbook)
Obligations: Contract Law
Obligations: The Law of Tort
Public International Law
Revenue Law (Textbook,
    Revision WorkBook and
    Cracknell's Statutes)
Succession

Mail order prices:	
Textbook	£14.95
150 Leading Cases	£11.95
Revision WorkBook	£9.95
Cracknell's Statutes	£11.95
Suggested Solutions 1998–1999	£6.95
Suggested Solutions 1999–2000	£6.95
Suggested Solutions 2000–2001	£6.95
Law Update 2002	£9.95
Law Update 2003	£10.95

Please note details and prices are subject to alteration.

To complete your order, please fill in the form below:

Module	Books required	Quantity	Price	Cost
		Postage		
		TOTAL		

For Europe, add 15% postage and packing (£20 maximum).
For the rest of the world, add 40% for airmail.

ORDERING

By telephone to Mail Order at 020 7381 7407, with your credit card to hand.

By fax to 020 7386 0952 (giving your credit card details).

Website: www.oldbaileypress.co.uk

By post to: Mail Order, Old Bailey Press at Holborn College, Woolwich Road, Charlton, London, SE7 8LN.

When ordering by post, please enclose full payment by cheque or banker's draft, or complete the credit card details below. You may also order a free catalogue of our complete range of titles from this address.

We aim to despatch your books within 3 working days of receiving your order.

Name

Address

Postcode   Telephone

Total value of order, including postage: £

I enclose a cheque/banker's draft for the above sum, or

charge my   ☐ Access/Mastercard   ☐ Visa   ☐ American Express
Card number

☐☐☐☐ ☐☐☐☐ ☐☐☐☐ ☐☐☐☐

Expiry date ☐☐☐☐

Signature: ....Date: ....